JUVENESCENCE
INVESTING IN THE AGE OF LONGEVITY

BY JIM MELLON & AL CHALABI

Foreword by Greg Bailey

Fruitful
PUBLICATIONS

"WE ARE BORN DYING"
CALEB FINCH, 2016

This edition first published in 2017

©2017 Jim Mellon and Al Chalabi

Registered Office:
Fruitful Publications, Viking House, Nelson Street, Douglas, Isle of Man, IM1 2AH.

For customer service and information about how to apply for permission to reuse the copyright material in this book, including permission to reproduce extracts in other published works, please see our website at www.juvenescence-book.com.

A catalogue record for this book is available from the British Library.

ISBN 978-0-9930478-1-7

Designed & printed by www.bookdesignandprint.com

MEET JIM MELLON

Jim Mellon is a British entrepreneur and philanthropist with interests across a number of industries.

Jim began his investment career in Asia and then moved to the US and worked for two fund management companies, GT Management and Thornton & Co. During this time he gained valuable insights into the companies and economies which would drive global growth over the following decades. He established his own business in 1991, which today persists as Charlemagne Capital and was recently acquired by Fiera Capital. He still controls Regent Pacific Group, a Hong Kong-listed company.

Through his private investment company, the Burnbrae Group, he has substantial real estate investments in Germany and in the Isle of Man, as well as shareholdings in private and public companies in sectors such as banking, commodities, leisure and healthcare.

Jim's investment philosophy, which has led him to be recognised as one of the most successful investors of his generation, is underpinned by his ability to identify so-called "money-fountains" – market trends which will lead to step changes and the resulting investment opportunities. His first book *Wake Up! Survive and Prosper in the Coming Economic Turmoil*, co-authored with Al, foresaw the global financial crisis of 2007-08, while his most recent collaboration, *Fast Forward*, also co-authored with Al and published in 2015, identified technologies and companies which are reshaping people's lives.

Jim and Al's latest book is this one - *Juvenescence*. It is about the 'money-fountain' idea of longevity science and is a result of a year's research into both the science and the companies

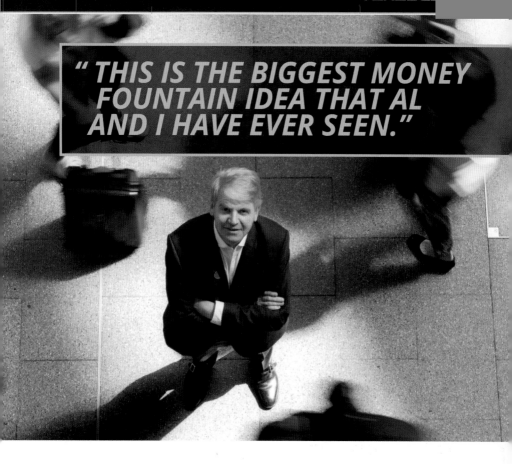

"THIS IS THE BIGGEST MONEY FOUNTAIN IDEA THAT AL AND I HAVE EVER SEEN."

involved in the developing field of enabling people to live longer and healthier lives.

Jim likes running and has completed 42 marathons, although his pace is slowing with each passing year.

Jim spends most of his time investigating and working on start-up ideas. He is an Honorary Fellow of Oriel College at the University of Oxford and is a trustee of the Biogerontology Research Foundation as well as of the Lifeboat Foundation. Jim has recently been appointed an Ambassador on the Buck Institute for Research on Aging's Advisory Council.

"This is the biggest money fountain idea that Al and I have ever seen. The longevity business has quickly moved from wacky land to serious science, and within just a couple of decades we expect average human life expectancy in the developed world to rise to around 110."

MEET AL CHALABI

Al Chalabi is an entrepreneur and business advisor with an impressive track record in a range of industries.

He grew up in the UK and studied Aeronautical Engineering at the University of Southampton. Al started his professional career in Canada, working as an engineer in process automation systems. After obtaining his MBA, he worked as a management consultant, specialising in technology, strategy and operations, and has been based out of Hong Kong ever since.

Since 2008, Al has been running CASP-R, a firm he founded to provide independent research and advisory services to investors and corporations, with a focus on real estate and technology. He is active in various Hong Kong-based angel investor groups that provide seed funding to Asian-based tech and healthcare companies.

Al has been writing books with Jim since they first joined forces to write *Wake Up! Survive and Prosper in the Coming Economic Turmoil*, published at the end of 2005.

Al lives in Hong Kong with his partner Fiona and their two children, Enzo (who is a godson to Jim) and Margaux. Al, like Jim, has always been health conscious and believes that, allied with current advances in science, the pursuit of a healthy lifestyle can reap significant rewards. Here, he presents his personal experience as well as the latest scientific information about diet and lifestyle most conducive to living a long, healthy life.

"If everyone read and followed our lifestyle recommendations, this book would help to solve the healthcare crises in most developed economies. Many diseases which manifest themselves today can be avoided by maintaining a healthy weight, eating a balanced diet rich in fresh fruit and vegetables, and engaging in a moderate amount of exercise, even for just a few minutes a day."

" IF EVERYONE READ AND FOLLOWED OUR LIFESTYLE RECOMMENDATIONS, THIS BOOK WOULD HELP TO SOLVE THE HEALTHCARE CRISES IN MOST DEVELOPED ECONOMIES."

CONTENTS

CONTENTS

CONTENTS

The Keys to Keeping Healthy - And to Getting Across that First Bridge 339

Conditioning for a Healthy Life 358

CONTENTS

HOW TO USE THIS BOOK

This book has been written to give readers an overview of the most recent and meaningful developments in the field of longevity science. The authors have made every attempt to reduce the complex topics into an easy to understand message, however, readers may not be familiar with some of the technical terminology. We have included a glossary at the back of the book to help. The first time a term is used in the text, it has been put in **bold.**

Juvenescence is organised into sections which are colour coded. Page references to relevant segments in the text have been included in that section's colour so that you can quickly and accurately find the information you need.

HOW TO USE THIS BOOK

ACKNOWLEDGEMENTS

We would like to extend our thanks to the following for all the help, support, and information they have provided during the production of this book:

Anthony Baillieu – friend, driver, wise owl and wine pourer at the end of a long day!
Anthony Chow – colleague, researcher, microscope enthusiast and all round good chap.
Greg Bailey – biotech superstar, business partner and friend.
Declan Doogan – best-connected man in biotech, business partner, friend.
Alexander Pickett – resident scientist and Managing Director of Juvenescence Ltd.
Emanuil Halicioglu – colleague, fact finder and superb graph maker.
Alex Zhavoronkov – new business partner, door opener and longevity guru.

And of course: **Trish Wilson** publishing workhorse, organiser par excellence, and one of Jim's three multi-talented sisters.

Jim was lucky enough to interview the following scientists who were very generous with their time and extremely patient with their explanations. Thank you!

Dr Aubrey de Grey
Professor David Sinclair
Professor Alex Zhavoronkov
Professor Leonard Hayflick
Laura Deming
Professor Nir Barzilai
Professor Walter Bortz
Dr Peter Attia

Dr Jay Bradner
Gabriel Otte
Dr Charles Roberts
Dr Matthew Freeman
Professor Alastair Buchan
Patrick Cox
John Mauldin

Dr Mike West
Professor David Gems
Professor David Glass
Elizabeth Parrish
Dr Joon Yun
Gary Hudson
Dr Eric Verdin

Scientific Reviewers:

- Biogerontology Research Foundation and in particular Franco Cortese and Dr Joao Pedro de Magalhaes.
- Professor David Gems.
- Dr Aubrey de Grey for his generous, meticulous and much needed review of the science – and of course, of the commas.

Many thanks to:

- Nick Martin for supplying the life insurance section.
- Franco Cortese for supplying the text for the biomarkers section.
- Dr Ian Walters for providing some of the text for the cancer section.
- Patrick Cox for writing the section on GHRH.
- Mike West who generously helped with the section on AgeX Therapeutics.
- Alan Kerr who took the photographs of Jim and of assorted dogs.

And of course, to all our friends at Can Curune in Ibiza, where the book was hatched and a lot of it was written. ¡Salud!

FOREWORD

by Greg Bailey, M.D.

It is rare that authors combine hard science with investment recommendations into single books with the success that Jim and Al have demonstrated in their previous publications. In my opinion, this one is no different - except that the subject matter is even more exciting. *Cracking the Code*, Jim and Al's 2012 book on the life sciences industry, could not have been more timely. After its publication, the Nasdaq Biotech Index went on a rampage, with the balanced portfolio recommendations in the book delivering 139% returns (in US dollar terms) since publishing in April 2012, about double the broad market indices. In this new book, Jim and Al anticipate another burst of science and commerce, one focused on a previously unassailable problem – the conundrum of ageing.

As a physician, biotech entrepreneur, financier, and founder I have enjoyed very good returns in the past few years. Medivation, a company I was involved with from 2004 to 2012, and in which Jim was also an investor, was acquired by Pfizer for US $14.3 billion in 2016. This was quite a remarkable journey from a US $12 million pre-money value just twelve years earlier. Subsequently, Jim and I have founded an immuno-oncology company, SalvaRx Group which was floated on the AIM, London in 2015 and recently reached new stock price highs.

Biohaven is another company that Jim and I, along with Declan Doogan, former Senior Vice President and Head of Worldwide Development at Pfizer, recently founded. We seeded it with US $3.5 million in 2014, and it has recently raised over US $200 million for the venture which has now gone public on the New York Stock Exchange with a substantial valuation.

For 8 years Jim, Declan and I have been co-investing in start-up biotech companies, and the latest and most exciting is *Juvenescence,* focused on longevity.

Life science companies, whether founded by us or by others, are normally based on novel science. This could be a new molecule, or it could be a better understanding of one of the many mechanisms or pathways that are involved in disease or in maintaining health.

In this book, you will learn about one of the hottest new areas of research, one that is being unravelled for the first time ever: how to treat ageing as if it were a disease. Jim, Declan and I, along with Alexander Pickett and Anthony Chow, are so excited about these developments that we have started a new company named after this book. Juvenescence has a mission to find diagnostic and therapeutic agents in order to treat ageing as well as associated diseases. We are hopeful that this business will be the most profitable of our companies to date and will provide at least part of the "solution" to ageing, should one ever be found. As Peter Diamandis of X-Prize Foundation fame has said, humans have not had an upgrade in 150,000 years - perhaps it is now time.

This book is fundamentally an attack on the old adage about the inevitability of *death and taxes*. I am being a little disingenuous, as *Juvenescence* will not lower your taxes, but could well increase your pre-tax returns via the investments that it recommends. As for death, the book recommends companies which are worthy of investment in most part because they are working to postpone the dates of our (still) sadly inevitable expiration.

Throughout history, a wide variety of people, ranging from Taoist sages, medieval alchemists, and Spanish conquistadors, have searched for a literal or figurative *fountain of youth:* an elixir which would restore youth to the aged.

Today, we are finally at a tipping point where what was once pure science fiction is transitioning into scientific reality. The research community is rapidly developing a proper understanding of the metabolic pathways involved in cellular ageing, and of course, we are now well aware of how lifestyle impacts the ageing of our bodies. *Juvenescence* will tell you about the scientists and companies who are working on these products as well as outlining the key pathways.

In my opinion, ageing is a unitary disease state that compromises our **cells'** natural abilities to sustain themselves or to regenerate. Interestingly, cancer cells are theoretically immortal. Furthermore, some organs are noted for their capacity to regenerate - specifically the liver and to a lesser degree the brain. This may give comfort to many readers who had an adventurous (ahem!) youth – not that this applies to any of us of course!

This amazing science is happening now only because of a unique new understanding. Until recently, most publicly and privately funded research was focused on the treatment of the many diseases and disorders that accompany ageing, such as dementia, diabetes, and heart

The Fountain of Youth *by Lucas Cranach the Elder, 1546.*

disease. While the pharmaceutical industry has made notable progress in the treatment of these diseases, none of that advance fundamentally altered the course of ageing or dramatically extended lifespan.

Juvenescence focuses on the recent progress that has been made in understanding the key molecular causes of ageing itself. Understanding these pathways is essential to the development of effective therapeutics, as well as of the **biomarkers** necessary to assess the likely success or otherwise of these therapies. Today, the life science industry is beginning to use insights coming out of a variety of universities and other institutions, in order to develop therapies for the disease of ageing itself. In the course of their researches, Jim and Al have

come to believe that the next 10 years will bring a material advance in our understanding of ageing and that we will see some genuinely anti-ageing drugs and treatments come to the market. In fact, Transparency Market Research of the US and India has estimated that by 2019 the global anti-ageing market will be worth nearly US $200 billion per annum.

One mechanism clearly involved in ageing is inflammation, which has long been recognised as a contributory factor to obesity, metabolic disease, cardiovascular disease (CVD), dementia, and to a litany of other ills.

Today some eminent scientists believe that chronic inflammation is itself a major driver of ageing. Recent results suggest that older, senescent cells may be responsible for chronic pro-ageing inflammation, due to their "bystander" effects, and a number of companies are working on removing these bad actors.

Other scientists are focusing on the role of insulin resistance in causing inflammation and ageing. As we get older, our organs gradually become resistant to insulin. Insulin resistance may also be a cause of ageing or its by-products, but it absolutely does drive metabolic malfunction and further deleterious inflammation. Most people's brains will become insulin resistant by the time that they are roughly fifty years old. Does the brain's inability to correctly absorb energy sources cause **proteins** like Aβ or tau to misfold, leading to Alzheimer's and other neurodegenerative diseases? Many anti-ageing scientists now believe that a daily dose of a generic anti-diabetic medication, **metformin**, may extend life and promote good mental health. You will read later in this book about the first clinical trial to try to slow ageing, using metformin as the lead compound.

It is not just ageing at the cellular level that science is now interested in, although that, of course, represents a transformative change in thinking. In this book, you will also read about breakthrough technologies involving **stem cells** and **gene** manipulation, the latter using an extraordinary editing tool called **CRISPR**, all of which will one-day attack ageing and its associated diseases. Then there are the regeneration treatments which are emerging to deal with age-related pathologies and loss of function.

I have been going to ageing-focussed conferences for five years and have noticed the transition from lifestyle solutions to address ageing – such as **caloric restriction (CR)**, daily flossing, regular sex and frequent exercise – to the point today where drugs are being developed that actually might prolong life, rather than simply improve it. Compounds such as **rapamycin** and metformin are now inspiring the conduct of proper anti-ageing clinical trials.

The current use of drugs for anti-ageing is still based on anecdotal information, but as you will read in this book that is about to change. Nonetheless, some crazy early adopters are on up to 250 supplements – a day! As a physician, I have settled on an imperfect 3 drugs plus a few vitamin combinations as I am concerned about drug to drug interaction if too many pills are taken: so, I take metformin to deal with insulin resistance, a statin and baby aspirin for inflammation and protection against cardiac events, along with fish oil, curcumin, vitamins D and B, nicotinamide mononucleotide (NMN) and episodic calcium to offset metformin's possible side effects.

MEET GREG BAILEY M.D.

Dr Gregory Bailey is an investor and entrepreneur in the biomedical sector having previously spent time as an investment banker and as a physician. Dr Bailey has arranged and participated in multiple financings and M&A transactions, and has taken several companies public. He is a co-founder and managing partner of MediqVentures and the Executive Chairman of Portage Biotech Inc.

Previously he was a managing partner of Palantir Group, Inc., a merchant bank involved in a number of life science company start-ups and financings. Palantir was also involved in acquiring intellectual property assets and founding companies around their intellectual property.

Greg is the co-founder of Ascent Healthcare Solutions, VirnetX Inc. (VHC: AMEX), Portage Biotech Inc. (PTGEF: OTCBB), DuraMedic Inc. and SalvaRx Group Plc (SALV: LSE). He was the initial financier and an independent director from 2005 to December 2012 of Medivation, Inc. (MDVN: NASDAQ). Medivation was acquired by Pfizer in 2016 for $14.3 billion.

Dr Bailey has served on the board of directors of many public companies and is currently on the boards of Biohaven Pharmaceuticals, Portage Biotech and of the SalvaRx Group. Grerg practised emergency medicine for 10 years before entering finance. He received his medical degree from the University of Western Ontario.

LONGEVITY TAKES FLIGHT

Just as with aviation a century ago, anti-ageing science is about to take flight.

On Jim's research trip around the US in February and March of 2017, he visited the Boeing factory near Seattle. Several large aircraft roll out of this vast structure every week, wiggling their wings as they take off to some distant airport.

It has only been slightly over 100 years since Mr Boeing built his first aircraft, a seaplane with two seats and only about 120 years since the Wright Brothers made history with their first flight at Kitty Hawk. Imagine being alive in 1915: could any one of us have ever believed what an aircraft would look like just one short century hence? Almost certainly not. But the really important thing was that by 1915 the mechanism by which aircraft could fly had been discovered – and

from that point onwards the design and capability of machines that were able to fly could only improve.

Knowledge, once learned, cannot be unlearned, and despite the occasional interruptions to fundamental human progress (war, famine and plague), it is simply wonderful that today we sit on such a huge repository of information – knowledge which is doubling, in quantity if not quality, every second year. Admittedly a lot of this "knowledge" is not very useful, but there is no doubt that the internet has facilitated a huge improvement in the transmission and use of scientific data – and this for the benefit of all of humanity.

That body of knowledge is the key reason why Boeing can now produce fuel-efficient aircraft made from composite materials, aircraft which can fly for upwards of 17 hours without refuelling while carrying hundreds of passengers in great safety. The pace of the accumulation of real, useful knowledge is accelerating and although no one can see around the corners of the future, we can imagine – and indeed believe – that our tomorrows will be even better than our todays.

That same pattern of accumulated knowledge applied to aviation is also manifested in the field of ageing and longevity. Until the Second World War, ageing was a marginal science at best, and this was because very few people beyond the realms of science fiction could envision many human beings living much beyond 100.

Today, just as when *Cracking the Code* was published in 2012, diseases are being either conquered or attenuated by the accelerating progress of medical science. With a few exceptions, this is leading to significant extensions in the average lifespans of people in almost all countries. Scientists now have a good understanding of the basic genetic makeup of humans thanks to the unveiling of the human genome at the turn of the 21st century and the discovery of the structure of DNA some 50 years prior. Researchers into ageing are now wrestling with two key issues:

1. How to cure or tame the diseases that become more prevalent and devastating as people age; and

2. How to research ageing as a unitary disease in itself - or putting it another way, as a type of disease state.

The fundamental ways in which our cells work are now being examined with a view to understanding how we might slow, stop or even reverse the process of ageing. There are multiple pathways implicated in ageing, and the science of discovering and altering them is still in its infancy, but it's an area undergoing explosive growth.

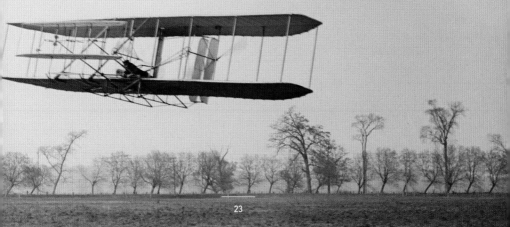

LONG LIVE JUVENESCENCE!

When we sat down at Jim's favourite local bar in Ibiza in 2016, which is by now a twenty-plus-year tradition, and discussed our next book project – the subject of **ageing** and **longevity** came up. Al wasn't initially convinced that ageing was a subject worth dedicating a year or so of effort towards as he, quite reasonably, believed that there really wasn't much that could be done to prevent the Grim Reaper from getting us when our time was up. All we could do to improve our chances of a long, healthy life was to not smoke, to exercise regularly, and to eat a balanced diet - and that was about the sum of it.

Subsequently, Al's view has changed – and is now aligned with that of Jim, who was born brimming with optimistic genes. Science is catching up with aspiration. We really can – and probably will – live much longer than most people think is feasible. Science is advancing so rapidly that it is hard to comprehend the full implications of many of these recent discoveries, so we have tried to distil the ones we are familiar with into this book.

We have spent a year researching, interviewing, collating, filtering, pleading, harassing and reading, as well as driving 7,000 miles around the US. Finally, we have arrived at our one central definitive conclusion: the current pause in rising lifespans in some developed countries, including in the UK and in the US, is only temporary. Babies born today are likely to live to well over 100, and probably a lot longer than that. Techniques which are available to us beyond those of the fairly obvious admonitions concerning diet, sleep, exercise, and the avoidance of sugar and tobacco could carry most adults alive today to well over 100.

Those techniques are building a bridge to a new world.

This new world is one where drugs, genetic engineering, cellular enhance-ments and organ replacements, amongst other interventions, will add decades to our potential lifespan, taking most people much closer to the maximal life length that only a few supercentenarians currently enjoy.

The bridge that is being built is one made partly of drugs and therapies that address the main diseases of ageing, namely cardiovascular disease, cancer, neurodegeneration, diabetes and respiratory disease.

In addition, the development of therapies to remove senescent cells, to restore cellular activity, to

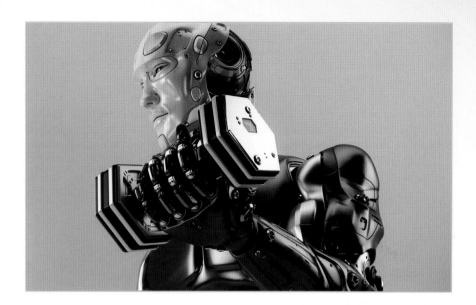

improve hormonal balance and to enhance mobility in older people is proceeding apace. If people can hold on to healthy life for the next decade or so, the chances are that they will eventually start to gain more than one year of life expectancy for each year that they live. The old nostrums about three score and ten, about being *illderly* in old age and of the inevitability of a preordained early expiration while in a diseased state are quickly being debunked.

The implications of the remarkably longer lives that are now about to be the norm are stupendous. The trajectory of our lives will change and the societal contract that dictates that we must first learn, then earn, then retire and expire is already being broken.

Family life will change, women will have children much later in life, education will be a necessary continuum, work will be something different to what we know today and *wellderliness* in older age will be the norm, not the exception. Older workers will be embraced and valued, and people living to 100, and thereafter to beyond 120 or so, will become commonplace and unremarkable.

There are those, such as Ray Kurzweil, who believe that an almost unlimited lifespan is possible and that humans will end up living forever as some sort of disembodied holograms – super-smart but in a very different form to what we now regard as "human". There are also those - and we talk about them in this book - who believe that we have already reached our maximal potential lifespans of about 115 years and that this ceiling will be a very hard one to break. However, most of these forecasters do accept that average if not maximal life expectancy will continue to rise.

Our own view is that there there will soon be the technology to advance human lifespan to beyond the longest ever recorded age of 122 (Jeanne Calment) and that we have the makings of that technology now. Future treatments could take us even beyond any historical "hard limit", although in predicting how soon that will occur we go into the realms of pure conjecture. However the future plays out, we are absolutely certain that achieving an average human lifespan of around 110 years is a realistic prospect thanks to a steady stream of recent discoveries.

Our quite remarkable bodies are going to reveal ever greater numbers of secrets, something vital to the process of re-engineering them to work longer, harder and more efficiently than they do today. And they do work pretty hard already.

The earthly vessels in which we reside contains a heart that pumps 750 litres of blood and beats over 100,000 times each day, a pair of lungs that take 17,000 daily breaths, a pair of kidneys that filter over a litre of blood every minute, a liver that works incredibly hard to produce cholesterol, vitamin D and blood plasma, billions of cells that regenerate at an astonishing rate, giving us a new set of bones every 10 years, a pair of eyes that blink 28,000 times each day - and all the other micromachinery working together in perfect harmony that makes us who we are will be fine-tuned into even greater perfection.

This book is about that process of re-engineering; and it's also about the description of an industry, nascent but growing at an astonishing pace – an industry that has the capacity to be the biggest money fountain ever.

New meaning is about to be given to the salutation: **"Live long and prosper".** We intend to do both – and we sincerely hope that our readers will join us.

*The Lab Mouse that Got Away! As a constant reminder of the complexity of life thus ordered, Jim has a large sculpture of the DNA double helix in his bedroom in Berlin, designed by the famous fashion house Ted Baker and one of several different representations of the helix used to raise funds for Cancer Research UK. The discovery of the DNA double helix structure by Watson and Crick in 1953 really kick-started the age of molecular biology – which is now moving into the age of Juvenescence. **See opposite.***

IS AGEING A DISEASE?

About two decades ago, Richard Doll, the eminent epidemiologist, argued that there was no such thing as a unitary disease of ageing. Rather, he suggested that ageing-related diseases should be regarded separately and treated as such. Subsequently, however, most scientists studying the biology of ageing – biogerontologists, as they call themselves – have come to regard the pre-symptomatic changes of ageing as being worthy of attention and to think of ageing as a type of disease in its own right. If the ageing syndrome could be treated as a disease, the associated diseases would be treated at the top of the cascade where they originate.

Research successes of the past twenty years, including those involving the manipulation of model organisms, such as fruit flies, yeast and worms, have shown that biochemical pathways are manipulable and malleable. The scientific *volte face* that has resulted – admittedly not embraced by everyone (see Key Opinion Leaders. Page 151) – means that ageing is no longer regarded as entropic and inevitable. Studies are gradually revealing the genetic factors that regulate our lifespans.

If the World Health Organisation (WHO) could be persuaded (in its once every two decades' review of the categorisation of diseases) to include ageing as a specific condition, this would have important and positive implications for the science of longevity. The next review is in 2018, and Alex Zhavoronkov (see Insilico Medicine. Page 120), one of our interviewees, is lobbying hard to make sure that ageing is included as a disease category.

Even without WHO categorisation, government and corporate funded research into ageing itself is beginning to grow. Since everyone on the planet is a carrier of the disease of ageing from birth onwards, there is a very large market indeed for people with this "disease".

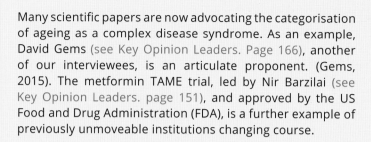

Many scientific papers are now advocating the categorisation of ageing as a complex disease syndrome. As an example, David Gems (see Key Opinion Leaders. Page 166), another of our interviewees, is an articulate proponent. (Gems, 2015). The metformin TAME trial, led by Nir Barzilai (see Key Opinion Leaders. page 151), and approved by the US Food and Drug Administration (FDA), is a further example of previously unmoveable institutions changing course.

It has been quite correctly pointed out that by increasing the productive lifespans of people in the developed world healthcare costs would be reduced. These are becoming unsustainable in quite a few major economies. Additionally, adding years of productive effort to people's lives would add significantly to economic growth (Zhavoronkov and Litovchenko 2013).

As recently as the early 1900s, most causes of death were stated on certificates as "old age" or "natural causes". For the last century, however, the majority of countries have insisted on a cause other than "old age" - but what is written instead is very likely to be an age-related disease. If ageing were properly re-categorised as a disease, it would once again be the cause of death in the majority of cases.

When ageing is correctly identified as a disease, many benefits will flow. The pharmaceutical industry and policy-makers would be much more inclined to undertake research, and money would also flow to academia.

IS AGEING A DISEASE?

ROCKING AND A-KNOCKING ON DEATH'S DOOR

On the long road trip Jim recently made around the US to research this book – in all, 7,000 miles of driving – he and his friend Anthony Baillieu made a pit stop in Las Vegas and took in a show. This show was called *Rock Vault* and is a tribute to the rock bands of the 70s and 80s, performed by well-depreciated session musicians. Their act, which was very good indeed, was juxtaposed with video of the original rock stars in their youthful primes.

The old guys on the stage dressed the part, but the contrast with their heroes of yesteryear was a bit tragic. Paunches straining out of overly tight leather trousers, straggly greying hair (wigs in some cases), and awkward rock struts, with no effort at acrobatic guitar playing. In any case, they wouldn't have been able to get up from the stage if they had taken a fall!

Quite clearly these guys have aged and, despite the best efforts of the make-up department and of the costume providers, it was very noticeable. So, even for the rock musicians who in their pomp projected invincible youth, time does not stand still.

Ageing, the UK way of spelling it, and aging, the American way, cannot currently be avoided. Ageing is marked by a progressive loss of physical integrity, with lessened functionality and increased vulnerability to death. This deterioration is the precursor for general frailty and for the commonest human diseases: cardiovascular, lung and neurodegenerative disease, cancer and type 2 diabetes. After age 70, most people will suffer from one or more such diseases.

Ageing does not, however, appear to be an inevitable part of life, although for now it remains so until medical science prevails. One indication that ageing is not preordained in an unavoidable way is that all of our cells contain the DNA code (the "sacred scroll") which in theory if rewritten, could keep our bodies functioning indefinitely. Indeed, there exist some ultra long-lived mammalian creatures as well as some possibly immortal marine creatures, each of which is able to stay alive much longer than we do. DNA influences ageing in two ways. Firstly, the longevity of a species is programmed by genes which are made of DNA – and the effects of genes on ageing can be bad as well as good, for example, through **antagonistic pleiotropy** (see Theories of Ageing. Page 87). Secondly, the accumulation

of damage to DNA contributes to ageing. Most drugs work through acting on the proteins that are encoded by genes but not by directly altering those genes. Since the process of our own cell division is imperfect, from time to time, there are errors in the copying of DNA that cell division entails. Additionally, other factors damage our DNA and as a result, our bodies accumulate these errors over our lifetime.

So, whether you are a rock musician, an athlete or a regular person, the glory days are fleeting. Although a rock-and-roll life of debauchery and drugs does tend to accelerate the process!

BIOLOGY 101

All organisms have a **genome** – which is the makeup or "map" of its entire cellular being. The basic building block of this genome is **DNA (deoxyribonucleic acid).** Stretches of the DNA are copied into **RNA (ribonucleic acid)** which in turn is copied into proteins.

DNA is a molecule that contains the genetic information for all forms of animal life, as well as for some viruses (the rest use RNA). DNA is a **nucleic acid**, and is described in chemical terms as being a "polynucleotide", as it consists of a long chain of **nucleotides**. For the sake of clarity, we need to describe these nucleotides in a little more detail.

Each of the nucleotides of DNA are composed of three ingredients:

1. A base, of which human cells contain about 3 billion, comprising the famous letters C G A T, which are cytosine, guanine, adenine and thymine, respectively. The ordering of these bases constitutes the "codes" of our existence: their arrangement and placement, in the form of "**codon**s" of three letters, specify the proteins of which we are made. It is in the manipulation of these bases – in their rearrangement or deletion, or in the addition of new ones – that gene editing has such promise. (see Genetic Editions of You. Page 235).

Additionally, DNA contains:

2. A sugar molecule consisting of 5-carbon sugar (also called deoxyribose)

3. A phosphate molecule

DNA is formed of two strands wound tightly around a central axis in the shape of the famous double helix. The helix itself is then further wound around proteins called **histones**, into structures called nucleosomes. Histones are the main proteins from which **chromatin** (the structure of DNA and proteins) is made, and there are additional, "higher-level" windings that compact chromatin even further.

DNA is in every single one of our 37 trillion cells apart from red blood cells. The human genome contains between 20,000 and 25,000 genes – these vary in how many "bases" they consist of, ranging from several hundred to a few million.

People, as well as all other organisms which are eukaryotic, i.e. with a nucleus at the heart of their cells, have two copies of the vast majority of their genes, one from each parent. These genes are held in common by everyone, with less than 1% variation between individuals. It is variations in this 1% that give us our individual characteristics, including diseases and defects.

Genes are thus the physical units of heredity, by which we and other organisms pass on our genetic identity, and by which our bodies function. The genome is divided into chromosomes; each cell normally contains 23 pairs of chromosomes, for a total of 46. Chromosomes are structures located inside each cell, and are composed of DNA and of protein (the chromatin described above). Twenty-two of these pairs, called autosomes, are identical in both males and females. The twenty third pair, the sex chromosomes, differ between males and females.

Genes "code" for proteins, which execute almost all our bodily functions. It is often convenient to view genes as consisting of three types of nucleotide sequence: exons, introns and regulatory sequences. Genes can now be much more readily altered, both by using drugs and by editing, to change their "expression" (the rate at which they are decoded into proteins) and thereby to change aspects of our bodies and those of other organisms including plants and animals. This relative ease of altering genes (see Genetic Editions of You. Page 235) is the result of CRISPR, a new development that every interested investor should take careful note of and which, amongst other scientific advances, that holds so much promise for longevity.

The Human Cell Atlas, a project funded by the Chan Zuckerberg Initiative, aims to identify every cell in every tissue – estimated to be about 37 trillion in total in each of us – and to create a "cell map" of the entire human body (www.humancellatlas.org). This "single cell" branch of genomics is fast becoming important and more than 20 labs around the world are now engaged in the micro study of cells.

BIOLOGY 101

" *LIFESPAN IS DETERMINED BY THE RATE AT WHICH WEAR AND TEAR OUTRUNS REPAIR.* "

WHAT IS AGEING AND CAN IT BE SLOWED, REVERSED OR ELIMINATED?

The short answers: it's bad, maybe, possibly, and probably not!

Ageing is a complex, tortuous and difficult subject, not easy to distil into a book. There are competing theses on all aspects of ageing and longevity and academic tempers can and do run high. The main reason for the difficulties involved in this particular branch of science is that the chemistry underlying natural organisms is not simple, even in the case of the smallest of beings.

What cannot be doubted is that, as Alex Comfort of *Joy of Sex* fame wrote in 1972, ageing results in "a decrease in viability and an increase in vulnerability" and in "an increasing probability of death with increasing chronological age." No one disagrees that ageing is an unpleasant fact of current existence, and one that is both causative of disease and which marks our progress towards death.

Wear and tear eventually outruns our repair mechanisms. Although this is a simplistic and in many ways outdated view of ageing, it is broadly on target.

Very few disagree with Ashley Montagu, the long-lived 20th century anthropologist, who said that "the idea is to die young as late as possible." Achieving Montagu's goal is the central aspiration of our book. There is a mountain of information/research/hype on the subject as to why we age and whether the process of ageing can, or indeed should, be altered.

Ideas that had traction just one or two decades ago are being speedily superseded as science advances, making everything even more complicated. For instance, the leading idea about ageing, espoused by German biologist August Weismann in 1889 and essentially unchallenged until 1952, was that ageing's sole function was to weed out the old and worn out. Thereby, the aged would be forced out to make way for a more vigorous generation. A kind of late-life *Logan's Run*!

This is an example of so-called natural selection of the fittest, and is now more or less discredited as a standalone and viable hypothesis for ageing, not least because it is circular (it basically says that evolution has created ageing because ageing happens).

We go through some of the many theories of ageing later, and we conclude that today some of them are (sort of) converging into a credible thesis, yet to be fully worked out. A consensus theory, no matter how woolly, would be very helpful to the cause of longevity science.

In a nutshell, we believe that it is possible to extend average human life expectancy significantly just by using today's technology, to within a decade or so of today's current "hard" ceiling of about 115 years. But then what? This hard ceiling is one that is rarely broken and only then for a few years and only by a small number of outliers. Exceeding it will be a difficult problem to crack, but cracked it will surely be. As to when, we readily admit we have no clear idea. But make no mistake: scientists today are engaged in building the metaphorical "time bridge" of cellular and other interventions that will take humans past this ceiling and to lifespans that today seem unimaginable.

This "bridge" is being built on a foundation of existing and developmental-stage therapies and they include, but are not limited to: stem cells, genetic engineering, drugs such as **rapalogs (analogs of rapamycin)**, drugs related to **sirtuins** (see NAD+. Page 189), drugs regulating insulin signalling, drugs regulating cardiac activity, new immunotherapies for cancer, and **Aβ** and **tau** clearance drugs for neurodegeneration – as well as bio-printed organs and tissues and the use of **transgenic** animals to produce new organs. (see Organs. Page 220).

Older, reformulated drugs, such as **metformin** and rapamycin, are the subject of much research, as are **resveratrol**, NMD/niacin/DHA and bromocriptine, in activating sirtuins (see Targets in Ageing. Page 189).

Also, apparently having some effect on extending life, to varying degrees, are aspirin (but with potentially dangerous bleeding side effects), 17α-oestradiol (non-feminising oestrogen), and nordihydroguaiaretic acid (from the creosote plant). Probably not working to promote life extension are green tea, curcumin, and anything in the omega-3 supplement category, other than highly purified fish oil, such as Vascepa from a company called Amarin.

Key **molecular pathways** such as **mTOR**/mTORC1/2 **(mechanistic target of rapamycin)** and **Insulin-like Growth Factor 1** (IGF-1) are now known to have an influence on ageing, and in this book we examine those. For instance, decreased signalling by the **Growth Hormone/**Insulin-like Growth Factor 1(GH/IGF-1) network is associated with longer lifespans in several models. In mice where GH and IGF-1 signalling has been decreased, lifespans increase by a third or so. (see mTOR. Page 184).

As examples, **nicotinamide riboside** and precursors or analogs of it are being avidly studied to see if they work in humans to extend or to improve life the same way they do in mice. There is also speculation that retroviral drugs, such as modified versions of those used in HIV treatment, might have an effect in slowing ageing, though there is nothing in the scientific literature on this subject, at least none that we can find.

Additionally, good progress is being made in addressing at least some of the diseases associated with ageing, such as cancer, type 2 diabetes and cardiovascular disease. To a lesser extent, this also applies to respiratory conditions and neurodegenerative diseases.

Apart from drugs, genetic techniques using the new CRISPR-like technologies (see Genetic Editions of You. Page 235) will almost certainly have utility in anti-ageing treatments, and stem cell therapies are now at last showing some anti-ageing promise.

Techniques are now being developed to "grow" replacement organs outside the body either in animals (mostly pigs) or on "cellular scaffolds", and to implant them in the same way that replacement parts are put into cars. Currently, these "grown"

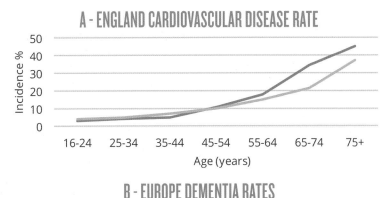

A - ENGLAND CARDIOVASCULAR DISEASE RATE

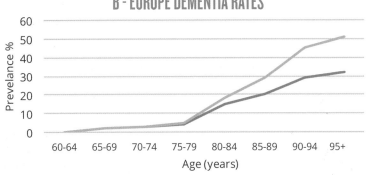

B - EUROPE DEMENTIA RATES

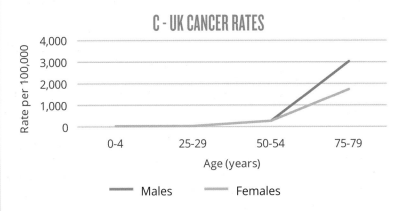

C - UK CANCER RATES

Males   Females

Disease or total death rates for the most common diseases of old age. (A) Cardiovascular disease incidence in England in 2006 (source: British Heart Foundation 'Coronary heart disease statistics' 2010). (B) Dementia prevalence in EU countries in 2006 (source: Alzheimer Europe, 2009). (C) Age-specific mortality rates per 100,000 population, UK (source: Cancer Research UK).

organs are too small to be effective in humans and are used primarily for research purposes. But the science is advancing fast. Body tissues can now be printed by 3D techniques, and these printed tissues will soon be used "in vivo" as opposed to just for academic research.

So a bridge is being built to "carry" us into another two or three decades of life. Built on existing and foreseeable technologies, this construct will buy us the time we need until the arrival of even more revolutionary technologies which will be based around the manipulation of our fundamental biological structures.

This bridge will be built despite the self-destructive lifestyles adopted in recent decades by many people across the world – lifestyles which have increased the prevalence of diabetes, of obesity and many other ills.

There will, of course, be many problems and obstacles in getting to the end of the first bridge. Will science indeed prevail? Can the imagination, endeavour and brilliance of the small band of scientists currently leading this longevity field be enough to make it happen? And if they do succeed, who will be able to afford the expensive treatments capable of extending lifespan? Only the rich and the elite? What are the demographic, work, and family implications of all this? These are some of the questions we address in our book, but at a bird's-eye level because the principal and distinctive purpose of the book is to make money for early investors in the area of longevity by switching on that money fountain!

A good pointer as to why ageing may eventually be treatable, if not directly reversible, is the fact that our bodies get stronger and add functionality over the early part of our lives. This suggests that if we could reincorporate youthful traits into older bodies, we who are older might in some ways become biologically younger.

As we have said, the paradigm shift in medicine – and one coming in the near future – is that ageing will be regarded as a single disease complex rather than as an inevitable process or condition. This change in attitudes and practice will happen by the gradual adoption of what has been best described as **regenerative medicine.** As Dr Nir Barzilai (see Key Opinion Leaders. Page 151), one of our interviewees, says, "treating the diseases of ageing as individual diseases, independent of ageing itself, has serious downsides; quite often the treatment of one disease, be it diabetes or heart disease, leads directly to another."

There are many diseases associated with ageing – cancer, cardiovascular disease, type 2 diabetes, respiratory impairment, muscle wasting and neurodegenerative disease being the principal ones. Some scientists such as Jay Olshansky (University of Illinois) have made the point that if the fundamental biological pathways involved in ageing could be altered, manipulated, blocked or substituted, then all age-associated diseases could be addressed in one fell swoop.

Ageing has in the past been regarded as separate to conventional diseases because it is perceived to be a "natural state." But, since pregnancy (also a natural state) is often subject to intervention (such as contraception, IVF, etc.) then why shouldn't ageing also be treated medically? Obesity was not considered to be a disease until relatively recently. Previously, being obese was thought to be the result of a failure of willpower, but today we all know it to be a deadly condition. And this is possibly due to a "switch" in the brain that never goes off in obese people – a switch leading to the permanent accumulation of **white adipose tissue** (Monash University 2017).

The diseases of accelerated ageing such as progeria, where the victims sometimes go from infancy to apparent old age within two short decades, are indeed considered diseases as opposed to conditions. So why should people who display the same symptoms as progeria sufferers, but some fifty years later than those

few patients, not also be considered to be carriers of a disease?

Diseases of accelerated ageing which are most notably Hutchinson-Gilford progeria, Werner syndrome and Dyskeratosis congenita are due to genetic defects, but their effects are in many ways like a sped-up version of "normal" ageing. It is true that progerias are not very accurate representations of normal ageing, but the study of these conditions has nonetheless produced some interesting insights into ageing as a syndrome.

Some scientists, noting that we are "selected" for reproduction (and that when we have reproduced we have no further utility and thus age and die (see Theories of Ageing. Page 68), believe that ageing has absolutely no useful evolutionary function, further strengthening the case that it should, therefore, be considered a treatable syndrome. (Caplan 1992, Gems 2011, 2013).

If ageing were to be categorised as a disease, there would surely be much more focus on the development of strategies to deal with it, to slow it down and to address the fundamental biological mechanics behind it. Serious money would then flow into ageing research, whether from governments, institutions or drug companies.

If we could address the causes of ageing such as chronic inflammation

(see Inflammaging. Page 60), cell breakdown, mitochondrial **DNA damage**, stem cell depletion, as well as **cellular senescence**, we might be a good way down the track to the life extension that we see coming.

Rather than degenerating over a prolonged period, the paradigm for exiting the world could in time become one of a speedy, or even unheralded, descent into death at the end of a much longer life than the one that most people currently live.

Some will be fearful that this type of "overnight" or sudden death without the traditional long period of anticipation and decline is somehow "unnatural". They might think that a death not preceded by disease and deterioration is somehow inferior to the anguished death bed scenes, pain and suffering that characterise a large percentage of deaths today. In this context, Pablo Neruda's line that the "graves are full of ruined bones, of speechless death rattles" is apposite.

Maybe they are wrong. Death that is peaceful, though unanticipated, may be what most people will aspire to. Certainly, we authors do – though at a much, much later date! But maybe people who are retaining their youthfulness will also retain their lust for life, however long ago they were born. Could it even be, in the realms of imagination but not of fiction, that there will be no death at all? That is a niche view – but no longer one that is considered to be totally outlandish.

The new field of anti-ageing medicine presents investors with an opportunity to participate in what will surely become one of the biggest industries in the world – if not, indeed, the biggest.

Our views on the subject of longevity have been shaped by many visits with key opinion leaders in the field, cold towels wrapped around our heads whilst reading a wide variety of source materials – and most importantly, by the close examination of the investment prospects of the key longevity companies.

Overall, our efforts have revealed that there is an incredible amount of activity in the longevity/anti-ageing area – some of it already bearing fruit, both in terms of products and strategies that we can already employ to live longer and in the context of making those money fountains gush with filthy lucre.

But why is now the time to look at longevity, rather than say in a few years' time? After all, humans have been around for a very long time, so what makes the people who live on the planet today so different from their ancestors?

First, the research tools available to scientists are improving rapidly, particularly in the field of **genomic sequencing**, in the management of big data, and in the use of non-animal models to get scientific answers much faster than by conventional means. (see Insilico Medicine. Page 120).

Second, because so much information has now been discovered about the pathways, genes and proteins that are implicated in ageing and so much chemistry has been done on what might interfere with them, the trials of therapies designed to influence lifespan are imminent. Indeed, as we shall see, some compounds which might influence lifespan are available right now, even if anti-ageing properties can't yet be definitively claimed for them.

One of the problems of ageing research is that people live a long time and trials involving humans have to be designed over long periods, making them expensive and very time-consuming. That's why alternative **models of ageing** (see Animal Models. Page 116) are so useful and computer simulations are becoming increasingly vital to getting to the important points of discovery.

Scientists in the field of **biomedical gerontology** (longevity and anti-ageing) have been working hard to identify the many genes and pathways that are implicated in ageing and in determining which ones are more important than others. A great deal of progress has been made here, and such things as mTOR, IGF-1/insulin signalling, **sestrins**, FOXO3A, sirtuins,

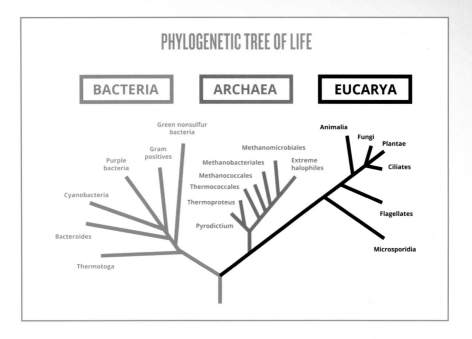

PHYLOGENETIC TREE OF LIFE

ApoE, CETP, daf-2 and AMPK, to name just a few, are now revealed as being important to the ageing process. (see Targets in Ageing. Page 183).

As an example, the **forkhead box family of transcription factors (FOXO)** has at least 40 variants in humans and hundreds in other species and plants. These genes are highly relevant to many human diseases because of their role in the specific disease syndrome of ageing, and are also important in controlling the cell cycles of organisms. The FOXO gene family is named after the fruit fly gene which, when mutated, causes the fly to have a distinctive fork head. Human FOX proteins are almost equivalent ("homologous")

to fruit fly forkhead genes – just one way in which flies are highly useful in research into ageing.

There is a much longer list of abstruse names given to genes, pathways, compounds and so forth related to ageing and we cover many of the key ones in this investment book. Since we are not scientists, please forgive us that this is not the comprehensive list you might find in a university textbook.

There is now a vast array of research into two of the most popular proxies of ageing, worms and yeast (see Animal Models. Page 116). Data from both species indicates that a commonality ("conservation") of the mechanisms that cause late-life decline exists in both of them. This is even though their evolutionary paths diverged at least a billion years ago.

Humans also appear to have these **conserved** pathways linked to ageing. Conserved simply means that some of the DNA sequences appear to have been remained relatively unchanged far back in time, as revealed by the "tree of life" (the so-called **phylogenetic** tree). This is in spite of **speciation**, which is the division of organisms into different species over a long evolutionary period.

Similarly, when we consider the far shorter timeframe of civilisation, the humans of today have almost exactly the same biological make-up as our ancestors stretching back many thousands of years, despite the fact that environmental improvement means that we are much longer-lived than those ancestors ever were.

It is the prospect of manipulating our fundamental biology and of overcoming the conservation of pro-ageing genetics that makes longevity such an exciting area. For the first time in history a concerted and significant effort is being made to unravel the roles that the multitude of bewildering pathways, genes and other factors play in ageing.

In the recent past, animals and other organisms have had their lifespans significantly extended in laboratories, something which points – sometimes tenuously – to the potential of finding a way of doing the same in humans. Although fruit flies and mice aren't human, the great genetic resemblance that they have with us and the fact that the genetic and chemical interventions in those models can have such dramatic effects makes scientists hope that similar types of interventions might just have a comparable effect in humans.

Just a few years ago, the possibility of an ultra-long life (over 110) becoming commonplace was envisioned only by people thought to be crackpots or charlatans. Today, one by one, the challenges to such ultra-long lifespans are being overcome. The ramparts protecting ageing as a defined and immutable condition are being stormed. Already, we can, and are, reducing the risk of dying from the diseases of ageing. For instance, cardiovascular disease (CVD) related deaths and cancer deaths are each falling in developed countries by about 2 to 4% per annum.

The five main causes of death in older adults are: cardiovascular malfunction, cancer, pulmonary malfunction, neurodegeneration and type 2 diabetes – are the main causes of death in older adults. Every day, across the world, about 160,000 people die, and 70% of them expire in older age because of one of those disease categories. The young tend to die of other things – accidents, drugs, suicides, etc. and only rarely from the deadly diseases of ageing.

In most developed countries, it is mandatory to specify the cause of death on the death certificates, and old "old age" isn't recognised as a disease for that purpose. This is despite the fact that very aged people appear to enjoy late-life protection against specific diseases and instead of dying of a specific cause, they just "wear out". Most people, however, do die of one or more diseases.

While progress is being made in reducing the incidence of the Deadly Quintet (CVD, cancer, lung disease, diabetes and neurodegenerative disease) even their total elimination would not fundamentally alter the fact that we would all steadily decline and die. We cannot yet grow younger. For that to be possible, scientists would have to understand how to manipulate cell biology at a much more detailed level than they can today.

Fortunately, the analytical tools available to scientists are improving dramatically. At the University of Oxford, we saw a molecule at its atomic level in 3D – something that only 10 years ago was thought to be beyond the limitations of physics (see page 66). Another important historic marker in this fairly new branch of

science was the discovery in 1983 (by Michael Klass) that the nematode worm C. elegans, now one of the favourite models of researchers, could be manipulated to live longer. Subsequent work by Cynthia Kenyon (then of University of California, San Francisco) as well as by others, has extended these worms' lives by up to 10 times.

In 2000 Steve Austad, who is a leading anti-ageing researcher, bet his friend Jay Olshansky that someone born in that year would live to at least 2150. There was, until recently, a sign on the road from San Francisco airport to the city stating more or less the same thing. Steve's descendants will collect on the bet if he himself doesn't make it long enough to see the 150th birthday of the lucky person. But for this wager to come true, combinatorial factors leading to extended lives have to be invented and to prove effective. As tantalising as that sounds, the first bar is to get average life expectancy up to a level close to current maximal lifespans.

For some time, researchers have been using non-human animal ("in vivo") and other laboratory-based ("in vitro") models to demonstrate that tweaking an organism's genes and its external environment can induce extended longevity. Indeed, it was as early as 1935 when it was discovered that caloric restriction (CR) could extend lifespans in rats by 50%, and this proved to be a landmark in studying ways in which longevity could be artificially induced.

It was also observed that chilled flies live longer than flies living in normal temperature conditions; the cold seems to influence **metabolism** and thereby to extend life in some creatures. This may apply, at least in a marginal way, to humans too, but it is an impractical intervention to make. Not many people want to live their lives with their teeth continuously chattering!

As we shall discuss in greater detail later, the "torture" of worms, yeast, fruit flies and mice has been going on for many years, as these are the principal models used to explore what works and what doesn't work in extending life.

Unfortunately, much of the pre-clinical animal research does not translate either fully or even at all to human biology, but in some areas, it demonstrably does. In most, but not all, models it appears that eventually wear and tear outruns repair.

As we described in one of our previous books, *Cracking the Code*, our bodies are incredibly complex cellular systems, and although scientists have made huge progress in understanding how cells live and die, we are still at a primitive stage in longevity science's potential.

The machinery that repairs the cells of our bodies is a key element of research because it is this machinery that eventually lets us all down as the process of cell division and the fidelity of chromosomal replication deteriorates with the ravages of time and as a result of our environment. Repairing and improving the cellular and tissue repair kit is thus a big focus for scientists.

But, what exactly is ageing? Ageing is rigorously described as **senescence**, the progressive degradation of bodily functions. Sir Peter Medawar, a British pioneer in ageing research in the 1940s, described ageing as an "unsolved problem of biology". Medawar proposed that some **genetic mutations** only have deleterious effects late in life and are not "selected out" by evolution, as evolution is concerned primarily with reproductive "fitness" and not necessarily with the prolongation of life. He suggested that increasing age features a decline in the strength of "natural selection".

In some cases, mutations may be helpful to us in earlier life but can turn against us in old age. This idea, due to George C Williams, is the theory of "antagonistic pleiotropy". It leads to the famous **Medawar-Williams Theory**, which is a fusion of both men's views. The combined theory posits that accumulated mutations will put an eventual limit on our existence. An apparent example of antagonistic pleiotropy is cellular senescence, which is described in Theories of Ageing. Page 87.

Molecules become unbound, genes become inefficient, waste products (cellular debris) build up and we (and other organisms) die. Organisms of all types accumulate damage to cells, tissues, organs, and indeed to all basic molecules causing genomic instability to set in. Along with this comes shortening of the **telomeres**, reduced mitochondrial function (limiting energy production), the depletion of the potency of stem cells, and impaired intercellular networks. Today, the Medawar-Williams Theory has been refined and updated. The "unsolved question of biology" of seventy years ago is not yet solved – but the answer is now tantalisingly closer.

Senescence is a pretty good word to describe the **pathology** (which is the study of the essential nature of a disease) of ageing – and, as we will discuss later, senescent cells appear to be one of the important factors in what should by now be described as the single disease of ageing.

For now, there are no specifically approved or recommended treatments to delay or to reverse ageing, other than fairly obvious lifestyle prescriptions, which include caloric restriction (CR) (see Targets in Ageing. Page 180) – i.e. fasting but not to the point of starvation.

Realistically though, we who live in the developed world enjoy food in abundance and so it's going to be hard to get people to even consider a drastic reduction in caloric intake even if it might result in living a little bit longer. Adopting a CR diet as a means of living longer was observed as being effective in animals over 80 years ago, but most humans will never attempt it over the long-term, or if they do, they will soon abandon it.

More practically, if we are to gain any small benefit from CR, we need to find a pharmacological way to mimic its advantages, without the downside of feeling perpetually hungry. Let's face it, most of us just enjoy eating too much.

At this juncture, readers might well be wondering why are we so optimistic about the opportunities in longevity science if we exhibit no fundamental biological superiority to our ancestors, and if there is nothing out there that is an approved treatment that slows or even reverses ageing.

The reason is that research has started revealing things about our bodies that will provide the basis for interventional techniques, some of which will lead to extending life. The health and longevity gains made as a result of sanitation, antibiotics, improved environments, and other factors play much of a role. Instead the leap forward will come by changing basic biology. And to speed this science on its path, research into animal and other models of ageing, as well as "machine learning," is growing rapidly.

As we get older, our bodies first develop faults, eventually becoming unstable and frail which is more or less the same thing that happens to laboratory models. The list of these faults, which eventually emerge in every animal that lives long enough, reads like a litany of despair.

The **mitochondria**, large structures **("organelles")** within our cells, are the machines that extract energy from nutrients and store it as **adenosine triphosphate** (ATP). Mitochondria are central to our metabolisms, but as we age, they function less effectively. We also accumulate more senescent or dormant/useless cells as we grow older (see Senescent Cells. Page 194) and our stem cells (see Stemming the Tide. Page 206) become less potent. Further, our whole cellular network becomes less efficient as communication between individual cells, tissues and organs deteriorate.

Ageing is physically manifested in a multitude of other ways, both visible and invisible. Examples of this are hair thinning and loss of pigment in our hair colour, loss of fertility in post-menopausal women, bone density loss, skin discolouration and loss of its elasticity, loss of muscular strength and memory problems. Our immune system also becomes compromised and our ability to maintain hormonal balance degrades.

The failure of our immune systems is why the potency of vaccinations starts to decline sharply in many people who are over 65 years old. Our reserves of T-cells and B-cells, the keys to fighting infections and cancers, decline with age as more and more of them lose their "naïve" or never-used qualities. Those are the cells that have not yet been "written" on to fight attacks by new invaders. But as we get older we tend to have been exposed to high levels of antigenic load and we have fewer and fewer naïve antigen-non-experienced T-cells, and this results in **immunosenescence**.

As we age we also become more prone to cancer, cardiovascular disease, type 2 diabetes, neurodegenerative disease, osteoporosis, arthritis and macular degeneration. We can't walk as well, we lose balance and our digestive system works less effectively.

In short, all the indignities and signs of old age emerge over time. Once they start to proliferate, we start to crumble. Meanwhile, the Grim Reaper awaits just around the corner – with his scythe at the ready. And from ashes to ashes, there we go.

Ageing in sexually reproducing creatures may have evolved about a billion years ago and resulted from

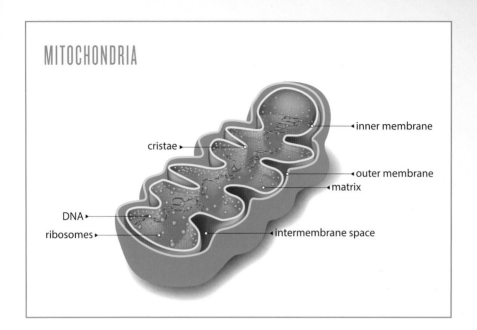

MITOCHONDRIA

inner membrane

cristae ►

◄ outer membrane

◄ matrix

DNA ►

ribosomes ►

◄ intermembrane space

what was once thought to be the evolutionary imperative of passing on genetic material to subsequent generations – in order to produce new and "better" versions of the species. Prior to that, and close to the dawn of the planet, single-celled organisms were (and still are) "immortal", in the sense that they could multiply into daughter cells and therefore did not "die". The earliest, **prokaryotic** cells formed the basis of early life. When **eukaryotic cells** (the ones that we are made of) evolved around 2.5 billion years ago, the early glimmers of the mortality which affects all multicellular creatures, including we humans, came into being. But not all living things die and this is an important clue as to why we might not have to either.

Even though all humans are currently destined to die, some of our cells are immortal. These cells remain immortal for as long as we remain alive. Even after we die they can remain immortal, at least in the sense that they can continue replicating in laboratories.

The fact that these immortal cell lines exist provides another clue as to why our ultimate destiny of being a pile of ash may not be written in stone. These immortal cells are cancer cells and **germ cells**, both of which can survive and replicate outside their hosts indefinitely, and they provide important clues to understanding cell life and death.

The most famous of the "immortal" cancer cells are those harvested from Henrietta Lacks, a woman, who died in the 1950s. These cells persist even today and are used widely in research because the original cells from her tumour have been multiplied many times over by propagated cells. Additionally, there are long-lived creatures, some of which may even be immortal, that provide pointers to the prospect of functional immortality in a broad sense for humans. But that point of immortality is so far away that it is not the focus of this book. We are more interested in the smaller, yet still dramatic, gains in life expectancy that are about to be harvested – gains which will employ existing techniques.

Death occurs not because we are preprogrammed to expire. We are not thus programmed; only a few scientists still believe that we have an internal "clock" of some kind hidden in our genomes, one which activates pro-ageing genes. But neither does it seem to be a single genetic determination that we must die. Paradoxically, the absence of such a single genetic "switch" makes finding a cure for "ageing" all the more difficult, since there are so many factors that are implicated in the ageing process.

So, for instance, **Professor Leonard Hayflick's** 1961 discovery – the **Hayflick Limit** – remains a barrier to overcome. (see Key Opinion Leaders. Page 160). Hayflick, with whom we have had dinner in San Francisco, identified a limit of 50 or so potential cell divisions in dividing cells. Programming our cells to divide and replicate more often than the Hayflick limit is a target for current and future research. But a note of caution: it is also known that increasing a cell's capacity to replicate might lead to more replicative errors and thereby to the vicarious activation of cancer-promoting oncogenes.

In parallel with the genetic component of ageing, it appears that the syndrome is also highly influenced by the environment and that if we could change our environment then we could change our life expectancy. We are not referring to climate change, important though that is. Environment in this context is the backdrop to an individual's life, our cumulative exposure to the sun and dangerous chemicals, as well as the types of food we eat, the amount of exercise we take, the amount we drink and smoke, the drugs we take, our stress levels, our sleep patterns, etc. This environment can and does make a difference to how long we live.

In a 2004 study of 5,400 twins, where an almost identical genome is shared by each pair, it was observed that the two members of any single pair very rarely die at anywhere near the same age. Moreover, genetics were responsible for only about 20% of any age-related diseases that they acquired in later life, with the other 80% being due to the different environments in which they lived – as well as to plain old luck (known in the scientific canon as random chance, or **stochastics**).

Ageing is currently inevitable because we haven't yet figured out how to use our medical and scientific armamentarium against it, but it is absolutely our prime risk or death, which we do of course intuitively understand.

Ageing raises many questions, for instance, there is an evolutionary component to our eventual demise, but what exactly is that? **Entropy**, based around the **Second Law of Thermodynamics**, may play a part – but increasingly this is not believed to be the whole story. **Genetic hyperfunctioning**, quasi-programmes, rate of living, accumulated DNA breakages/other damage, failure of body repair mechanisms – these are all worthwhile theories, and all being researched at a furious rate, as are other emerging explanations. (see Theories of Ageing. Page 78).

As some of these theories converge into what will ideally be a single and elegant explanation of ageing, the truth about how we can defer death will come into sharper and sharper focus. Just as hidden depths have recently been revealed about cancer,

leading to its containment and possibly to its functional elimination, so it will be with ageing. Ageing will be slowed, and then slowed further and possibly in some aspects, reversed. It will take time, but this train is leaving the station. Boy, is it a complex and contentious area!

What does appear to be incontrovertible – although why is a matter of some debate – is that the exposure of our bodies to two types of assault on our DNA – external (or **exogenous**) damage, and internal (or **endogenous**) damage – gradually contributes to genomic instability. The software that guides us begins to freeze, malfunction and eventually crashes. Thus, **homeostasis** – the steady state when our bodies are in balance – can't and doesn't last forever.

Because some of our cells divide so often, mistakes are sometimes made and these can slip through the cracks of our internal quality control. These mistakes, combined with external, physical, chemical and other "insults" to our DNA, accumulate until there comes a point when they can no longer be tolerated.

All animals generate energy through the process of cellular respiration (oxidative phosphorylation) and, over time, defects in this process begin to cause problems. This includes the increased production of free radicals (**reactive oxygen species – ROS**), a major source of damage to our cells, tissues and to the entire body.

The process of cellular respiration consists of the use of oxygen to extract energy from nutrients. This metabolic process produces waste products, notably carbon dioxide. The exchange of oxygen for carbon dioxide takes place through the circulatory system, otherwise known as the "vasculature" – consisting of the heart, blood vessels, and of other transport networks. Imbalances build up between the ROS, which are products of our metabolic systems, and, on the other side, our normal cellular repair mechanisms. ROS are generally negative but they do also play a role in attacking pathogens, so their total elimination would not be good. Because of the presence of ROS and of other factors which damage our DNA, mistakes in the DNA replication process happen all of the time. Most are corrected, but eventually our repair toolkit becomes rusty and begins to fail us.

The big question here is: can we promote, improve, or rejuvenate our cellular repair mechanisms, such that excess ROS and other "bad stuff" doesn't damage our cells to the extent that it inevitably does today? And by so doing, could it thereby slow, or indeed, reverse ageing? Over-the-counter pills and supplements won't do it, although vegetables and good food might

help a bit, so fundamental science needs to come to the rescue.

Oxidative stress, the name for what ROS and other harmful compounds cause in our cells, is mostly produced in our mitochondria, the machines that produce our energy. In their normal states these organelles have several ways, using **enzymes** (proteins which catalyse chemical reactions) such as superoxide dismutase, catalase and glutathione peroxidase, to detoxify excess ROS. But they are never perfect at this task, and with age they become even less perfect.

This failure of cellular repair processes leads to disease, metabolic imbalance, and eventually death. Although ROS and other toxins are not the only reason that we die, they are heavy contributors to the eventual breakdown of our homeostasis. Along with the fact that our repair systems become compromised, sluggish and ineffective, other weakening factors appear. We get undesirable losses and gains to our chromosomes, genes get disrupted by **transposons,** mutations develop, and our telomeres get shorter (see Transposons and Telomere sections. Page 252).

What's more, mitochondrial DNA (mtDNA), the key to our efficient energy production and effective metabolism, becomes adversely affected. As a result, time and the luck of our environmental and genomic draw eventually kills us, as well as almost all other living organisms.

Think of this process as a slow leakage of energy, one which stems from the loss of our cellular integrity. The flame that burned so bright in youth is gradually reduced to embers – and then to ashes. What scientists are now working on are ways to keep the flame burning and the machinery turning for longer. And we believe there is a very good chance of them succeeding.

Ageing starts right at the point of conception, and of course, our skeletons stop developing by about the time we are 20 years old. Men tend to age and die slightly younger than women, though the gap is narrowing in most countries. It does seem that women have stronger immune systems than men (important for longevity), but as a result, women are also more prone to autoimmune diseases, such as arthritis, lupus and asthma. This is because their more finely tuned immune systems are more likely to over activate than those of men. For organisms that reproduce sexually, such as human beings, the rate of ageing is different from individual to individual, due to both heritable and environmental factors.

Although observationally the pace at which we humans age is different among people, the specific "rate of biological ageing" can now be measured. This is done by using an **epigenetic clock**, developed by Horvath and team in 2013 at the University of California, Los Angeles. This epigenetic clock, which uses 353 epigenetic markers, is a pretty accurate indicator of the rate of ageing (+/- 2.7 years margin of error), and uses measurements of DNA methylation (substitution of a hydrogen atom by a methyl group) to estimate biological age between individuals and species. The change in methylation is directly proportional to age. Other more accurate and complex clocks are being developed including one by Insilico Medicine.

There is plenty of controversy and debate around almost every aspect of ageing research, including its most fundamental aspects. For instance, perceived wisdom of many scientists is that ageing is the result of accumulated damage to DNA, principally through oxidation, and involves so-called "free radicals". Others believe that in addition to damage, some innate processes are at work, whereby DNA is damaged by so-called **epimutations** on a "timer" basis, which alters the methylation of **nuclear DNA** and similar modifications of histones.

There are also scientists, including **Aubrey de Grey** (see Key Opinion Leaders. Page 154), one of our interviewees, who believe damage to nuclear DNA is not relevant, except insofar as it can lead to cancers, but that damage to mtDNA is far more important. His view is that we need to replicate in older people all of the biochemical advantages that younger people have and thereby keep humans alive for extended periods.

There are elements of truth to all of these and to many of the other hypotheses about ageing – and it seems to us that the differences which separate many of them are beginning to be narrowed by discoveries over a wide front. A consensus theory of ageing is slowly emerging.

Whatever the reasons for ageing and its biology, the fact that we age remains unavoidable. The question, is how do we get to 110, 135 – or even older, if indeed this is possible?

Although we live long lives compared to most species on the planet, we are by no means the longest-lived. It is certainly the case that although almost all organisms appear to die at some point, some seem to have exceptionally long lives, and indeed some are capable of dramatic regeneration, even after suffering major injury or trauma.

Sea anemones are one such example, as are hydra (a relative of the jellyfish); others include tortoises and turtles, some types of shark, sturgeon fish, and certain reptiles. Some trees can live exceptionally long, even if they are not part of a clonal or shared system. This steady state as far as we humans are concerned is called homeostasis. In our continuous exposure to environmental and internal DNA damage, however, homeostasis cannot persist, and the processes of ageing appear to become irreversible. So, if these species can live ultra-long lives, why can't we? They have seemingly overcome what we have not and their ability to do so must lie in genetics. Maybe humans can indeed live much longer and if that proves to be the case, the implications would be pretty dramatic.

Lifespan is the result of the speed at which wear and tear outruns repair. So, in the present world, we humans live life in three stages – infancy and education, work, and retirement: leading up to eventual death. This progression is not a biological imperative, but is today a conformist response to the ordered view of society that lifespan is preordained, within certain parameters. As people's lifespans increase notwithstanding that the pace of increase has recently (and, in our view, temporarily) slowed, societies will start to rethink the fundamental tenets of this established routine of growth, homeostasis, and decline.

The implications for populations everywhere are huge; education will be continuous throughout life, family life will be very different, and work will be something that goes on way beyond the current retirement ages of developed economies. This is because, in short, our research indicates that lifespan (and, importantly, healthy lifespan, or "healthspan") is on the verge of a significant shift upwards, possibly by more than 30%.

Within decades, a fresh understanding of the principles of cell biology will allow for the manipulation of age-specific pathways and of so-called cell senescence – which, combined, will take mankind beyond the record of 122 that Jeanne Calment set over two decades ago.

As with so much technology in recent years, the realisation of this vision is now becoming a blurry possibility, and although the ways in which it will happen are unclear, we are certain it will happen.

Of course, there are plenty of doubters of the view that we are on the verge of a lifespan revolution. These include some genuine luminaries of the scientific world, including some (a dwindling band) who believe that the Second Law of Thermodynamics (see Theories of Ageing. Page 78), combined with the fact that our toolkit is still relatively primitive, will make life extension beyond 120 impossible for many years to come, except for some very rare outliers.

One such doubter, Jan Vijg, of the Albert Einstein College of Medicine in New York, is convinced that the human body has innate limits. People who make it to beyond 115 are rare, and life expectancy even for them is highly limited thereafter. Only two people are officially verified to have ever lived beyond 118.

Dr Vijg believes that average life expectancy, and indeed average healthspans, can and will increase but that the upper limit is about 115, after which our bodies will simply collapse and die. According to Vijg and the Einstein researchers, this upward arc for maximal lifespan has a hard ceiling and some people, though not most, have already touched it. Dr Vijg used data from the Human Mortality Database, which compiles mortality and population data from more than 40 countries. This data suggests that, since 1900, survival improvements for people 100 or over have been more or less maximised, and that the chance of anyone living over 125 anywhere in the world is only one in 10,000 – and that is for any time in the foreseeable future.

Judith Campisi is a respected scientist from the Buck Institute for Research on Aging just north of San Francisco, one of the most important centres for ageing research (and one which Jim has visited). Professor Campisi believes that ageing is becoming postponed and will be postponed further in coming decades. But she cautions, as we do, that any further gains in maximal lifespan will have to come through the modification of genomes. She is more pessimistic than we are on the timing of this as she rightly points out that there are so many genes implicated in ageing, it will be hard to modify most or all of them within the space of two generations. But we note that only a few such modifications may in fact be needed.

However, the more optimistic camp is gaining some decent traction. For instance, Tom Kirkwood of Newcastle University in the UK, who is an important opinion leader in the longevity field, disputes the notion that there is a limit to human lifespan: "The idea does not really fit with what we already know about the biology of the ageing process. There is no set programme for ageing – the process is driven by the build-up of faults and damage in the cells and organs of the body, which is malleable." This malleability of our bodies provides the main grounds for optimism. If science can change our fundamental path, it changes the world.

It is entirely possible, in our view, that because ageing does not appear to be specifically evolved, but is a function of evolutionary neglect, (i.e. that evolution has no reason to prevent it – Foddy 2012), that at some point in the future the basic mechanisms of getting older will be understood,

slowed and halted, or even reversed. That point of reversal is some way away, and we have to admit, may never be achieved, even though it cannot be ruled out.

Most scientists share the contention that we are "selected" for reproduction, and that when we have reproduced we have no further utility so age and die. They believe that ageing has no useful evolutionary function, but some conclude that it should be considered a treatable syndrome. (Caplan 1992, Gems 2011, 2013).

Though we must again stress that our estimates of timeframes are immensely speculative, here they are anyway. We judge that the coming improvement in lifespans and healthspans is about 20 years away and will mean that average life expectancy (the typical person's age at death regardless of health) around the world will rise from about 73 today to close to 100. In developed countries, it will rise to over 110 at around that same time. This is not some sort of outlandish fiction – in our considered view it has a very good chance of happening.

This change in lifespan will be the result of the most important scientific developments in history. It will alter the whole trajectory of our lives and also the ways in which our physical and societal world operates. It will be achieved partly by improving the environment (the sum of factors that currently lead to exogenous DNA damage and disease), and also by new drugs and interventions that will manipulate the molecular pathways known to be implicated in ageing.

Importantly, this is a book for investors. The incremental addition of 30 years or so to average lifespans over the next two or three decades will represent the single greatest investment opportunity in recorded history. Normally, we start to really decline after age 60 and in a highly visible and precipitous way. This is the key reason why we, sadly not in the first flush of youth, are going to be among the first in line for the life-extending treatments that we outline in this book.

It is at this point of more rapid decline – around 60 years old – that we tend to lose metabolic "information", the system which allows us to perform normal and efficient cellular repairs. We then become the victims of what has been described by Professor David Sinclair (see Key Opinion Leaders. Page 149) as "epigenetic noise" which is the cumulative randomisation of genomic behaviour that results from being alive for six decades or more. Although in the developed world we generally live for another 23 years after hitting sixty, for the last two decades of our lives most of us are likely to suffer the increasing burden of the diseases of ageing.

The bad news is that, according to what we have discovered, there can be no true immortality in our current form. Immortality would require us to change all of our cells, all of our organs, and most improbably, our brains, which represent our "self".

Additionally, the elimination of all the key diseases of ageing would not be enough to confer in itself a huge increase in average life expectancy. Even if the Deadly Quintet of diseases could be completely eliminated, this would confer a maximum of about 15 years of extra life to human beings, a figure well below the 30 extra years that we believe is genuinely possible in the relatively short term. And the deaths that will always happen simply because our bodies are fragile – murders, accidents, suicides – will be with us for all time as far as anyone can tell. That said, if you can stay alive for another ten to twenty years, and if you aren't yet over 75, and if you remain in reasonable health for your age, you have an excellent chance of living to over 110 years old.

If you can survive a full 30 years, there is a chance that you might live to 150, as a number plucked from the air. And if you do live that long, you're going to need some good investments to finance this extended lifespan (those on defined benefits pensions are the more fortunate ones). Quite possibly, the best of those investments will emerge

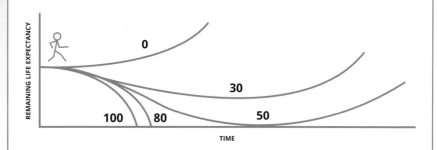

ACTUARIAL OR LONGEVITY ESCAPE VELOCITY

REMAINING LIFE EXPECTANCY

0

30

100   80   50

TIME

At present, more than one year of research is required for each additional year of expected life. Longevity escape velocity occurs when this ratio reverses, so that life expectancy increases faster than one year per one year of research, as long as that rate of advance is sustainable. Illustration provided by Aubrey de Grey.

because of the very phenomena we are writing about. Increasing lifespan through genetic, pharmacological or other methods will surely yield very large rewards for investors with foresight and appropriate knowledge. After exhaustive (literally) and much more extensive research than for any of our previous books, we have conclusively formed the following view:

We, as a species, are going to live longer. This will happen in stages: first, the attainment of 100 as a regular and unsurprising event; second, far more people living to what is currently considered effective maximal lifespan, that being around 115; and third, attainment of "longevity escape velocity" (a term coined by Aubrey de Grey) to take us to a currently unimaginable longevity. This third one remains in the realm of aspiration, but there is always the chance.

We are already benefitting from the gradual erosion of the effects of the key diseases related to ageing. Cancer, now often viewed as a broad spectrum of around 200 individual diseases, and caused by multiple different factors, will cease to be the death sentence it once was. In fact, we are pretty certain that within two decades cancer will not be among the leading causes of death. Immunotherapies are becoming increasingly sophisticated, and early diagnosis of cancer will soon become a clinical norm.

Additionally, cardiovascular disease is significantly less impactful than it once was, due to improvements in treatments, both prophylactic and curative, as well as to a reduction in the number of people smoking in developed societies (this fall in smoking applies positively to cancer also, of course). It is interesting to note that the UK rates of coronary disease have fallen by 20% since an indoor smoking ban was introduced a decade or so ago. New drugs which augment the established stable of statins, mini-aspirin, ACE inhibitors and beta blockers now include PCSK9 inhibitors (marketed by Amgen and Regeneron). In addition, and the the surprise of many, in June 2017 Merck announced the REVEAL trial of its CEPT inhibitor (anacetrapib) met its primary end point. So pending the filing of anacetraib's NDA, this could be another therapy to add to the toolkit. But for now, statins remain the undisputed kings in dyslipidemia (excess cholestrol). And, by the way, the best of those in our opinion is Crestor.

At present, neurodegenerative diseases such as Alzheimer's remain intractable to long-term treatment. However, sooner or later, the burden of these diseases will also be lessened by early diagnosis and by intervention – and that joyous day, despite the many drug trial failures so far, is probably not too far away. The **Aβ drugs** that have been trialled multiple times actually do clear **amyloid plaque** very well. The problem, as Aubrey de Grey has pointed out, is that amyloid plaques are not the only story in Alzheimer's. **Tau protein** tangles play a part, as do other pathologies. The discovery of the exact mechanisms by which Alzheimer's and other dementias occur is probably closer than most people think.

There are also new drugs coming to market for diabetes, for both type 1 and 2, and grounds for optimism that this modern-day scourge can be better contained. To cap off the good news, there are some interesting things happening in respiratory disease, another big killer of the old. But the big change in lifespan will come when we can improve the error correction mechanisms upon which continued good health and life depend.

INFLAMMAGING AND THE DECLINING IMMUNE SYSTEM

Inflammaging is a new word, first coined by Franceschi et al. in 2000, to describe aspects of the breakdown of intercellular communication and the gradual failure of the immune system. This occurs with age and results in increased inflammation and susceptibility to disease.

When the immune system, which is made up of two components – the innate, or inborn, system and the adaptive, or "learned," system – begins to fail with age, "immunosenescence" sets in. At this stage, the immune system can't fully challenge infectious pathogens or other foreign bodies as well as it once did, and the result is increased vulnerability to illnesses. In parallel, the immune system is mis-targeted to attack waste products that it cannot actually destroy, leading to the persistent inflammation which is known as "inflammaging".

As we age, inflammatory regulation becomes less powerful (and notably in the production of regulatory hormones by the endocrine system) and the innate and **adaptive immune systems** both begin to weaken. The **innate immune system**, in particular, is very important in regulating cytokine balance and in controlling inflammation. This age-associated increase in inflammation happens for various reasons, including secretions of **cytokines** by senescent cells, the general weakening of the immune system, greater activity of **NF-κB**, and a less effective **autophagy** response. (See Authophagy. Page 132). The failure of the hormonal system, in particular, means that the body's ability to monitor the intrusion of pathogens and of pre-cancerous cells is lessened.

The site where much of this inflammaging occurs is in the gut, which harbours the vast array of bacteria now often known as the **microbiome.** Decades of exposure to refined foods, including fructose sugars and carbohydrates, encourage autoimmune diseases and allergies. And older people generally have compromised guts.

Heavily implicated in inflammaging is the NLRP3 gene, which encodes the cryopyrin protein. Cryopyrin proteins recognise specific

THE FIRE INSIDE

INFLAMMAGING AND THE DECLINING IMMUNE SYSTEM

molecules including bacterial particles, uric acid, asbestos, silica and the secretions of damaged cells, and become less useful and specific in later life.

Cryopyrin molecules normally form what is known as the inflammatory response, where white blood cells and signalling molecules rush to the site of an inflammation caused by injury or disease. When this signalling goes awry, inflammation becomes persistent.

The adaptive immune system comprises the processes by which B-cells, produced in bone marrow, and T-cells produced in bone marrow and matured in the thymus, "learn" how to cope with individual threats (known as antigens) to the body, and "remember" their responses. With ageing, the thymus, in particular, becomes subject to involution or shrinkage, and the amount of mature T-cells it can produce declines. In addition, depletion of B-cells is a significant contributory factor in obesity in the elderly (Blomberg, University of Miami 2017). More generally, the bone marrow and thymus produce fewer of these cells, and most of the ones which were produced long ago are no longer "naïve" and therefore, no longer useful in fighting new types of pathogens.

The innate immune system is made up of phagocytic leukocytes, dendritic cells, plasma proteins and "natural killer" cells which, when working well, rapidly attack infections and act as "wake up" alarms to the adaptive immune system. The decline in the innate immune system contributes to chronic inflammation in the elderly, as well as microbial infections such as oral aspiration, pneumonia and periodontitis.

Concurrently, existing T- and B-cells become less potent, and the decline in the adaptive immune system leads to the elderly becoming more susceptible to, for instance, the flu or to pneumonia, especially as vaccinations often lose their potency in old age.

Vaccinations, and we've all had them, are where a harmless molecule is injected into the bloodstream, along with a microbial immunostimulant called an adjuvant, that is normally an attenuated version of the virus that the immunisation is designed to protect against.

The adaptive immune system is able to mount highly specific responses against individual pathogens, recognising tiny differences in molecular structure – and is thus exceptionally good at conferring protection right up into people's seventies. As already mentioned, the adaptive system is composed of two types of white blood cells called T and B **lymphocytes;** when these cells bind to **antigens**, and destroy them the innate immune system will "eat" them using other white blood cells known as macrophages.

Over time, the adaptive immune system T- and B-cells become "used up", and fewer fresh ones are created within the bone marrow. **Immunosurvelliance** of persistent viruses and in particular of the **cytomegalovirus** (CMV), causes stress to T-cells. The CMV virus is carried by a majority of older people and it absorbs the attention of a large number of immune cells, rendering them unable to fight any other intruders.

Inflammaging has been linked to Alzheimer's, Parkinson's, macular degeneration, type 2 diabetes, cancer, and atherosclerosis. In addition, bone loss – resulting in balance issues and in osteoporosis – has been linked to chronic inflammation. It appears that resveratrol and metformin have an effect in suppressing inflammaging. Resveratrol seems to dampen the effects of inflammaging by activating the gene Sirt1, leading to the deacetylation of NF-κB and down-regulation of TNF (tumour necrosis factor) alpha-induced inflammatory responses.

It also seems that zinc, flavonoids, and icariin are candidates to treat inflammaging. A drug that could interfere with the gene Cdc42 (cell division control protein), which is heavily implicated in inflammaging, is also being explored.

INFLAMMAGING AND THE DECLINING IMMUNE SYSTEM

Closer to today's reality, it seems that classic hormones, such as growth hormone and Insulin Growth Factor 1, could stimulate the regeneration of the thymus. Old mice who are administered one of these hormones experience a growth in their thymuses, though upon the cessation of treatment, the thymus shrinks once more. The administration of growth hormones also has to be carefully monitored, as they may well cause cancer if mis-prescribed or mis-dosed. In fact, the general view is that taking growth hormones unless specifically needed for growth is a bad idea.

Separately, feeding FGF7, which is a growth factor marketed as Kepivance, to old mice has shown remarkable results, including increased cell proliferation and a down-regulation of expression of the gene Ink4a. This is important because deletion of Ink4a in thymic cells in mice leads to a significant delay in thymus shrinkage, but Ink4a is also a known tumour suppressor so it is important that its role in this respect is more carefully investigated before we can conclude that suppressing it would be beneficial.

Researchers are also looking at deleting "programmed" (non-naïve) lymphocytes, where CMV has caused them to take up too much space, and rapamycin is being examined as a way to do this. But because any regeneration of the T and B-cell population would still have them living in an ageing microenvironment, this can only be a partial solution to restoring an effective immune system in the elderly.

One part of a future armoury of therapies to address immune senescence is to improve the microbiome that coexists with our cells. Intestinal microbes outstrip our individual cell count by 10 to 1. Research into the microbiome is growing and the Human Microbiome Project, started in 2012, incorporates a serious effort to understand the effect of the microbiome on ageing. What is known is that most intestinal microbes are non-pathogenic, but rather, symbiotic with our own biological structures or at worst, neutral or "commensal". But in older people, the microbiome can turn more hostile. There are clear and important links between microbiome changes and ageing in humans; for instance, Clostridium difficile, colon cancer, and atherosclerotic disease have strong links to the microbiome and to the health of the gut.

Manipulation of the microbiome in older people to restore function looks like a promising strategy. One way is to look at transplanting healthy flora into older people and this is being actively researched already. Scientists at the Max Planck Institute in Germany have transferred faecal matter from young fish to old ones, and increased median lifespan by more than a third.

Additionally, metformin, which is shaping up as a key anti-ageing compound and which has **AMPK** see Targets in Ageing. Page 183), as one of its key targets, is interesting. AMPK is conserved among species, and is an important nutrient sensor, which has been shown to have positive effects in **dietary restriction** when inhibited. Metformin fed to worms works on the AMPK pathway to increase lifespan (Kenyon 2010). In one interpretation, it seems to happen via the metformin acting on the worms' gut bacteria rather than the worms themselves. Metformin fed to worms bred to have no bacteria, for example, has no effect. Researchers at the Universities of Gothenburg and of Gerona have identified changes that metformin induces in gut bacteria, inducing proliferation of helpful Akkermansia microbes, which seem to make metformin reduce blood glucose levels. This is aside from the fact that metformin also reduces the production of glucose in the liver.

Thus, rapamycin, metformin, and resveratrol all seem to have an anti-inflammaging role to play. Additionally, the close examination of the microbiome will surely yield anti-ageing secrets, as will closer examination of the role of growth factors in the restoration of the human immune system.

INFLAMMAGING AND THE DECLINING IMMUNE SYSTEM

CHAPTER 2.0 – NEW FLAGSHIP INSTITUTE AT OXFORD

Oxford University plans to capitalise on a series of recent breakthroughs that, when integrated into a single interdisciplinary institute, will provide a foundation for transformative discoveries in human health. The central idea is that to cure disease, we must understand the underlying biology, and that as part of understanding biology, we must understand how cells work.

Cells are the fundamental units that make up our bodies, and their malfunction underlies almost all ill-health, including the lifestyle and environmentally influenced diseases of ageing that are prevalent in the developed world. By learning how cells function, what goes wrong with them, how to fix them, and how drugs work (or sometimes don't), we expect to develop entirely new approaches to tackling the diseases of the 21st century.

In the 1950s science was altered forever by the discovery of the double helix structure of DNA, which led to an understanding of how genes work. We are now on the verge of a second transformation: understanding how cells work.

An extraordinary convergence of breakthroughs across different scientific disciplines is enabling us to investigate the full complexity of cells for the first time. In the biological realm, the discovery of CRISPR-mediated gene editing technology provides scientists with unprecedented ability to engineer the way cells work, and even to fix defects. This was not possible until very recently. Another truly ground-breaking approach, only recently discovered, is the use of induced pluripotent stem cells, which provide the ability to regenerate human tissues from a person's own cells.

There have also been game-changing discoveries in the physical sciences that help us to reveal the inner workings of cells. Cryo-electron microscopy allows molecules to be seen directly in cells; super-resolution light microscopy uses clever computing to break the so-called 'resolution limit', thereby allowing us to observe dynamic processes in cells in real time; and advances in mass spectrometry and other physical techniques provide methods for identifying the components of the nano-machinery that control cellular processes.

Oxford University is already a world leader in many of these new technologies, but to derive maximum impact from them they need to be brought together into a single focused effort. The University has therefore committed to developing a world-leading new institute. Interdisciplinarity will be the key: breaking down traditional subject boundaries by integrating physicists, chemists, engineers and computer scientists to work with biologists. This will constitute a powerful new engine of discovery that will drive the cellular biology revolution and, in turn, produce extraordinary advances in human health. It's a radical idea, but the time is ripe.

The vision for this new institute is:

- To capitalise on the recent revolutionary changes in both genetic and physical methods to discover how cells work at a molecular level;

- To pioneer the second chapter in modern biology: transforming the molecular biology revolution of the 20th century into the cellular revolution of the 21st;

- To exploit this mechanistic understanding; and

- To build platforms that will tackle the major human health challenges of the 21st century.

Text provided by Matthew Freeman, Head, Sir William Dunn School of Pathology, University of Oxford.

CHAPTER 2.0 – NEW FLAGSHIP INSTITUTE

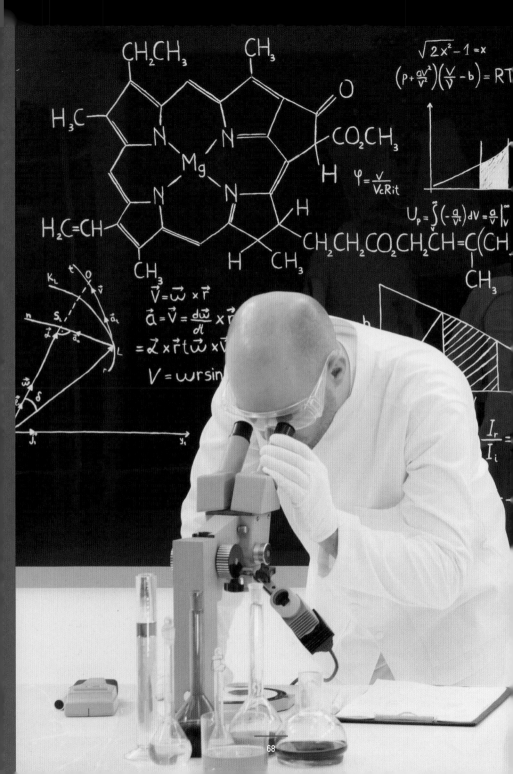

THEORIES OF AGEING
VIEWS SLOWLY CONVERGING

Nowhere in this complicated and emerging field of longevity do the practitioners disagree more than on this question – what is ageing and why does it happen?

What is more, many of the people on the competing sides exhibit strangely closed minds – they just know that they are right, and the other side is wrong! There are glimmers of hope, however, and a convergent opinion is developing among a core number of serious scientists that ageing is multifactorial and ordained, and that science will be able to figure out a way to slow it, halt it or even reverse it.

All these scientists agree ageing is currently inescapable, that it is characterised by the progressive loss of functioning of our bodies and that it is the principal cause of what we call the Deadly Quintet and that its path is inevitably towards death.

A bird's eye view suggests that there are two broad camps of opinion: those who believe that ageing is in some way preprogrammed, and those who take the entirely opposite view and believe the so-called random or stochastic theory of ageing. Those in the preprogrammed camp believe that there are some kind of biological "clocks" ticking away in our cells, affecting gene expression and/or hormonal signalling, and/or that there are other gravitational forces that prevent us from outrunning death.

The random or stochastic theories regard the accumulation of damage to different types of DNA, mitochondrial and nuclear, as well as the effects of free radicals or ROS and cellular senescence and failures in cell signalling, as being responsible for ageing.

The best solution, as in most conflict of opinion, is to seek a middle ground. It seems to us that we do now know that ageing is related to genetic pathways and to biochemical reactions, some of which are conserved in evolution, and that ageing is related to damage of a variety of sorts, caused by the simple fact that we exist and can't escape our environment. Thus, the process of ageing might best be defined as stochastic and quasi-programmed.

It is also now established that there are several important pathways related to ageing, with notable ones being the nutrient sensing pathway, known as **insulin**/IGF-1 (Kenyon, 2005), which is the most **conserved pathway** across multiple species, ranging from worms,

to mice, to us. As an example, mutations that interfere with IGF-1, causing growth hormone to become dysregulated, are well known to influence longevity in some types of mice (Barzilai et al., 2012).

The results of caloric restriction (CR) validate the following fact: longevity is increased through the regulation of nutrient-sensing pathways and genes, such as mTOR, AMPK, sirtuins and IGF-1, when an organism or a human is exposed to a calorically restricted regime, i.e. eating fewer than the recommended daily calories. But CR has only a marginal influence on human longevity, so science needs to drill down into how these pathways work, along with several others, and determine how (if at all) they can be influenced to amplify the positive effects of CR. In addition the recent trend towards "clean eating" has been shown to be potentially dangerous, depriving its strict adherents of vital nutrients.

A group of eminent scientists, Carlos López-Otín, Maria A. Blasco, Linda Partridge, Manuel Serrano and Guido Kroemer, recently described what they regard as the nine hallmarks of ageing. These hallmarks are evident regardless of whether ageing is believed to be preprogrammed or stochastic.

In summary, there are many theories of ageing, and most are interconnected. Below we try to identify and to critique the principal ones.

THE HALLMARKS OF AGEING

López-Otín, Carlos et al., Cell, Volume 153, Issue 6, 1194-1217

PROTEOSTASIS - BENT OUT OF SHAPE

As we age, we begin to lose **proteostasis.** This is a component of homeostasis, or the maintenance of steady state, and it specifically refers to the approximately 100,000-250,000 proteins (the proteome) that we need for life. In all cells, proteins occasionally misfold, and become misshapen and so the normal 3D shape of native proteins degrades. Proteostasis involves refolding or destroying such proteins. When proteostasis declines and misfolding occurs, the bent proteins accumulate and diseases start to develop.

Proteostasis is now a major focus of research, and the degradation of proteostasis is regarded as one of the causes or accelerants of ageing.

"Chaperone" molecules are proteins or drugs that refold misshapen proteins. Small-molecule chaperone drugs are being developed to aid in the accurate folding of misshapen proteins. Chaperone proteins are the basis of the normal mechanisms which assist other proteins to position and fold correctly, without ending up in the completed structure. Chaperones also transport proteins across membranes and act as signallers for proteins.

Two systems are used by the body to destroy misfolded proteins: the first is the autophagy-lysosomal system (see Autophagy. Page 132) which sequesters and degrades badly-shaped proteins. Macro-autophagy, the best-studied form of autophagy, is a system where cellular junk is segregated into compartments called autophagosomes, which are fused with acidic compartments called lysosomes for degradation. The second is the ubiquitin-proteasome system, which chops them up into small chunks for recycling. Both of these systems degrade with ageing.

Multiple studies have shown that proteostasis is impaired as we age (Koga et al., 2011). Too many unfolded, misfolded or clumped proteins are heavily implicated in age-related diseases such as

Parkinson's and Alzheimer's (Powers et al., 2009). Misfolded proteins can lead to the formation of aggregates with an amyloid-like structure, characterised by plaques.

It is not yet fully understood why these amyloid-type aggregates occur, but it is thought that the aggregation of misfolded proteins is in some way toxic, and the plaques are a response to this, developing as a protective measure. The role of these aggregates in neurodegenerative diseases is not yet fully understood.

If proteostasis could be maintained for longer, lifespans would almost certainly be favourably impacted. In animal research, this is very much borne out by results. As an example, transgenic worms which overexpress chaperones (proteins that refold misshapen proteins rather than destroying them) are long-lived (Morrow et al., 2004; Walker and Lithgow, 2003). Also, mutant mice deficient in a chaperone of the so-called heat shock family exhibit accelerated ageing, whereas long-lived mouse strains overexpress heat shock proteins (Min et al., 2008; Swindell et al., 2009). Moreover, activation of HSF-1, which is a master regulator of the heat shock response, increases longevity in worms (Chiang et al. 2012; Hsu et al., 2003).

The successful renewal or removal of damaged proteins and their components is the aim of such research. Whatever the truth, the successful removal of these aggregates is a major focus of Alzheimer's and Parkinson's research.

PROTEOSTASIS - BENT OUT OF SHAPE

EVOLUTION AND AGEING

Although ageing is not a fixed imperative of biology, it does have "conserved" characteristics.

The evolutionary theory of ageing is bound up with Charles Darwin's work on natural selection, outlined in *On the Origin of the Species by Means of Natural Selection,* which was published in 1859. This thesis of natural selection is a way of describing the different survival and reproductive outcomes of individuals due to differences in their **phenotypes.** Exposure to the environment and simply being alive causes random mutations in people's genomes and these mutations can sometimes be inherited by their children.

Since almost all organisms eventually die of diseases, accidents, predation, etc., genes or gene variants called **alleles,** which are beneficial early in life, are favoured by natural selection over genes beneficial later in life.

PHENOTYPES AND GENOTYPES - WHAT'S YOUR TYPE?

Phenotypes are the observable characteristics of an organism – in other words, its physical properties. Additionally, the phenotype includes the organism's development path, its behaviour and the extended products of its behaviour (e.g. a bird's nest or a beaver's dam).

Phenotypes are the physical and behavioural expression of **genotypes.** Genotypes are what we inherit from our parents and phenotypes are what that genotypical inheritance produces in the natural environment. August Weismann took this distinction into account when he distinguished between the cells of heredity, the "germ plasm" cells, and the cells of the body, our **somatic** cells.

PHENOTYPES AND GENOTYPES

When the pressure to reproduce abates, ageing seems to slow. Steve Austad of the University of Alabama, a leading light in longevity science, showed in 1993 that opossums, a type of marsupial living in North America, age more slowly if they live in a predator-free environment, with less time pressure on their reproduction – and presumably, on their nerves!

Because some genes that allow for more success in reproduction are selected for by natural selection, the people with those genes are more likely to successfully reproduce and therefore to pass on those genetic characteristics to subsequent generations. This phenomenon results in the genetic evolution of the population. Although genotypes can and do slowly change by "random drift", natural selection is by far the main cause of evolution. It sounds a bit clinical and devoid of romance, and is only part of the story, but there is, of course, a significant element of truth in it.

In 1966, William D. Hamilton demonstrated by using fruit flies, which were then (and still are) a popular model for ageing research, that the force of natural selection decreases with age. In *The Moulding of Senescence by Natural Selection,* he described the power of natural selection at an early age, and expanded his thesis to include the nature of ageing and the timing of

and nature of the cessation of ageing – and of death.

He derived a mathematical formula that is known as *Hamilton's Forces of Natural Selection.* This suggests that the mechanisms of ageing have evolved to include germinal (i.e. heritable) mutations with a series of initially minor harmful effects, which do not have significance until later in life, allowing unimpeded natural selection to take place in the earlier part of life.

Interestingly we and all other mammals evolved from reptiles. Reptiles are a taxon (family of species) with many members who apparently age at an almost imperceptible rate. They do eventually die, but don't exhibit the classic signs of ageing. It is also a fact that all mammals experience **oocyte** senescence, i.e. egg production diminishes with age – but somehow that phenomenon doesn't happen in reptiles. Furthermore, reptiles' teeth continue to grow into old age, unlike those of mammals. In the case of the salamander, an amphibian, tissue regeneration is rapid even in the context of significant trauma, such as the loss of a leg or even, in some circumstances, parts of the brain. These are simply regrown.

So why is it that many reptiles (and some fish) age at a much slower pace than we mammals do, even though we all evolved from the same source, and we mammals are supposedly of a higher order than reptiles, amphibians and fish? One suggestion is that mammals first started to age as a result of "r-selection" in the age of the dinosaurs. R-selected species are those that place an emphasis on a high physical early growth rate, and, typically live in less crowded ecologies, and these r-selected species also tend to produce multiple offspring, each of which has or had a relatively low probability of surviving to adulthood.

In the age of the dinosaur, mammals were small creatures about the size of today's mice, and were highly vulnerable to predation. So, they evolved to have many offspring, and to have a rapidly ageing phenotype, rather than a phenotype based on long-term survival. With the disappearance of the dinosaurs, mammals such as elephants and humans evolved the condition which we now call longevity. But the underlying ageing phenotype has persisted all the way through to today, and as a result all mammals experience some form of menopause and ageing.

And it does seem that after humans and other animals have fulfilled their "duty" in respect of reproduction and the raising of offspring, functional decline really does set in. This normally happens after 60 years of human life. But, because we now generally live a long time after 60, this makes the neat and simple evolutionary theory of ageing a bit of a dead end. On the pro side of the natural selection theory it does indeed seem that evolution has favoured the young over the old, particularly after reproduction and for most mammalian species. But, as with so much in the science of ageing, this isn't totally clear cut either. For instance, why is it not the case that those who have already reproduced die faster than those who haven't yet produced offspring?

This isn't always the case, however. People who do have children can and do often live longer than those who haven't reproduced, although this is maybe because they suffer less isolation and loneliness in old age (Karolinska Institute Sweden, 2017). It is certainly the case that popular people live longer than "Billy No Mates" types (study by The Brigham Young University).

And yet, there is a lifespan difference between those who are capable of reproduction and those who are not; in some studies, castrated men have been shown to live longer than those who have not been castrated, demonstrated in large-scale and macabre studies in Kansas dating back to the 1950s. In these studies, 300 men with mental health problems were castrated early in life and went on to outlive 700 men who were not – by an average of 14 years! The result of this study is generally, but

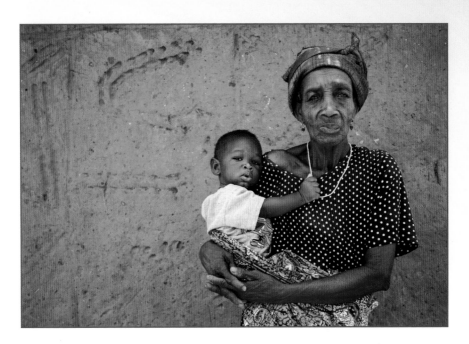

not always, borne out by historical precedents; it seems that Korean eunuchs at the 17th century royal court lived 14 to 19 years longer than their counterparts who had not been castrated (*Science* 2012). In contrast, Chinese counterparts had no such longevity advantage over their more fortunate brethren, and nor did Italian castrati, who were chopped to preserve their treble voices. Those sorts of trials, practices and rituals could not, of course, be contemplated today – at least not, hopefully, anywhere near where we live!

Human beings typically live long lives post-reproduction and such hypotheses as "the grandmother theory", which suggests that women live long lives post-reproduction in order to ensure that their daughters are able to have more children, also don't seem to make much sense in today's world.

If it is the case that women are saved from death to be helpful grandmothers, why do men live almost as long as women? It is true that men can be fathers into old age, but according to evolutionary theory, with plenty of men around only the "fittest" would survive and men wouldn't live as long as they do. Of course, some men can be helpful grandfathers too, though most seem to prefer pubs and sports to grandfatherly duties!

THE SECOND LAW OF THERMODYNAMICS

This Second Law of Thermodynamics is complex and has been refined over two centuries. Concisely, it states that the total entropy (disorder, or randomness) of an enclosed system (for instance, the universe) always increases with time, or, in ideal conditions, stays constant, if a steady state can be maintained. We here on earth live in a physical system that is not enclosed, because it is constantly receiving energy from the sun and in turn giving some of that energy up to space.

According to the Second Law, everything eventually crumbles – tables, chairs, roads, ships, cars, and us. As Henri Amiel said "Chaos is the law of nature; order is the dream of man". The Second Law would seem to suggest that to reverse the molecular degradation that accompanies ageing, we would have to find a way to keep cells healthy for longer, or forever, or to replace all of the cells, organs and tissues that make us who we are and on a regular basis. And that would include the cells that typically don't often divide, or don't divide at all, such as heart cells and neurons/brain cells. This theory makes the point, inaccurately but succinctly that with age and prolonged exposure to the Second Law's effects, homeostasis gradually collapses.

But such theories of ageing as entropy are now generally discredited in academic circles, because humans and cells are not closed systems and therefore not subject over time to the Second Law of Thermodynamics and to increasing entropy. Putting it another way, living organisms exist by virtue of the importation of energy, which they use to (among other things) "export" entropy.

However, **Leonard Hayflick** (see Key Opinion Leaders. Page 160), whom we have met during our research, remains an advocate of the entropy thesis and believes that thermodynamics is an unavoidable feature of life and death.

Peter Hoffman, who wrote *Life's Ratchet* in 2013, also believes that what he calls "nanoscale thermal physics" guarantees our eventual decline into senescence, despite all the medicine available to treat the diseases of ageing. In his book, Hoffman explains how molecular machines create order within our cellular structures. He then describes how protein machines, like tiny ratchets, turn chaos into order by directing the water bombardment that all cells receive a trillion times a second into useful energy. This process of conversion of thermal motion into energy is also one of a constant battle with the Second Law, and eventually the Second Law always wins.

This never-ending battle results in protein bonds being broken, at different rates for different people, but nonetheless broken. Hoffman's views are consistent with Hayflick's opinion that ageing is caused by "an increasing loss of molecular fidelity or increasing molecular disorder." Hoffman believes that ageing cannot be neatly explained by DNA damage, or telomere shortening, or by protein aggregation; rather that these are biological responses to a fundamental cause, which is the accumulation of damage through thermal and chemical degradation.

But Hoffman appears to be wrong, because although protein bonds are broken and this fact cannot be changed, it might be possible that an increased rate of repair could counteract this. Additionally, germlines are immortal and this on its own shows that the Second Law does not always win.

Hoffman thus believes that ageing is a natural process that can be reduced to nanoscale thermal physics, and that it is therefore not a disease. This is even though to our minds it seems that many individual diseases could be reduced to nanoscale thermal physics, counteracting his argument. In fact, Hoffman's view is mostly at odds with the modern canon of longevity research. That research is now converging on the broad view that there are complicated fundamental drivers of ageing which are potentially correctable.

Others don't believe that this Second Law applies to ageing at all. Aubrey de Grey (see Key Opinion Leaders. Page 154), for instance, believes that although entropy is indeed a feature of life, humans are pretty good at dealing with it and exporting it. Aubrey believes that science should focus on improving our ability to export entropy by using cellular repair mechanisms to counterbalance its effects. Currently, entropy that is not exported takes the form of accumulated damage.

Another example of why entropy is not insurmountable, according to Aubrey, is maternity. When a woman gives birth, she produces a baby which is "new". Her germline cells, immortal as they are, produce a child with no signs of age, despite the fact that the mother is a mature adult. If the woman was bound by the Second Law, how could she produce this "new" being? What actually happens is that the mother uses energy to sequester the entropy she carries, and to stop too much of it from getting into the baby, in just the same way that throughout life we push entropy out into our environment and minimise the amount that we carry.

Interestingly, although Peter Hoffman doesn't believe that the laws of physics can ever be defeated, he does think that if scientists could discover the key molecular components whose early breakdown leads to a "cascade of failure", then those components might be regularly repaired. He is definitely more optimistic in this respect than Hayflick. And we, of course, are in the camp of the believers.

THE DISPOSABLE SOMA THEORY

The "disposable soma" theory states that ageing occurs due to the accumulation of damage during life and that the burdensome need to constantly defend and repair our bodies contributes to ageing (Kirkwood and Austad, 2000).

The idea that we die because we have outlived our biological usefulness is contained in this theory of ageing, first described by Tom Kirkwood in 1977, now of Newcastle University. He does go on to say that he believes that in due course this force of nature can and will be overcome.

The disposable soma theory states that we have effectively been designed as vessels useful only to ship our genetic code (via germ cells – sperm and eggs) to the next generation. Kirkwood does not regard this as an impediment to potentially living much longer than we currently do, and his view represents a refinement to the evolutionary theory of ageing because, in this case of a trade-off

between reproduction and somatic maintenance, evolutionary "weakness" can be turned to our advantage.

This could happen if we were able to identify the features of biology that make us "disposable" in the first place and adjust and correct them. Then, presumably, we could live much longer than for just the period of our reproductive usefulness. And, of course, we already do live much longer than we "should", according to both the disposable soma and other evolutionary theories.

If we look at this from a different perspective, if we really were born simply to pass on our genes, then there should be no need for the maintenance of our bodily functions after reproductive success (defined as child-rearing to maturity). Indeed, it would be expected that we wouldn't live long after reproduction, because from an evolutionary standpoint, we would have little, if any, remaining purpose. But in fact, we do maintain our bodies, albeit at a progressively lesser rate, in contrast to some animals that die almost immediately after reproduction.

To its credit, the disposable soma theory does recognise that in periods of food shortage but not starvation, reproduction, which carries a heavy energy cost, is curtailed, and this is a point which no one disputes. As a result, the theory predicts that lifespan should increase when reproduction is deferred or eliminated. Somewhat supporting this is that women who have numerous children tend to die younger than those who don't, and the supply of testosterone, which in men is many-fold higher than in women, seems to accelerate death. Testosterone suppresses immune function, and is therefore a negative factor in longevity. As Richard Bribiescas has put it: for men, life is "stud, dud – and thud" – as well as "macho makes you sick".

Reproduction is expensive in a biological sense and uses resources that could be better employed for DNA maintenance in the straitened circumstances of food shortage. And so, reproduction is deferred when animals are subject to diminished food intake. There is no doubt that reproduction can, in some circumstances, take years off your life. Women who have many children tend to live shorter lives than those who don't, and men carry the burden of excess skeletal muscle mass, which is known as dimorphic mass. This excess musculature may have some bearing on men's somewhat shorter average lives.

If we could mimic and amplify this evolved reproductive reaction to caloric restriction (CR) or even to dietary restriction (DR), such as vegetarianism, then we might gain the benefit of the positive stress elements of food shortages, and extend our lives. In fact, reducing food intake does seem to be one way of doing just that, but with a dubious cost/benefit equation for humans. There are even cleverer ways of mimicking cell stressors and of delaying the "throwaway" date of the human soma, and we will detail them later in this book.

Over many generations, we humans have worked out how to limit threats to life. This has been accomplished by improving the environment in which we live, and as a result we enjoy a lifespan normally considerably longer than just the period required for reproductive success.

Kirkwood is a believer that if there could be an improvement in somatic (body) maintenance, ageing could be slowed down significantly. More optimistically, and definitely espousing an outlying opinion, Aubrey de Grey believes that if youthful repair and maintenance processes could be enhanced in the human body, then ageing could be delayed, possibly forever.

FREE RADICALS, DNA DAMAGE AND THE OXIDATIVE THEORY OF AGEING

A paper by Leo Szilard published in 1959 (followed by Vijg and Zetterberg) proposed the role of damage to the nuclear DNA in our bodies, which we now know occurs in the form of mutations (change to sequences) and epimutations (such as alterations to methylation, or changes in histones, the spools around which DNA wind). He called these "ageing hits", the result of lifelong exposure to ionising radiation as well as other environmental factors. The molecular details came along later, but Szilard's paper formed the basis of the scholarly study of damage to DNA as being at least partly causative in ageing.

This paper led to the now widespread view that nuclear and mitochondrial DNA damage is central to ageing throughout the animal kingdom, and it is also believed by many scientists that one of the key factors in causing this damage is reactive oxygen species, or ROS (which are popularly known as free radicals, but in fact also include other molecules such as hydrogen peroxide). ROS cause oxidative stress and are now incontrovertible factors in ageing, not least because mutational damage to the DNA cannot be repaired and accumulates.

This damage to our cells and to our DNA occurs at a remarkable rate and on a daily basis. As cells replicate, mistakes occur and these need to be repaired, and at the same time other damage, including trauma, adds to the stress levels of our cellular apparatus. These combined stresses cause breaks in DNA, numbering on average about 50 breaks per cell cycle and this adds to the burden of the 10,000 or so oxidative "insults"

that each and every cell receives every single day of our lives.

As repairs are carried out, epigenetic alterations get introduced, and some of these can persist after the repairs are completed. These include altered methylation of so-called CpG sequences, and this can result in interference with proper gene expression and regulation.

The damage that ROS and other factors, such as injury and toxic chemicals, cause is cumulative and is important, inter alia, in the development of cancers in mammals. We all need to breathe, and we will die very quickly without oxygen, but ROS are generated by the mitochondria which process that oxygen. Oxygen is transported by blood to all the cells in our bodies and it is vital to the process of creating the ATP that the mitochondria churn out. This aerobic respiration is a fiendish molecular balancing act, and in the process, we can end up with partly-metabolised oxygen, which is the cause of free radicals – and these go on to wreak havoc in cells, mitochondrial DNA, nuclear DNA and in surrounding structures. These free radicals, which are collections of atoms with unpaired electrons, cause damage by "stealing" electrons from nearby molecules.

Our bodies do of course have effective antioxidants, particularly in early life, which act to mop up free radicals before they do any damage. These include superoxide dismutase, catalase and glutathione peroxidase. But this chemical security force can and does fail to disarm all the free radicals that the cell makes. And it is because some ROS evade antioxidants that genetic mutations, damage to our lipids (fats) and damage to our proteins start to occur.

Intriguingly, it is now pretty certain that many antioxidant supplements play no, or little, positive role in preventing this type of damage. This may be because having some ROS is actually positive and necessary for cell life. Among other things it seems to act as a "stressor" to the cells, which is good if in limited quantity. This phenomenon is known as *hormesis*. It may explain why worms fed low doses of paraquat weed killer (which promotes ROS production) seem to thrive and to have extended lives, while a larger quantity would kill them. Don't try this particular experiment at home though!

Additionally, although excess ROS is certainly negative for humans, the theory that cellular oxidative damage increases with ageing does not universally apply to other species. As an example, mice that are bred to overexpress antioxidant genes do not have longer lives than their "wild type" (or normal) counterparts but mice following a CR diet do.

What is known, however, is that the aggregation of unrepaired DNA causes genome-wide epigenetic change over time, manifesting in the alteration of **chromatin** (the materials that make up chromosomes) and thereby leading to age-related diseases. It is now thought by some eminent scientists that if the repair process of DNA could be enhanced, then the build-up of such epigenetic change could be reversed or at least slowed.

CR (caloric restriction), which is eating less without starvation, is a mild positive stressor for our cells, which seems to stimulate the body's production of natural antioxidants. We talk elsewhere in the book in more detail about dietary and caloric restriction.

Additionally, ageing seems to result in our tissues and cells receiving less oxygen, creating what is known as hypoxic (insufficient oxygen) conditions. Hypoxia is another cellular stress factor and (paradoxically) generates added ROS. Although the influence of the development of cellular hypoxia is not fully understood, it certainly has some role in ageing, and it is one of the many factors which add up to cause decay.

Apart from excess ROS, some other "bad stuff" gets through our cells' "nets" – and these nasty compounds are also toxic in aberrant quantities. These bad actors can also add to the many "breaks" in the strands of our DNA that are incurred daily and as a result, these breaks have become a highly important focus of anti-ageing research.

DNA DAMAGE

DNA is damaged all the time, throughout our lives. This damage is rapidly repaired, usually accurately, but not always. DNA damage often takes the form of single or double strand breaks in the structure of the DNA, caused by reactive oxygen species (ROS) a.k.a. "free radicals", but there are other types of damage to DNA as well. These include damaging hydrocarbon adducts and hydroxydeoxyguanosine residues, such as from exposure to diesel fumes. DNA damage takes place at least 10,000 times per day on average in every cell of the human body, and 50,000 times a day in every rat cell.

Unrepaired DNA damage is particularly noticeable in non-dividing or slowly dividing cells, such as neuronal, heart and skeletal cells because the mutations tend to persist. Whereas in dividing cells, such as those of the liver, DNA damage that is not repaired will normally automatically induce cell death, though occasionally it can lead to the development of aberrant cancerous cells.

DNA damage repair is central to our existence and an improvement to repair is vital to expanding lifespans by a large amount. In energy terms, the human body invests heavily in the constant repairs that it undertakes. As an example, one double-strand break of DNA needs about 10,000 molecules of ATP (adenosine triphosphate) to repair.

All organisms, from bacteria to humans, employ ATP as their primary energy "currency". Nutrients contain energy in low-energy covalent (molecular) bonds and this form of energy can't do much within our cells. So, ATP is used as the conduit to transform nutrients into usable energy. ATP is a molecule used to perform just about all of our bodily functions, constructing molecules, contracting muscles, and firing neurons. ATP liberates energy by being converted into ADP (adenosine diphosphate), by removing one of the phosphate groups. ATP becomes spent when it is converted to ADP. The ADP group is then recycled in the mitochondria, recharged, and re-emerges as ATP and the cycle continues. The removal and subsequent replacement of the phosphate is what causes energy to be continuously and efficiently supplied in the body.

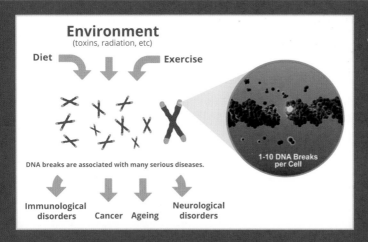

Environment
(toxins, radiation, etc)

Diet   Exercise

DNA breaks are associated with many serious diseases.

1-10 DNA Breaks per Cell

Immunological disorders   Cancer   Ageing   Neurological disorders

Humans have an estimated 37 trillion cells and each cell has about one billion ATP molecules, so the total number of ATP molecules in a human body is mind-blowing. In fact the figure in the average person is about one hundred sextillion. And the energy in ATP is generated and recharged about three times every minute and in every single ATP molecule. The amazing thing is that at any time there are only 50 grams of ATP in the body, and this amount is recycled so often that the process means that up to 180kg or 400lbs worth is turned over per day; and that's with an intake of just 2500 calories per day for the average human male.

So cells and mitochondria have to work very hard, and it isn't surprising given the volume of work, that many mistakes are made and damage occurs. That damage becomes an increasing burden with age, and our repair mechanisms eventually become overwhelmed and exhausted. When mutations occur, diseases happen, and ageing proceeds.

It is also well known that higher levels of nuclear DNA damage and mutation mean a greater risk of cancer and this is the key reason why cancer is mainly a disease of the old. The more cells that suffer DNA damage, the more likely it is that one or more cells experience exactly the type of damage needed to go rogue and to proliferate as cancerous growths. In addition, mutations to DNA can't be corrected, and are passed on when cells divide and replicate. This is because the corrective enzymes which repair DNA damage can't "see" the mutations once they are incorporated into each of the DNA strands. Mutations are generally adverse because they interfere with protein regulation and function.

It is a matter of debate as to whether mutations in slowly dividing cells, and particularly in their **mitochondrial DNA** (mtDNA), are causative of ageing. Some scientists argue that the lack of histones (which bind DNA in the nucleus) means that there is less protection for the mtDNA and that they are therefore more vulnerable to damage. Furthermore, mitochondria operate in an oxidative micro environment and lack sophisticated repair mechanisms. This is the view of the **SENS Research Foundation** (see Key Opinion Leaders. Page 158), headed up by Aubrey de Grey.

There is evidence that mitochondrial DNA mutations mostly occur early in life and are not caused by accumulated damage. This view may seem contradictory to the large body of research which indicates that mutational load is much higher in aged cells (Khrapko et al., 1999), but it is possible that early-life mutations are just amplified and replicated throughout life, and that indeed the originating mtDNA mutations are something that happens in our early years.

Experiments in mice seem to bolster the side of the argument that mutations, however caused, are implicated in ageing. These mice (Vermulst et al., 2008) were bred to be deficient in mtDNA replication fidelity and exhibited premature ageing signs and impaired mitochondrial functioning. It is not yet known whether this is ageing-related, as ROS production was not elevated as a result of impaired mtDNA functioning.

What is clear is that rejuvenating cells, improving the repair mechanisms of DNA, and protecting mitochondrial activity will be fundamental to any process that significantly increases lifespans beyond the "hard ceiling" of 115 or so.

DNA DAMAGE

THE THEORIES OF ANTAGONISTIC PLEIOTROPY AND HYPERFUNCTIONING

Yet another theory of ageing is that of antagonistic pleiotropy, developed by George C. Williams in 1957, and representing an evolutionary explanation for ageing. Put simply, antagonistic pleiotropy is where a gene variant is beneficial to our survival in earlier life, then becomes harmful in later life. If the harm occurs early enough in adulthood to impact the individual's reproductive capacity, evolution can be expected to develop a fix. As an example, adolescents experience an upsurge in hormonal levels from puberty to full development and maturation. This upsurge is beneficial to growth, but ends after full development, probably because, if left unchecked, cancers could result. But if the deleterious effect only emerges in old age, after reproductive success, evolution doesn't care.

The principle was first proposed in 1957, but it was in 1991 that Michael Rose coined the phrase "antagonistic pleiotropy". It was also Rose who hypothesised that ageing can and does stop in very aged humans, usually after 93 years of age. The idea that ageing just stops is controversial.

Rose used fruit flies to determine whether breeding from the longest-lived flies in each generation would produce longer lived versions over time. And it did. He managed to quadruple the original lifespan in some flies, and the obvious prediction based on antagonistic pleiotropy was that these superaged flies would have much lower fertility in earlier life, making them live longer until eventually, reproduction took place.

In fact, that prediction was proved wrong; the long-lived flies produced more eggs at every stage of life, and this is now thought to be because of the protected environment that these flies lived in (the nice, warm laboratory). If exposed to the natural elements, these flies might just revert to the normal and less long-lived type. Additionally, the long-lived lab flies displayed weaknesses that would have made them poor survivors in the wild. Faced with this and looking to refine the pleiotropy hypothesis, Rose developed a theory that is the antithesis of antagonistic pleiotropy – late-life immortality.

Here, Rose proposed that if natural selection gradually comes to an end, then so should ageing, and as a result he does not believe that ageing is like rust, a series of accumulated chemical damages. At some point, the process of ageing seems no longer to be necessary and literally stops. According to this refinement, very old people do not die of ageing, or of ageing diseases, but just of plain exhaustion. This is a contentious view and millions of fruit flies have lived and died while it has been examined; it seems that once the forces of natural selection peter out, ageing seems to stop. So, in studies of women over 93, some stopped ageing although they all subsequently died.

More recently, **David Gems** of University College London (see Key Opinion Leaders. Page 166), whom we have met on several occasions, has described what he calls the Williams-Blagosklonny or hyperfunction theory. This theory proposes that ageing is not solely the result of decline caused by accumulated molecular damage, but because of antagonistic pleiotropy (hence Williams-Blagosklonny) which leads to the pathologies of ageing through the excessive activity or "hyperfunction" in late-life of genes that should ideally be active only in youth. This idea was proposed by Mikhail Blagosklonny, a professor of oncology at Roswell Park Cancer Institute in Bufalo, New York, who is a key researcher in cancer and ageing.

This so-called hyperfunctionality is exemplified by the normal but excessive activity of signalling pathways such as **mTOR** (the mechanistic target of rapamycin), and insulin/IGF-1. Too much activity in later life in these and other pathways leads to the diseases of ageing, thereby limiting lifespan.

Inhibition by genetic or by chemical means of, say, the mTOR pathway can extend life (in mice for example), but not indefinitely so. There are clearly other pathways which may be hyperfunctioning in later life as well – and more and more of these are being discovered.

Tom Kirkwood, among others, has argued that ageing is not programmed, in that it serves no purpose in evolutionary terms. Blagosklonny agrees with this but points out that, through antagonistic pleiotropy, ageing is programmed by genes. So it is programmed and it isn't programmed: as he puts it, it is *quasi-programmed* (which gets back to our earlier conclusion). He uses the analogy of a bath running; as the bath fills (the programme), that is a good thing, but if it runs over (the quasi-programme) it isn't, as it tends to annoy the neighbours.

David Gems uses his treasured worms, and the yolk that they produce in their own reproductive process, to illustrate how quasi-programmes generate late-life disease. The genes responsible for producing yolk don't get turned off after reproduction, and this yolk overproduction leads to senescent obesity and the promotion of tumours: tumours that coincide with, but don't seem to cause, death, at least in the hermaphroditic self-reproducing version of these worms. Here normal genes just performing their allotted task, not stochastic damage, are causing ageing pathology: their action is good in early life, but its continuation in later life causes ageing. This implies a new approach to inhibiting ageing: use drugs or other interventions to switch off disease-promoting quasi-programmes in later life.

RATE OF LIVING THEORY

Then there is the **"rate of living" theory,** which in a simple sense suggests that the slower the metabolism of an organism, the longer its lifespan. Max Rubner first came up with this idea in 1908 and Max Kleiber produced what is known as **Kleiber's Law** in 1932. This suggests that on a mouse to elephant curve, weight divided by basal metabolic rate correlates with animal longevity.

In other words, the bigger the better, from a longevity point of view. In 1927, Raymond Pearl foolishly opined on "why lazy people live the longest" – with women supposedly living longer because they did less physical labour than men. That particular nonsense has been totally disproved; men do much less manual work today and most women work, but women still outlive men.

But what is true is that people do age at differing rates. This is unlikely to be due to a limitation on the number of heartbeats that humans can generate during their lifespans or to differing metabolisms, with the faster living less long. Indeed, animals who are on a calorically restricted diet process more calories (higher metabolism) than their ad libitum fed equivalents, but live much longer. Metabolic rate has little bearing on longevity in birds and in mammals.

A good and useful predictor of biological age, mentioned earlier, is provided by analysis of DNA methylation, Horvath's epigenetic clock. It is a measurement though and the markers that are used to determine its forecasted outcomes are not necessarily causative of ageing, rather are simply as described – markers.

So, lots of theories! What to make of them, as most have at least some merit? In the 1990s, scientists Peto and Doll opined that "there is no such thing as ageing", as a means of underlining the fact there is no one thing that determines ageing.

KLEIBER'S LAW

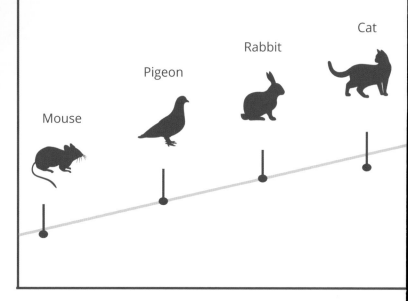

METABOLIC RATE (LOG SCALE)

BODY MASS (LOG SCALE)

The theories outlined above are not necessarily mutually exclusive, but rather there are elements of truth to all of them. The hope is that the convergence of these and other, alternative theories will eventually produce something more cohesive and unitary.

If we knew what caused ageing today, we would probably already have a cure or treatment and we wouldn't be writing this book. It is the fact that we are at an early stage in the science of longevity that gives us to the opportunity to be ground floor investors in what comes out of the

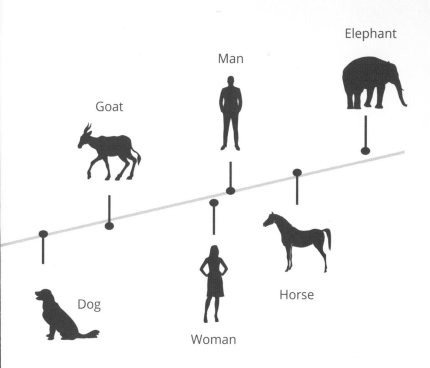

The average elephant weighs 220,000 times as much as the average mouse, but requires only about 10,000 times as much energy in the form of food calories to sustain itself. The reason lies in the mathematical and geometric nature of networks that distribute nutrients and carry away with wastes and heat. The bigger the animal, the more efficiently it uses energy.

myriad of avenues of research being undertaken.

One very good summary – and an implied plea to treat ageing as a unified pathology – comes from David Gems who says that "we must draw aside the rosy veil of tradition and face ageing for what it is, and in all its horror: the greatest disease of them all."

THE DEADLY QUINTET

THE HEART OF THE MATTER

About 15 million people around the world die each year from a heart attack or a stroke, making cardiovascular disease (CVD) the number one killer globally. That having been said, deaths from CVD are falling almost everywhere. As an example, American death rates per capita from heart disease and strokes have fallen by 20% in the last 20 years, and this is despite the fact that 27 million people in the US still suffer from heart disease, and an estimated 50% of Americans over 65 have some form of heart condition.

So-called "bad" **cholesterol** or **LDL** (low-density lipoprotein) is a major factor in the formation of heart diseases. This type of cholesterol furs up arteries and other blood vessels, and the phenomenon is highly age-associated. Over the past fifty years or so, effective medications have been developed to reduce cardiac diseases. The most widespread of these are the statin class of drugs, many of which are now generic and thus inexpensive. Statins reduce the amount of bad cholesterol in the blood, and so lessen the amount of arterial blockage from the build-up of plaques. Statins also change the heart structure, reducing thickness and volume and reducing the chance of a heart attack (University College London, 2017). In elderly people, Lord et al., (University of

Birmingham, 2017) have shown that statins improve neutrophil function, increasing immunity against infections.

In addition to statins, a wide and effective range of drugs are now available to people with heart disease. These include beta blockers, which slow heart rates and decrease blood pressure, (half of all Americans are above the target range of 120/80) and nitroglycerin, which dilates coronary arteries, alleviating pain. There are also angiotensin-converting enzyme (ACE) inhibitors, and angiotensin II receptor blockers (ARBs), which also reduce blood pressure. Additionally there are, niacin, fibrates, bile acid sequestrants, omega-3 fatty acids in purified fish oils, alpha-linolenic acid (ALA), Artichoke Barley Beta sitosterol, specialised blood thinners, as well as plain old daily mini aspirin (75mg to 81mg) (although watch out for bleeding risk). A recent study published in the *Lancet*, using the medical records of 3.5 million people in the UK from 1995 to 2015 found that these drugs are all useful to varying extents in reducing the risk of a fatal heart attack or stroke. If aspirin might be a factor in bleeding risk for some patients, then using proton pump inhibitors are 90% as effective. These are the anti-ulcer drugs such as Tagamet and Zantac, and have no bleeding side effects.

A new class of drugs, humanised monoclonal antibodies, called PCSK9 inhibitors, have recently been approved, to mixed reviews, these being: evolocumab (Repatha-Amgen) and alirocumab (Praluent-Regeneron Pharmaceuticals/Sanofi). PCSK9 (proprotein convertase subtilisin/ kexin type 9) inhibitors work by binding to the LDL receptors in the bloodstream, promoting removal of LDL from circulation. PCSK9 inhibitors reduce LDL levels by as much as 70% and have few, if any, adverse effects.

The first approval for both of these drugs was for a fatal hereditary disease called homozygous hypercholesterolemia, a disease in which individuals die prematurely because of extremely high levels of LDL, which can't be controlled by statins. Here, both of the PCSK9-inhibiting drugs work very well, although it is not yet known whether the exceptionally low level of cholesterol that these drugs are responsible for is safe or not (as cholesterol has an important role in moderate quantities).

A recently reported trial (funded by Amgen, called FOURIER), involving over 27,000 patients who were randomised into taking the drug evolocumab or a placebo, showed the drug to have a clear benefit over statins in reducing LDL in the patients receiving the injected drugs. However, the cost-benefit analysis over statin therapy is not clear cut. In normalised populations, it appears that evolocumab only "saves" about one in 65 people from a major cardiac event, in comparison to trials where people took only statins.

Evolocumab and alirocumab are expensive, costing about US $15,000 for each patient per year in the US. A patent war rages around the two drugs, with Amgen winning the early stages of a royalty battle with Regeneron/Sanofi based on infringement of its patents, although both drugs remain on the market while the case rises higher up the legal chain.

It is debatable what market size there is for PCSK9 inhibitors, given that statins already work well in most cases. But for those with very high LDL levels, where the only alternative is apheresis (which is very expensive and acts as a kind of dialysis to remove LDL from the blood), PCSK9 inhibitors are a life saver. Our own view is that the market for PCSK9 inhibitors will be large – possibly as much as US $10 billion a year worldwide – and as a result Amgen is one of our favourite large company investment targets.

Further advances have been made recently when Novartis announced positive results of its CANTOS study using canakinumab for the reduction in risk of cardiovascular events in patients who have had a prior heart attack. The headline figure was a 15% reduction of major adverse cardiovascular events, including a 24% relative reduction in risk of heart attack. The reason for the excitement over these results is because most other drugs targeting cardiovascular diseases target cholesterol, whereas canakinumab targets inflammation via interleukin-1 beta.

A number of new thinning agents for the blood are on the market or about to hit it. Two types of blood thinners exist, both generally effective - anticoagulants, such as warfarin and Eliquis, and antiplatelet drugs, such as aspirin. Both types are important in stroke prevention. The main cause of a stroke is atrial fibrillation, which affects about 3 million Americans annually. Atrial fibrillation (AF) causes irregular heart rhythms and in some cases, leads to pooling of the blood, which increases the likelihood of stroke-related clots. AF rates are seven times higher in the US than anywhere else, and all of this is due to lifestyle.

Additionally, clots can form as a result of deep vein thrombosis or pulmonary embolisms. Anticoagulant drugs or "thinners" are the answer for most people, though increasingly "ablation" (surgery) is being used in patients with severe AF disease.

Apart from aspirin and warfarin – the old standbys for thinning the blood, but ones where there are severe side effects and dosing issues – new drugs are being developed, as well as ones that have recently appeared. These new entrants include Eliquis (apixaban-Pfizer/Bristol-Myers Squibb), Pradaxa (dabigatran - Boehringer Ingelheim) and Xarelto (rivaroxaban - JNJ/Bayer), and all of them work by preventing pooled blood in the heart from clotting. The market for these drugs is very large, worth over US $10 billion a year in the US alone, and Pfizer/BMS look to be the winners. The JNJ/Bayer drug is currently subject to patient lawsuits alleging harmful side effects, involving excessive bleeding.

The US biotech company Portola is also close to commercialising an interesting anticoagulant. This is an oral, once-daily Factor X inhibitor, targeting the blood coagulation pathway. It has been granted fast-track status for authorisation in the US, for blood clots in venous thromboembolism, as well as in very seriously ill patients, particularly those at risk of a second stroke. It is expected to be on the market in 2018 and is likely to sell very well. Additionally, a new drug for congestive heart failure, which is where the heart of the patient is incapable of pumping blood sufficiently hard, has recently been approved. The drug, Entresto (valsartan/sacubitril), developed by Novartis, has achieved a 20% reduction in death or hospitalisation among patients with heart failure. Sales in the US are already running at over US $500 million per annum,

although a companion drug from the same company, seralixin, recently failed a Phase 3 trial. There are an estimated 5 million people in the US who suffer from congestive (or left ventricular ejection fraction) heart failure. Entresto is a combination of an angiotensin blocker (valsartan) and a neprilysin inhibitor (sacubitril), which is the key ingredient that differentiates the drug and the one that makes it expensive (about US $5,000 per annum).

Oh, and apparently six bars of dark chocolate (a rich source of flavanols, but choose the ones without lots of sugar) a week are very good at warding off atrial fibrillation as well!

Surgical interventions in cardiac disease are also improving. Already, coronary bypasses are commonplace, and the use of stents has now been widespread for over two decades. Pacemakers are extremely long-lasting, safe and sophisticated. Scientists from the University of Washington have invented a device which "retrains" the undamaged half of a stroke victim's brain to take over the functioning of the damaged half, and early results have been very good indeed.

A new form of valve replacement surgery (trans-catheter aortic valve replacement, or TAVR) has in recent years become internationally widespread. Here, aortic valves that are malfunctioning (usually because of a

LEADING CAUSES OF DEATH IN THE US, 2014

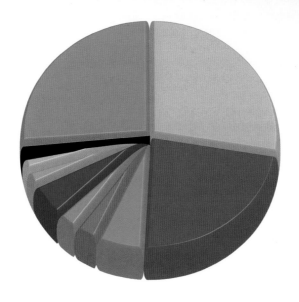

HEART DISEASE 28%

CANCER (MALIGNANT NEOPLASMS) 23%

CHRONIC LOWER RESPIRATORY DISEASE 6%

ACCIDENTS (UNINTENTIONAL INJURIES) 3%

ALZHEIMER'S DISEASE 3%

DIABETES 5%

INFLUENZA AND PNEUMONIA 2%

KIDNEY DISEASE 2%

SUICIDE 2%

OTHER 26%

Source: Centers for Disease Control and Prevention.

type of calcification causing stenosis of the valve) are replaced without invasive surgery, and this has become the gold standard of treatment for older people who suffer from aortic valve disease.

Five million Americans are diagnosed with aortic valve disease each year, and about 250,000 of them have a severe version of the disease. Of those, half would not survive five years without a valve replacement, and TAVR operations have risen to almost 100,000 a year, from none five years ago. In older people, not having to open the chest cavity is a major benefit in survival outcomes. Edwards Lifesciences (US listed, EW: NYSE) is the major player in this area, although it is not recommended by us as an investment, as it is a slow-growing colossus.

New "wearables" which measure heart health are emerging, (for example, the Withings Blood Pressure Monitor). Additionally, it is now clearly established that the banishment of trans fats from food absolutely reduces cardiac risk, that exercise and eating vegetables does too, and that a molecule called C Reactive Protein (CRP) is an excellent biomarker for inflammation in general including heart health. A low reading is a sign of good cardiac health and the CRP test can be bought over the counter.

CANCER IN RE(TREATMENT)

Age is the principal risk for cancer. In industrialised nations, about one in two people will develop a form of cancer during their lifetimes, and generally, between the ages of 40 and 80. Just under 8 million people die of cancer worldwide every year.

Controlling cancer is thus an important part of extending human lifespans. While our risk of cancer goes up as we age, most cancers are caused by genetics, environmental exposure to toxins (such as smoking), or sheer bad luck, the latter being the most important. Increasing maximum lifespans without defeating cancer would mean that most of our lives would end with chemotherapy, surgery or radiation.

Fortunately, the good news is that cancer treatment has changed dramatically over the past decade. Readers are of course familiar with cytotoxic chemotherapy, which are toxic chemicals given to cancer patients in the hope that their tumours would be killed before the patient. While chemotherapy does indeed save lives, and has helped countless people, most physicians and scientists have shifted their focus to the new paradigm of cancer treatment – **immunotherapy.** This involves stimulating the patient's immune system to better fight cancer. Because our bodies are always in the process of dealing with cancerous or pre-cancerous cells, especially when we are younger, this immunotherapy treatment is effectively a way of restoring the body's natural immune balance.

This mobilisation of the immune system against tumours appears to be a simple concept, but in practice it is a sophisticated therapy which must not only activate the immune system, but also properly target the specific tumour, as well as suppressing the checkpoint molecules that tumours use to block the immune system.

Immune system mobilisation can be thought of like driving a car: you have to first release the brake, then press on the accelerator and steer where you'd like to go. Early attempts to mobilise the immune system involved giving patients immune cytokines, which was analogous to pushing the accelerator pedal right to the floor. In these earlier therapies, the immune system then attacked everything in sight, and patients often died when normal tissue became highly inflamed. This is called a "cytokine storm" and is often fatal. Nonetheless, despite early setbacks, it was observed that some patients had long term responses when their immune system successfully overcame the cytokine storms and allowed the targeting of tumours, thereby

eradicating them. Additionally, it became apparent that this type of treatment offered long-term protection against recurrence, something that traditional cancer treatment only does in about half of the cases.

These "cytokine" treatments are still used, but they are reserved to limited types of cancer in relatively healthy patients, that are able to tolerate the side effects. While oncologists showed some tentative results in the early days by "pressing on the gas pedal" with cytokines, it was Medarex Inc. that led a breakthrough in cancer immunotherapy, when the company developed antibodies to a protein called CTLA4. CTLA4 is expressed on the kinds of immune cells normally tasked with destroying tumours (so-called T-cells). When CTLA4 interacts with its target, it shuts down the immune cell. This checkpoint serves to prevent the immune system from destroying healthy tissue, but tumour cells sneakily upregulate this checkpoint molecule and prevent the immune system from attacking them.

Anti-CTLA4 antibodies like ipilimumab prevent CTLA4 expressed on T-cells from "seeing" their target on tumour cells – a bit like Odysseus ordering his men to close their ears to the Sirens' songs. Ipilimumab has had fantastic results in advanced metastatic melanoma, a diagnosis where in the past patients had a 10 year survival rate of less than 10%. In contrast, approximately 20% of patients in early trials showed a long-term response to the disease with ipilimumab, meaning that most doctors would consider those patients to be functionally cured. (*Journal of Clinical Oncology* June 2015)

Although treatment with ipilimunab does sometimes lead to severe and possibly fatal immune reactions, it is better tolerated than treatment with cytokines and patients enjoy a much better prognosis. Bristol-Myers Squibb (BMS) purchased Medarex in 2009 for US $2.4 billion, acquiring ipilimumab and a portfolio of early-stage checkpoint inhibitors. BMS quickly followed ipilimumab with a second Medarex antibody, nivolumab, which targets another checkpoint protein called PD1. Nivolumab proved an even more selective way of mobilising the immune system against cancers. Approximately 34% of melanoma patients treated with nivolumab have survived until at least five years after their diagnosis, and nivolumab causes less non-specific immune activation (AACR 2016).

Even more importantly, since these two drugs work on distinct parts of the immune system, they work in concert when they are given together, benefiting more than 50% of patients. The success of ipilimumab and nivolumab (now approved as Yervoy and Opdivo) have spurred scientists and companies working in this area to focus on new combinations that can bring more patients into a long-term response.

Anti-PD1 drugs are now approved for use in melanoma, lymphomas, bladder, lung, kidney, and head and neck cancers, and they are being studied in many more. Analysts have predicted that over 60% of all cancers in the developed world will eventually be managed with these types of cancer immunotherapy treatments. Estimates of the global market range from US $50 billion to over US $80 billion annually.

The FDA in the US and other regulatory health authorities have fast-tracked these types of new drugs to the market, given their pronounced benefit and generally good tolerability. Excitement about cancer immunotherapy from patients, clinicians, scientists and regulators has led to increased investment in innovative technologies, more aggressive merger and acquisition activity, and huge returns for investors. Scientists are now busy exploring other approaches to cancer immunotherapy, in addition to the now established checkpoint inhibitors.

Another type of immunotherapy focuses on removing some of a patient's immune cells from their blood and re-engineering them outside the body in order to fight cancer more effectively. Taking samples of a patient's tumour and immune cells, expanding them and manipulating them in a lab, and then re-infusing the amplified cancer-fighting cells back into the patient is an exciting new treatment. These approaches are called CAR-T (chimeric antigen T-cell receptors) and, as their name suggests, are engineered T-cell therapies. While currently cumbersome and expensive to produce, they have shown remarkable - indeed, biblical - results in treating blood cancers, such as leukaemia. Until recently, it was difficult to predict which peptide a T-cell receptor would bind to, but research by Dash et al., and Glanville et al (2017) has demonstrated that it is now possible to do so.

In addition, the demand from larger companies to "buy" from the labs of smaller companies is now at historically high levels: aggregate private M&A values over the past few years are 3 times what they were in 2010-2012. Much of this investor excitement has specifically come from advances in oncology and cancer immunotherapy. Dr Walter's company, SalvaRx (SALV:LSE), is focused on developing compounds that can be used in combination with Yervoy or Opdivo or the like, to improve response rates in tumour types that have already been pre-treated with immunotherapies. As well, SalvaRx is working to improve responses to tumour types that are resistant to current treatments.

Pharma giants such as Merck, Novartis, Pfizer and Bristol-Myers Squibb, as well as smaller entrants like Juno Therapeutics and Kite Pharma, are among the leaders in the field. Also, Johnson and Johnson and Danish partner Genmab have produced stunning data for Darzalex, their new and now approved immunotherapy for multiple myeloma, which is a disease of the blood that is more prevalent among the elderly. Darzalex, in combination with other drugs, appears to completely eradicate the disease in about two-thirds of all cases.

As earlier detection of cancers becomes possible with improved screening technologies, as immunotherapies are better dosed and personalised using genomic sequencing, as combination therapies involving checkpoint inhibitors, CAR-T technology, and new compounds are developed, the chances of dying of cancer will continue to diminish. Even currently relatively intractable tumours, such as pancreatic, lung and liver cancers, will shortly be addressable with much more effective drugs. The world's second biggest killer, a close runner after cardiovascular disease, is about to drop down the death charts.

With thanks to Dr Ian Walters, CEO SalvaRx Group Plc, who contributed to this text.

BREATHING EASIER IN OLD AGE – RESPIRATORY DISEASE

Recently, Jim went to the brand-new concert hall in Hamburg known as the Elbephilharmonie. It is absolutely state of the art, supposedly boasting the world's best acoustics. The orchestral performance was amazing, but the sound of the audience was anything but.

This is because so many of them were coughing; a combination due to them being mostly elderly and, probably, of being or having been smokers. They had respiratory diseases, and even the best venue in the world couldn't disguise that fact. Whether in smokers or non-smokers, age reduces lung elasticity, respiratory strength and the efficiency of the chest wall in respiration.

Respiratory disease has been rising as a cause of death in the developed world. This has been mostly due to the incidence of smoking in people who were born in the 1930s to 1950s. As the habit becomes increasingly taboo in most rich countries, the prevalence of smoking-related disease will probably decline, while, sadly, they will become more commonplace in the developing world.

Respiratory disease is a major health burden, and its correlation with ageing is high. Many lung diseases are related to each other. About ten million people worldwide die of lung diseases every year, representing about one sixth of all deaths, even more than cancer, if lung cancer were included in the respiratory category. Lung diseases are responsible for about one tenth of all days lost to illness, and the unpleasantness of most lung diseases makes it a feared opponent in anti-ageing strategies.

We have to breathe about 17,000 times a day, and we rely on the efficient exchange of oxygen and other gases for our survival.

Respiratory disease increases with age and our lungs, bronchi, tracheas, and the nerves and muscles associated with breathing all decline in efficiency. Key diseases of respiration in the elderly include lung cancer, mesothelioma, asthma, pneumonia, chronic obstructive pulmonary disease (COPD), emphysema (a form of COPD), pulmonary embolisms, pulmonary hypertension, idiopathic pulmonary fibrosis (IPF), a fatal type of pneumonia and, of course, the common cold.

Broadly speaking, these diseases can be divided into four categories:

1. Diseases of the airways, which are the tubes that transport oxygen and other gases into and out of the lungs. The diseases that affect the airways cause blockages or

constrictions and make it harder for sufferers to breathe. Such conditions include asthma, COPD and bronchitis.

2. Diseases of the lung tissues. Diseases resulting from workplace and environmental exposure to asbestos and other toxins fall into this category. Here, the tissues of the lungs get scarred or inflamed and expansion of the organs becomes more difficult. Idiopathic (i.e. unexplained) and other forms of pulmonary fibrosis are prime examples of this, and **idiopathic pulmonary fibrosis**, in particular, has a high correlation with age. In addition, lung infections such as pneumonia are common in the elderly.

3. Pulmonary circulatory diseases. Pulmonary hypertension is a good example of this, as this disease is highly associated with cardiovascular problems. Pulmonary circulatory diseases occur when blood vessels get clogged up, or scarred.

4. Lung cancers, roughly divided into three types: non-small cell lung cancer (NSCLC), accounting for about 80-85% of lung cancers, small cell lung cancer (SCLC), accounting for about 10-15% of lung cancers, (very difficult to treat), and mesothelioma, which is generally the result of exposure to asbestos or to coal dust, and is rare. Cancers of the lung generally start in the cells lining the bronchi and the alveoli. Several cancers originating elsewhere in the body can also spread (metastasise) to the lung.

A large portion of respiratory disease, particularly the lung cancers and COPD, are associated with smoking. Lung cancers, which about three-quarters of the time are the result of smoking, account for about one in six of all cancers, and about a one in three deaths from cancer. Lung cancer is now being addressed by the new types of cancer immunotherapy and the outlook for this once almost always fatal disease is considerably better. It also represents a US $20 billion potential market for the leading companies in the lung cancer immunotherapy field, namely Roche, Bristol-Myers Squibb, AstraZeneca and Merck. However, giving up smoking is absolutely the best way to ward off the possibility of contracting cancers of the lung and is far better than waiting for a "cure" to come along.

COPD is the second largest category of respiratory disease, having overtaken lung-related infections. COPD is also linked to smoking, and can also be the cause of pulmonary arterial hypertension, which is connected to heart disease. Quite often, patients will have two or three forms of respiratory disease at the same time.

New treatments are being developed for lung diseases in the elderly, and particularly for lung cancers, the single largest cause of death among cancers. For example, early detection tests being developed by scientists at the Francis Crick Institute, London amongst others, are very promising. The Crick scientists have developed a way of detecting "chromosomal chaos" many months before scans do – potentially saving the lives of many at-risk patients.

COPD is a very difficult disease to treat, and most care is palliative. However, an innovative surgical procedure developed at the Royal Brompton and Chelsea and Westminster Hospital in London is now being employed. Here, sufferers of COPD (which is really a term for several types of lung disease, including bronchitis and emphysema, with about three million sufferers in the UK alone), involves burning away the parts of the damaged vagus nerve of the lungs, which stops the overproduction of mucus and the consequent constriction of the airways. This seems to be an excellent long-term substitute for the bronchodilator drugs that COPD patients currently use. Vagus nerve therapy is also being heavily studied in autoimmune disease (*Nature,* May 2017).

For COPD and other lung diseases, most therapies are designed to improve the quality of life for the victims, but are not disease-altering.

The objective of scientists now is to find ways to block the pathways that stimulate blood vessel growth, and which are a large factor in blocking arteries, and are implicated in the development of many types of lung disease.

Pulmonary hypertension, an often-fatal disease involving excessive blood pressure in the lungs, is generally caused by a defect in the BMPR2 (bone morphogenetic protein receptor type II) gene. Blocking or sidestepping this receptor appears to have the potential to reopen the arteries, whose clogging is the principal characteristic of pulmonary hypertension.

A trial involving the drug imatinib (Gleevec, a Novartis cancer drug) failed in this indication, but the idea of intervening at the genetic points of weakness which causes so much respiratory disease has now taken hold. At the moment, for instance, dilators and heart drugs (believe it or not, including Viagra) are becoming viable drug treatments for COPD and pulmonary hypertension patients – but none are curative of the underlying disease.

Therefore, Asthma UK, AstraZeneca, the British Lung Foundation and MRC Technology are looking at a bigger picture by incorporating epigenetics in the study of respiratory disease. Epigenetics involves the changing of gene expression because of lifestyle and environment, rather than change in a person's DNA sequence.

To our minds, genetic intervention in lung and other respiratory diseases will be a game-changer. But such a solution is at least a decade away, so in the meantime, drugs such as the tyrosine kinase inhibitors offer the only hope of halting or partially reversing COPD and pulmonary hypertension.

In addition, Verona Pharma (VRP), a British company, is also developing a compound known as RPL554, a maintenance treatment for asthma with apparently significant benefit for lung function over current standard-of-care. It is not curative, however, and nothing will be on the market for some considerable time.

There is, however, an additional interesting angle worth noting. In a recent study led by the Mayo Clinic, idiopathic pulmonary fibrosis, (IPF) has been shown to be linked to the fundamental biology of ageing. Dr Nathan LeBrasseur, director of the Healthy Ageing programme at the Mayo Clinic, headed up this particular study. Currently, there is no effective treatment for IPF, which has a very poor prognosis of three to five years of remaining life for newly diagnosed patients.

The Mayo Clinic study found that senescent cells are related to IPF and that the secretions from these cells probably drive inflammation, thereby leading to fibrosis in tissues, which is the principal characteristic of IPF. The numbers of these senescent cells increase along with the disease progression leading to a developing hypothesis that the process of ageing itself is accelerated as IPF takes hold.

Using a combination of the drugs dasatinib and quercetin, the researchers eliminated all of the senescent cells in mice models. These mice, which had been bred to mimic symptoms of IPF, then showed remarkable improvements in markers of lung function, including treadmill tests. From this research it appears that senolytic drugs (drugs that remove old and damaged, or senescent cells) might help IPF patients, but equally, that senolytics used in a non-IPF population might have the potential to restore a more youthful respiratory system in elderly subjects. Now, that would certainly be breathtaking.

DIABETES – SWEET NEWS AHEAD

Diabetes has been around for a long, long time, but only in recent decades has it developed into the epidemic that it is today. Its ancient Greek meaning is "to pass through", is because of its association with frequent urination, but, in general, mentions of the disease in ancient texts are rare. Diabetes is considered to be a life-shortening disease in all three of its forms (possibly four, if Alzheimer's becomes generally considered as a form of diabetes).

The disease takes a long time to manifest, and the principal destructive factor associated with it is cardiac disease, notably damage to blood vessels. Its emergence into the modern plague it has become has fairly obvious causes. It's partly because of the modern Western diet that has today brought type 2 diabetes into the lives of over 450 million people worldwide (8% of the adult population). And partly because fifty years ago people didn't then live long enough to get the disease, as it is a condition whose incidence is highly correlated with age.

If left untreated, diabetes can cause multiple complications. These can include cancers, foot ulcers, eye problems, heart disease, kidney failure, and stroke. Diabetes is also associated with a 1.2 to 1.5 times greater rate of cognitive decline and more physical falls in the elderly. Heart disease is twice as prevalent in diabetics as it is in the general population. Three-quarters of diabetics die from cardiac problems, stroke, or circulatory diseases. The American Diabetes Association estimates that the average patient diagnosed at age 50 dies six years earlier than a person without diabetes. If the current trajectory of the disease continues, one in three adults in the US will have diabetes by 2050. At least 90% of diabetics in the West have the type 2 form of the disease, which in most, but not all, cases is lifestyle induced.

In 2014, the International Diabetes Federation estimated that diabetes causes around 5 million deaths worldwide every year, and that the total cost of the disease is about US $600 billion, with nearly half of that spent in the US. Diabetes is divided into three types, 1 and 2, and gestational, with type 1 manifesting in earlier life, and type 2 later on. Gestational diabetes, is much less common.

Type 1 cannot be reversed yet, and has a genetic component in most cases. Type 1 affects only about 1% of adults worldwide and is medically controlled by the administration of insulin. It results from the pancreas's inability to produce enough insulin.

Type 2 diabetes begins with insulin resistance, a condition in which the body becomes resistant to the insulin hormone. Additionally, in the later stages of the disease, patients produce less insulin. The most common causes of type 2 diabetes are obesity and insufficient exercise, but the disease can also manifest for other reasons. The principal reason underlying all types of diabetes is metabolic derangement and hyperinsulinemia (Fung and Berger, 2016). Type 2 diabetes can be reversed with lifestyle changes, and a wide variety of therapies are available to patients who suffer from it. The incidence of type 2 diabetes is high in developed nations, at between 7% and 10% of adult populations, and is growing in the developing world as well.

For instance, in China, in 1984 only 1% of adults had diabetes (mostly type 1) but today that figure is closer to 12%. Diabetes is age-associated: its incidence rises with successive age cohorts. There are 30 million diabetics, mostly type 2, in the US, and about 4 million, also mainly type 2, in the UK.

The first effective form of treatment for any type of diabetes didn't emerge until the 1920s, when human insulin was purified for use in diabetics. Since then, a wide range of effective therapies have been developed but mostly for type 2 diabetics: insulin that is synthesised and with much more specific and tailored doses, insulin that is inhaled, a wide variety of new drugs, artificial pancreases, and the nascent use of stem cells.

Because diabetes in its second and much more widespread form is obesity-associated (although not exclusively, as there are millions of diabetics of normal weight), dieting is a major part of effective diabetic therapy. As an example, a 2017 study by Valter Longo of the University of Southern California and published in *Cell* magazine has demonstrated that a brief, periodic fasting type of diet can reverse both type 1 (very

interestingly) and type 2 diabetes in mice by reprogramming pancreatic cells into once more being insulin-producing. Valter is now selling a US $300 per week diet that mimics periodic fasting – including kale chips, quinoa, and other cardboard substitutes. Nice work if you can get it!

Additionally, exercise and other physical activity reduce the risk of diabetes by about a third in prediabetic patients. The types of food that are helpful to people at risk of diabetes, or people who have it, include grains, fibre, nuts, fish, and of course, a strict limit on sugar intake (see Sugar - Deception. Page 344). The main treatments for diabetics are pharmacological, although an artificial pancreas (used to regulate the level of insulin in the body, rather than to replace the organ) and bariatric (gastric band) surgery have been shown to be effective, as has the Elipse gastric balloon which does more or less the same thing.

The pharmacological interventions for diabetes are mostly designed to reduce blood sugar levels. Our old friend metformin, which is a drug taken orally, is an ideal first-line of treatment for type 2 diabetes. In addition, if metformin fails, there are other equivalent drugs. Januvia (sitagliptin) produced by Merck, inhibits the dipeptidyl peptidase 4 (DPP-4) enzyme, and this works to increase insulin production. Monotherapy using metformin on its own is slightly more effective than Januvia alone, but the combination of both drugs is highly effective – and convenient, as they are both orally taken.

Other marketed drugs include injectable GLP-1 (glucagon-like peptide 1 receptor) "agonists". These are for type 2 diabetics and replicate the action of natural GLP-1 by increasing the insulin production of the body and by inhibiting glucagon. A stimulant for insulin production is called an incretin, and these drugs, which are quite new, are now becoming widely prescribed. The brand names under which they are sold include Byetta, Bydureon, Victoza, Lyxumia and Tanzeum. In contrast to insulin, GLP-1 agonists tend to reduce the weight of patients, and also reduce the risks of hypoglycaemia, as well as of cardiac disease. GLP-1 agonists in combination with insulin have now been approved in the US.

Additionally, there are SGLT2 (sodium-glucose cotransporter 2) inhibitors, known as gliflozins, which are oral medications. These are new, having only been introduced in 2013, and go by the brand names of Jardiance, Farxiga and Invokana. They have been shown to reduce mortality risk by as much as a third in diabetics. They work by reducing blood glucose levels, and operate through the kidneys, in order to prevent glucose

that has been filtered from being reabsorbed into the bloodstream. They are also associated with weight loss, reduced cardiac disease and reduced hypoglycaemia, except when taken with insulin. They do carry the double the risk of ketoacidosis (too much acid in the blood) (BMJ 2017) and the FDA has recently highlighted this potentially adverse effect.

There are also a large range of long-acting and short-acting insulins on the market, most produced by recombinant methods, and together with effective glucose testing these keep the diabetes of most patients under control.

Inhaled insulin, sold by Mannkind, under the brand name Alfreeza, has been on the market in the US since 2014, but sales have been hugely disappointing. Sanofi has been developing a compound that seeks to mimic the satiety reaction that occurs after gastric bypass surgery – a surgery which in many cases can reverse type 2 diabetes.

"Smart insulin", which would automatically increase insulin supply when blood sugars are too high, and switch off the supply when sugars are at normal levels, is also being developed by Merck and by Sanofi. If successful, this would significantly reduce the risk of hypoglycemia, which remains a serious risk for insulin-injecting diabetics.

Early stage trials of a LMPTP (low molecular weight protein tyrosine phosphatase) inhibitor are underway at the University of Southern California in San Diego. The inhibition of LMPTP reverses diabetes in mice fed a high-fat diet. LMPTP is a promoter of insulin resistance, so its deletion or inhibition would seemingly be favourable in treating the disease.

Currently, around 500 trials of new medicines for diabetes are underway. The most intractable form of the disease, type 1, still suffers from a lack of viable alternatives to the injection of insulin, which carries a lifetime risk of higher mortality. Pancreas transplants have been attempted on a very small number of patients, but this cannot be a global solution.

New forms of alternative diabetes treatments, including wearables such as pumps which inject insulin but don't monitor glucose levels, are being made, by amongst others, Insulet, Medtronic and Tandem, all public companies, and these are now widely available. The dominant players in the diabetes markets for pharmaceuticals include Sanofi (our preferred investment), Novo Nordisk, Merck, Eli Lilly, and AstraZeneca.

For type 2 diabetics, there are many promising new drugs and therapies coming into the market in the years ahead. However most people, including the elderly, can avoid type 2 diabetes by eating well and by exercising. A recent Danish study of 70,000 people suggests that both men and women who drink red wine significantly reduce the chance of developing type 2 diabetes. Oh, and by avoiding or curtailing sugar (see Sugar - Deception. Page 344).

DON'T FORGET – THE LONG ROAD FOR DEMENTIA

The incidence of dementia and other neurodegenerative diseases rises with age. Despite public angst about the burden of diseases such as Alzheimer's and Parkinson's, the prevalence of dementia and neurodegeneration is actually falling in the developed world. As an example, from 1989 to 2011, the proportion of people in England and Wales over 65 with dementia actually dropped by a fifth.

This is good news, but of course the number of people over 65 is constantly rising as life expectancy increases, so these are still serious life-shortening diseases, with many millions of sufferers around the world. About 32% of people over 85 years old in the US have been diagnosed with Alzheimer's, the leading form of dementia. Worldwide, there are thought to be, at a minimum, 50 million people with dementia, and if no new treatments are forthcoming, that number will rise to 130 million in 2050.

Around 60%-70% of people with dementia suffer from Alzheimer's, and the balance have vascular dementia of one kind or another. In addition, about 2% of adults over 65 will have Parkinson's disease, which has a similar aetiology to dementia, and is characterised by protein build-ups (as aggregates termed Lewy bodies), a characteristic which is the same for patients with dementia (amyloid plaques and tau protein tangles). Until recently, it was thought that statins provided some protection against Parkinson's, but research by Xuemei Huang of Penn State College of Medicine has disproved that. In fact, it seems that lipophilic statins, such as atorvastatin and fluvastatin, may actually increase the risk of Parkinson's. For people concerned about the disease – and there are 50,000 new diagnoses of Parkinson's every year in the US – it may be best to switch to a non-lipophilic statin.

In addition, Living Cell Technologies, listed on the Australian and US stock exchanges, has been engaged in promising research in implanting PiB (Pittsburgh compound B) brain cells from the pig's choroid plexus into the brains of Parkinson's patients using an alginate (seaweed-based) capsule to bypass immune reactions. The first four patients thus implanted are reported to be doing well, and have improved significantly in recognised cognitive tests. Another 18 patients have recently been treated. In the Chinese city of Zhengzhou, Parkinson patients are being treated with human embryonic stem cells directly implanted into their brains.

David Perlmutter in his book *Grain Brain* (2013) proposes that dementia and diabetes are linked because of the high incidence of poor diet in patients with both conditions. He believes that gluten and processed foods are linked to cognitive impairment. The authoritative Hisayama study from Japan, which measured an elderly population from 1985 to 2005, also demonstrated a strong link between diabetes and Alzheimer's and vascular dementia. Other studies including a recent Harvard study, suggest that a gluten free diet might actually be damaging to health, except in the case of the 1% or so of the population who are coeliacs – so on this point, confusion reigns. Gluten in moderation is probably OK for the other 99%.

What does seem to be the case is that people who rank higher on the scale of "cleverness", such as IQ tests, generally live longer than those who don't. This is probably due to the fact that such cleverer people benefit from greater "system integrity" which is probably because they listen to health advice!

THE DIFFERENT KINDS OF DEMENTIA

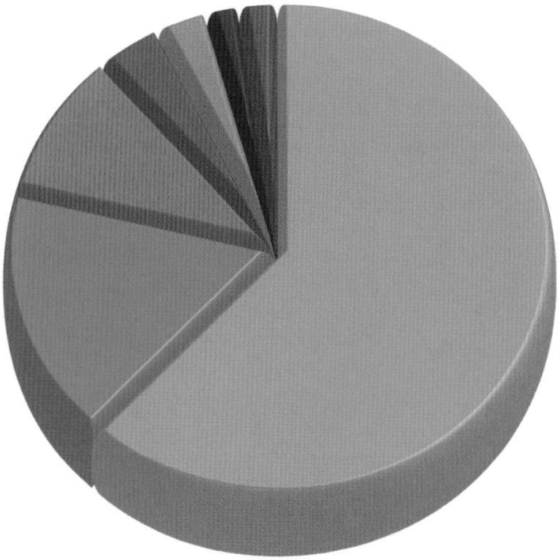

ALZHEIMER'S 62%

Causes problems with memory, lanaguage and reasoning. 5% of cases start before age 65.

VASCULAR DEMENTIA 17%

Impaired judgement, difficulty with motor skills and balance. Heart disease and strokes increase its likelihood.

MIXED DEMENTIA 10%

Several types of dementia contribute to symptoms. Most common in people over 85.

DEMENTIA WITH LEWY BODIES 4%

Caused by Lewy Body Proteins. Symptoms can include hallucinations, disordered sleep.

FRONTOTEMPORAL DEMENTIA 2%

Personality changes and language problems. Most common onset between the ages of 45-60

PARKINSON'S DISEASE 2%

Can give rise to dementia symptoms as the condition progresses.

OTHER 3%

Conditions such as Creutzfeld-Jacob disease; depression; multiple sclerosis.

Source: alzheimers.org.uk

While dementia has a high genetic component, it is not an inevitable feature of old age. People can remain on the mental ball well after the age of 100, and many old people, despite "slowing down", can handle mental tasks on a par with much younger people.

Alzheimer's remains pretty much a mystery, as are many diseases of the brain. Our brains are by far the most complex organ we have, and we are a long way from understanding exactly how it operates. For instance, many people die with a large quantity of amyloid plaques in their brains but with no symptoms of Alzheimer's. And beta amyloid clearing drugs don't yet seem to work in the way intended. A recent University of Florida study (*PLOS Biology* 2017) suggests that a human enzyme, cyclophilin 40 may reduce amyloid levels, which is forming the basis for early stage research for a novel approach to amyloid plaques.

The main pathway of dementia and of Parkinson's disease is characterised by the build-up of protein aggregates in the brain, possibly occluding normal brain function. These proteins become misfolded and form aggregates. It is possible that plaques arise as a form of cellular protection, and that the real villains are intermediate forms of the misfolded protein consisting of just a few molecules stuck together.

It is thought that the accumulation of misfolded proteins is the result of the failure of the so-called **chaperone** system, whereby proteins are guided into their 3D structures by helper molecules. The failure of autophagy (see Autophagy. Page 132) to remove these misfolded proteins, as well as damaged organelles, through lysosomal degradation aggravates the situation in both Alzheimer's (tau peptides) and in Parkinson's (α-synuclein protein aggregation).

Patients with dementia are more likely to have had a parent or sibling with the disease. There are about 20 gene variants that are associated with dementia, the most famous of which is in the ApoE gene. The ApoE4 variant is implicated in late-life dementia, though it is not as deterministic to getting the diseases as mutations in the genes associated with early onset Alzheimer's, notably APP, PSEN1, and PSEN 2.

About 70% of Alzheimer's is genetic, so that means that about 30% comes from environmental factors, including obesity, poor diet, insufficient exercise and not remaining "engaged" and keeping the brain active. The recent FINGER study in Finland validated this conclusion, with people who maintained brain and physical health avoiding dementia far more often than those who did not. We are lovers of a puzzle called WordStorm, which is available for download and is highly addictive!!

Although the incidence of people with dementia is declining, those who do suffer from it become increasingly dependent on others, and the burden of care can and is often overwhelming for relatives and social services.

About 200 drugs for Parkinson's, Alzheimer's and other forms of dementia have been trialled in the past two decades and almost all have failed abjectly; only a few are now available on the market and none of them radically alter the diseases' properties. A further 260 compounds are currently being investigated in trials. The drugs currently being sold for Alzheimer's are Aricept (donepezil), galantamine (Razadyne), rivastigmine (Exelon) and memantine (Namenda). These drugs alleviate the symptoms and possibly slow the progression of the disease, but this is a condition which always ends up in cognitive catastrophe. All of these drugs are known as cholinesterase inhibitors.

The standard-of-care drug for Parkinson's is L-Dopa, which is used to treat movement symptoms, but unfortunately is known also to induce hallucinations. Additionally, antipsychotics as well as anti-depressants are often administered to PDT patients. Deep brain stimulation has been known to help victims; this is a technique which uses embedded electrical signals generated by a pacemaker-like device which blocks harmful neuronal signals. Additionally, transplanting fetal cells into Parkinson's patients is now being trialled and scientists at the Karolinska Institute in Sweden are reprogramming the brains of dopamine-deficient mice, using a virus carrying four genes to reprogramme the astrocytes (the brain's "support" cells) into dopamine-producing neurons. By the age of 60, approximately half of all dopaminergic cells have been lost in most people.

Upregulation of autophagy is now regarded as a novel target for drugs to treat Parkinson's and Alzheimer's, using the **mTORC1** (see Targets in Ageing. Page 184) pathway as a channel for intervention. The removal of protein aggregates, which are toxic to the surrounding brain tissue, is a promising area of research.

Separate studies at the University of Edinburgh and at University College London have revealed that people's brains age at different rates. Scans on 669 patients in Scotland, all of them over 73 years old, showed that brains that appeared older were associated with earlier death. Men dying before age 80 had brains that were eight years "older" than those of men who died at a later age. With women, the age difference was two years.

The obvious conclusion of this research is the possibility of administering scans to older people and of determining if lifestyle changes and brain-stimulating activities need to be prescribed to those whose brains are ageing at a more rapid rate. Additionally, the active ingredient of cannabis, while possibly deleterious in teenagers, appears to be positive for older people. This ingredient, THC **(tetrahydrocannabinol)**, appears to restore memory in elderly mice (using mazes as a test), according to a study conducted by the University of Bonn in Germany.

It appears that THC increases the number of connections between neuronal cells in the hippocampus, which is where short-term memories are stored. Future trials using cannabinoids will use purified THC rather than spliffs or reefers, so that elderly potheads will not be a regular sight in any town near you.

A high-profile trial of an anti-Aβ immune therapy for Alzheimer's, a monoclonal antibody, solanezumab (Eli Lilly) failed, but the drug category focused on clearing beta amyloid plaques may not yet be dead in the water. These drugs really do remove plaques, so it may be that the amyloid plaques themselves are not central to the disease of Alzheimer's, but it could be other forms of the same protein. Merck has recently done a deal with Japan's Teijin Pharmaceuticals to further the development of a drug to block tau hyperphosphorylation (the modification that appears to promote aggregation) in Alzheimer's patients. The move away from beta amyloid removal is understandable – after all, 99% of all Alzheimer's drugs have failed. Tau may be the new holy grail – and there is certainly a growing body of "Tauists" who are banging the drum. The jury, as with so much in neurodegenerative disease, remains out.

A recent article in *Brain* magazine, by Professor Giovanna Mallucci of the University of Cambridge, has described a neuroprotective effect of a combination of trazodone and dibenzoylmethane (DBM) in mouse studies. This drug combination appears to block the misfolding of beta amyloid proteins, as well as what is known as the unfolded protein response, which is thought to drive decreased protein synthesis, the mishandling of misfolded proteins and neurodegeneration itself. Too much unfolded protein response is a common feature of Parkinson's, Alzheimer's and Huntingdon's disease.

Trazodone, which is a long-established anti-depressant, and DBM, which is an extract of Chinese herbal liquorice, appears to be neuroprotective in Professor Mallucci's mice - but often - drugs for neurodegenerative disease trialled in animal models don't work well or at all in humans. Despite the curious combination of drugs in this study, Professor Mallucci is a highly-acclaimed scientist, so we will watch her work with interest.

So-called PERK (protein kinase RNA-like endoplasmic reticulum kinase) inhibitors have been trialled by GlaxoSmithKline, although they were subsequently dropped. These are effective in stopping neuronal cell death in mice, but had serious unwanted side effects.

The holy grail of pharmacological intervention in neurodegenerative disease, drugs that do more than just alleviate symptoms, is still some way off. Brain mapping, a collaborative effort by scientists around the world, and a work in progress, is certainly making a difference. Additionally, a huge amount of funding from governments, charities and companies will hopefully yield better therapies than those currently available.

What is clear, however, is that moderate exercise is important in warding off Alzheimer's — as it seems to induce autophagy and the clearance of amyloid plaques and of tau protein tangles. A naturally occurring compound called BDNF (brain-derived neurotrophic factor) is upregulated with exercise and has an absolute effect on cognition and on lessening depression. Pharma companies are now looking at finding ways of mimicking the BDNF response to exercise, and are particularly interested in the metabolite beta-hydroxybutyrate, which seems to act as a promoter of BDNF production, acting through the genes HDAC2 and HDAC3 (members of the histone deacetylase family of transcription factors).

Genetic intervention to silence the gene related component of Alzheimer's will be available in due course, and the link between diabetes and dementia may turn out to be more than observational, with treatments for both disease categories possibly being able to act in tandem. Of all the diseases of ageing, however, neurodegeneration remains the least tractable, and the scariest.

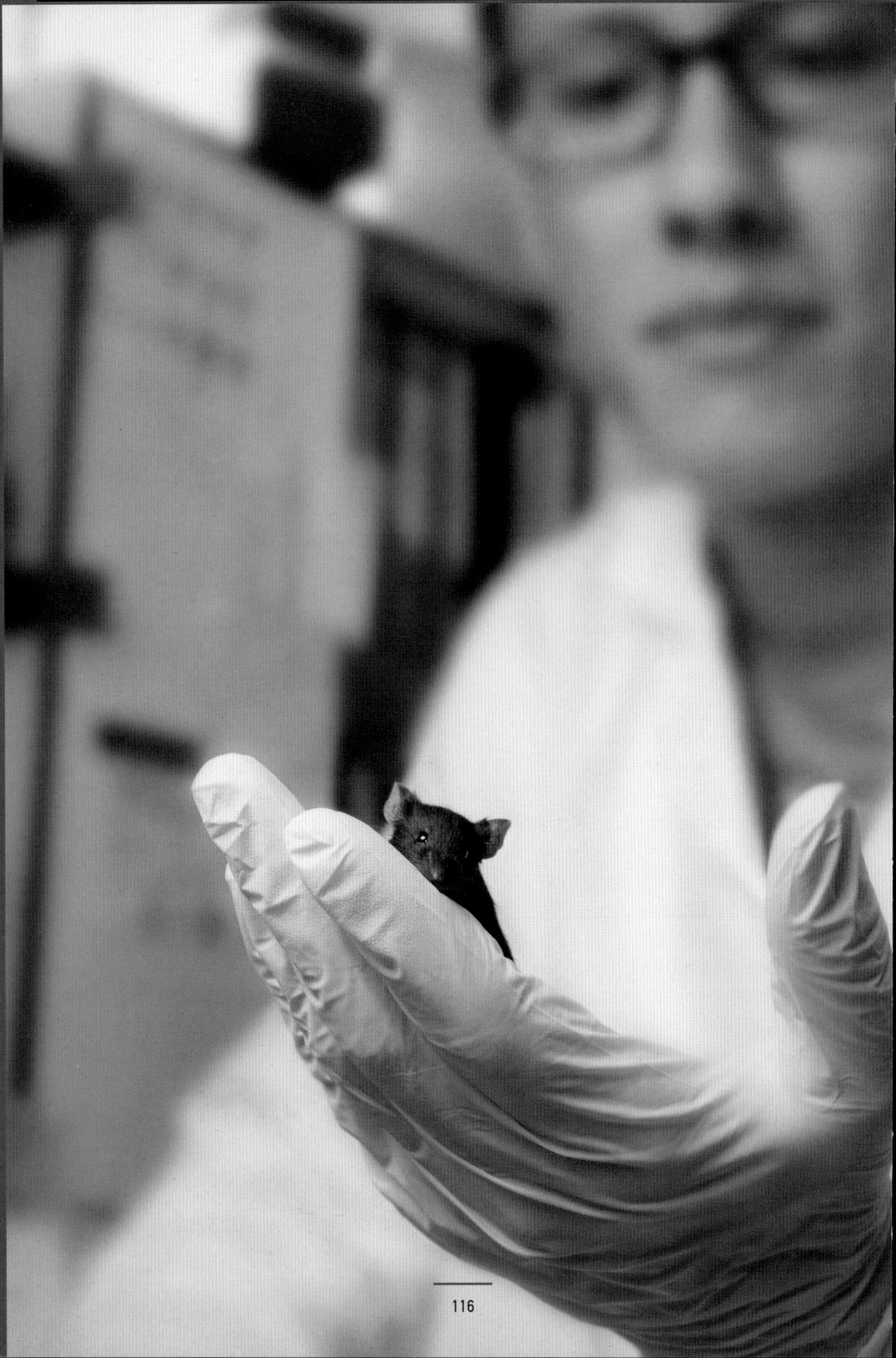

ANIMAL MODELS
THE ELEGANCE OF WORMS, THE FRUITS OF FLY RESEARCH, MOUSE HUNTS — AND A LEAVENING OF YEAST

For many years, animals and other organisms have been used in both fundamental research and in trialling drugs. In the US and in Europe, it is in fact a requirement that new drugs be tested on animals before being tested on humans.

Ethical issues come into play, as being a laboratory animal is not a pleasant existence. Mice, for instance, are kept in plastic boxes and confined to a small space with other comrades. While these mice are not subject to the predations of the wild, they are used in sometimes gruesome experiments.

There is a move, now partly approved by the FDA in the US, to remove animals from drug testing altogether (at least in the early stages), and companies are working to do more research in silico, i.e. on a chip. This not only removes animals from the picture but also speeds up the process of finding compounds that work on humans.

Emulate Bio has devised "organ on a chip" technology that replicates organ activity on tiny devices and these are already being used to trial drugs for liver diseases.

Noble as these efforts are, there is a fundamental problem in the study of longevity: humans live a long time. That makes it hard for scientists – who are themselves mortal – to use their fellow beings, except observationally, as "models". Instead, researchers turn to shorter-lived, inexpensive and manipulable "models" for their endeavours. This is necessary both because human beings are long-lived, and because we are not inclined to take part in tests that may cause us inconvenience, pain or even death.

Apart from human cells and tissues, the key "models" used are fruit flies (Drosophila melanogaster), roundworms (Caenorhabditis elegans, C. elegans), laboratory mice (Mus musculus) and the unicellular baker's yeast (Saccharomyces cerevisiae). According to the GenAge database of ageing-related genes, there are over 700 genes connected to ageing amongst the key model organisms, 555 of which are in the worm, 87 in yeast, 75 in the fruit fly and 68 in the mouse. These four models are chosen for their short lives, their high fertility and relatively low expense.

Other models that are used, although less extensively, include non-human primates, rats, dogs, and reptiles. Some longer-lived birds are also potentially useful models for understanding human ageing, due to their slow ageing rates when compared to size-equivalent mammals (Holmes and Austad,1995; Holmes et al., 2001), as well as some type of fish.

In the past thirty years or so, many labs, such as those of Cynthia Kenyon and David Sinclair (see Key Opinion Leaders. Page 169), have done extensive work using these models. Kenyon points out that some animals seem to have protective mechanisms that keep them alive much longer than their mammalian counterparts. For instance, why do some small bats live up to 40 years, despite being metabolically and size-wise similar to mice, which normally die after 2? Why do small dogs live longer than big ones?

Kenyon and Sinclair have altered the genes and other characteristics of their favourite models of ageing to see what factors lead to extended longevity. From these experiments, they also try to determine if an extended life can be one in which healthspans could also be extended.

As an example, the lifespan of the round worm can now be manipulated to be up to ten times longer than its wild type or normal state, (Ayyadevara et al., 2006). Removing parts of its reproductive equipment, altering some genes, and keeping the worms on a calorie restricted diet and at cold temperatures (worm "torture") has this effect.

C. elegans (Caenorhabditis elegans)

These worms have been studied since the 1960s, when Sydney Brenner, the "Father" of worm research, realised that three features of these creatures made them ideal models, namely that they have a uniformly fixed number of 959 cells (always in the same position), they can exist in high concentrations, (10,000 in one petri dish), and they have high fertility (each worm can produce 300-500 progeny as self-fertilizing hermaphrodites). Furthermore, these worms are highly manipulable by using gene editing techniques.

The C. elegans' genome was first fully sequenced in 1998, and consists of about 100 million base pairs, about 3% of the number that humans possess, but a comparable number of genes to humans. The C. elegans' genome's similarity to our own is about 40%. Worms can also be frozen and then thawed, which means that they can be transported easily between labs and all around the world.

There are problems with all of these established models, however. An obvious one is that as they are selected for high fertility and relatively short lifespans, i.e. they are subject to different evolutionary forces than the ones that we humans experience.

Wild-type mouse strains, when not subject to predation, live much longer than laboratory strains, and reproduce much later, which seems to support the thesis that lab models are imperfect replicas of human biology.

In addition, animal models tend to be homogenous and rigorously standardised, which gives consistent results in tests, but doesn't reflect the diversity of humans (Partridge and Gems, 2007).

INSILICO MEDICINE, INC.

Insilico Medicine is a machine learning company headquartered at the Emerging Technology Center at the Johns Hopkins University campus in Baltimore. The company is one of the pioneers and leaders in applying artificial intelligence (AI) to drug discovery, biomarker development and ageing research. It has contracts with four of the top ten pharmaceutical giants and some of the largest cosmetics and regenerative medicine companies, as well as research collaborations with over 100 academic and non-profit collaborators. Since 2014, the company has assembled one of the world's largest curated repositories of human gene expression profiles, from healthy tissues of various ages as well as from tissues affected by disease. It also holds a repository of small molecules linked to multiple "omics" data types and it also works with population-level data gathered from multiple countries in Europe, North America and Asia. It maintains a close relationship with NVIDIA, one of the main providers of hardware solutions for AI, and owns several deep learning clusters, now exceeding 240 teraflops in computing power. As an aside, it seems important to us that patient data from around the world, suitably anonymised, should be shared as widely as possible in order to advance medical science.

Another important area of Insilico's R&D is in biomarker development using deep neural networks. There are two ways to evaluate the efficacy of anti-ageing interventions: running lengthy clinical trials or alternatively, and much more efficiently, analysing a large number of biologically-relevant ageing biomarkers. Scientists at Insilico realised that it is possible to use a human's age as a unifying parameter for integrating multiple data types, using AI. Since every living creature has a date of birth, it is now possible to develop the really large data sets required to train the deep neural networks to predict the age of the patient in a healthy state using blood tests, tissue samples, clinical records, medical imaging and even pictures. These predictors are used to understand the relative contribution of

each data type and individual parameters to the accuracy of the system. This technique allows the company to understand what parameters are most important in ageing as well as their biological relevance. Dr Alex Zhavoronkov, Insilico's CEO started his career in computational sciences before switching to longevity biotechnology in 2004.

In 2016, the company published 23 papers in *Nature Communications, Molecular Pharmaceutics, Aging* and many other peer-reviewed journals along with collaborators from Johns Hopkins, the University of Oxford, Novartis and other prestigious organisations. In addition to publishing in peer-reviewed journals, the company has presented at multiple industry conferences and organises two annual scientific forums on ageing research and AI in Basel, Switzerland.

This overview of Insilico Medicine was kindly provided by Alex Zhavoronkov.

INSILICO MEDICINE

INSILICO MEDICINE
22 PEER-REVIEWED RESEARCH PAPERS IN 2016

First application of Adversarial Autoencoder (AAE) generating new molecular structures with desired properties

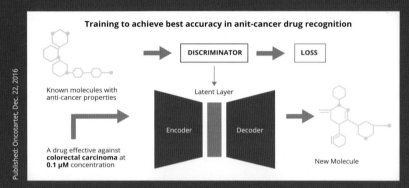

Generative Adversarial Networks (GANs) "imagine" new cancer drugs on demand

First transcriptomic and structural DNN ensemble predictors of therapeutic class, side effects and Phase I/II clinical trials outcomes

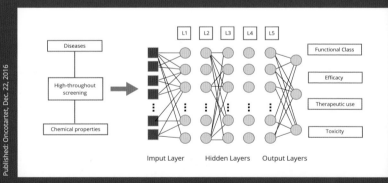

Pharma.AI
A Set of Predictors of Toxicity and Efficacy

Published: Oncotartet, Dec. 22, 2016

Published: Oncotartet, Dec. 22, 2016

First deep learned biomarkers of aging using DNN ensembles; multimodal one-shot learning disease markers; navigator of differentiation state; First nutraceuticals to be launched in 2017

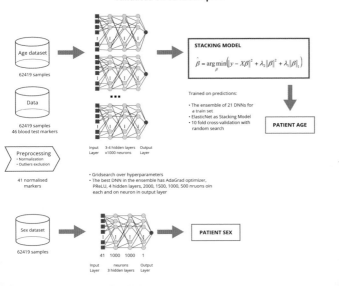

The ensemble of 21 different DNNs trained on 56177 samples and validated on 6242 samples

Age dataset

62419 samples

Data

62419 samples
46 blood test markers

Preprocessing
· Normalization
· Outliers exclusion

41 normalised markers

Input Layer   3-4 hidden layers ×1000 neurons   Output Layer

STACKING MODEL

$$\hat{\beta} = \arg\min_{\beta}\left(\|y - X\beta\|^2 + \lambda_2 \|\beta\|^2 + \lambda_1 \|\beta\|_1 \right)$$

Trained on predictions:

· The ensemble of 21 DNNs for a train set
· ElasticNet as Stacking Model
· 10 fold cross-validation with random search

PATIENT AGE

· Gridsearch over hyperparameters
· The best DNN in the ensemble has AdaGrad optimizer, PReLU, 4 hidden layers, 2000, 1500, 1000, 500 nruons oin each and on neuron in output layer

Sex dataset

62419 samples

41   1000   1000   1

Input Layer   neurons 3 hidden layers   Output Layer

PATIENT SEX

Embryonic.AI
Aging.AI

Generative Adversarial Networks (GANs) "imagine" new cancer drugs on demand

Insilico Medicine's pioneering work in deep learning, adapted from the NVIDIA Keynote Presentation 2016.

INSILICO MEDICINE

DOGS AND AGEING — BARKING UP THE RIGHT TREE

Those of us who love dogs – and the authors both do – hate the fact that they live so short a life compared to our own. This is particularly the case with big dogs, which suffer from a form of progeria, or accelerated ageing, and typically live less than 10 years.

Expenditure on pets is rising in every major nation, and the treatment and upkeep of dogs and cats is big business, estimated to be worth around $70 billion in the US in 2017. There are about 89 million dogs and 94 million cats in the US, and most are loved as family members.

If products designed to extend life could be trialled on dogs and cats, it would accelerate interest in similar products for humans. It would also potentially validate some of the developing science and represent a large commercial opportunity. Also, the "bar" to designing trials is less in dogs and cats, making it easier to try experimental medicines than in humans.

In this respect, a non-profit called the Dog Aging Project (DAP) in the US is conducting trials on middle-aged dogs to see if their lives can be extended, and these trials are the first ever to examine ageing in dogs. What makes these trials exciting is that they are short longitudinal studies, given the curtailed lives of dogs, whereas similar trials in humans would take decades to perform.

Mice have had their lives extended by rapamycin, acting on the mTOR pathway, and DAP is currently conducting an intervention trial using a variety of low doses on middle-aged dogs. Age-related disease markers, including cognition, cardiac function, immune system functioning and cancer incidence, are "end points" of the trial, which is now in phase 2. The objective is to find a way to extend the healthy lifespan of large dogs by between 2 and 5 years. The trial is expected to include over 10,000 dogs and appears to be close to being fully funded.

Elsewhere, at Cornell University, a sort of 23andMe service for dogs, named Embark, analyses dog genomes for a fee. Adam Boyko, the man behind the project, provides data to the owners such as ancestry, character traits and disease susceptibility, and in return gets useful information from thousands of dog profiles. Another company, called Dognition (yes, the names are all cute!) studies cognition in dogs and provides reports to dog owners.

In a couple of years, Jim's two dogs, Horatio and Isis, might well be taking a version of rapamycin – and enjoying a much longer life as a result!

DOGS AND AGEING - BARKING UP THE RIGHT TREE

Certainly, some pathways of ageing are well conserved between all organisms, from yeast to humans, but not all ageing is equivalent across different species. Telomere research (see Telomeres. Page 200) is a good example of this. **Telomerase** insufficiency in mice doesn't impact their rate of ageing, but it does so in humans. Telomere dysfunction in humans can lead to a disease called dyskeratosis congenita (Marrone and Mason, 2003), but this is shared with mice only when telomerase deficient mice reach the sixth generation, making it very hard to use mouse models to determine the impact of telomeres and telomerase on humans.

The standard models of ageing are undoubtedly useful, but researchers are now exploring other avenues, including the use of big data and in silico research. Additionally, new models are being looked at, including the use of longer-lived mammals such as the naked mole rat, the white-faced capuchin monkey and the bowhead whale, all of which are exceptionally long-lived relative to their sizes. The naked mole rat, as an example, has genes which seem to process oxygen more effectively than in other rodent species, which may contribute to its potential 20 to 30-year lifespan. Additionally, this type of rodent is very resistant to cancer.

The bowhead whale appears to be the longest-lived mammal, considerably longer-lived than humans (one is known to have lived to 211 years old). But bowhead whales are quite hard to study given their size and movement

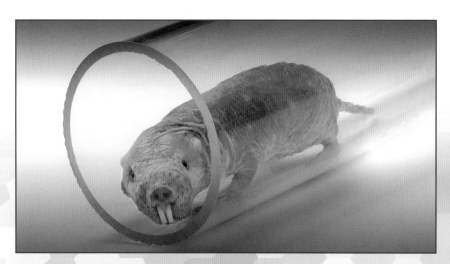

Naked Mole Rat - Beauty is in the eye of the beholder!

across the ocean. Whales have anti-cancer mechanisms which may provide clues as to how we too might develop therapies that protect us from cancer.

It is increasingly asked why we don't study these longer-lived species rather than the short-lived models currently used. Creatures with low or negligible senescence may in fact be better to study than those with shorter lifespans (Strehler, 1986). Studying creatures that have resistance to ageing is undoubtedly a path worth following – but, of course, these long-lived creatures are both more expensive to observe and take a long time to reach old age.

Whatever their limitations, animal and other organism models have thrown up exceptionally useful results in the past half-century, and a great deal of progress has been made in longevity analysis as a result. For instance, our understanding of how CR impacts longevity is largely the result of genetic manipulation of yeast and of worms.

Each of the four standard models has independent and aggregated merits in ageing studies, and will not be discarded any time soon.

C. elegans, the nematode worm, has an average lifespan of just 2 to 3 weeks, and has two sexes, male and self-reproducing hermaphrodite. Manipulation of a variety of genes including DAF2 (dauer larvae formation

2), a gene similar to the human IGF-1, and insulin receptors have more than doubled worm lifespans (Kenyon et al., 1993). This lifespan increase only happens in the presence of a working version of DAF-16, which encodes a FOXO homolog, important in the ageing process of most organisms, including humans.

Similarly, many common pathways and genes between worms and humans that are implicated in ageing have been explored. This includes mTOR (see mTOR. Page 184), which is downregulated to the benefit of lifespan when food is short, possibly by upregulating autophagy (see Autophagy. Page 132); additionally, AMPK, Sir1 and Sir2, and Heat Shock Protein 1 have been shown independently to reduce levels of ROS in worms, thereby increasing lifespan. This is roughly analogous to what happens in humans.

The lifespan of C. elegans can also be affected by the manipulation of the reproductive system. Removal of a worm's germ cells extends life by 60% (Hsin and Kenyon, 1999). The removal of germ lines stimulates DAF-16 in nuclei, and has a positive effect on intestinal cells in the worms, and this seems to be the cause of its expanded lifespan.

Fruit flies have a lifespan of about a month and it is known that downregulation of the IIS (Insulin and

Insulin-like growth factor system) extends lifespan in these flies. The IIS is conserved in humans as well. Mutations of the female flies' insulin-like receptors cause life extension of about 80%. These flies are known as "chico" because they emerge as dwarves.

In both flies and worms, the regulation of the insulin pathway is critical to longevity – and it is thought to be so in humans as well. Autophagy can be directly induced in flies by increasing expression of the gene ATG1, and experiments have shown that the anti-ageing effects of AMPK disappear when ATG1 is blocked.

Among mammals, mice are the unfortunate species that have been chosen to carry the burden of research. Mice have more or less the same number of genetic base pairs as humans (3.1 billion). The protein-coding regions of mice and humans are about 98.88885% equivalent. In addition, mice and humans have almost identical sets of genes. And whereas 4,000 genes that have been studied are common to both species, fewer than 10 are lacking in one or the other between humans and mice.

Novel insights have been gained by experimenting on mice engineered to exhibit premature ageing, CR, cancers, muscle wasting, neurodegeneration, and any number of human disease characteristics. Mice are relatively cheap to keep, adjusting for mice that die from cancers or something else prematurely (and that means before two years of age) or those that display signs of unintended cancer beyond 2 years old. It costs about US $1,000 to raise a usefully functioning mouse.

Mice can be bred to be "reporters", i.e. they have gene-specific promoters controlling the expression of some measurable or identifiable stimulus which is only produced in cells or tissues where the gene in question is actively transcribed. A common reporter is what is known as green fluorescent protein (GFP); by attaching a gene-specific promoter to a GFP transgene, only the tissues where the gene in question is being expressed will fluoresce as green.

Such reporters are increasingly important to ageing research because they allow researchers to identify the tissues in which ageing-related genes are most active and where they are not.

Lastly, there is the Hydra, or jellyfish model of ageing. This is a unique model as it is regenerative to the point of immortality. The Hydra is an organism which reproduces asexually. The three stem cell lineages that allow for continuous self-renewal of the organism express high levels of FOXO genes, genes which clearly play a key role in the Hydra's apparent biological immortality. FOXO plays a key part in human longevity also, and is now the focus of extensive research.

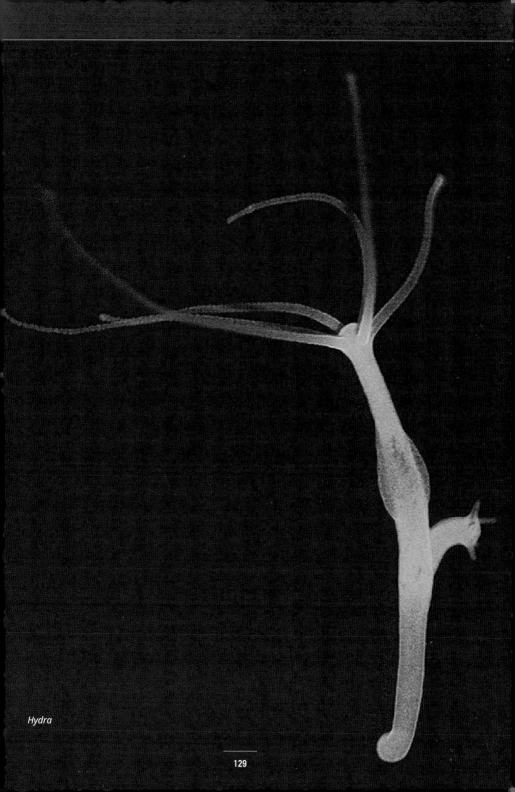

Hydra

FERTILITY — ANOTHER SHOT ON GOAL!

It is estimated by the World Health Organisation that 48 million couples worldwide are unable to conceive, even after five years of trying. This is normally due to the age of the prospective parents, and even the relatively new technique of in vitro fertilization (IVF) has a poor chance of success with older women.

The IVF industry is big business. In 2015, 1.6 million IVF procedures were undertaken in the US, at an average cost of US $13,000 each. And the chances are not good, approximately one in eight implantations succeed. There is also the discomfort and side effects of using hormones to stimulate the ovaries to yield eggs.

Efforts are now underway to improve the outcomes of IVF. David Sinclair of Harvard (see Key Opinion Leaders. Page 149) foresees a role for NAD+ precursors in fertility. Together with his colleagues in Jumpstart Fertility (private), Lindsey Wu and Hayden Homer, he is working on activating SIR2 by increasing NAD+ availability to improve oocyte (egg) harvesting outcomes in IVF. Women will be treated for three months with an NAD+ precursor to improve chances of IVF success, an improvement which is estimated to be about a doubling. JumpStart believes that the market size in the US alone for this product could be US $1.5 billion.

Recently a clinic in Athens, Greece released data suggesting that it has treated 180 women with a method called PRP, platelet-rich plasma. This involves the injection of PRP into the uterus or ovaries, stimulating repair of the female reproductive system. The clinic, Genesis, also claims to have treated 27 menopausal women, of whom 12 have managed to ovulate. The research behind the PRP treatment, which is already used in cosmetic surgery, has yet to be published, making many scientists sceptical. However, if menopause can be reversed, the options become wide open to women who are currently constrained by their fertility window.

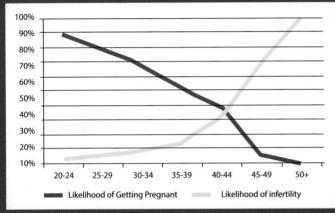

Declining Fertility (source: www.babycentre.co.uk)

A company named Prelude has recently raised US $200 million to create a network of egg-freezing centres for women (the technique is called vitrified oocyte preservation), as more and more women defer reproduction to improve career and family choices.

Northwestern University researchers have now produced a 3D printed ovary structure on a cellular scaffold that when implanted into infertile mice actually ovulates, pointing to the same type of thing for women in the future.

FERTILITY - ANOTHER SHOT ON GOAL!

THE GARBAGE COLLECTORS — AUTOPHAGY

Autophagy is a cellular garbage disposal system which delivers unwanted components from within the cytoplasm (the contents of a cell) to the lysosome, which reduces them to amino acids and other cellular building blocks. This is a different process to the ubiquitin-proteasome system, which degrades ubiquitinated (tagged for disposal) proteins within the cytoplasm itself.

An organelle (a specialised structure within a cell) called an autophagosome is key to the best-studied type of autophagy, termed macroautophagy. In this process the autophagosome engulfs the unwanted part of the cytoplasm, including damaged mitochondria, and delivers the contents to the lysosome for disposal. The other two types of autophagy are called microautophagy and chaperone-mediated autophagy.

Damaged mitochondria are dangerous, and so the autophagy process is vital to keeping them at bay. Unfortunately, as we age, the lysosome becomes less efficient. When this happens, unwanted junk is quite often not fully degraded and stays within the lysosome, which then increasingly becomes unable to accept new material for destruction. Thus, drugs targeting an induction of autophagy back to youthful levels could well prolong lifespans, but only if the lysosome can also be rejuvenated.

It has been observed that transgenic mice with an extra copy of the gene encoding the chaperone-mediated autophagy component LAMP2a have little age-associated deterioration in autophagic activity and as a result keep good liver function as they age (Zhang and Cuervo, 2008).

In mouse models, administration of rapamycin, an mTOR inhibitor, (see mTOR. Page 184) has been shown to increase lifespan and to delay many aspects of mouse ageing (Blagosklonny 2011). Though rapamycin has a clear effect on inducing autophagy in non-mammalian models such as yeast and worms (and without that induction, life

Stress signal

AUTOPHAGY PROCESS

Regulatory
complex

PI3K complex

Conjugation
cascade

Elongation

Image reproduced courtesy of Mind The Graph - www.mindthegraph.com

extension doesn't happen), it is not clear yet that this is the case in mammalian models such as mice. Additionally, rapamycin has potentially dangerous immunosuppressive effects. There is also some recent commentary that rapamycin may work in anti-ageing solely because it reduces the incidence of cancer; it seems to us that whatever mechanism it works through, even if it is acting to reduce cancers and not to delay ageing generally, that's still a good thing, as of course cancer is a disease of ageing.

However, another substance, spermidine, has been shown to be an autophagy inducer that has no obvious side effects, unlike rapamycin, and also promotes longevity in yeast, worms, and when combined with similar polyamine preparations, also in mice (Eisenberg et al.,2009; Matsumoto et al., 2011).

THE GARBAGE COLLECTORS — AUTOPHAGY

Spermidine acts to reduce inflammation, to improve lipid metabolism and to better regulate cell growth and death in mammalian models. Spermidine seems to act as a sort of "cell cleaner" and may be another target compound to assist in longevity. Its action is largely through autophagy. Spermidine also seems to have an effect on hair growth, and also to be neuro- and onco-protective in various model organisms. In the meantime, as proper trials get underway on the effect of induced autophagy using spermidine, there are food supplementations that could well have a positive effect. High concentrations of spermidine exist in wheat germs, in salad and in pears, as well as in particularly smelly, fermented cheeses!

Additionally, it appears that metformin induces autophagy under certain circumstances. This happens through activation of adenosine monophosphate-activated protein kinase, better known as AMPK. (see Targets in Ageing. Page 183).

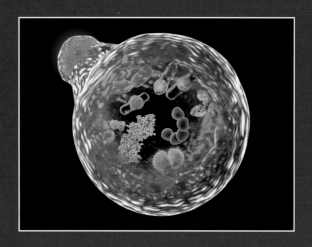

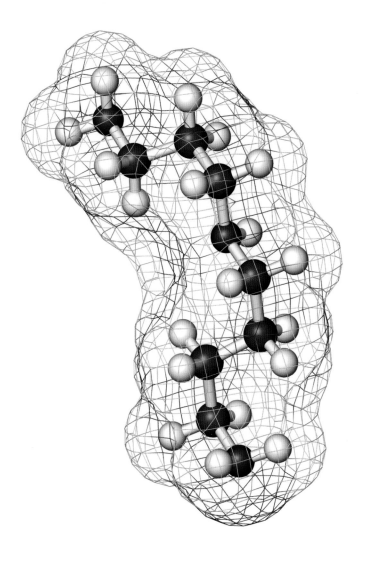

Spermidine molecule

TOOLS OF THE TRADE — TIME TO UP THE GRADE

We have visited quite a few labs in the course of researching this book. The most opulent, as one might expect, was at Harvard, where the endowment cup runneth over. But generally, they all look more or less the same, full of test tubes, microscopes, lab fridges and people in white coats.

Biotech and academic research is way behind the curve in terms of adopting new technology. It takes far too long and absorbs far too much money to get a new drug to market. On average it costs upwards of US $1.5 billion and about ten years, and comes with a 90% failure rate on the way. If cutting-edge technology were more widely adopted in bio research – and it will sure be – then the scale of animal testing could be greatly reduced, drugs could get to market faster, and the nature of human disease and ageing could be better understood.

Only about one-in-twenty robots is sold to the biotech industry (and included in that figure are those sold to research and academic institutions), and visits to labs highlight that very point. Skilled researchers spend too much time manually manipulating samples and not enough time using their intellects to produce new discoveries.

In the same way that a visit to the doctor still sometimes involves stethoscopes and knee hammers, which seems so primitive in an age of genomic medicine, our sense is that most labs are out of date in terms of their machinery and equipment, and possibly even their thinking.

The University of Oxford has a collection of mass spectrometers and microscopes that enable the university's scientists to "see" molecules at an atomic level. Harvard University has a state of the art animal model facility, and UCL has three "models" all under the same roof – the worms, the fruit flies and the yeast.

But none of the labs we visited has yet fully embraced the 21st century.

This is about to happen, and not before time.

Several inventions and developments will soon revolutionise the way that research labs look and operate. These are: genome sequencing, cloud computing, improved microscopy, AI and deep learning, as well as the disruption of the academic publishing industry.

Genome sequencing is becoming cheaper every year (US $499 at genos.com) and the machines that do the sequencing are getting ever smaller. Not only will sequencing become a ubiquitous feature of doctors' clinics in about ten years, but it will also be found in research labs, and as a matter of routine. At the moment, it is not, and most sequencing takes place off premises, adding time and cost to the process.

As an example, Illumina, the dominant player in sequencing, has teamed up with IBM's Watson Health supercomputer to work on cancer diagnostics panels, known as Trusight Tumor 170. The Trusight panel does a deep dive into about 170 of the most important oncology genes, with a view to identifying mutations and finding therapies. Not everyone is a fan of Watson, some believing it to be over-hyped, but the concept of a computer driving patient diagnosis is a valid one. And indeed, it is probably at least ten years away before any of us visit the doctor-plus-computer combo.

Cloud computing is enabling collaboration and exchange of large data sets to occur much more rapidly and efficiently than before, as well as speeding up the complex computations involved in modelling genes, molecules and potential new drugs.

This is despite the fact that Silicon Valley types seem to believe that to "solve" the problem of ageing, only a few thousand lines of code are needed (see Futurists. Page 259).

"In silico screening" (see Insilco Medicine. Page 120), the mechanism whereby drugs are discovered and improved using silicon based arrays which are subjected to an AI-like deep learning process, is becoming increasingly important – and big pharma is taking note.

Deep learning will become a standard in drug discovery, and quite a number of deals are being done to take advantage of its potential. Generative adversarial networks (GANs) are being used, where two neuronal networks act almost as debaters would in a contest.

As an example of a deep learning system being applied to biotech, a search engine named Bioz has "learned" to trawl hundreds of millions of pages of life science research papers to provide recommendations and reviews on lab equipment, assays, and individual researchers.

Also, Exscientia, a Scottish company, recently inked a deal with Sanofi to collaborate on finding small-molecule drugs for metabolic disease. The deal, worth up to €250 million, involves Exscientia's AI platform. BioAge is also using machine learning to search for biomarkers that predict mortality and then expects to computationally design drugs to affect those markers.

Sophia Genetics, a Swiss company, has an AI-driven database to predict and diagnose diseases such as cancer, and Freenome (see Portfolios. Page 302) is using similar techniques to generate biomarkers.

Being able to see and manipulate compounds at the molecular and atomic level is also a recent and encouraging development. We have seen this in operation at the University of Oxford, where the diffraction barrier of optical microscopy has now been overcome and cryo-electron microscopy is able to render colour images at the atomic level; images never seen before. By firing electrons in a vacuum and by focusing them using magnets, scientists are now able to do so much more accurately, than just a decade ago. These transmission electron microscopes which use cryo (freezing) techniques can magnify up to 10 million times, with viruses, cells and even molecules visible, as well as atoms.

One of the regular complaints we have heard in our research is about the stranglehold over researchers that large publishing houses have – and about the fossilised nature of academic publishing in general.

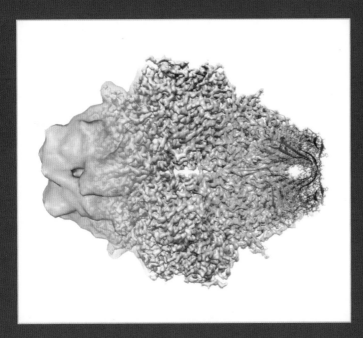

This image, showing a single molecule of the protein beta-galactosidase, is a montage. It was created to demonstrate how dramatically cryo-EM has improved in recent years. In the past, cryo-EM was only able to obtain a blobby approximation of a molecule's shape, like that shown on the far left. Now, the technique yields exquisitely detailed images in which individual atoms are nearly visible (far right). Colour is artificially applied. Credit: Veronica Falconieri, Subramaniam Lab, National Cancer Institute.

TOOLS OF THE TRADE - TIME TO UP THE GRADE

This lucrative industry is dominated by four large companies: Elsevier, Wiley, Taylor & Francis, and Springer. The combined revenue for the academic publications of these companies was about US $25 billion in 2015, with very high profit margins. Publishers don't generally pay for the research that they publish; they rope in low-paid academics to review the material, own the copyrights and charge exceptionally high prices for subscriptions. As the buyers of those subscriptions are usually university libraries, the consumer and the producer of the material are generally the same. Reminds us a little of Facebook!

And this massively profitable business carries on despite the fact that so much of the academic work done which then gets published in these expensive journals is government or charity funded – and really should have open and free access.

Disruptors are emerging (Academia Inc, ResearchGate and PubMed) but the incumbents are fighting a stalwart rearguard battle, pressurising professors to abide by tight copyright restrictions that they contracted years ago. There are some moves by a couple of publishers to introduce "fair sharing" but they strike us as too little, too late.

It will probably take government intervention to prevent the oligopoly power of the publishers from "tolling" research ad infinitum. We hope it happens soon.

THE BUCK INSTITUTE FOR RESEARCH ON AGING

The Buck Institute for Research on Aging is the world's first and leading independent research institution focused on using ground-breaking scientific insights into age-related pathways to identify new ways to prevent and cure age-related chronic diseases. Simply put, the Buck is working to increase healthspan, or the healthy years of life. The Institute's unique culture fosters interdisciplinary collaboration among diverse fields including oncology, immunology, neuroscience, metabolism, and regenerative medicine. Its mission is to cure diseases by altering the ageing process. The scientists at the Buck firmly believe that their work will one day transform the practice of medicine.

Located 30 miles north of San Francisco, the non-profit Buck Institute occupies a 365,000 square-foot campus designed by world-renowned architect I.M. Pei. The Buck draws the best and the brightest from laboratories around the globe: its 200+ employees come from more than 30 countries. Their scientific programmes tackle ageing with a wide variety of complementary approaches such as: (1) The genetics and biochemistry of ageing, including oxidative stress, mitochondrial function, protein homeostasis, cellular senescence, and genetic determination of lifespan; (2) Age-related conditions including Alzheimer's disease, Parkinson's disease, cancer, stroke, diabetes, frailty, cardiovascular disease, osteoporosis, and macular degeneration; (3) Regenerative medicine (stem cell research) and ageing; and (4) New technology to support age-related research including genomics, proteomics, and metabolomics.

Buck scientists publish widely in *Nature, Science, Cell* and other top peer-reviewed journals. Because of this stellar record of accomplishment, the Buck Institute enjoys a prominent position among the top biomedical institutions in the San Francisco Bay Area, and has long-standing collaborations with the University of California-San Francisco (UCSF), the University of California-Berkeley, the Gladstone Institute and Stanford University. The Buck also has a wide variety of industry partnerships in both basic and translational science in the Bay Area, the birthplace

Jim, Gordon Lithgow, Aubrey de Grey and Eric Vardin at the Buck Institute, 2017.

of biotech, and around the world. The Buck Institute is also an incubator for companies developing treatments for age-related diseases. Most recently, Unity Biotechnology, co-founded by a Buck faculty member, closed a significant US $151 million Series B financing round.

The Buck Institute is internationally recognised for its role in pioneering and shaping the field of ageing research. While its leadership is proud of the Institute's achievements, it believes that the best is yet to come. With the last decade's advances in technology and biological insights, there has never been a better time for biomedical inquiry into the ageing process. As the Buck Institute approaches its 20th anniversary, it is more optimistic than ever that its scientists will succeed in increasing healthspan by preventing, delaying and curing the chronic diseases of ageing.

Professor Judith Campisi heads up the Campisi Laboratory at the Buck. She has made significant contributions to the understanding of why ageing is the largest single risk factor for developing cancer and is widely recognised for her work on senescent cells.

This section has kindly been provided by The Buck Institute.

THE BUCK INSTITUTE FOR RESEARCH ON AGING

BIOMARKERS OF AGEING

Biomarkers of ageing are quantitative variables indicative of biological age. They are biological parameters that should vary in accordance with the chronological age of the patient, and that also serve as reasonably accurate measures of morbidity and risk of mortality. Biomarkers of ageing are necessary for the eventual clinical evaluation and approval of any healthspan-extending therapy, as the only alternative is enormously expensive longitudinal studies that measure actual patient lifespan extension. As such, the search for accurate biomarkers of ageing is a vastly popular pursuit within ageing research.

Clinically significant blood-based biomarkers of ageing include inflammation agents (Il-6, TNF-a, CRP, network analysis of inflammatory markers), glucose metabolism biomarkers (HbA1c, plasma glucose), adipokines, thyroid hormones, NT-proBNP, troponin, unconjugated bilirubin (Wagner, et al., 2016), albumin or albumin/creatinine ratio (Mitnitski et al, 2015; Putin et al., 2016), etc. Recently, a number of large studies identified sets of blood-borne biomarkers of ageing which retrospectively predict morbidity and mortality in large cohort studies and clinical trials (Horvath, 2013; Belsky et al., 2015; Mitnitski et al., 2015; Moreno-Villanueva et al., 2015; Putin et al., 2016; Sebastiani et al., 2017). These kinds of studies provide valuable tools for predicting clinically significant ageing-related outcomes, like mortality, cognitive decline or frailty.

Frailty indices have gained in popularity greatly over the past 15 years as useful and accurate proxy measures of chronological age. A frailty index is intended to serve as a quantification of the health status of an older individual. It is defined as the ratio of deficits present in a patient to the total number of potential deficits measured (Rockwood et al., 2005). The deficits typically considered include disease signs and symptoms, laboratory abnormalities, cognitive impairments, and disabilities in daily living activities. Frailty indices are often used in epidemiological and clinical studies to characterise ageing and to predict mortality and morbidity. The frailty value assigned to a patient is a continuous variable, and as such assigns a score based on health status rather than classifying patients as simply frail or non-frail.

While frailty increases with age, it is more commonly related to biological age than chronological age (Romero-Ortuno and Kenny 2012). The most widely-used FI was created by Rockwood et al., and consists of a 7-point frailty scale (Rockwood et al., 2005). Rockwood et al., initially applied their FI to 305 elderly patients who participated in the second stage of the Canadian Study of Health and Aging (CSHA), where they followed the cohort and after 5 years used it to predict death or the need for institutional care, and correlated the results with those obtained from other established tools to measure its effectiveness at serving as a measure of mortality and the need for institutional care. Upon performing statistical analyses of the ability of the Rockwood FI to serve as an indicator or biological age and a predictor of the likelihood of mortality, many groups have found it to characterise biological age and the likelihood or mortality independently and more effectively than chronological age ((Mitnitski et al., 2001; Kulminski et al., 2007; Romero-Ortuno and Kenny 2012; Ommundsen et al., 2014). In this sense, the use of the Rockwood FI as a diagnostic and prognostic tool for characterising ageing would appear to

BIOMARKERS OF AGEING

be more effective and more meaningful than the use of chronological age. This is both in terms of disease diagnosis and prognosis and as a measure of the effectiveness of interventions designed to attenuate the biological ageing process (wherein a decrease in a subject's FI score would serve as a quantitative measure of the therapeutic efficacy of the intervention) during clinical trials. A number of similar frailty indices currently in use (Rockwood et al., 2005) correlate with many clinically significant endpoints better than calendar age, including mortality (Ravindrarajah et al., 2013), postoperative outcomes (Lin et al., 2016), sexual health (Lee et al., 2013), and cancer survival (Ommundsen et al., 2014). It even appears that frailty indices serve as better indicators of biological age than methylomic clocks, which possess the greatest predictive accuracy in measuring chronological age of all biomarkers of ageing based upon biological parameters (Kim et al., 2017).

While many singular biomarkers of ageing have been proposed, and have been shown as effective indicators of biological age and of the functional status of multiple organ systems, in general gerontologists are now moving toward a systemic analysis approach that integrates multiple biomarkers to create biomarker signatures, and have found that such signatures are more effective predictors of mortality and morbidity, and serve as more robust quantitative measures of biological age.

For example, Sebastiani et al., measured 19 blood-based biomarkers including constituents of standard hematological measures, lipid biomarkers, and markers of inflammation and frailty in 4,704 participants of the Long-Life Family Study (LLFS), (aged 30 and 110 years) and used an agglomerative algorithm to group them into clusters yielding 26 different biomarker signatures. They then correlated them with longitudinal changes in physiological functions and incident risk of cancer, cardiovascular disease, type 2 diabetes, and mortality using longitudinal data collected in the LLFS to test whether such biomarker signatures could effectively serve as an indicator of biological age. Ultimately, they found significant associations of these biomarker signatures with physical function, morbidity, and mortality (Sebastiani et al., 2017).

Mitnitski et al., measured 40 biomarkers of cellular ageing, inflammation, haematology and immunosenescence using baseline data and 7-year mortality data from the Newcastle 85+ Study (n = 845; mean age 85.5). Then characterised the discriminatory ability of this biomarker-based frailty index (FI-B) to predict mortality compared to individual biomarkers, and then combined this biomarker-based frailty index with a clinical deficits frailty index (FI-C) to see whether the combined FI-B and FI-C index possessed greater ability to predict mortality than the FI-B alone. The biomarkers which were significant predictors of mortality included blood-based inflammation biomarkers such as high sensitivity C-reactive protein, leptin, adiponectin, homocysteine, albumin, haematological biomarkers (haemoglobin, platelets, white blood cells, neutrophils, lymphocytes), biomarkers of immunosenescence (CD4 T-cells (% T-cells), CD8 T-cells (% T-cells), CD8 TEMRA T-cells (% CD8 T-cells), CD4/CD8 T-cell ratio, Memory/naïve CD4 T-cell ratio, Memory/naïve CD8 T-cell ratio, Memory/naïve B-cell ratio), as well as TGF beta and IGFBP1. The group found that the FI-B has significantly greater discriminatory accuracy to predict mortality than any one biomarker or biomarker subgroup alone, and that the combined FI-B and FI-C index possessed the greatest overall ability to predict mortality (Mitnitski et al., 2015).

However, a good ageing clock, especially as it pertains to quantifying the effect of interventions upon the rate of biological ageing, should be judged not only by how accurately it correlates with chronological age and predicts morbidity and mortality, but also by how actionable (i.e. practically measurable) it is. As such, there is great need for the development of biomarkers of ageing that are both accurate and actionable.

This section has kindly been provided by Franco Cortese, Deputy Director of the Biogerontology Reseach Foundation.

KEY OPINION LEADERS

PROFESSOR DAVID SINCLAIR & LIFE BIOSCIENCES

Professor David Sinclair and his colleagues, Dr Lindsay Wu and Tristan Edwards, of the newly formed Life Biosciences, have been hugely influential in guiding the shape and content of this book.

David is a Professor at Harvard Medical School in the Department of Genetics, and is a thought leader, entrepreneur and highly acclaimed scientist. We have visited David's labs at Harvard, met with his large collection of mice, and spoken with him on many occasions. David has 45 patents or pending patents to

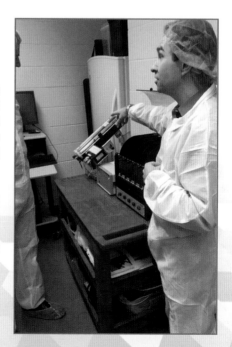

his name, at least 150 scientific publications, and 35 honours and awards. He has been cited in many recognised publications, including *Time* magazine, and recently won a NASA prize for his work in obviating cosmic radiation for astronauts travelling long distances in space.

David is a leading entrepreneur in the longevity field having founded twelve biotech companies, four of which have been taken public, and one of which, Sirtris Pharmaceuticals, was sold to GlaxoSmithKline for US $720 million in 2008 – a deal which to this day remains somewhat controversial.

David and Lindsay, his scientific collaborator at Life Biosciences, are highly approachable, patient in explaining complex science and all round good guys. Their colleague Tristan Edwards runs the financial side of the enterprise, which is expected to be very well capitalised and is creating a number of companies in the longevity business.

Life Biosciences is a longevity research platform dedicated to developing and commercialising new therapies for both rare and common age-related diseases. These therapies also have the potential to delay ageing and to extend human lifespan. Life Biosciences' philosophy is to bring the world's most promising research

in longevity under one umbrella, allowing scientists to collaborate and work together, rather than working in isolation and funded on an ad hoc basis by different sources.

Life Biosciences has attracted some of the best people in the longevity space including Dr Nir Barzilai, as well as seasoned drug development expert Dr John Amatruda (Yale Professor and former Vice President at Merck & Co, whose team developed the diabetes drug Januvia, which currently generates US $6 billion a year in revenue).

The founders of Life Biosciences believe that knowledge and technology have reached a tipping point that is enabling major breakthroughs that will extend human lifespan. These therapies would treat ageing itself, rather than the diseases of ageing, and would overshadow and outcompete existing therapies that are designed to treat one disease at a time. Such therapies would would have an impact on human health rivalling antibiotics, and would revolutionise medicine. By forming companies in separate but parallel scientific avenues to extend lifespan, Life Biosciences has more "shots on goal" than any other group to develop such revolutionary treatments.

Because no regulatory agency of any country currently designates ageing as a disease, Life Biosciences takes a commercially rational approach of ensuring that any new therapeutics that it develops must have an obvious disease indication that can be targeted in the immediate term. The team ranks opportunities based on their ability to (i) ensure early clinical success and the highest impact on human longevity, (ii) meet the largest unmet medical needs, and (iii) achieve the most cost-efficient, fastest routes to regulatory approval. Echoing the story of statins, which started as a therapy for rare lipid disorders, clinical trials for anti-ageing related drugs will first be undertaken for specific disease indications, and then go on to be trialled for anti-ageing properties.

Life Biosciences operates as an incubator that builds companies from early-stage research, and generates value by using its cross-company team of seasoned biotech entrepreneurs, drug development veterans, intellectual property specialists, life sciences managers and venture capital specialists. This team works with its daughter companies to translate basic scientific findings out of academic labs into new companies. Life Biosciences has founded cutting-edge, early-stage companies in the first half of 2017 in the areas of metabolic regulation, fertility enhancement (see Fertility. Page 130), rare diseases, and senolytics (see Targets in Ageing. Page 194) to treat cancer and fibrosis.

NIR BARZILAI AND TARGETING AGEING WITH METFORMIN — TAMING THE AGEING BEAST

Dr Nir Barzilai is the founding director of the US Institute for Aging Research and is affiliated with The Paul F. Glenn Center for Biology of Human Aging at the Albert Einstein College of Medicine. He is one of the key leaders in ageing research, and has had a starred career, including being the head of the Medical Corps of the Israeli Army, before moving to the US. He is also co-founder of CohBar, Inc., a biotechnology company developing mitochondria-based therapeutics to treat diseases associated with ageing (see Portfolios. Page 317).

Among his accomplishments, he has studied centenarians from a group of 600 Ashkenazi Jewish families to find common characteristics as to why they lived/live so long. This is a genetically homogeneous group of people, which makes identifying common traits an easier task. Nir found that many of these ultra-long-lived people had very high levels of **HDL** (high-density lipoprotein) cholesterol, the "good cholesterol", which has made HDL an important component in longevity research.

Nir has also discovered that such long-lived people appear to have protective variants of specific genes, including cholesterol metabolism (CETP and APOC3), of metabolism (ADIPOQ and TSHR) and of the growth gene IGF1R. This collection of genetic variants appears to confer protection against cardiovascular disease, type 2 diabetes, dementia and cancers. These centenarians produce unusually high levels of a peptide called humanin, which is encoded in mitochondria.

Dr Barzilai works closely with Steve Austad, another longevity luminary who is based at the University of Alabama, and their latest exciting investigation is into the possible effects of the diabetes drug metformin and its analogs on ageing and age-related diseases. Their trial, TAME (Targeting Ageing with Metformin), is the first of its type. Normally, trials involving longevity are difficult to undertake given that it is costly and takes a long time. Typically, the measurement of the rate of ageing in a population is done via Kaplan-Meier survival curves overlaid with Gompertz analysis. But that would all take too long for viable research, and so TAME has to be novel. TAME is constructed to use the time to appearance of diseases such as cardiovascular, cancer or Alzheimer's over a six-year period. The trial will also seek to confirm whether or not metformin extends life and prevents diabetes, as well as the other key diseases of ageing.

We spoke with Dr Barzilai in the course of our research. A charming man, he is careful to emphasise that the upcoming TAME trial should not be taken as an indication that the drug works beyond diabetes, merely that it has observed benefits which the trial can either validate or not. That having been said, just about every single person we have met in the longevity space – and there have been many – takes metformin prophylactically. Lewis Cantley, director of the Cancer Center at Weill Cornell Medicine, has said that "metformin may already have saved more people from cancer than any other drug in history!"

Metformin is a drug that has been around for 60 years, it is off patent, cheap, generic and widely used to treat type 2 diabetes. The trial that should start in mid-2017, will be a placebo-controlled one involving 3,000 older, non-diabetic people. Its aim is to see whether or not age-related diseases are delayed in the active (i.e. those who take the drug as opposed to placebo) arm of the trial. Nir and his partner Steve Austad have apparently received funding from the American Federation for Aging Research for the trial, which will in reality be the first ever proper trial of a potentially valid anti-ageing compound.

Observationally, metformin appears to protect against heart disease, cancer, and possibly Alzheimer's. Nir has suggested that metformin might add two to three years of healthy living to patients, but this has yet to be verified. It certainly has more than this effect in rodents, possibly by reducing oxidative stress, but rodents are not the same as people. It does appear that in healthy outbred mice, the effects of metformin are either small or non-existent.

However, there is a great deal of observational evidence that metformin protects against some of the diseases of ageing. An earlier examination of the records of 78,000 diabetic patients taking metformin as compared to the records of a similar number of non-diabetic patients not on the drug, matched for characteristics such as smoking and age, showed an

equivalent mortality level across all age spectrums, except in the over 70s. In those people, the metformin treated patients experienced a 15% reduction in all causes of mortality. This is an extraordinary outcome, given that the life expectancy of type 2 diabetics is generally considerably shorter than that of non-diabetics.

Being a pre-diabetic himself, Nir takes metformin and has done for five years. He says that the proven safety of metformin is vital to the TAME trial, as it removes the possibility of serious toxicities emerging, a recurring worry in drug trials.

But, and here we introduce a cautionary note, there have been recent studies out of Taiwan suggesting that metformin taken by diabetics for prolonged periods (12 years plus) might increase the risk of Alzheimer's and/or Parkinson's by as much as a factor of two. In the Taiwanese sample of about 9,300 type 2 diabetic patients, half on metformin and half not, the incidence of Parkinson's disease rose to 6.8% in the metformin-treated patients, compared to 2.8% in the untreated half of the trial; additionally, patients on metformin experienced an all-type dementia incidence of 11.5% versus 6.5% not taking the drug. This is something to watch carefully, and is the first time we have seen negative coverage of metformin. This is apart from the standard recommendation that people who take metformin, particularly women, should also take vitamin B12 supplements.

AUBREY DE GREY – BEGINNING TO MAKE SENS

Aubrey is a terrific guy and a passionate and eloquent advocate for the science of anti-ageing and longevity. He is one of the most recognised people in the field, partly for his vision, and partly for his appearance, which makes him instantly recognisable. The bohemian look that he sports is calculated to reassure people that he's not in the longevity space for personal gain; indeed, he has handed most of his wealth over to his charitable foundation, the SENS (Strategies for Engineered Negligible Senescence) Research Foundation. This idea of "negligible senescence" comes from the book *Longevity, Senescence, and the Genome* by Caleb Finch, in which Finch pointed out that some organisms – notably lobsters and jellyfish – don't seem to visibly age at all.

The SENS Research Foundation is based in Mountain View, California and we visited its facilities and labs on our trip to the US, as well as subsequently enjoying dinner with Aubrey himself. We also met up with him, at a packed conference in Cambridge, UK, where the theme was the *ageing cell*. The conference itself is another sign that longevity science is now coming out of the shadows. He has written multiple papers and books, which have had a wide influence. Partly as a result of his efforts, **biogerontology,** which is the science of ageing and of age-related diseases, is going mainstream. Hence the enthusiasm for us as investors to get involved.

Aubrey leads the group of "life extensionists" and "longevists" who believe that stem cells, tissue rejuvenation, molecular repair, pharmaceuticals, and organ replacement can alter our fundamental biology and in a positive way.

Aubrey is a believer that regenerative medicine is close to addressing the seven forms of cellular and molecular damage that he has identified as accumulating over time, causing decay and eventual death. He is on record as saying that the first person to live to 1,000 years old is alive today, and may even be 50 or 60 years old. His are the most optimistic views of all the researchers we have met, and he has a very concrete vision of how ageing can be tackled.

He believes that a whole-body solution of tissue rejuvenation and repair should be the focus of longevity research and practice. This he calls "SENS" (see SENS Foundation. Page 158), which stands for "strategies for engineered negligible senescence", and is a strategy of repairing damage and degradation as it happens, thereby pre-empting the associated diseases of ageing.

He thinks people deliberately "block out" any serious discussion on ageing, as a self-protective mechanism to put its horrors out of their minds. He thinks this is because most of us associate ageing with "illderliness", a vision of dribbling away in a catatonic state in some vile nursing home. What people don't yet get, in his view, is that poor health in old age is not necessary, and

that "wellderliness" over prolonged lifespans (or "healthspans") is close to being achieved.

He compares people's blinkered views on ageing to the trap of Tithonus, and this trap means that people are inured into thinking that bodies are just disposable "soma", or vessels designed to carry our genes into the next generation, with a "hard" limit to life, very rarely exceeded, of 115. Ageing is thought to be miserable and unavoidable. Tithonus was a Trojan warrior who was granted immortality by Zeus, but his immortal nature was always at the extreme end of painful old age, and he ended up as a grasshopper.

The seven types of molecular and cellular accumulating damage, according to Aubrey, are as follows:

1. MUTATIONS AND EPIMUTATIONS IN CHROMOSOMES, I.E. CHANGES TO NUCLEAR DNA

This leads to cancers which are responsible for about a quarter of all human deaths. Unlike most scientists, Aubrey does not believe that mutations to nuclear DNA are responsible for other aspects of ageing. Nuclear DNA is the blueprint for our physical structures and regulates the production of proteins and processes that make us "us". This nuclear DNA sits, fairly obviously, in the nucleus of our cells. Mutations occur as a result of time and continuous damage to DNA, and these can result in cancers. Most scientists now think that those mutations are causative of ageing as well, but Aubrey disagrees. He points to the fact there is as yet no clear proof that damage to nuclear DNA detectably accumulates during adulthood.

2. MUTATIONS IN MITOCHONDRIA

However, Aubrey does believe that mutations in mitochondria are important to ageing, as they affect energy production. Mitochondria do not possess highly tuned repair mechanisms and so are prone to more rapid damage accumulation. Aubrey suggests repairing mitochondria by allotopic expression, which means copying the mitochondrial DNA into the cell's nucleus, which is much better protected, thereby making mitochondrial mutations harmless.

This is an interesting angle and SENS reports some success in using this strategy and the foundation has shown that ATP6 and ATP8 genes (both important in mitochondrial functioning) can be successfully expressed directly in vivo in the nucleus. In addition, Gensight Biologics, a US-based private company, is currently working on a clinical programme to express the ND4 gene (also important in mitochondrial activity) in the nucleus in order to prevent retinal disease.

3. CELLULAR JUNK

Aubrey calls this material "intracellular aggregates", and it is the rubbish that cells generate but lack the machinery to incinerate. These aggregates are causative of Alzheimer's, macular degeneration, and cardiovascular diseases. Aubrey suggests bolstering the internal garbage disposal system of the cell, the lysosome, by adding new enzymes to better "dispose of" this cellular rubbish.

4. EXTRACELLULAR JUNK

This is another form of "rubbish" which sits outside of cells, and one such type is the amyloid plaques which are the principal characteristic of Alzheimer's. Aubrey advocates using antibodies to remove this material – an approach that already works for plaques and should be equally effective elsewhere in the ageing body.

5. LOST CELLS

Aubrey recommends replacing cells that are depleted (and these are typically non-dividing or slow dividing cells such as brain or cardiac cells). These lost cells are implicated in diseases such as Parkinson's and in the degradation of our immune systems. Exercise and certain growth factors can help this, but Aubrey also believes that stem cells will play an important role in improving the outlook for people suffering from cellular depletion.

6. SENESCENT CELLS

These are cells stuck in the limbo between healthy function and apoptosis (programmed cell death) and can be pro–inflammatory. Senolytics (a word fusion of senescence and lytic – meaning to destroy) – are small-molecule drugs that selectively destroy these limbo state cells. If these cells could be eliminated or reduced in number, the inflammatory diseases which they cause could thereby be reduced. Senescent cells have also been implicated in cancers and in type 2 diabetes.

Senescent cells generate inflammation via secretory signals, and their action is known as senescent-associated secretory phenotype (SASP). Even though there are few senescent cells relative to healthy cells (perhaps 1%), their effect is devastating.

7. EXTRACELLULAR PROTEIN CROSSLINKS

This is the phenomenon, linked to age, where too many connections are formed between the proteins that cells lay down outside of their surface. This causes tissues to lose elasticity, and has been implicated in arteriosclerosis and skin wrinkling. SENS is developing drugs to break accumulating links known as sugar bonds or advanced glycation end-products.

There are plenty of critics of Aubrey's work, with most of them not believing that the mitochondrial and other genetic engineering he proposes is remotely possible, or at least any time in the near future. In fact, a group of worthies penned an open letter a decade ago describing SENS as "pseudo-science". It has to be said though, that some of Aubrey's prophecies are slowly wending their way into the realms of reality. Senolytic drugs, for example, are arousing genuine excitement in the longevity community and large-scale funding is being directed into their development.

The key thing about Aubrey is that he is a challenger to conventional thinking and while his seven "commandments" may not all be borne out, he is defying the inertia that has kept longevity science subdued for far too long. We like him and his work, which is done on a shoestring budget, and we have made a donation to his foundation. Let's face it, all innovative ideas appear to be wacky at some point otherwise we would all be adopting them sooner than we eventually do.

SENS RESEARCH FOUNDATION

SENS is a public charity that is transforming the way the world researches and treats age-related disease. The research that SENS funds at universities around the world and at its own research centre in Mountain View, CA, uses regenerative medicine to repair the damage underlying the diseases of ageing. SENS' goal is to help build the industry that will cure these diseases. SENS believes that a world free of age-related disease is possible.

SENS research emphasises the application of regenerative medicine to age-related disease, with the intent of repairing underlying damage to the body's tissues, cells, and molecules.

SENS is, at its core, a research-focused outreach organisation. Its outreach efforts include the SENS conferences at Cambridge, the annual Rejuvenation Biotechnology Conference, summits, speaking engagements, and general advocacy. SENS strives to inform policymakers and the public at large about the promise of the damage-repair approach to treating age-related disease.

Finally, SENS engages in educational work through a vibrant student program, SENS Education. SENS Education operates a summer internship program that places students at the SENS Research Centre and outside institutions; provides students with guidance, mentorship, and materials grants for SENS-related research projects; and is developing online coursework.

Many things go wrong with ageing bodies, but at the root of them all is the burden of decades of unrepaired damage to the cellular and molecular structures that make up the functional units of our tissues. As each essential microscopic structure fails, tissue function becomes progressively compromised – imperceptibly at first, but ending in the slide into the diseases and disabilities of ageing.

SENS' strategy to prevent and reverse age-related ill-health is to apply the principles of regenerative medicine to repair the damage of ageing at the level where it occurs. We are developing a new kind of medicine: regenerative therapies that remove, repair, replace, or render harmless the cellular and molecular damage that has accumulated in our tissues with time. By reconstructing the structured order of the living machinery of our tissues, these rejuvenation biotechnologies will restore the normal functioning of the body's cells and essential biomolecules, returning ageing tissues to health and bringing back the body's youthful vigour.

Decades of research in ageing people and experimental animals has established that there are no more than seven major classes of such cellular and molecular damage: cell loss and atrophy, cancerous cells, mitochondrial mutations, death-resistant cells, extracellular matrix stiffening, extracellular aggregates and intracellular aggregates. We can be confident that this list is complete, first and foremost because of the fact that scientists have not discovered any new kinds of ageing damage in nearly a generation of research, despite the increasing number of centres and scientists dedicated to studying the matter, and the use of increasingly powerful tools to examine the ageing body. In its own way, each of these kinds of damage make our bodies frail, and contribute to the rising frailty and ill-health that appears in our sixth decade of life and accelerates thereafter.

This SENS overview has kindly been provided by Aubrey de Grey, Chief Science Officer and Co-Founder, SENS.

sens research foundation
reimagine aging

LEONARD HAYFLICK AND LAURA DEMING – MIND THE GAP

It's February 2017 and Jim and his three dinner guests are in an old-style restaurant in San Francisco. One of them is Len Hayflick, a prominent expert in the longevity field, and incidentally also the inventor of the main way in which common vaccines are manufactured. Len starts our evening by pointing out that everything ages, not just living organisms. He gestures at the wood panelling in Sam's Grill and says that the wood is ageing, that we are ageing, that worms and mice are ageing and that the solar system

is ageing – in short everything is getting older. Nothing and no one is immune from the chaos of time and the second law of thermodynamics. Everything will eventually crumble to dust. It's pretty bleak stuff and the wine bottle is quickly emptied.

Len is 88 years old, though he looks younger, and one of Jim's other guests was another prominent longevity specialist, Laura Deming. She is just 23 and has been researching the field since she was 12. Really! She started out in the labs of Cynthia Kenyon, then of UCSF and now at Calico, who is a real luminary of the science of ageing.

So, the two experts are at the opposite ends of the age spectrum but despite this they agree in many ways about the fundamental tenets of their field. First, that everything is subject to entropy, or molecular chaos; second, that, while useful, the results of longevity experiments in animal models don't always translate well into humans. This is because studies in animals are artefacts of particular experimental conditions, generally in laboratories, and may well not accurately represent the "wild type" truth. The other point that they agree is that many of the anti-ageing tactics used today are primitive and not properly understood.

With reference to animal models, Len talks about a specific study. One

Later on in the evening, it transpires that Len and Laura definitely don't agree with each other on many profound issues, although as with most notable scientists, they are civil and respectful of each other's opinion. Len, who is famous for two important discoveries (see overleaf. The Hayflick Limit) including the vaccination technique described above is not optimistic that mankind will breach the upper age barrier of lifespan, one that appears to have been in place for several decades. Sure, he says, human life expectancy has risen dramatically since the turn of the 20th century, and many more people are living to over 100. But Len believes that the pathways that lead to senescence (the gradual wearing down of our bodies and of their fundamental mechanisms through cellular breakdown) are too complex for us to understand anytime soon. He does not subscribe, as Laura (and others) do, to the view that we are on the verge of a step-function leap in terms of average life expectancy. Laura is an articulate advocate of life and of healthy life – beyond 150 and upwards – and sometime in the "near future".

of the largest increases in lifespan (44%) in C. elegans was generated in a study which involved feeding worms a synthetic antioxidant called EUK-8 (Melov et al., 2000). Other scientists, however, could not reproduce these results (Keaney and Gems, 2003), even though EUK-8 was shown to increase antioxidant levels (Keaney et al., 2004). This suggests that very specific conditions are necessary for this antioxidant and any other life-extending compound to successfully work, and that results across trials may be aberrant. At least, that's Len's argument.

This basic conflict between Len and Laura – centred on the key question "can we extend life beyond its seemingly proscribed limits and can we extend it within two or three decades as well and to a wide population?" – runs through the whole of longevity science.

THE HAYFLICK LIMIT

The Hayflick Limit is the point at which cells in a normal human cell population stop dividing. This point is reached when the telomeres at the end of chromosomes in cells get to a critical length. Len Hayflick reported in his seminal work in the 1960s that this endpoint of cell division occurs after 50-60 population doublings, but varies between cell types. In addition, it is important to note that cells in old people are distinct from old cells, those nearing their replicative limit. Even in old people, many cells are nowhere near their Hayflick limit.

Hayflick's discovery was very important, overturning a series of received wisdoms that had persisted for decades (pioneered by Alexis Carrel). However, the term "Hayflick Limit" was only coined in 1974, when Macfarlane Burnett used it for the first time. Hayflick's observations suggested that there is a mechanism that is "counting" the number of divisions a cell has made and that when the replicative limit is reached, further division is halted. This replicative senescence is now known to be inducible by any of several factors, and not just the shortening of telomeres.

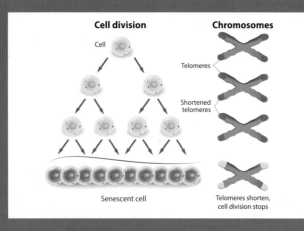

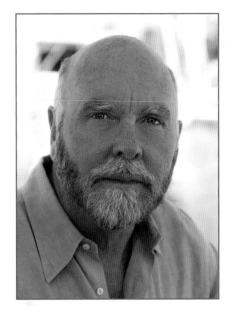

CRAIG VENTER – IN-VENTOR

Craig Venter is one of the handful of well-recognised longevists; an American, born in 1946, he was one of the first scientists to sequence the human genome in the early 2000s. He founded Celera Corporation, the Institute for Genomic Research, and is the co-founder and Chairman of Human Longevity Inc. with Peter Diamandis and Robert Hariri. This company is focused on extending the healthy "high performance" lifespan and the venture has so far raised US $300 million in funding. Venter is the executive chairman, and has stated that the company plans to sequence 40,000 genomes a year in the near future, with a focus on cancer detection.

Venter and Human Longevity Inc. are not currently looking for anti-ageing drugs per se, but are using an array of DNA sequencing machines to look for specific genes associated with individual diseases, such as heart disease and cancer. By using proprietary sequencing techniques, they are seeking to predict an individual's risk from mutated genes in the genome.

Venter, whom Jim met briefly in London at an event at the Science Museum, is a charismatic and energetic individual and brims with evident passion for the cause of longevity. He was the first person to "transfect" a cell with a synthetic genome, by making a very long DNA molecule containing an entire bacterial genome. He and his colleagues then introduced this genome into a new cell, and the resulting cell contained "watermarks" in its DNA to identify it as synthetic and to help trace its lineage. Whimsically, two of these watermarks were an email address for the genome and the names of the 46 scientists who contributed to the project. There is a sinister side to this: if terrorists could develop a synthetic virus, the question of how long we might be able to live would be a moot one. An incurable disease could spread around the world in a matter of days. This is a risk that needs serious monitoring.

Walter is recognised as one of America's most distinguished scientific experts on ageing and longevity. Walter's research has focused on the importance of physical exercise in the promotion of healthy ageing. He recently lost his wife to Alzheimer's, and is now actively dating, and as he says remains "fully engaged" with life, though he has long since retired from his clinical practice.

Walter has written seven books and is famous for being an advocate of regular exercise. He is also a good friend of Len Hayflick, with whom he agrees on the fundamental causes of ageing as being entropy, loss of heat and energy leading to degradation – the Second Law of Thermodynamics. Interestingly, Walter, as one of the two oldest people we met on our research trip, is also, along with Len, one of the two people to think that maximal lifespan is unlikely to be extended. We speculate that maybe the older you are, and the closer to life's exit doors, the less optimistic you are that something can be found to help you overcome life's apparent limits. Nonetheless, Walter is determined to make it to 100. He has good familial genes on his side, with his father and mother both living extended lives.

DR WALTER BORTZ – THE ENERGETIC ELDER

Dr Walter Bortz is 86 years old and lives in what he calls his very own paradise in Portola Valley, south of San Francisco. We cannot disagree, as when we visited him we absolutely loved his house and its surroundings. Walter M. Bortz II, M.D., is a retired Clinical Professor of Medicine at Stanford University School of Medicine and a graduate of Williams College and of the University of Pennsylvania School of Medicine.

Familial longevity does indeed have some bearing on our own lifespan expectation. The caveat here is that long-lived parents may have more positive influences on their offspring in terms of lifestyle behaviour than less long-lived parents. As an example of familial connection to lifespan, researchers from the University of Exeter have recently established that if you have one parent who lives to 100, your own chance of living to 70 is 68% greater than if you don't. And as an aside, the world's verifiable oldest person ever (Jeanne Calment) had a brother who lived to 97. Her family was known to live very long lives and she certainly outlived them all. Currently the oldest person alive is a Jamaican lady named Violet Brown who is 117. Her prescription for a super-long life is church, no pork, no chicken and (it being Jamaica) no rum! Violet might well be tempted to go for the prize of a million dollars offered by Dmitry Kaminsky, a well-known Russian venture capitalist, and a friend of ours. Dmitry has promised the cash pay-out to whomever lives to their 124th birthday. He or she will not only make history, but will get a nice enhancement to their pension pot.

Meantime, Walter Bortz keeps a positive attitude, along with a workload of book writing, speeches and meetings, as well as romantic dates – and all of these keep him active. He has given up running long distances, due to general creakiness and to a heart operation in 2016, but still runs a couple of miles most days.

He has some basic principles which we summarise here:

1. The influence of the obvious. Moderate exercise, non-sugary diets, moderation in most things and not smoking will affect life expectancy positively. High stress levels influence longevity negatively, as do dangerous sports or work. And of course, the quality and quantity of sleep is a sine qua non.

2. "Engagement" with the world, according to Walter, will improve mental health and certainly mitigate neurodegenerative disease. Staying interested and useful is a hallmark of longevity and this has been proved in numerous studies.

DR JAY BRADNER – NOVARTIS INSTITUTES FOR BIOMEDICAL RESEARCH

Dr Jay Bradner, whom we spoke to in the course of research for this book, is President of the Novartis Institutes for Biomedical Research, and is based in Cambridge, Massachusetts. Previously, Dr Bradner was on the faculty of Harvard Medical School at the Dana-Farber Cancer Institute. He has over 130 scientific publications and 30 patents to his name, so is well qualified to opine on matters relating to ageing.

He is keen on Myc, a regulator gene important to cell cycle activity, as a target, both for cancer and for ageing (see Targets in Ageing. Page 249), and as head of Novartis "innovation" recognises ageing as an important new area for research. Novartis is a Swiss company and one of the largest pharmaceutical companies in the world, with annual sales of close to US $60 billion.

Involvement in specific ageing research is rare among big pharmaceutical companies; after the failure of Sirtris, a resveratrol-focused company bought for US $720 million in 2008 by GlaxoSmithKline, there has been a reluctance among major pharmaceutical companies to contemplate specific anti-ageing therapeutic developments. However, recently Novartis and AstraZeneca have put their corporate heads above the parapet with everolimus, a rapamycin analog, and AstraZeneca's AZD8055, another mTOR inhibitor (see Targets in Ageing. Page 184).

Dr Bradner was understandably circumspect in talking with us; the constraints of big company internal secrecy and of the long arm of public market regulation are fairly obvious. Nonetheless, the emphasis on Myc gene targeting is interesting, and everolimus (an immune suppressant) is also an fascinating opportunity.

DAVID GEMS — THE JEWEL IN THE CROWN OF WORM RESEARCH

David Gems is a Professor at University College London and a noted expert on the ageing processes in C. elegans; he works closely with Linda Partridge, another longevity specialist, also of UCL, as well as of the Max Planck Institute in Cologne. David has been very helpful and patient in the construction of this book.

His office at UCL adjoins his laboratory, which is organised into neatly separated sections containing fruit flies, yeast and of course his speciality, nematode worms.

On his wall is the *Fountain of Youth* by Lucas Cranach the Elder, a depiction of the search for immortality – one dating back to 1546, and a daily reminder to him of his work in the field of ageing.

David has both a negative and optimistic view of the science of longevity. He is negative because he is disappointed by the lack of a deep understanding about the nature of even C. elegans ageing despite decades of work by many labs. He is frustrated by the inadequacy of the traditional view that ageing is caused by molecular damage; and because no central process of ageing has yet emerged that would make treatment

of ageing as a single disease viable. He is also a critic of the process by which academic publications operate, where the producer is also the consumer.

He is optimistic, on the other hand, because so much has now been discovered about the multifactorial processes involved in ageing that the prospect of fully understanding ageing and treating the diseases of ageing will undoubtedly become easier in the next couple of decades.

David's lab is partly funded by the Wellcome Trust, which is surely the most far-sighted medical charity of major substance in the world. We have also bought a new fancy microscope for David's lab, one that allows him to see his beloved worms in their luminous glory!

Although he does not believe that there is a single, central ageing process, David is a promoter of what he calls the "Williams-Blagosklonny" theory of ageing, which is that our wild type genes become hyper-functioning as we age and "run on", causing life-limiting pathologies, including many of the diseases of ageing. By this view, our bodies are a bit like a joint of beef in an oven, cooked to perfection till maturity and, then becoming overcooked, dry and inedible as the oven carries on heating the joint.

He explains that C. elegans provides a key example of this principle: it reproduces for about three days of adulthood, and then stops, but it carries on producing yolk which eventually causes senescent obesity and promotes tumour growth.

Worms are essentially machines for turning bacterial food supply into eggs; once the egg-producing function has been accomplished, the genes that created the yolk which enables the production of the eggs are not turned off but rather "run on". It isn't the tumours that kill worms though, but other pathologies, including something resembling a gut infected through injury.

That having been said, worms can be made to live very much longer than normal (as much as 10 times longer) and the factors that enable that phenomenal life extension do have some relevance in human ageing research.

In the case of the fruit fly, intestinal disease is the major cause of death, and in other organisms, many other factors are the principal causes of death. There is no one thing that is central to the death of animals and organisms, and that's why the science is so complicated and still at a primitive, though fast developing stage.

According to David, the major driver of human ageing is late-life gene action. For example, in senescent cells triggering cancers and other diseases. There is currently a certain futility to treating late-life diseases individually as they are a bit like the multiheaded Hydra of Greek mythology; remove one, and two more will appear to take its place.

But, and here his optimism begins to seep in, keeping healthy, and looking after your gums and your teeth, will typically extend healthy lifespans. Compounds such as rapamycin (and rapalogs) and senolytics, which are emerging to treat a wide range of pathologies, will also improve late-life health and extend lifespan.

He is not certain that modulating mTOR and growth hormone will have big effects on maximum lifespan, and points to the experience with the 350 or so Ecuadorean Laron dwarves. These are born insensitive to growth hormone and so have low IGF-1 levels. The absence of IGF-1, which is very much implicated in ageing, means that these people, who are exceptionally short, don't suffer from cancers, diabetes (despite being universally overweight) or Alzheimer's but they are prone to alcoholism, seizures and accidents, and as a result they don't die any later than the general population. This is disappointing, because mice bred to be insensitive to growth hormone are exceptionally long-lived, with at least a 50% increase in average lifespan.

The conundrum of ageing remains one to be solved and people like David Gems – working not for personal enrichment, but for the future of humanity – are key to the step-by-step understanding and eventual treatment of the single disease syndrome of ageing – a terminology which David very much thinks we should adopt.

CYNTHIA KENYON AND CALICO — TEAR DOWN THAT WALL!

In the course of researching this book, we sought to meet as many of the key opinion leaders in the field of longevity as we could. Cynthia Kenyon has undoubtedly been important in the area, especially for her early work with C. elegans, and for her innumerable contributions to ageing science.

But, and it's a big but, she has taken the Alphabet/Google/Abbvie dollar and is now, at least partly, silenced. She was the only longevity leader to refuse to talk to us outright, citing corporate secrecy. Calico (California Life Company) is the Alphabet subsidiary at which she now works, Cynthia having formerly been a leading light and Professor at the University of California, San Francisco. Getting information on what she, or Calico, is up to is a bit like getting the KGB to reveal its secrets in the old Soviet days. Nonetheless, Clive Cookson, Science Editor of the *Financial Times,* did secure an interview with Cynthia and so a lot of what of we know is down to his sleuthing prowess.

But for mere authors such as us, there is no way that we could get past the gatekeepers of a company whose motto was until recently "Don't be Evil". It has now been changed to "Do the right thing", however, it might have been better changed to "Say Nothing". We do, of course, know that Alphabet's principal subsidiary, Google, is a money machine, recently tarnished but still churning out huge amounts of cash. A bit of that cash has been diverted to a variety of so-called "moon-shot" projects, some of which are whimsical, and some of which would in normal circumstances be labelled "vanity".

It is not known whether Calico, into which a reputed US $1.5 billion has been sunk (half from the biopharma company Abbvie), falls into the latter category, because precious little is known about it, other than that the provenance of its key employees is, on paper at least, outstanding. Calico's objective appears to be to extend lifespans, something that Cynthia proved adept at in her previous incarnation at UCSF – although that was in worms and not in humans. It is rumoured that 1,000 mice are now being housed at Calico, with a view to examining every aspect of their ageing process, to establish biomarkers and to investigate drugs that might target pathways of the ageing process.

In September 2013, Art Levinson was named chief executive officer of Calico. He is another huge name in life sciences, having been the CEO of Genentech from 1995 to 2009. He is also the chairman of Apple, so is Silicon Valley royalty. He has authored or co-authored 80 scientific papers and is cited in 11 US patents.

Recently, Calico announced a joint venture with C4 Therapeutics to discover and commercialise therapies for the diseases of ageing, including cancer, using C4's expertise in protein degradation. This is very much a preclinical deal, so nothing concrete has yet emerged. The announcement accompanying the venture was as anodyne as one from the Politburo, and scientists generally have been disappointed with Calico's progress. Nir Barzilai has been quoted as saying: *"The truth is, we don't know what they're doing, but whatever it is doesn't really seem to be attacking the problem."*

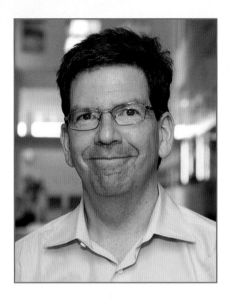

It is certainly great news that a billion and a half dollars have been committed to the study of ageing, but whether Google should be providing any of it is entirely another matter.

By all accounts, Cynthia Kenyon is a passionate, articulate and charismatic advocate of advancing the longevity industry. It is such a shame that she has been constrained by a corporation supposedly founded to help mankind, but now cloaked in a veil of secrecy which ill suits it.

DR DAVID GLASS – NO WASTING HERE

We have spoken with Dr David Glass, the Executive Director of the Novartis Institutes for Biomedical Research in Cambridge, Massachusetts. Novartis is one of the few large biopharma companies to be making serious efforts in the field of anti-ageing, although as a first step they are addressing the diseases of ageing.

David is particularly interested in ageing skeletal muscles and in the mechanisms which cause cellular senescence. He highlighted the experimental compound RAD001 otherwise known as everolimus, a Novartis drug in development which is a rapalog (currently used as an immunosuppressant) and is now being repurposed to boost the immune systems of the elderly (see Targets in Ageing. Page 194).

The idea is to overcome immuno-senescence, which is the failure of the immune system in old age, and thereby to improve the efficacy of vaccines, for instance of influenza and of shingles. Trials suggest that RAD001 can increase the potency of these vaccines in the elderly (70+) by about 20%. RAD001 is an inhibitor of mTORC1, and a promoter of autophagy (see Autophagy. Page 132), as indeed are all rapalogs.

In addition, David is involved with BYM338 (otherwise known as bimagrumab), which in 2016 failed in a pivotal trial for a rare muscle disorder. This is a joint venture (with MorphoSys) and has been studied in relation to sporadic inclusion body myositis.

Bimagrumab is designed to inhibit myostatin (growth differentiation factor 8 or GDF-8), a protein produced and released by myocytes to inhibit myogenesis (myogenesis is muscle cell growth) and differentiation. BYM338 is also cited as being potentially effective in other muscle diseases, including cachexia (illness-related wasting) and sarcopenia (illness-independent muscle wasting, mostly in the elderly).

David believes that our skeletal musculature is the last significant undrugged area of our bodies and that new drugs in this area will help the elderly to achieve better balance, strength and mobility. In his opinion drugs to address sarcopenia will be on the market in the next 5 to 10 years.

David is also a sceptic when it comes to the opinions of people such as Amy Wagers of Harvard University and Richard Lee of Brigham and Women's Hospital in Boston. These scientists think that that there is a specific factor in young blood, GDF11, that is particularly beneficial to the elderly – and that this factor is good for muscle regeneration. On the contrary, David asserts that GDF11 is actually maintained in old age and that much more important for anti-ageing is the inhibition of myostatin. Hence, BYM338.

We aren't sure which way this goes, but we like David's optimism – and we like the way that Novartis is now involved in the ageing market. Increasingly, big pharma companies will be forced to think the same way. After all, it is the future of medicine. As long, of course, as regulators don't stand in the way of progress.

TARGETS IN AGEING

RULES AND REGULATIONS

The regulatory landscape for anti-ageing interventions around the world is far from perfect. However, we do see several positive trends that are going to contribute to the expansion of the preventative and restorative medicine industry.

The US already allows the testing of anti-ageing interventions within a classical clinical trial regulatory framework. The TAME study, due to start in 2017, has shown that it has probably become more difficult to get these sorts of trials funded than it is to register them. In this respect, it's worth readers keeping an eye on the companies that have "ageing" as the specific disease indication for their interventions. The US government website ClinicalTrials.gov contains a centralised registry of all clinical trials and is accessible to all.

Some longevity scientists such as Franco Cortese and Alex Zhavoronkov, both Trustees of The Biogerontology Research Foundation, feel that it is important to classify ageing as a disease (Classifying Aging as a Disease in the Context of ICD-11, Zhavoronkov and Bhullar, 2015).

It is no great secret that regulatory burdens are the major impediments

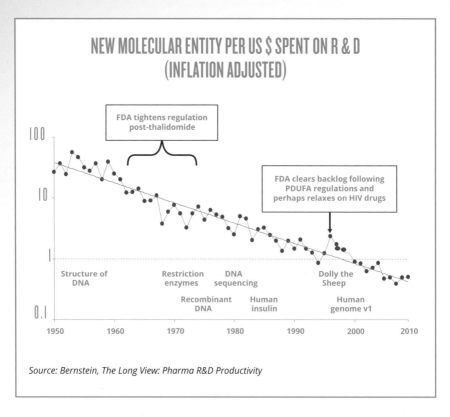

NEW MOLECULAR ENTITY PER US $ SPENT ON R & D (INFLATION ADJUSTED)

FDA tightens regulation post-thalidomide

FDA clears backlog following PDUFA regulations and perhaps relaxes on HIV drugs

Structure of DNA

Restriction enzymes

DNA sequencing

Dolly the Sheep

Recombinant DNA

Human insulin

Human genome v1

Source: Bernstein, The Long View: Pharma R&D Productivity

to progress in biomedicine. Since the FDA strongly tightened its rules in the 1960s, the number of drugs, referred to in the industry as new molecular entities (NMEs), has been in steady decline. The average cost to take a drug from lab to market had, by 2015, increased to over US $1.5 billion (with some estimates running as high as US $4 billion).

One of the major reasons for these relentlessly increasing costs is, of course, the high failure rate among experimental compounds. On average, about 90% of all drugs fail in clinical trials and, in oncology, the failure rate reaches 95%. In the US, as well as elsewhere, the first phase of clinical trials is intended to prove the safety of the drug in humans and nearly two-thirds of all drugs which go into this phase pass. The real "valley of death" is the second phase, which is intended to prove efficacy. Barely a third of all drugs which make it into phase 2 make it to phase 3.

PROBABILITY OF SUCCESS

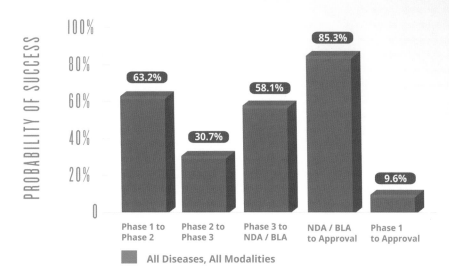

All Diseases, All Modalities

PROBABILITY OF SUCCESS WITH OR WITHOUT SELECTION BIOMARKERS

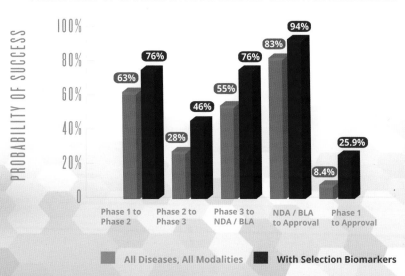

All Diseases, All Modalities   **With Selection Biomarkers**

Source: Biotechnology Industry Organization, Clinical Development Success Rates 2006–2015

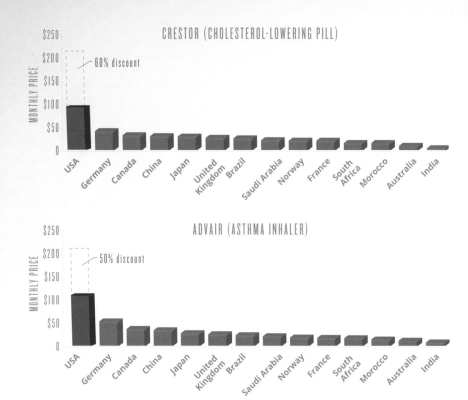

Source: Centers for Medicare & Medicaid Services, 2015.

The costs of clinical studies increase exponentially from phase to phase, with the third phase exceeding a billion dollars. High failure rates contribute significantly to drug prices, as drug companies naturally seek to recover the costs of R&D for failed compounds from the (few) successful ones and this results in what can only be described as exorbitant prices for drugs in the US.

In 2015, total national health expenditure (NHE) in the US grew by 5.8% to US $3.2 trillion, or 17.8% of GDP. Prescription drug spending increased 9% to US $324.6 billion, about 10% of total health expenditures. 28.7% of the total NHE was paid by the federal government, i.e. taxpayers, and the rest by insurers and by consumers.

It is very likely that in the near future there will be changes in the ways that drugs enter and progress through the regulatory system. There will be substantial support for greater openness and

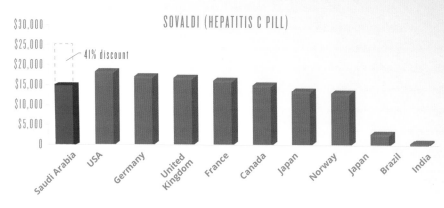

SOVALDI (HEPATITIS C PILL)

41% discount

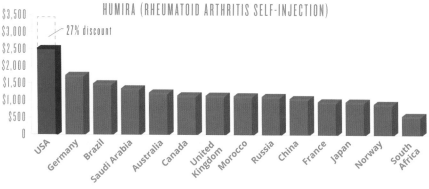

HUMIRA (RHEUMATOID ARTHRITIS SELF-INJECTION)

27% discount

transparency with clinical trials data, and the transitioning of this data onto blockchain. Additionally, integration of AI into biomarker development, into drug discovery and into the "prediction" of the outcomes of clinical trials will soon become the norm.

An example of where clinical trials can and will be improved is the use of ageing biomarkers to determine the age-adjusted responses of participants in trials in advance of their conduct. This is needed because,

at the moment, trials don't take into account the relative efficacy of drugs at various biological age levels.

Insilico Medicine, which has developed a range of deep learning-based predictors of clinical trial outcomes, is a likely beneficiary of such a move. Osiris, a US company, is offering a DNA methylation biomarker of ageing at an affordable price.

This text was kindly provided by Alex Zhavoronkov, CEO, Insilico Medicine.

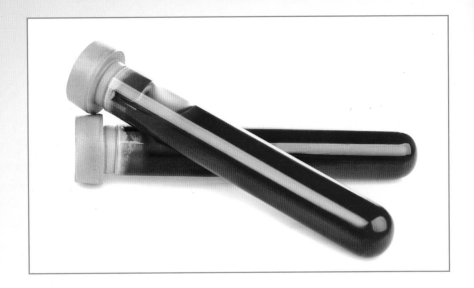

AGEING VAMPIRES

Should everyone over 40 don a cape and grow fangs?

The idea that young blood transfused into older people has a rejuvenating effect has been around for a long time. A German doctor as far back as 1615 hoped that the "hot and spirituous blood of a young man will pour into the old one as if it were from a fountain of youth". Recently, the idea of somehow reinvigorating the old using the blood of the young has enjoyed a renaissance – and has been the subject of serious debate. Big money is already being spent in unregulated clinics.

The practice has an unfortunate history. The physician Alexander Bogdanov injected himself with the blood of younger people in 1924, and while feeling great to begin with, he contracted tuberculosis and malaria from one such infusion – and consequently died.

In 2016, before the US Presidential election, the comedian Stephen Colbert cautioned teenagers that a President Trump might replace Obamacare with compulsory **parabiosis** – the practice of joining a young organism to an older one. "He's going to stick a straw in you like a Capri Sun", Colbert joked.

If all of us over 40 became Dracula-like, would it improve our survival chances, or is the idea as fanciful as Bram Stoker's creation? Tom Rando of Stanford University announced in 2005 that heterochronic parabiosis, where two mice of different ages were conjoined by surgery, restored the livers and muscles of the older one. In both mice and rats that are conjoined, the entire blood supply is exchanged between the parabionts about ten times a day.

The positive effect of blood transfusions from young to old may be because older people have a lesser supply of blood stem cells in their bone marrow than the supply that younger people enjoy. These blood stem cells are progenitors for our red and white blood cells, and so a diminished quantity of them leads to anaemia and a weakening of the immune system (which is dependent upon **haematopoiesis**).

Hartmut Geiger of the German University in Ulm has discovered that older mice suffer from a lower level of osteopontin, a protein found in blood. By mixing this protein with the stem cells of older mice, he noticed that the older stem cells began to produce more white blood cells, effectively reverting to a youthful state. This might open the possibility of re-energising old blood without the need for transfusions (or, even worse, heterochronic parabiosis).

The benefits of heterochronic parabiosis in the older of the animals takes the form of stronger skeletons in the case of conjoined mice (yes, they really are sewn together).

Additional benefits to the older "parabiont" include improved cardiac muscle tissue, enhanced cognition and what is known as remyelination (bolstering the sheaths of axons in the central nervous system) in the old "parabiont". This is a word to describe the unfortunate creatures that end up as a sort of Siamese mismatched twins. That said, there is no doubt that regeneration occurs in the older animal during this process, which is encouraging for longevity research.

This work, by Stanford researcher, Tony Wyss-Coray, has led to a company called Alkahest (whose meaning is the alchemists' holy grail), being formed, in an attempt to use this technique to address Alzheimer's, using a cocktail of proteins.

The downside of parabiosis is that the younger animal of the unfortunate couple ages faster by being exposed to the older animal (normally mice are used in these experiments). It also seems that a lot of the improvement comes not from sharing blood, but from the stronger circulatory system in the younger parabiont extending its strength to the conjoined pair, and possibly also by the action of the youthful liver of the younger mouse. There is certainly some effect from the blood exchange itself, though, and researchers are looking for other rejuvenating contributors.

It appears that members of the Wnt 193 and TGF-β family of signalling genes, including GDF11, as well as the hormone oxytocin and the cytokine CCL11 (a secretion of the immune system), can be activated in older mice without the need for combining the circulatory systems of aged and younger mice. Plasma from young mice can be injected into older mice on a regular basis, and this increases cognition and muscle strength just as effectively.

Apart from parabiosis, which seems to us to be unnecessary, other transfers between the young and the old are being explored. Somewhat unappealingly, the transfer of faecal matter may have a positive effect on older models and might have a role in extending life. Dario Valenzano, of the Max Planck Institute for the Biology of Ageing in Germany, transferred the gut microbiomes from young killifish to old killifish, and found positive effects on longevity. Ambrosia, a California start-up, is selling blood from younger people to about 100 longevists, mostly Silicon Valley types, at about US $8,000 a pop.

So, is there anything to it? Yes, there probably are factors in young blood that could usefully be amplified in older people, and the transplant of faecal material to older people will perhaps bring benefits also.

However, it is a process that needs a lot more investigation, and will require rigorous quality control, as any defects of young donor blood or faecal matter could easily be transferred to the older recipient. And then the law of unintended consequences will apply.

A recent study by Zhang et al. (*Nature* 2017) has shown that aged mice injected with stem cells from the hypothalamus of newborn mice are accorded an extra 2–4 months of life (the human equivalent of about 10–20 years). It seems that after the age of 2 (70 in humans) mice lose all their brain stem cells, so injecting them with stem cells from a newborn mouse appears to improve longevity.

CALORIC RESTRICTION (CR)

It is now well known that CR, which is eating less without starvation, extends lifespans in all studied species. It also lessens disease burden in ageing mammals. However, it is a very unpleasant and impractical way of going about living longer. You might end up living a little longer but in constant hunger, and, as the old joke goes, it will feel a looooot longer.

Very few people have successfully lived on calorie restricted diets, at least since the finding emerged about 80 years ago that by doing so life (at least of rodents) can be extended. This is mainly because most people lack the willpower, circumstances and inclination to pursue such a course.

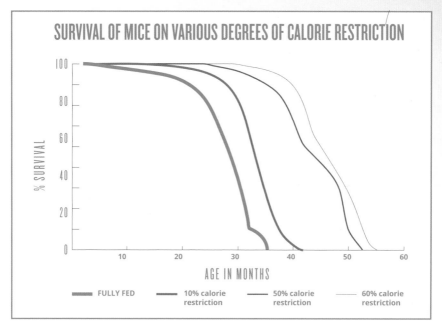

SURVIVAL OF MICE ON VARIOUS DEGREES OF CALORIE RESTRICTION

% SURVIVAL

AGE IN MONTHS

FULLY FED   10% calorie restriction   50% calorie restriction   60% calorie restriction

Where restricted dietary intake does take place, there appears to be empirical evidence that centenarians are more abundant in the general population. Studies in Okinawa, Japan, whose population historically ate less than people elsewhere in Japan, illustrate just that, or at least it did until the arrival of McDonald's and its ilk. Okinawa had (and still has) a high frequency of centenarians, and average life expectancy in the population was (and is) remarkably high.

But, despite there being strong data that lifespan is significantly extended due to CR in mice, fruit flies, worms, yeast and indeed, primates, when it comes to humans, there does seem to be some effect on lifespan by cutting

calories (and we are talking here about a 30% reduction in calories on a per diem basis). So, one of the objectives of longevity researchers is to try and find drugs that mimic CR (i.e. CR mimetics) and amplify the effects of CR on lifespan.

In primates, the closest species to humans, there has been conflicting evidence as to the efficacy of CR, but after more recent research, the longevity effect seems to be incontrovertible. The most recent available data suggests that rhesus macaque monkeys fed since their young adulthoods on two-thirds of a normal dietary intake are significantly longer-lived than those that are not. Furthermore, their all cause-mortality is less skewed to the usual diseases of ageing than in the case of normal monkeys.

These less-fed monkeys are stronger, experience less fur thinning, and have less cancer, diabetes, muscle wasting and bone loss than their better-fed counterparts. Their immune systems appear to be more efficient, and in short, they display all the signs of healthy ageing and live longer as a consequence.

A long-running study, dating from the 1980s, by the National Institute on Aging in Baltimore, USA and by the University of Wisconsin, has shown that macaques on a CR diet live about three years longer than normal, that being 26 years, the human equivalent of about an extra nine years. Some of the monkeys are still alive, and four of them have lived to over 40, which is the human equivalent of a supercentenarian.

Some of these trials were imperfectly designed, but the overall evidence is very strong that the CR monkeys live longer on average than the control monkeys. And it is interesting that the age gain was only about two years in males compared to six years in females. Since monkeys do live longer on CR diets, it is likely that humans would do too, though those who practise it report feeling permanently cold and having reduced libido.

CR regulates a large number of biological pathways, and it is difficult to isolate exactly where the positive effects come from. But reducing IGF-1 and insulin levels and increasing insulin sensitivity seems to be a major factor, as does the reduction in ROS by the means of provoking mild stress in mitochondria. As mentioned earlier, this is known as mitohormesis, a subset of the more general phenomenon of hormesis where a stressor is positive at low levels and negative at high levels. An example is the feeding of low-dose paraquat weed killer to worms, where a modest increase in ROS awakens stress resistance systems and has the effect of lowering free radicals and lessening oxidative damage.

In addition, CR appears to affect the three key nutrient sensing pathways – mTOR, AMPK and SIRT1. The modulation of mTOR and SIRT1, using metformin and NAD+ precursors in particular, looks promising in respect of the mimicking of CR.

It also worth noting that monkeys, mice, worms and yeast that are subjected to CR are generally introduced to it in early life, whereas this is not feasible in humans. So, the effects of CR on humans in middle or older life may be lessened relative to the models. Indeed, it may be undesirable for older people, who are trying to ward off muscle wasting (sarcopenia), to take up CR.

Mimetics of CR and intermittent fasting (think 2:5 diets) are avenues

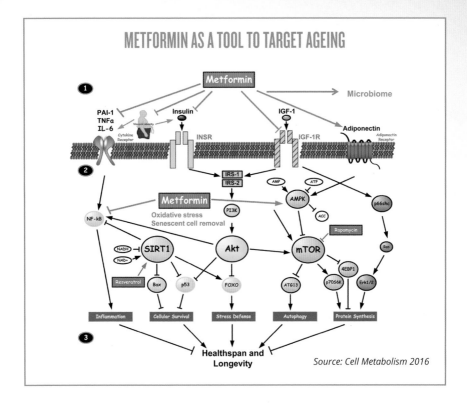

METFORMIN AS A TOOL TO TARGET AGEING

Source: Cell Metabolism 2016

that researchers are actively exploring to achieve some incremental lifespan benefit, without the unpleasantness of actually having to eat one-third less on a daily basis.

AMPK AND METFORMIN

Metformin is an antidiabetic drug that increases insulin sensitivity (important in mammalian longevity) as well as activating the gene AMPK (adenosine monophosphate activated kinase), thereby positively modulating glucose levels and levels of circulating lipids in the body. It also seems to regulate a variety of processes relating to ageing (Foretz 2010).

AMPK seems to play a critical role in the regulation of our energy balance, particularly in restoring mitochondrial function. Exercise and caloric restriction have an effect in activating AMPK, as does metformin. AMPK also appears to inhibit the mTOR pathway, which is an important clue to metformin's role in anti-ageing. mTOR has been linked to several age-related diseases such as cancer, cardiovascular disease, and Alzheimer's.

Metformin originates from a synthesis and reformulation of an active ingredient guanidine, which is found in French lilac, a compound whose effects had been observed, but not understood, as early as the Middle Ages. The synthetic versions belong to a family of drugs known as biguanides, and the star member is metformin. First approved in Europe in 1957 (but not until 1994 in the US), 37,000 tonnes of metformin are produced annually, mostly in India. The drug is as cheap as chips.

Metformin inhibits oxygen consumption in the mitochondria, thereby lowering the metabolism of patients. Metformin achieves a lowering of blood glucose levels This also decreases liver glucose production; by decreasing intestinal absorption of glucose, and by improving insulin sensitivity through an increase in peripheral glucose uptake.

The TAME trial (see Key Opinion Leaders. Page 151) is designed to lead the way for other, possibly more sophisticated, trials of compounds including rapamycin, which appear to have specific anti-ageing benefits. The main reason for the TAME study is to convince the FDA to approve ageing as a specific druggable indication so that it can become a target for future and improved medications.

Jim's dogs when they heard they were going to be given Rapamycin!

MTOR, RAPAMYCIN AND RAPALOGS

mTOR is an extremely important target of research in the field of longevity. mTOR stands for "mechanistic target of rapamycin", and is a kinase, a word for an enzyme that catalyses the transfer of phosphate groups to molecules.

mTOR is divided into two complexes, both found in every cell. These are mTORC1 (complex 1) which is the most important in ageing research, and mTORC2 (complex 2), of less significance for the purposes of this book, although still part of the story. mTORC1 is a controller of cell growth and proliferation and is inhibited by rapamycin (sirolimus), which is a naturally occurring macrolide (a class of antibiotics derived from soil-borne bacteria), discovered in Easter Island (Rapa Nui), in the 1970s. mTOR's effects increase with age, and this increase occurs partly as a result of increased signalling from white adipose fat tissue. Judicious suppression of mTOR (and in particular of mTORC1) is more than likely to be anti-ageing. This is certainly the case in invertebrate and mammalian animal models (e.g. mice), though its effects tend to be sex- and genotype-dependent, i.e. better in women than in men, and better in some types of people than others. mTORC1 is activated by nutrients and by growth factors whereas mTORC2 is triggered by extracellular cues, such as the activation of PI3K (phosphoinositol 3-kinase) signalling.

Rapamycin was initially used as an antifungal drug and subsequently was developed into an immunosuppressant against transplant rejection (Afinitor – Novartis). In the 1980s, rapamycin was discovered to have anti-cancer properties, though its early development as an oncology drug failed due to severe side effects. The discovery in the 1990s of temsirolimus, a soluble rapalog, once again put the compound into the anti-cancer line-up, and since then several cancer drugs based on rapamycin have been developed. Activation of the PI3K-AKT and ERK pathways, both of which are related to cancer, is a complication of mTOR inhibitor therapy and this activation is something that the rapalogs in development seek to avoid.

Activation of PI3K is not a good thing in cancer treatment.

Amongst the rapalogs in development, everolimus and ridaforolimus stand out, but there are plenty of others: a recent count showed that over 200 trials of rapamycin analogs had already taken place or are currently in progress, for cancer as well as other indications. These rapalogs are either designed to be monotherapies or to be part of combinations with other drugs. In treating cancer, rapamycin has relatively limited use; it is confined to mostly rare types of cancer and is not curative but intended to stabilise the disease.

As with so many compounds developed for one specific indication and then used for something else (like Viagra), rapamycin and its descendants' major purpose will change from being anti-cancer to being integral in anti-ageing therapies. Rapamycin may thus turn out to be the most important repurposed drug of all time.

In 2009, researchers at three separate (but collaborating) institutions discovered that rapamycin had a remarkable property: it extends the lifespan of mice by an average of 20%. Rapamycin was already known to have anti-ageing properties when used in other organisms such as fruit flies, but up to that point no significant evidence of its lifespan effect on mammals had emerged. The key to this extension of lifespan was the

Rapamycin and its Effects

Model	Intervention	Median Increase in Lifespan	Paper
S. cerevisiae	S6K1 deletion	200%	Fabrizio et al., 2001
C. elegans	S6K1 inhibition	30%	Jia et al., 2004
C. elegans	TOR inhibition	200%	Vellai et al. 2003
Middle aged mice (600 days old)	S6K1 suppression	9% males / 14% females	Harrison et al., 2009
Mice possessing two hypomorphic alleles of mTOR	mTOR inhibition	20%	Wu et al., 2013

inhibition of mTOR, and specifically, of mTORC1.

The way this inhibition happens is that rapamycin forms a "complex" with a protein called FKBP12, which binds to mTORC1 (but not to mTORC2). Rapamycin is therefore an allosteric (control) inhibitor of mTORC1, and as a result of the administration of the drug, mTOR goes into life-extending survival mode.

It is known that the inhibition of mTORC1 activates autophagy and improves lifespan in animal models (Laplante & Sabatini, 2012). Rapamycin and its analogs seem to replicate this effect, and there is every reason to believe that these drugs will be lifespan-prolonging in humans, though any estimate of the magnitude of that effect is entirely speculative.

Inhibition of mTORC1 (or of its substrate, S6K1) leads to significant life extension in models. Because mTOR activity increases in ageing mammals that are obese – obesity being age-related in many cases – this obesity can be reversed in mouse models by directly infusing rapamycin into the hypothalamus of the mice (Yang et al., 2012).

In humans, rapamycin has side effects which limit its direct usefulness in longevity medicine. Adverse effects of rapamycin include poor functioning of the metabolic system, such as hyperglycemia, and insulin resistance. It appears that this is because rapamycin inhibits both mTORC1 and mTORC2; mTORC1 inhibition is a good thing, but inhibition of mTORC2 appears to be the cause of metabolic dysfunction (Lamming et al, 2012).

For that reason, rapalogs, i.e. derivatives (analogs) of rapamycin, are being developed. Such rapalogs may end up being a key component of the anti-ageing strategy designed to build the bridge to a genetically engineered extreme long life and one that we, somewhat optimistically, believe possible in about twenty or thirty years.

mTOR inhibition, however, is not a one-way happy street as it has some negatives as well. These include increased insulin resistance, even just with mTORC1, and impaired wound healing. Additionally, mice fed rapamycin can suffer testicular atrophy (Wilkinson et al., 2012). The focus of much rapalog research is to separate out the positive from the negative effect of the differing compounds. But overall, rapamycin and its successors are of enormous interest to longevity researchers.

As well as the lifespan-prolonging effects of rapalogs, there are other advantages that are being uncovered. RAD001, a rapamycin analog, improves vaccination response in elderly subjects, increasing the efficacy of, say, the flu vaccine, which normally falls off rapidly after the age of 70. Additionally, rapamycin has been shown in animal models to reverse $A\beta$ plaque aggregation in Alzheimer's, and also stop neuronal death in Parkinson's models (Malagelada et al., 2010). Thus, rapamycin has provided a positive first step to addressing mTOR inhibition, but it needs to be done safely and at proper dosages.

For this reason, rapalogs are urgently needed and some are already available, though not specifically designed or prescribed for anti-ageing. A second generation of rapalogs is being developed, some that block the feedback activation of P13K/AKT signlling and others that only target mTORC1 and not mTORC2, the inhibition of the latter can play havoc with metabolic systems. Strictly speaking these are not really rapalogs, but specific mTORC1 inhibitors, but they do share a common lineage with rapamycin. At the moment, they are usually designed for cancer treatments, but their potential in anti-ageing is obvious.

As a result of the discovery of the anti-ageing properties of rapamycin and of its progeny, a real gold rush is developing. A key company involved in this area is PureTech Health, which is London-listed but US-based. This company has recently done a deal with Swiss pharma giant Novartis to take over the anti-ageing development of everolimus, the Novartis rapalog. This will be positioned as a compound for delaying or reversing immunosenescence, in order to boost immunity in the elderly. PureTech has established a subsidiary to develop these rapalogs, called resTORbio, the most contrived a name we have ever seen!

Life Biosciences (see Key Opinion Leaders. Page 149) is also involved in rapalogs, and its broad suite of anti-ageing strategies makes it one of the more interesting candidates amongst the private businesses we have looked at. We would suggest keeping a weather eye out for a listing or any spin-out of one of Life Biosciences's subsidiaries.

Additionally, AstraZeneca, the UK pharma giant, has an important rapalog in late stage development. AZD8055 is an oral, potent and selective compound, and also prevents the feedback to AKT which causes problems with the simultaneous inhibition of both mTORC1 and mTORC2.

And, of course, dogs are currently providing us with useful information on how rapamycin might work (see dogagingproject.com and Dogs and Ageing. Page 124). Dogs are perfect for the examination of genes because the different breeds of pedigree dogs are essentially identical clones, resulting from inbreeding over many generations and as a result, the subtle differences between the breeds can provide useful clues as to our own genetic makeup. Woof!

SESTRINS – ANOTHER ANTI-AGEING TARGET

Sestrins are a family of proteins, found in many species, expressed in cells that have been exposed to stresses. In mammals, there are three types of sestrins – SESN1, SESN2, and SESN3. Their principal role is to regulate ROS, free radicals and other nasties, some of the worst factors in promoting ageing.

Sestrins activate what is known as the adenosine monophosphate-activated protein kinase gene (AMPK) and act as inhibitors of mTOR. Sestrins appear to be antioxidants (Budanov, 2004) and if they are depleted, at least in mouse models, age-associated disease increases.

Sestrins are, in turn, regulated by p53, which is an extremely important tumour suppressor, and there is a strong link between p53, sestrins and mTOR. It appears, from recent studies in the Cleveland Clinic, that sestrins can reinforce an antioxidant "firewall", mitigating damage by free radicals and improving cell signalling. The regulation of sestrins by the oncoprotein p53 seems to protect cells from death induced by stroke or by peroxides generated from ROS. Intervention in the activity of sestrins could therefore have major therapeutic implications. Quark Biotech, a California-based private company, is supposedly involved in very early trials of finding a way of upregulating the activity of sestrins using small interfering RNAs (siRNAs).

NAD⁺, BASIS, NMN AND SIRTUINS

When Jim visited the labs of David Sinclair at Harvard University in March 2017, he was given a small vial of the experimental compound NMN, which is the precursor of NAD+ that David and his colleagues have developed. A drug precursor is a chemical used in the production of pharmaceuticals and so NMN acts a "promoter" of the production of NAD in the body. Professor Sinclair has recently published data in the prestigious *Cell* academic journal, showing that treatment of mice with NMN significantly reduces the functional age of the mouse tissue. The NMN compound seems to mimic the effect of exercise and CR – at least in mice.

If similar effects of NMN found in the mice – i.e. improved skeletal tissue, reversal of age-related infertility in women and cardiac function – could be replicated in humans, 60-year-olds would end up with 20-year-old bodies. Sign us up!

Natural NAD+ levels decrease with age, and this makes it harder for bodies of all species to convert glucose into carbon dioxide and, thereby, generate ATP in mitochondria, ATP being necessary for cellular energy utilisation.

In 1906, British biochemists Arthur Harden and William Young discovered the NAD molecule, and in 1938, vitamin precursors of NAD+, including niacin, were identified by Conrad Elvenhjem. In 1949, Americans Friedkin and Lehninger discovered that NAD was the link between the citric acid cycle, a fundamental part of metabolism, and the synthesis of ATP, the currency of cellular energy.

Uses of NAD+, apart from redox (transfer of electrons – see below), have only recently been discovered. In the 1980s and 1990s, NAD+ and its metabolites were found to have a role in cell signalling. Then in 2000, Shin-ichiro Imai and colleagues at MIT found that NAD was linked to the function of the sirtuin family of protein deacetylases.

nicotinamide riboside

Sirtuins are conserved across many species and are dependent on NAD+. Sirtuins are now known to be important in the longevity of many organisms, including yeast and mice, and may well be useful in extending human life as well. Hence the huge academic and commercial interest in all things NAD+

as well as in sirtuins. Despite a great deal of NAD+ supplementation being already on the over-the-counter market, it is unlikely that these compounds can successfully get into cells, as their molecular size is just too large. So, we are excited about the arrival of NMN and other smaller compounds.

The reason why NMN and other compounds acting as precursors to NAD+ are so tantalising to longevity specialists is because they seem to work in the rejuvenation of cells and they can get into those cells in vivo. They restore cells by augmenting the body's ability to perform DNA repair, and they also act on the sirtuin family of enzymes, which we describe later.

Jim's vial of experimental NMN, designed to last about two weeks, went with him to Nashville, his next stop after Harvard, but sadly he forgot it in the fridge of his hotel room. Juvenescence has had to wait a little longer!

NAD+ is a signalling molecule, now also established as important in DNA repair as it regulates protein-protein interactions. Sinclair has shown that NMN lessens age-associated DNA damage and is protective against radiation exposure. In fact, on the day Jim was at the Harvard facilities, it was announced that Sinclair and team had won a prestigious NASA prize for their work in exploring the effects of cosmic radiation on astronauts planning to go to Mars. Those astronauts would age

drastically without the geroprotection offered by NMN, and on their return to earth would be biologically much older than their peers. The protection afforded to the prospective astronauts by NMN, as well as by equivalent drugs related to NAD+, is thought to be potentially beneficial to us earthbound people as well.

NAD is somewhat complex, so it's cold towel time for this one.

NAD+ goes by the full name nicotinamide adenine dinucleotide, and it necessary for the deacetylase activity of the silent information regulator 2 (Sir2) family of enzymes. NAD+ is a coenzyme and it is found in all mammalian cells. NAD is a called dinucleotide, because it consists of two nucleotides joined through their phosphate groups.

One of its nucleotides contains an adenine base and the other contains nicotinamide. **Nicotinamide adenine dinucleotide** takes two forms, an oxidized and a reduced form, abbreviated to NAD+ and NADH.

NAD is central to metabolism because of the redox reactions it is involved in; redox is the transport of electrons from one molecule to another. In other words, NAD acts a bit like a freight system. NAD+ is the oxidizing agent, accepting electrons from other molecules, and thereby becomes what is known as reduced. When reduced,

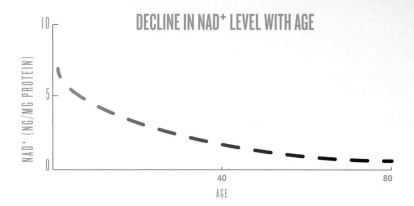

DECLINE IN NAD⁺ LEVEL WITH AGE

NAD+ becomes NADH, which in turn becomes a reducing agent, donating electrons. NADH is a crucial coenzyme in making ATP, the energy fuel we use in our bodies.

In its reduced form of NADH, the NAD molecule acts as a shuttle for electrons during cellular respiration, along with another molecule, FADH2. Using these molecules, electrons are removed from nutrients within the mitochondria, and their energy is then concentrated into ATP. This part of NAD's role is within what is known as the citric acid cycle.

These electron transfer reactions are the principal function of NAD. However, it is also important to other cellular processes, the most notable one being as a substrate of enzymes called sirtuins, which add or remove chemical groups, notably acetyl, from proteins. Because of the importance of these functions, the sirtuins enzymes involved in NAD metabolism are targets for drug discovery.

NAD concentration declines with age, and as it declines, it becomes less able to stop the harmful interplay between two proteins, DBC1 and PARP1, an interplay that is known to be damaging to cells and tissues. As a result of this negative interplay, DNA strand breaks are less able to be repaired, with the result being cell damage, loss of organ function and, ultimately cell death. PARP1 is an important protein in cellular repair, and its work is interrupted when interfered with by DBC1, a highly abundant protein.

DBC1 also interrupts the work of the SIRT1 protein, known to delay ageing in mice, flies and yeast and now, based on recent research, in humans. It is therefore important to cell vitality and repair that the interference of DBC1 in the actions of PARP1 and of SIRT1 be halted. Gomes and Sinclair have established that DBC1 and PARP1 bind harmfully to each other in a low-NAD environment. PARP1 (poly-ADP ribose polymerase 1) is vital to cell maintenance and has particular application in DNA repair and telomere repair. But when NAD levels are increased, these harmful bonds between PARP1 and DBC are significantly lessened.

Research into SIRT1 (known as the longevity gene) has shown how the molecule delays ageing and protects against obesity, diabetes, neurodegeneration and atherosclerosis. Sirtuins in general, not just SIRT1, are heavily involved in multiple biological processes and have broad enzymatic activity in all animals, including humans. All of these activities require NAD, which unlocks the sirtuins' activity. Sirtuins are an evolved component of cellular and DNA repair.

Sirtuin research started off relatively clumsily, and the unfortunate case of Sirtris Pharmaceuticals did set it back somewhat. In 2008, a sirtuin-focused company that David Sinclair had been a co-founder of, Sirtris, was sold to GlaxoSmithKline for US $720 million, but its technology didn't deliver. However, sirtuin-activating compounds are now once again the focus of excitement.

Sirtris was initially involved in discovering sirtuin-based treatments for type 2 diabetes. This work had begun at MIT in the labs of Leonard Guarente, where Sinclair had been a postdoctoral fellow and discovered the effect of resveratrol on yeast longevity. That early research on resveratrol proved to be flawed, and the whole area fell into controversy. GlaxoSmithKline shut down Sirtris in 2013, although work has continued on a resveratrol derivative termed SRT2104, one designed to activate sirtuins.

Resveratrol is a plant-derived polyphenol known to activate SIRT1; it has been shown to have antioxidant and anti-inflammatory properties. Activation of SIRT1 and Sir2 is thought to promote the mimicking effects of a CR diet and to increase lifespan in animal and other models. However, in the case of resveratrol-based sirtuin activation, the scientific work in worms and in fruit flies has been inconclusive, though overall, we do believe it to be beneficial.

Resveratrol research continues, but much more exciting are the studies into NAD derivatives which are already yielding more conclusive results. As a result of this research, NAD appears to be an activator of sirtuins as well as an un-binder of DBC1 and PARP 1.

Because we know that NAD levels decline with age, this in turn reduces sirtuins' activity and negatively affects mitochondrial function. This generates a negative feedback loop which can lead to the development of the diseases associated with ageing. Supplementation of NAD using NAD precursors to boost intracellular levels is now being explored in several labs, including Sinclair's (his product being the aforementioned NMN).

The workload of ageing cells is already very high: they have to neutralise ROS, repair DNA and maintain fidelity in cell division. In Sinclair's lab experiments, old mice suffering from high levels of PARP1/DBC1 bonds were fed NMN. After just one week, these mice showed a huge improvement in NAD levels and in PARP1 activity. Molecular markers of DNA damage lessened and when irradiated, the NMN-treated mice showed no ill effects.

In mammals, several of the seven sirtuins paralogs (similar genes to Sir2 that have evolved different functions) appear to have anti-ageing effects, but in different ways. Studies of transgenic mice bred to overexpress mammalian SIRT1 have demonstrated that, although their lifespans are not increased, aspects of ageing are improved. SIRT1 is the closest human relative to Sir2, the first sirtuin to be discovered and found in yeast. SIRT improves genomic stability and enhances cellular efficiency (Noguieras 2012), as well as restoring nutrient sensing.

SIRT6, another sirtuin, has been shown to be pro-longevity in mammalian models, and is the first sirtuin to demonstrably increase lifespan. SIRT6 regulates NF-κB (nuclear factor kappa B) signalling (see page 251) as well as insulin signalling. Mice which are bred to be deficient in SIRT6 age faster than normal mice (Mostoslavsky et al., 2006) and male transgenic mice which are bred to overexpress SIRT6 live longer than controls.

Recently, overexpression of SIRT3, another member of the sirtuin family, has been demonstrated to improve the capacity of hematopoietic stem cells to produce red and white blood cells in bone marrow (Brown et al., 2013). So it appears that at least three of the seven sirtuins are pro-longevity, or at least positive for healthy ageing. These are SIRT1, SIRT 3 and SIRT6.

As we said earlier, there are supplements for both NAD+ and resveratrol on the market. However, these are probably not sufficiently bio-absorbable, and it would be better for those inclined to wait for Life Biosciences's (see Key Opinion Leaders. Page 148) and others' products. NMN has yet to come onto the market.

Elysium, a private company in which Leonard Guarante is involved as Chief Scientist, promotes a product called Basis which is a combination of an NAD+ precursor with resveratrol. In exchange for shelling out US $480 for a year's supply, they claim they have a formulation which is more bioavailable than standard NAD+ and resveratrol supplementation. A bottle is delivered every month to buyers, and they suggest that in early tests in humans, NAD+ levels have been boosted by 40%.

The scientific advisory board of Elysium reads like a who's who of luminaries in the longevity space, including George M. Church, Professor of Genetics at Harvard, and James Kirkland, Professor of Aging at the Mayo Clinic.

We are confident that NMN and its follow-ons may prove to be the better compounds with genuine efficacy, but in the meantime, we suggest that there is little downside (if you have sufficient money) in subscribing to the Basis package (2 capsules a day) from Elysium. Elysium is likely to go public at some point and it has already raised US $20 million in venture capital. But its central proposition is scientifically somewhat dubious, and the whole enterprise has a touch of the snake oil to it. Having said that, Jim does admit to taking two Basis pills every day.

SENESCENT CELLS, SENOLYTIC DRUGS, CAVEOLIN I AND FIBROSIS IN AGEING

Cellular senescence is a major target for drug discovery in the new science of longevity. Companies such as Life Biosciences, Oisin and Unity Biotechnology are involved in attempting to find "senolytic" drugs that clear the body of harmful senescent cells. Cell senescence is when a cell doesn't remain healthily active, but it doesn't die through programmed cell death (apoptosis), trauma and injury (necrosis) or through pyroptosis, which is a central part of the immune system.

Senescence in cells is a sort of limbo-like state, positive in some ways but mostly negative. It has mostly been studied as an interruption of the normal cell cycle, when the Hayflick limit of divisions has been reached and telomere length has been exhausted. This is called replicative senescence.

Cells can also senesce because of DNA damage, which can occur in response to excess ROS, activation of oncogenes, as well as the presence of senescent neighbours. In these cases, cells are not aged, as the name "senescent" might suggest, but altered in ways that share many features. Whatever the route by which cells become senescent, they release harmful proteins called cytokines. These cytokines are cell signallers, which have important physiological roles but in the case of senescent cells mostly send the wrong signals, generating an unwanted immune response and causing havoc in surrounding cells and tissues.

This harmful release of cytokines is called the SASP, or "senescent-associated secretory phenotype", and it is the reason why it only takes a small number of senescent cells to do a great deal of damage. This damage is done in many ways. First, the SASP is pro-inflammatory, causing overexpression of immune responses, Second, it promotes tumour development in nearby cells. Senescent cells also, on the other hand, can positively affect the healing of wounds – but as a clear

Baker et al., Nature (2016). Left: normal aged mouse (equivalent to 75 human years), Right: Aged littermate, with senescent cells destroyed.

example of antagonistic pleiotropy, they play an evident role in ageing-associated diseases.

It is thought that senescence in cells has evolved to protect cells from becoming cancerous. This is one reason why increasing levels of telomerase in the body (see Telomeres. Page 200) is considered potentially dangerous; it might drive cells to become cancerous. If the cells with added telomerase become immortal, they could take on the characteristics of cancer cells, which are naturally immortal. Senescent cells are increasingly common in the ageing body.

In a nutshell, therefore, they are generally, though not exclusively, negative and the safe removal of at least some of them should add significantly to lifespan.

When progeroid mice, animals bred to display signs of accelerated ageing, have been treated to remove their senescent cells, they display greater resistance to the diseases of ageing.

But because of the positive aspects of senescence in cells in wound healing, the application of senolytic drugs has to be on a one-off or interval-based basis. It is also important that the administration of senolytics occurs in a supervised environment.

Judith Campisi of the The Buck Institute for Research for Aging near San Francisco, along with colleagues Baar, Brandt, Putavet et al. (*Cell* 2017), has shown that targeted apoptosis of senescent cells dramatically restores tissue homeostasis in mice experiencing the effects of chemotherapy, or in mice exhibiting the signs of ageing. She has used a FOXO4 peptide to achieve these results and it is this peptide that is now the basis of Unity Biotechnology's senolytic drug. (see Portfolios. Page 337).

It is now known that there is a clear link between senescent cells and certain specific diseases. Idiopathic pulmonary fibrosis (IPF) is one of them and this is a condition with a very poor prognosis. After diagnosis, patients typically live only about 3-5 years. IPF is characterised by shortness of breath, eventually leading to such badly impaired lung function that death becomes inevitable.

Life Biosciences, the company formed by David Sinclair and colleagues, has established a Spanish subsidiary which is involved in developing a senolytic drug with initial applications in fibrosis. Since tissues surrounded by senescent cells lose their power of regeneration, leading to the formation of scar tissues, it is thought that a one-time clearance of senescent cells will help people suffering from IPF. The Life Biosciences senolytic uses a novel system to deliver cytotoxic drugs to senescent cells, thereby eliminating them. If successful, the application could be extended to cardiac fibrosis, which leads to congestive heart failure, as well as to liver scarring, both age-associated diseases. Other diseases known to be associated with senescent cells include muscle wasting (sarcopenia), cataracts, and osteoporosis.

Another interesting avenue for reversing fibrosis, particularly in cardiac fibrosis, is the use of the peptide caveolin 1 scaffolding domain, (CSD), which in animal models has been shown to significantly improve heart function. Researchers have been aware for some time that excess collagen production in skin, heart and lung cells, which generates fibrotic tissue, is associated with a deficiency in caveolin 1. A reversal of fibrosis using the CSD peptide thus holds significant promise.

The removal of senescent cells in mice has generated some startling results. In the Mayo Clinic, Jan van Deursen has achieved a 20–25% increase in lifespan in his rodents by genetically engineering senescent cells to self-destruct when triggered. This increase in lifespan was done by one single treatment. James Kirkland, also of the Mayo Clinic, showed that senolytic drugs fed to normally ageing mice improved vascular activity, delayed frailty, and reversed osteoporosis.

Because senescent cells resist apoptosis, it's no surprise that they exhibit an upregulation of pro-survival pathways. These pro-survival traits are the weak link in such "limbo state" cells, and it is now known that by targeting these pathways, including those mediated by the genes Bcl-2, AKT, and p21, apoptosis can be induced. This has had the important effect of reducing the secretory effects of senescent cells on neighbouring tissues in animal models.

Unity Biotechnology, which has raised over US $150 million dollars from a variety of well-known biotech investors, is another company which is targeting senescent cells. In early trials in mice, its drug appears to delay cancer, to halt cardiac hypertrophy and to increase mouse life by an average of 30%. Ned (Nathaniel) David, the boss of Unity Biotechnology, is on record as saying (hyperbolically and probably unscientifically) that: "We think our drugs vaporize a third of human diseases in the developed world". Unity Biotechnology's drug, along with that of Life Biosciences, is not yet in the clinic, and the company, clearly destined for the public markets, maintains an Alphabet/Calico-like cloak of silence.

Additionally, it has been observed in animal models that the combination of two compounds, Dasatinib (a very expensive cancer drug) and quercetin (an anti-histamine and anti-inflammatory) can kill senescent cells. The mode of action in this combination takes the immune system's natural ability when youthful to recognise and to kill senescent cells, and seeks to rejuvenate this more robust immune response in older people.

Dasatinib appears to eliminate senescent human fat cell progenitors, while quercetin is more effective against senescent human endothelial (vessel lining) cells, as well as those in mouse bone marrow stem cells. This combination of the two has been found in some studies to be effective in restoring heart function in mice, as well as in improving overall body flexibility and performance.

Quercetin is a plant extract, found in many fruits and vegetables, including cranberries, plums, red onions and capers. Dasatinib is a cancer immunotherapy drug made by Bristol-Myers Squibb and currently used

to treat CML, a type of leukaemia. Quercetin on its own has no effect so it is the expensive combination that appears to have promise.

What is clear (Serrano, *Nature*, 2017 and Baar et al., *Cell*, 2016) is that senescent cells depend on the transcription factor FOXO4 for survival, a factor which points to the mechanisms that may be used to control them. Additionally, because inhibition of the BCL-2 protein seems to push senescent cells into apoptosis, this is a further area in which prototype senolytic drugs research is being directed.

In our view, this developing family of senolytic drugs is one of the most exciting features of longevity science. Apart from applications in diseases such as IPF, senolytics and gene-based interventions involving senescent cells, they could well have utility in the broader area of regenerative medicine. Clearing the body of senescent cells by forcing them to apoptose, using genetic engineering or by pharmaceutical methods, will probably help human lifespans as well as those of our friendly and much-burdened mice. What is more, these drugs and genetic techniques are closer to being proven as effective than many other anti-ageing techniques and compounds. The fact that large amounts of money are being poured into senolytic drug development is something of a validator of the technology. We are actively exploring ways of participating.

APOPTOSIS

Apoptosis is programmed cell death and it occurs in all multicellular organisms. The word is derived from the Greek for "falling off", as in leaves falling off trees, and the process of apoptosis involves a number of steps. These include blebbing (or bulges in the cellular membrane), the shrinking of the cell, chromatin compaction or condensation, and ultimately cellular death.

In adult bodies, 50–70 billion cells die every day and they typically die in a programmed way. Apoptosis contrasts with necrosis, which is cellular death due to injury. Necrosed cells can be dangerous because, unlike apoptosed cells, they are not quickly engulfed by phages that are primed to "eat" them. Apoptosis, whether caused intrinsically (that is because of cellular "suicide") or extrinsically (because of signalling from other cells), is normally highly choreographed.

In programmed death, cells recognised as potentially dangerous are "instructed" to kill themselves. These include ones that might become cancerous or ones that might "attack" the body (where they recognise "self" as threats, as in autoimmune reactions), as well as cells infected by viruses.

Caspases, a sub-family of proteases (protein-degrading proteins), act as executioners and signal the death of normal cells. Apoptosis is very important; where there is too little, cancer results, and cells grow in an unchecked way. Where there is too much apoptosis, atrophy or wasting results, because bodies end up with too few cells.

In 1986, Horvitz and Ellis found two death genes in the worm C. elegans which are necessary for apoptosis, and subsequently have uncovered the equivalent human genes. As a result of this discovery that apoptosis is genetically manipulated, researchers are looking at how apoptosis could be pharmacologically or genetically controlled. Any such treatments, if properly administered, could be useful in treating ageing-related diseases.

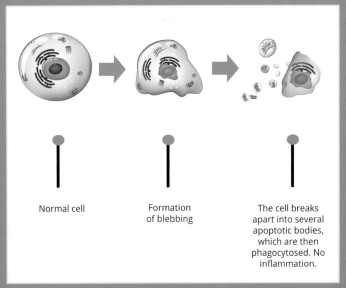

| Normal cell | Formation of blebbing | The cell breaks apart into several apoptotic bodies, which are then phagocytosed. No inflammation. |

Viruses, for instance, use a variety of strategies to stop cells which they have infected from committing suicide. Some will craftily make proteins to mimic the apoptotic pathway and use them to signal a halt to the cell suicide process. HIV, as an example, can block the pathway itself, stopping the cells from sacrificing themselves. This allows the viruses to keep on replicating.

The viral evasion or blockade of apoptosis is giving scientists an interesting insight into the process of apoptosis. If cell death could be better controlled, it could lead to interesting longevity strategies. There are studies underway to see if HIV retroviral drugs might have some effect on longevity.

APOPTOSIS

In youth, the enzyme telomerase comes to the rescue when cells are damaged and extends telomeres to normal length in the course of repair but as people get older they produce less telomerase. This telomere "exhaustion" forms the basis of replicative senescence, otherwise known as the Hayflick Limit (Hayflick and Moorhead, 1961). This limit describes the finite proliferative capacity of some types of cells in laboratory conditions. The limit is thought to be somewhere around 40–60 divisions (see Hayflick Limit. Page 162).

Jim with Elizabeth Blackburn.

SHORTER TELOMERES – SHORTER LIFE?

Elizabeth Blackburn is President of the Salk Institute in San Diego and has won a Nobel Prize for her work on telomeres. We have met her in the course of our research and her book *The Telomere Effect* is well worth reading. She did not discover telomeres, but she has worked out what they do, described in papers presented in the 1970s and 1980s, as well as in subsequent research which continues today.

She suggests that telomeres are like plastic caps at the end of shoelaces, and that when they fray or shorten, this is bad for our health. Telomeres are what she calls the "aglets" at the end of our chromosomes. Telomeres are repeated sequences, and they tend to shorten in dividing cells, leaving older people with shorter versions than in younger people.

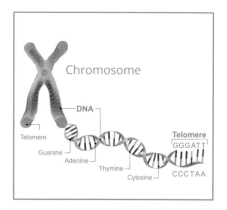

In other mammalian species, however, short-lived creatures can and do have longer telomeres than those of longer-lived creatures like humans, making the role of telomeres in influencing ageing a confusing one.

Blackburn, however, has convincingly demonstrated that telomeres are particularly prone to age-related deterioration even if they don't necessarily cause ageing by themselves. Furthermore, it is known that cancer cells reconstruct telomeres, facilitating the unchecked cell division that is the hallmark of the disease. And looking at how cancer does this is an important window on how telomeres operate.

In her initial studies, Blackburn used *Tetrahymena thermophila,* a pond-dwelling organism, as her "model". This creature has 20,000 chromosomes, instead of the 46 that humans have, making them exceptionally fertile ground for research into telomere maintenance. Today, Blackburn is researching how telomeres and the enzyme telomerase, which is the chemical basis of the aglets, might be used as therapies for breast, bladder and prostate cancers. There are drugs currently in development to promote the restoration of telomeres. A naturally-derived telomerase activator, TA-65, is already on the market, and is being studied to see if it reduces the number of senescent cells in patients. TA-65 appears to increase telomerase levels in mouse tissue, but does not have any effect on lifespan. Indeed, mice with a shortage of telomerase do not live shorter lives than wild-type mice.

The other factors that make many scientists sceptical about the restoration of telomeres in humans is that many cells do not divide (i.e. neuronal and heart cells) and so do not normally experience telomere shortening. Therefore, therapies involving the restoration of telomeres to the body will have no effect on those particular cells. Additionally, the oncogenic effect of telomerase is a worry – what if infusions of telomerase end up causing cancer.

GROWTH HORMONE RELEASING – HORMONE (GHRH)

Restoring GH levels in older individuals with adult growth hormone deficiency (AGHD) has been pedelled as a way of causing general rejuvenation of tissues. The purported effects of GH include improved body mass index (or, more informatively, changing fat to muscle ratio), skin tone and organ health. And this discovery has inspired widespread use of growth hormone in the anti-ageing and athletic communities. However, abuse of GH has revealed sinister side effects. These side effects, together with ambiguous observational evidence of any improvement in longevity, have reduced interest in GH as an anti-ageing therapy. Endogenous (e.g. in the body) production of GH by stimulating GHRH, however, might be the answer, as such production addresses the side effects of GH while amplifying the benefits.

The hypothalamic hormone GHRH stimulates synthesis and production of GH from the anterior pituitary.

John Mauldin, Patrick Cox and Jim.

from multiple species including mice, rats, dogs, pigs, horses, and cattle. Indeed, GHRH enhancement using DNA vaccines is approved for farm agricultural animals in Australia and elsewhere.

Using these vaccines only involves relatively few cells in the production of GHRH because the hormone impacts GH production at extremely low levels of GHRH (circa 100 pg/mL) in the blood. Moreover, this endogenous production of GH takes place within the overall normal biological regulatory axis. Unlike exogenous administration of GH (by injection or any other method), GHRH manufactured within the body produces no measurable spikes of GH blood levels. Most importantly, the GH produced is controlled by the normal endocrine feedback regulation inherent within the GHRH axis, so that normal hormone production remains in homeostatic balance.

Furthermore, the use of GHRH for the enhancement or restoration of growth for rejuvenation purposes has been extensively researched, generating considerable scientific and pharmaceutical interest. Though virtually no adverse events have been linked to GHRH, (unlike growth hormone on its own), it is not widely used because it is very expensive and short-acting. With a half-life in serum of only six to seven minutes, GHRH would have to be injected frequently to produce significant benefits.

The solution is thus to genetically engineer cells that produce endogenous GHRH. This can be accomplished by the implantation of cells genetically engineered to express GHRH or by the introduction of GHRH-producing plasmids via DNA vaccines. The latter delivery system has been utilised in tens of thousands of animals

GH and IGF-1 levels increase proportionally to the GHRH dose. Consequently, treated animals exhibit no short- or long-term systemic adverse effects that might otherwise accompany exogenous GH therapy. These side effects include cardiac hypertrophy (enlarged heart), insulin resistance, enlarged organs (organomegaly), and acromegaly, which is a disease specifically caused by excessive growth hormone. This is characterised by enlargement of the forehead, jaw and nose. Sufferers of abuse of growth hormones also have high blood pressure, joint pain, and diabetes.

But with the endogenous production of GHRH, there seem to be no notable side effects. Animal studies of plasmid-based GHRH delivery have demonstrated reversal of cancer-induced anaemia and cachexia. Survival rates of treated animals compared to untreated animals improve, as do lessening of disease incidence, acuity, activity level, fertility, immune system function, and exercise tolerance. Animals which receive a single treatment benefit for more than a year. The cost of a cell-based or DNA vaccine-based GHRH therapy would be significantly lower than the cost of a regularly ingested drug and the significant labour involved in numerous daily administrations.

This view stands in contrast with other opinions in that animal model studies clearly point to GH/IGF-1/TOR as promoting ageing. Mice with knockdown of the GH receptor (the mutant is called the "little" mouse) are long-lived. Mice with GH deficiency or insensitivity are long-lived, and GH-insensitive humans (in Ecuador) show resistance to some diseases of ageing.

The text for this section was kindly provided by Patrick Cox, Editor, Mauldin Economics' Transformational Technology Alert.

HORMONES – FEELING FRISKY

The industry of hormone supplementation and replacement is large. It is at least a billion dollars a year in the US, and much larger if "natural" products are included.

Hormones have been used in anti-ageing for a long time, and their administration has very mixed blessings. Hormones are chemicals produced in our bodies and they regulate the behaviour of our organs and as well as many cells. Hormones are produced by specific glands, notably the thyroid, adrenal glands, the hypothalamus, the ovaries, testes, and the pituitary gland.

Many different hormones, about 50 in total, are produced by our bodies, including GH, adrenocorticotrophic hormone, insulin, oestrogen, testosterone, progesterone, and adrenaline. The glands producing hormones, together with the hormones themselves, are collectively known as the endocrine system.

Replacing hormones is a well-trodden but controversial anti-ageing strategy. Levels of hormones decline in both men and women with age, so the idea of replacing "lost" hormones has an obvious allure. And in one or two cases, the strategy makes sense. Apart from oestrogen replacement **(hormone replacement therapy or HRT)** for women, and testosterone replacement for men, the biggest hormonal markets are insulin for diabetics (the biggest market of all, and of course a lifesaving one) as well as the much more dubious administration of GH for athletes and bodybuilders.

This latter one, GH, is administered to stimulate the production of IGF-1 as well as of DHEA (dehydroepiandrosterone), a precursor of oestrogen and of testosterone. A *New England Journal of Medicine* study dating back to 1990 studied the injection of HGH in 12 men over 60, where the men experienced modest weight loss and improved muscle mass and bone density. From that point onwards, despite the small scale of the study and evidence of problems with some of the men on follow-up, a myth has emerged that GH is a good thing. But it probably isn't.

Administering GH is illegal if a patient doesn't have abnormally low levels of the hormone. However, this is subjective, and that's why there are plenty of fly-by-night clinics willing to prescribe the treatment, possibly causing serious problems for their gullible patients at some time in the future. GH administration exogenously (i.e. from outside the body) seems to us to be a dangerous practice. It may well lead to cancer and/or cardiovascular disease and indeed, it appears that people who

live exceptionally long lives have low IGF-1 levels. It is clear that the risks of GH seriously outweigh any benefits. Don't do it!

The use of hormones in anti-ageing strategies is the subject of much debate and study. It does appear that HRT (hormone replacement therapy) in menopausal and perimenopausal women is, on balance, positive. As 80% of women are postmenopausal by the age of 54, there is a huge medical need to counteract the symptoms associated with "the change".

The administration of oestrogen and progesterone can relieve the symptoms of menopause, including vaginal atrophy, and improve the quality of life. Oestrogen supplementation also slows bone loss and lowers colon cancer risk.

However, the Women's Health Initiative study of 2002 demonstrated that HRT increased the risk of breast cancer, stroke and cardiovascular disease. On the plus side, lower bone fracture rates are observed with the use of HRT, and overall quality of life was reported to be significantly improved.

Prescriptions of HRT which had peaked at about 90 million a year in the US, covering about 15 million women, fell sharply after the Woman's Health Initiative study and have remained subdued ever since. Women have been turning

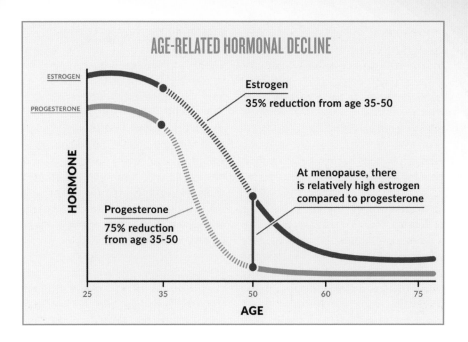

AGE-RELATED HORMONAL DECLINE

ESTROGEN

PROGESTERONE

HORMONE

Estrogen
35% reduction from age 35-50

At menopause, there
is relatively high estrogen
compared to progesterone

Progesterone
75% reduction
from age 35-50

25   35   50   60   75

AGE

to so-called bio-identicals, derived mostly from plants, which are less potent analogs of hormones. These include oestradiol and bioidentical progesterone. Oestradiol appears to boost the immune system.

There are over 50 different combinations and types of HRT currently on sale. The market for safe hormonal replacements for women in later life is large; this is because women spend at least one-third of their lives being hormonally deficient.

In both sexes, production of DHEA (dehydroepiandrosterone) declines with age, and because DHEA is important in steroid production, it is

thought that DHEA supplementation may actually be positive.

Additionally, in both sexes, insulin-growth factor 1 (IGF-1) declines with age. The progressive loss of IGF-1 and DHEA results in muscle wasting, mood swings, cognitive dysfunction and lower libido. Skin ageing occurs, as does bone loss. The main purpose of the skin, our largest organ, is to provide a physical protective barrier. It also regulates the immune system and temperature.

Mostly specific to men, testosterone supplementation has been used for many years. This has the effect of making men feel better, of boosting libido, and of improving strength. It is used as a sort of mid-life therapy for men, much as HRT is for women, although some younger men also need additional testosterone. The most commonly used testosterone preparations are topical gels. There are two main brands: AndroGel and Testim. Testosterone in pill form is known to cause liver toxicity.

Testosterone is generic and is profitable for drug companies, but it is not a path to great riches for investors. Men suffer testosterone loss at a rate of about 1% per year from their forties onwards, and eventually hypogonadism ("hypo" meaning low) sets in. About 40% of men above 45 suffer from hypogonadism to varying degrees. There are concerns, however, that testosterone supplementation may increase the risk of cardiovascular disease and prostate cancer.

The latter risk has not been confirmed by recent studies, and should therefore not (yet!) be considered a significant problem for the administration of the testosterone hormone. About 500,000 men have been studied around the world to look for a link between testosterone and prostate cancer, and at worst there is only a very weak correlation. Undoubtedly, however, anyone with heart failure or cardiac issues absolutely must not be taking testosterone supplements.

STEMMING THE TIDE OF AGEING

Stem cells are becoming an increasingly important part of anti-ageing research and their use will surely help to turn back the senescence clock. Furthermore, stem cells will be available for this purpose within a relatively short period of time. In our opinion, stem cell replacement or replenishment will play a vital role in extending lifespan, and animal models provide clear pointers to this outcome.

Stem cells are the ancestors of all cells, and sit at the foundation of the tree-like depiction of life that scientists like to use.

We believe that the initial application of stem cells will be in restoring damaged cardiac function (something that is already happening); repairing spinal cord damage; restoring mobility to those with damaged cartilage; and treating type 1 diabetes. Progeric mice (those with an induced disease that causes premature ageing) lived 30% longer in a study into stem cell replenishment led by Professor Juan Carlos Belmonte of the Salk Institute in the US. He and his team recently reprogrammed stem cells using the **Yamanaka transcription factors,** described below, and the longer-lived mice did not, as in previous experiments, develop cancers. This, along with multiple other animal studies, suggests that stem cells will quickly come to play an important role in anti-ageing strategies.

The single most important cell for all of us is a type of stem cell; it is the single, fertilised **zygote** from which we, and all our trillions of cells, are formed. This zygote is known as a totipotent cell, because it can produce every kind of cell. After a few days, the zygote divides into multiple cells, and becomes what is known as a blastocyst.

This blastocyst consists of an array of stem cells, which over time divide into the approximately 200 different types of cells in our bodies. After the blastocyst stage, stem cells divide into embryonic (or pluripotent) cells, and thereafter adult (or multipotent) cells.

Embryonic stem cells can be found in umbilical cord blood, and many people are banking the cord blood of their babies in the hopeful expectation that this blood, rich in stem cells, might be useful in later life, though in practice this is rarely the case. Indeed, the American Academy of Pediatrics warns that the odds of using one's own banked cord blood sometime in the future is 1 in 200,000, while the Institute of Medicine says that only a few such procedures have ever been performed using a patient's own cord blood – and not always successfully.

However, over the past two decades, more than 20,000 patients have received blood factors from donated umbilical cords, and about 3 million units of cord blood have been banked in over 500 repositories worldwide. The procedure is particularly popular in Asia; for instance, 25% of all babies born in Singapore have their cord blood stored, and in China, which boasts of a NYSE-listed company (China Cord Blood Corp) specialising in cord blood banking, about 3% of newborn babies have their blood stored. This company has over half a million subscribers, who pay an upfront fee, then an annual fee (of about US \$130) for 18 years. One of the problems with cord blood stored by the parents' babies for later use is that at least twice the volume of initially harvested cord blood is needed for a successful transplant into a grown adult. Nonetheless, it is possible that cord blood could be synthetically induced or amplified in the future. The jury is out on this one.

Adults have stem cells and progenitor cells (which produce only one type of cell, or a few) and these together act as important repair systems for tissues. Their numbers, as with so much else in the body, decline with age.

This age-related reduction is important because as these adult stem and progenitor cells get damaged and become less effective, tissue is not as easily replaceable as it once was. If adult stem cells could be somehow rejuvenated or their numbers amplified, heart tissue (as an example) might be more successfully repaired after a cardiac arrest or in the context of congestive heart failure. In addition, it is possible that the islet beta cells which are lacking in type 1 diabetics could be replaced, arthritis could be warded off by replenished cartilage, and tissue and bone density could be restored.

This is the marvellous promise of stem cells, and it is a mighty promise. Sadly, however, it is also a promise made by charlatans, some of whom operate fly-by-night clinics offering the gullible "curative" or miracle injections of stem cells. The problem with stem cells is that they can cause cancer when misused, and that the wrong administration can be fatal or have hugely damaging health consequences.

However, science is catching up with hope in the stem cell field and there are now really good reasons to be optimistic. Today, about 85 diseases or conditions are being treated with stem cells, up from only 27 in 2005.

A type of stem cell that is currently the focus of much late-stage research is **mesenchymal stem cells** (MSCs), ones which can differentiate into a variety of cell types such as osteoblasts (bone), chondrocytes (cartilage) and adipocytes (fat cells). When the number of chondrocytes declines, as an example, the ability to repair cartilage falls, and when osteoblast numbers decline, bone formation suffers. So, if these could be replaced, bones could successfully regrow, and cartilage could be replenished. Additionally, adipocytes will possibly be used to treat victims of type 1 diabetes, as they have been shown to replenish the beta cells in the pancreas that are destroyed by the disease.

Recently, scientists at Edinburgh University have demonstrated that it is possible to actually reverse the ageing of adult MSCs, using a pluripotency-associated transcription factor, NANOG (discovered by James Thompson, of the University of Wisconsin, with whom Jim has met in the past). This factor reverses the age of an MSC cell back to that of a newborn baby. MSCs are donated by people other than the intended recipient, ideally by younger donors.

If scientists could work out a way to reverse the age of harvested MSC cells post-harvesting, then the pool of potential stem cell donors could be vastly widened, beyond just the young and the vigorous.

Another and very important type of adult stem cell is **haematopoietic stem cells** (HSC). These are derived from mesodermal haemangioblast cells, which are able to differentiate into either HSCs or endothelial (blood vessel lining) cells. HSCs are responsible for the production of all of our blood cells, and they can be found in bone marrow, peripheral blood, umbilical cords and (it has also been recently discovered) in the lungs.

HSCs are vitally involved in blood oxygenation, in stemming bleeding, and in our immune system. HSCs are vital to health, and therapies involving them are evolving rapidly. These therapies involving HSCs go by the name of haematopoiesis stem and progenitor cell gene therapy (HSPC-GT) and an earlier variant of this treatment, involving the transplantation of healthy HSCs into a "cleaned" system (where the bone marrow is depleted of existing stem cells by using chemotherapy) is now a well-established therapy.

Several rare diseases are the direct result of defective HSCs, because defects in these cells can cause pathologies as diverse as leukaemia or multiple sclerosis. Replacing defective HSCs, using transplantation of fresh cells into the bone marrow, is now a standard treatment for leukaemia, and indeed has been for 50 years. These transplants have taken place many thousands of times, particularly in people with life-threatening blood cancer, but also for people with hereditary lysosomal storage disorders.

HSPC-GT is now emerging as a new type of stem cell therapy, where HSCs produced by donors are manipulated by genetic engineering to produce HSPCs, which are then administered in a "one-off" fashion to a patient, to produce healthy blood cells – and these last a very long time once administered.

The first regulatory approval for a HSPC-GT took place in Europe in 2016 for a procedure called Strimvelis, developed by GlaxoSmithKline and by an Italian research institute. This therapy is designed for a rare condition called ADA-SCID (Severe Combined Immunodeficiency due to Adenosine Deaminase deficiency – a.k.a. "bubble boy" syndrome), where children are unable to produce lymphocytes and therefore can't fight infections. Other companies and institutions developing HSPC-GT treatments include Genethon (an institution), BlueBird Bio (a public company in the US) and Orchard Therapeutics (private). Initially, these treatments are likely to be extremely expensive, but the potential for wider applications and lower costs is absolutely apparent.

Overall, stem cell therapy has advanced considerably since we published *Cracking the Code* in 2012. It is now known, for instance, that stem cells can be used to regenerate tissue in the victims of heart attacks. In the case of cardiac infarction, typically a quarter of all the heart cells in the left ventricle, which is the most important chamber of the heart, die due to oxygen starvation. This, plus the subsequent growth of scar tissue, means that the heart thereafter performs sub-optimally. Even if the victim survives, the chance of another attack is high. The injection of stem cells into the heart can help to regrow healthy tissue, and a large-scale trial is underway. This European BAMI clinical trial, involving 3,000 patients, is one where bone marrow-derived stem cells are reinfused into the heart. The study began in 2014, and is expected to report its results in 2018.

It is known that some animals can spontaneously regrow heart tissue, with the catalysts for this being what are known as endothelial progenitor cells. The application of these in a human heart regenerative medicine is now a major focus of research.

Additionally, considerable work is going into the use of stem cells to regenerate pancreatic beta cells, by using precursor cells and transplanting them into in the islets of Langerhans, the part of the pancreas where insulin is produced. This is an intriguing effort to generate a treatment for type 1 diabetics, where not much is available for patients other than insulin. The problem here is how to overcome auto-immune reactions to the transplanted cells, and in this regard, a variety of techniques are being explored.

As we age, adaptive immune cells (see Inflammaging. Page 60) are produced in smaller numbers because haematopoiesis (the ability of the bone marrow to create new cells) declines and because the thymus withers away. This is called immunosenescence and leads to: a reduction in the body's ability to fight infection: to anaemia; and an increase in blood cancers. The decline in our stem cells' potency and quantity is replicated in all areas of the body where stem cell "pockets" (or "nests") exist. Specific areas where this depletion occurs include the bones, the muscles, and the brain, where there are two "nests".

With age, HSCs divide more slowly (Rossi et al., 2012), and this is probably because of the accumulation of DNA damage and an overexpression of certain proteins (especially Ink4a), all of which inhibit cell-cycle division. Additionally, the shortening of telomeres doesn't help. The use of exogenously administered stem cells to boost stem cell reservoirs is being investigated as a way of reversing the effect of this depletion.

Stem cells derived from bone marrow, white adipose tissues, umbilical cord blood, the pancreas, as well as MSCs, hepatocyte cells, and neural stem cells, are all being trialled in humans as we write this book. The objectives of these trials are, broadly speaking, to effect changes in specific diseases or injuries. Trials are being undertaken for liver disease, lupus, spinal injury, heart failure, diabetes, palsy, Huntington's, Alzheimer's, Parkinson's,

Professor Shinya Yamanaka

force cells that have already been differentiated (i.e. into for instance, skin, hair or blood cells), back into "induced pluripotent stem cells" (iPSCs) that are almost exactly equivalent to embryonic stem cells. Furthermore, once regressed into iPSCs, these stem cells can be made to differentiate into specialised cells of any type once again. So, for example, a heart attack victim can have his or her own skin cells extracted, manipulated into iPSCs, and then differentiated back into transplantable heart progenitor cells. Naturally-occurring embryonic cells are pluripotent and are the progenitors of all of our cells. The induced embryonic stem cells discovered by Professor Yamanaka are what results from the use of the combination of the four factors bearing his name.

familial hypercholesterolemia, multiple sclerosis, Crohn's, amyotrophic lateral sclerosis (ALS or Lou Gehrig's disease), rheumatoid arthritis – and the list goes on.

In the field of stem cell studies, the absolutely biggest breakthrough so far took place over a decade ago, but it is only now that it is being widely used. Shinya Yamanaka of Kyoto University in Japan, now a hugely deserving Nobel Prize Laureate, discovered what are now known as the Yamanaka factors.

These are the transcription factors (factors which turn DNA into RNA) OCT4, SOX2, KLF4, and c-Myc. Each one is a protein which when combined

However, as is often the case with an early version of a breakthrough technology, there are problems. Merkle et al. (*Nature*, 2017) have shown that pluripotent cells cultured in vitro, derived from human embryonic stem cells (hESCs), are liable to develop mutations in the gene TP53, leading to cancer, so very careful screening is required.

Scientists now aspire to create pharmacological compounds to replicate and amplify the actions of these four transcription factors, thereby rejuvenating cells without the associated mutational side effects.

A Chinese team, Huangfu et al, have investigated histone deacetylase (HDAC) inhibitors, notably valproic acid (normally used in epilepsy), and initial results suggest a 100-fold increase in the reprogramming efficiency of cells compared to the Yamanaka factors alone. HDAC inhibitors prevent histones from losing their **acetyl** groups, thereby restoring the transcription of tumour suppressors.

Additionally, iPSC cell production is now being improved by using recombinant viruses, new forms of vectors (delivery systems) and liposomes, as well as new chemical agents, all to improve on the Yamanaka factors acting in isolation.

It is important, however that any use of Yamanaka factors and derivatives to revert normal cells to a stem-like status is not prolonged. Nasty teratomas, or jumbles of tissues, teeth, bone and hair, as well as other tumours, can result if the treatment is more than transitory.

Infusing Yamanaka factors as a whole-body treatment has proved disastrous in animal models. Attempts to do this in 2013 and 2014 resulted in the deaths of all of the animals, either because the cells had lost their "identities" or because of cancers. Since embryonic cells are primed for rapid growth, too much of a good thing can, and does, have adverse consequences.

So, scientists are now using highly precise and targeted exposure to Yamanaka factors, and "pulses" – with some success. The eyesight of an elderly woman in Japan has recently been improved using retinal pigment epithelial cells, derived from induced pluripotent cells. Yamanaka and his colleague Mandai treated the woman with this type of cell to attempt to stabilise her age related macular degeneration (AMD), and since then, the "brightness" of her vision has improved and has remained stable for a number of years.

Yamanaka has opened the door to a highly promising cell therapy, one which is being continuously refined. Subsequently, Alejandro Ocampo and colleagues at the Salk Institute have found a way to only partially reprogramme cells by successfully inducing undifferentiated cells, which are not yet full induced pluripotent stem cells (iPCS). This involves a transient, very brief, exposure to the four Yamanaka transcription factors. They have created cells of a "plastic" progenitor nature, and subsequently used these to create healthy cells which, when infused, successfully integrate into tissue architecture, therefore restoring its vitality.

It is interesting to note that stem cells which are "autologous", i.e. from the patient's own body, are associated with lower levels of rejection than "donated" or allogeneic stem cells. But even autologous cells can carry risks. Relatively recently autologous haematopoietic cells which were injected into a patient with kidney disease resulted in death, and similarly three patients injected in the retina with adipose-derived autologous stem cells resulted in partial or total loss of vision.

The science of stem cells is certainly becoming more accurate and successful, but there are still multiple areas in which the full consequences of stem cell transplantation are not fully understood. That having been said, successes are fast outnumbering failures. For instance, several patients have been treated by scientists at the University of Pittsburgh with their own thigh-derived stem cells, which were then used to grow muscle cells, and reinjected into the bladder. The result was a reversal of the urinary incontinence blighting the lives of these patients. This particular technology is being developed by a private company, CookMyoSite, a subsidiary of Cook Medical of the US.

In addition, the ubiquitous Professor Yamanaka, as well as other scientists, is currently focused on creating off-the-shelf stem cell treatments, using iPSCs from donated cells. Off-the-shelf stem cells avoid the costly and time-consuming analysis of a patient's own cells. Using standardised cell lines would dramatically cut the cost and the time to successfully use stem cells in patients. Yamanaka's team is looking at Parkinson's disease as a target for these off-the-shelf cells, and will be using them to deliver new dopamine-producing cells into patients. There are over 10 million people worldwide who suffer from Parkinson's, the key characteristic of which is the loss of dopaminergic neuronal cells.

Because it is now more or less established that a major contributor to ageing is epigenetic change, the possibility of using the Yamanaka factors (or easier-to-handle alternative chemicals) to reprogramme cells could be of benefit even to centenarians, according to Ocampo.

But, in the short-term, the most exciting use of stem cells is the prevention of death in heart attacks and in congestive heart failure. This is not only because heart disease is still the number one killer in the developed world, but also because stem cell trials have already shown great promise in treating patients with heart issues. For instance, the Heart Cells Foundation in the UK is now funding the treatment of heart attack victims in St Bartholomew's Hospital, London using the patients' own bone marrow-derived stem cells. Hundreds of patients have been thus treated in the past decade, and with generally positive results.

A private company named OxStem, spun out of the University of Oxford, has recently raised US $21 million to pursue research around stem cells. The view of its founder is that injecting stem cells is not an efficient way of treating patients. He points out that most injected stem cells are flushed out of the body, or act to regenerate other cells rather than being particularly useful in themselves. So, OxStem is developing small-molecule drugs to actually regulate stem cells in the body, but little is known about the exact way in which it is going about this.

An Australian public company named Mesoblast, although previously consistently disappointing in its performance, is now seemingly set for success. The company is engaged in late-stage trials using MSCs for the treatment of cardiac patients. Mesoblast's products are "off-the-shelf" mesenchymal stem cells, and the company uses cells from young donors, then expands their number, and in this way can theoretically treat multiple unrelated recipients without negative immune effects which occur with other forms of stem cell infusion. MPC-150-IM is a late Phase 3 product candidate being developed as a treatment for both advanced and end-stage chronic heart failure (CHF) and recently cleared an important regulatory hurdle.

This disease is expected to affect over eight million Americans by 2030 and has a very poor prognosis. It involves insufficient blood flow to the main organs and extremities. Mesoblast's product for CHF consists of 150 million MSCs being directly injected into the heart muscle to introduce factors which are designed to reactivate cardiac function. The idea is to reverse scarring and fibrosis and to induce vascular network regrowth. The treatment is currently being trialled on 600 patients in a late-stage study in North America, and Mesoblast is also developing stem cell therapies for rheumatoid arthritis and for diabetes, amongst other conditions.

A recent spinoff from BioTime, a US-listed company which is based in California and headed by Mike West (whom we have met), is AgeX. This company owns a large number of stem cell patents aimed at conditions such as cardiovascular disease and diabetes. The ultimate goal of AgeX, which will probably be public by the end of 2017, is to reverse ageing. AgeX is also working on what it calls induced tissue regeneration (ITR), and we are investors. The following is a short transcript below from a presentation given by Mike West at the World Stem Cell Summit in 2016:

"We don't talk much about it, but we're working on something now that I think will be massive – I call it "induced tissue regeneration." Just as you can induce pluripotency by adding specific gene products to a cell, I believe you can induce an adult cell or tissue to regenerate. Everyone knows that some animals, like salamanders, can regenerate whole limbs. It seems obvious that the mechanisms of regeneration in these animals are the same mechanisms that form the tissue in the first place – they just never turn it off. Human embryos also have the ability to regenerate to some extent – for example, prior to eight weeks of gestation, human skin has scar-less wound repair. Once embryogenesis is complete, these pathways get turned off and scar tissue is formed whenever certain tissues and organs are damaged. We believe that the genes that control tissue regeneration can be identified and used therapeutically to reintroduce the regenerative potential that exists during development. To that end, we announced a collaboration with Inilico Medicine to use artificial intelligence to analyze large amounts of transcriptomics data to compare early embryonic development with adult cells and tissues. I think the impact of induced tissue regeneration on medicine will be even more powerful than the stem cell approach, because it exploits an intrinsic ability of the body."

There are two further promising areas for research in stem cells as they apply to ageing. The first is that it now appears that the FOXO (forkhead) family of transcription factors plays an important role in tissue homeostasis and in stem cell biology. For instance, FOXO1 controls two factors critical to maintaining stem cell health.

FOXO1 is necessary for maintaining pluripotency in embryonic stem cells, and it appears that the administration of the antioxidant N-acetylcysteine upregulates stem cells and downregulates ROS or free radicals - and so N-acetylcysteine is added to our list of compounds which we think are worth considering in the battle against ageing.

The second is that it has recently been discovered that blood stem cells are produced in quantity – more than ten million platelets an hour, about half of which is produced in the lungs of mice, and probably, therefore, in human lungs also. Thus, if bone marrow cells are depleted, it might be possible that the lungs, acting as a kind of bioreactor, could be induced to produce blood cells instead. This is a recent discovery, but adds to the excitement now building around stem cells as a legitimate part of longevity science.

AGEX THERAPEUTICS, INC.

AgeX Therapeutics, Inc. is a biotechnology company formed in 2017 as a subsidiary of BioTime, Inc (NYSE MKT: BTX). Its mission is to apply technology related to cell immortality and pluripotency to human ageing and to age-related diseases. The company's technology platform has three facets: Pluripotent stem cell-derived progenitor cell lines representing over 200 types of cells in the body (PureStem technology); HyStem matrices, and induced tissue regeneration (iTR), the latter being an emerging technology directed at inducing the immortal regeneration of tissues in the body.

The history of the AgeX technology can be traced back to Geron Corporation (NASDAQ: GERN). AgeX's CEO Michael D. West, Ph.D. founded Geron in 1990 and this was at the time the most visible public company in ageing biotechnology. At Geron, Dr West led efforts in two highly significant advances. The first was the isolation of the telomerase gene. His team was able to demonstrate that telomerase could immortalize diverse human cell types that would otherwise age due to the Hayflick phenomenon. In addition, this telomerase gene is implicated in approximately 90% of cancer types and is therefore important in cancer therapy. The second area Dr West led while at Geron was the first isolation of pluripotent stem cells. Unlike the cells in the body that have finite lives, pluripotent stem cells never age due to the permanent presence of telomerase, Additionally, they provide a means for the first time in the history of medicine to manufacture young cells of any type in the body and on an industrial scale.

Via BioTime, AgeX has licenses to a consolidated technology estate of over 500 patents and patent applications worldwide, including the technologies Dr West invented at Geron and at his subsequent companies.

AgeX is starting off with cell-based regenerative therapeutics for significant unmet needs in age-related disease. These include type 2

diabetes using a manufactured brown adipocyte product (AGEX-BAT1), as well as cardiac ischemic disease using a young vascular progenitor cell product (AGEX-VASC1). In addition, AgeX will also be advancing an entirely new technology platform aimed at the central molecular processes of ageing itself designated "induced Tissue Regeneration (iTR)."

AgeX scientists believe that the combination of telomerase therapy and iTR may unlock the potential of immortal tissue regeneration in humans. Model organisms exist that display immortal tissue regeneration and display no evidence of ageing.

AgeX scientists believe that interventions that marginally extend healthspan in model organisms – such as dietary restriction, or modulation of sirtuin and mTOR pathways – may operate through partially increasing the body's ability to regenerate. Therefore, the direct modulation of iTR pathways may more profoundly impact the biology of ageing than interventions in the more downstream biology of sirtuins and mTOR.

Initial planned milestones for AgeX will be the completion of animal preclinical studies for AGEX-BAT1 and AGEX-VASC1, and the probable registration of shares and distribution of shares to BioTime shareholders, which will allow AgeX to trade separately on a national market. The combination of pluripotent stem cell and iTR technology provides AgeX with a highly differentiated and valuable platform to address large markets associated with chronic degenerative age-related disease. We like this company and will be highlighting its development in our blogs. We have invested a significant amount in AgeX.

AGEX THERAPEUTICS, INC

MITOCHONDRIAL UNCOUPLING AND BROWN ADIPOSE TISSUE (BAT) – NEW DRUGS AND THERAPIES ARE COMING

The mitochondria, and their gradual degradation, are key factors in ageing. Mitochondria, the fuel cells of our bodies, control metabolism and regulate the balance between nutrient inflow and energy output, as well as stopping ROS from doing too much damage. They are responsible for what is known as cellular respiration, and are present in most cells, though not in all of them. When the mitochondria start to lose efficiency with age, this has negative implications, and so mitochondrial dysfunction is a consequence of ageing.

Mitochondrial uncoupling is a phenomenon where the extraction of energy from nutrients into ATP, the cell's energy store, is not fully accomplished. Mitochondrial uncoupling is a natural process and is one system for limiting the production of free radicals. Now it can also be counted as a process which is useful in delaying cellular senescence (Papa and Skulachev, 1997; Brand, 2000).

The reduction in ROS and in the production of excess heat when mitochondrial uncoupling occurs is accomplished while at the same time keeping ATP production at viable levels. In a way, it's a bit like letting steam off in a pressure cooker, where the steam represents excess energy. This is done by activation of what is known as an uncoupling protein, named UCP1.

There are other specific uncoupling proteins, but the first to be identified was UCP1 (uncoupling protein 1) and this controls what is known as non-shivering thermogenesis. This is where the body produces excess heat, even when the body is not cold. Subsequently four other proteins were discovered in the "uncoupling" family, imaginatively named as UCP2, 3, 4 and 5. The functions of UCP2-5 are not well understood, but UCP2 and 3, along with UCP1, appear to be involved in limiting free radicals. The tissue where this non-shivering thermogenesis was first observed was in brown adipose tissue (BAT), but it is also present in the thymus (Adams et al., 2008).

Mitochondrial uncouplers are therefore proteins which act to separate oxidation from the process of ADP phosphorylation (the precursor to making ATP is ADP; phosphorylation is the metabolic process whereby ATP is produced by the transfer of a phosphoryl group (PO_3) to ADP). As a result of mitochondrial uncoupling, energy that has been released from nutrients is converted to heat rather than to ATP, and this can absorb as much as 30% of our baseline energy use – otherwise known as metabolic rate.

Mitochondrial uncoupling can thus be thought to be equivalent in some ways to caloric restriction, and mitochondrial uncoupling drugs work in a way similar to CR. And indeed, mitochondrial uncoupling can now be induced by drugs, and as a result this is a really exciting area of research. It appears that mitochondrial uncoupling does indeed promote a longer lifespan, both because of the reduction in ROS damage and because of the benefits of pharmacologically-induced dietary restriction.

Previous attempts to make mitochondrial uncoupling drugs failed because of toxicity, most notably with a compound popular with dieters in the 1930s. This was dinitrophenol (DNP), a chemical used in explosives and in herbicide manufacture. When DNP was discovered to induce rapid weight loss, it became a popular over-the-counter remedy, but one with very serious side effects. In 1938, it was deemed to be exceptionally dangerous and banned. It is still for sale today through the internet, however, and people (mostly gym bunnies) are still dying from its abuse, mainly as a result of lethal hyperthermia.

Recently, Dr Kyle Hoehn, associated with Life Biosciences (see Key Opinion Leaders. Page 149), has apparently discovered safe uncoupling molecules, of which the lead molecule is BAM15. This molecule doesn't, unlike DNP, affect the cell membrane and should therefore be non-toxic. BAM15 has been developed at the University of New South Wales and in models has been shown to extend life quite significantly. This compound, it should be stressed, is at a very early pre-clinical stage of development.

The other area of interest in mitochondrial uncoupling is the potential for the transplantation of BAT, into the back of the neck. BAT is only present in pockets of the thorax, mostly between the shoulder blades and under the neck and is a very different type of fat to the white fat we all carry around with us. In the foetus, BAT is apparent and relatively bountiful, but as we grow beyond our earliest years, its supply diminishes rapidly to the point of negligibility, except in a few outlier individuals. BAT is present in small animals in proportionately greater volumes than in humans.

BAT is made up of brown coloured adipocytes and well as adipocyte stem cells. BAT is richly populated by mitochondria, which is why its absence, is thought to play a role in obesity and type 2 diabetes. Therefore, BAT may well be geroprotective, especially as it is the site of a great deal of mitochondrial uncoupling, and its induction or transplantation is likely to be positive for the release of "excess energy".

Moreover, studies in mice have shown that the brown adipocytes generated from stem cells can be successfully transplanted into adult mice and this results in a greater consumption of excess energy, as well as in extending lifespan. The same approach for humans is currently being investigated by the aforementioned AgeX.

ORGANS – DO IT LIKE THE CLASSICS (CARS)

The transplantation of organs is vital for people who have end-stage disease and would die or suffer miserably without a replacement organ. The key organs in terms of transplant are kidneys, liver, heart and lungs – in that order. The successful transplant of the first organ occurred in 1954 and was of a kidney, which is still the most common organ to be transplanted. This is partly because we each start off with two of them, and we can function with only one.

Improving the ways in which organs are transplanted into humans is an exciting area of research. Not only are we encouraged by developments in what might be termed traditional transplants, i.e. human to human, but we are also watching with interest the beginnings of an industry that could be very big indeed; animal to human transplants, as well as the use of stem cells to create new organs outside of the body, either by using cellular scaffolds or by bioprinting.

Interestingly, Lei Yang of the University of Pittsburgh has made a beating "heart" using human skin cells transformed into iPS cells, and then attached onto what is known as a "scaffold". This prototype "heart", derived from a mouse heart, contracted at 50-60 beats a minute. While far from being a real heart, it's an indication of how hearts will be engineered from stem cells at sometime within the relatively near future.

Around the world many people die every year as a result of waiting for an organ of whom 4,500 are in the US. Large numbers wait either in vain or for a long period, for heart, lung, liver and other organ transplants. In the US, the number waiting at any given time is 120,000+, of which 100,000 are awaiting a new kidney.

Part of the problem is the lack of compatible organs, due to the fact that our bodies reject organs that don't match our own organs to the satisfaction of our immune system. Compatibility has to be of two types: the blood and also six key antigens which can, if not properly matched, trigger rejection. Matches aren't easy to come by. In the case of kidneys, for instance, the chance of a match is about 1 in 100,000. Additionally, even if an appropriate organ is found, there are time issues involved in getting it to the recipient, since organs decay quickly even if they are appropriately cooled.

Then there is the issue of the large number of people waiting for

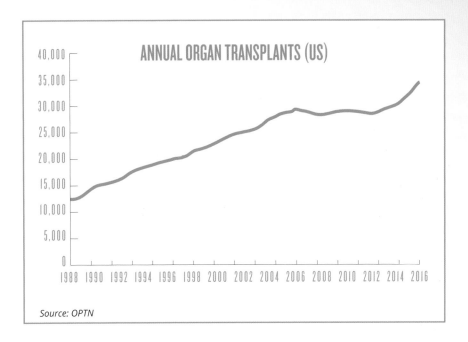

ANNUAL ORGAN TRANSPLANTS (US)

Source: OPTN

organs versus the number who are either prepared to donate while alive (kidneys or sections of liver, as examples) or who have given authority for their organs to be harvested when they die. So, while the science of organ transplantation is evolving, it needs to evolve faster to save the lives of the many thousands who need organs to lead successful and healthy lives.

Apart from the people who are in need of new organs urgently, there is also the potential for prophylactic organ transplants, akin to changing worn out car parts, where in theory our organs could be periodically replaced as part of a broader anti-ageing strategy.

Progress in organ replacement is now taking several forms:

1. Cryopreservation of organs to allow for a longer time between harvesting and implantation;

2. Improved immune suppression, allowing less specific organ matches to be successfully made;

3. Organs grown in animals, probably in pigs, to be harvested for human use, and without adverse immune reactions. This process is known as **xenotransplantation.** Human-to-human transplantation is known as allogeneic transplantation. Genetic engineering, using techniques such

as CRISPR, will soon be able to fully "denature" pig organs, without the possibility of an adverse immune reaction or the transmission of porcine diseases;

4. Organs grown from stem cells, probably derived from a patient's own body (autologous), and created around a cellular matrix; and

5. Bioprinting of tissues and organs, using 3D printing techniques.

At present, immunosuppressive drugs have to be used in most organ transplants, and are then used for life. The downside of these drugs is that patients with replacement organs end up being susceptible to many infectious diseases, due to the immunosuppressant medication they have to take after transplants.

Although people can live long lives post-transplant, particularly with new kidneys, most recipients who get new organs don't live nearly as long as those without a transplant history. The average percentage of people who don't require a second transplant, or who die before the fifth anniversary of their transplant, is 52% in lung, 57% in pancreas, 70% in liver, 76% in heart, and a much higher percentage in kidney. With a kidney transplant, especially with those from live donors, the new kidney will on average be functional for 15-20 years. There are problems with transplants apart from the curtailment of normal life and the lifelong requirement for post-surgical drugs. A major one is the danger of hidden diseases in the transplanted organs, even with screening; West Nile virus, rabies and particularly hepatitis B and C are examples of these.

New techniques to dampen the automatic immune reaction of most people against transplanted organs are being developed. This type of immune reaction can be serious. In some earlier cases of transplantation, such is the strength of the immune response that patients have died almost immediately.

The Johns Hopkins School of Medicine has now found a way to "quieten" the immune system, at least as far as transplantation is concerned. By filtering antibodies from a patient's blood (and they have now trialled this technique in thousands of patients) they can lower the risk of rejection, and the results have been startling. After eight years, about 77% of those who had received an incompatible transplant were still alive, compared to 44% of those patients who were still on the waiting list. This process of dampening the immune response is known as desensitisation.

In the case of transplanting organs from animals into humans (xenotransplantation), early efforts proved worse than futile. Although organ transplantation has been attempted for centuries, it only entered canonical medical literature in the early 20th Century.

Princeteau implanted slices of rabbit kidney into a renally insufficient child in 1905, without success. As recently as 1984 in California, Baby Fae received a baboon heart, and survived for three weeks. Her death was due to the fact that baboon blood is incompatible with human blood, and in fact it is now known that non-human primates, despite their affinity to us, are poor donors for transplantation.

Because the risk of cross-infection and rejection is too high in transplants from non-human primates into humans, pigs are now the main focus of research into xenotransplantation. The risk of cross-species disease with pigs is less than with primates because they are much further away from humans in the phylogenetic tree. Furthermore, pigs' organs are roughly the same size as those of humans, and because pigs have lived in close proximity to humans for centuries, the risk of cross-infection is lessened.

To prevent rejection, a variety of techniques are under investigation. One way that has been suggested is the use of cobra venom factor, which would probably halt the immune cascade response, but after analysis this appears to be a poor choice, because of the toxicity of the venom.

The best path is now believed to be the use of engineered pigs which are bred without the gene that codes for proteins called 1,3-galactosyltransferases, meaning that their immunogenic antibodies are knocked out. This is the α-Gal epitope (an epitope is the part of an antigen molecule to which an antibody attaches itself); the result is that the organ is much less immunogenic to humans.

α-Gal is found in all mammals apart from monkeys and humans, and can cause what is known as Mammalian Meat Allergy (MMA). This MMA, if present, would activate a highly negative reaction in human recipients of pig organ transplants and for that reason the α-Gal has to be eliminated for successful transplants to take place.

This technique of gene knock-out appears to reduce α-Gal expression by about three-quarters, which is probably sufficient to remove the immune response risk. In addition, reducing the human host T-cell responses and macrophages is an additional way in which rejection can be suppressed. As well, in order to prepare the patient for transplant, pig donor stem cells are introduced into the bone marrow of the human recipient to cause progenitor T-cells to migrate and mature in the thymus, causing a lineage that is part porcine, but one which will be eliminated in due course by the human immune system.

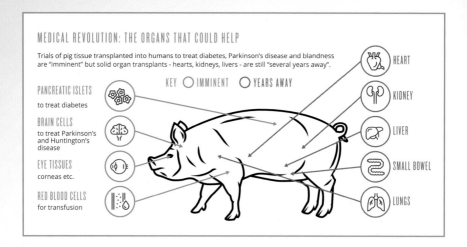

MEDICAL REVOLUTION: THE ORGANS THAT COULD HELP

Trials of pig tissue transplanted into humans to treat diabetes, Parkinson's disease and blandness are "imminent" but solid organ transplants - hearts, kidneys, livers - are still "several years away".

KEY ◯ IMMINENT ◯ YEARS AWAY

PANCREATIC ISLETS
to treat diabetes

BRAIN CELLS
to treat Parkinson's and Huntington's disease

EYE TISSUES
corneas etc.

RED BLOOD CELLS
for transfusion

HEART

KIDNEY

LIVER

SMALL BOWEL

LUNGS

There are, of course, serious obstacles associated with pig organ transplants; one is the size of a pig's body and another is that pigs only live about 15 years, so xenografts might not last any longer than that. There are also differences of body temperature between us and pigs; a pig's body temperature is 2 degrees Celsius higher than a human's.

And pigs carry diseases that might be passed to humans, including rotavirus, parvovirus and herpes, and most importantly, PERVs (porcine endogenous retroviruses) which is why donor pigs have to be specifically bred for transplantation harvest and isolated from other animals.

The PERV are not normally a problem that manifests in the animals themselves, but might do so in humans. Pig cells can be engineered to remove the 62 types of PERV using CRISPR (see

Genetic Editions of You. Page 235), which represents a real breakthrough for xenograft technology. Indeed, George Church's lab at Harvard has managed to eliminate all PERVs from pig tissues within 14 days using CRISPR. We have teleconferenced with George Church, one of the leading lights in biogerontology, and he is convinced that xenotransplantation will happen quite soon. Indeed, he is involved with eGenesis Bio, one of the 20 or so companies he has co-founded (including one of our favourites, Editas Medicine – (see Portfolios. Page 317) eGenesis Bio is focused on xenotransplantation and recently raised US $38 million in private funding.

There are also, of course, ethical and religious implications involved in pig organ transplants; some religions regard pigs as being unclean, and some people do not approve of animals being bred to provide humans with spare organs. In addition, because of the risk of animal-to-human transfection, the FDA has stated that in the event that such transplantations do take place (and they haven't as yet) the recipient must be monitored for his or her whole life.

Elimination of pig proteins that are rejected as not being "self" by human bodies is the pre-eminent goal of scientists working in transplantation. And there have been many successes. Several pig-to-primate transplants have been conducted without major incident, though the primate recipients still require immunosuppression drugs for the balance of their lives.

Recently, scientists have been experimenting with plants, specifically spinach leaves, as a way to grow human heart cells. The idea is that multiple spinach leaves could be used to build layers of human-compatible healthy tissue, particularly for the heart.

Worcester Polytechnic Institute in the US is the leader in this field, and this imaginative idea arose because spinach leaf stems look somewhat like human blood vessels. The spinach leaves are used as a scaffold: once the plant cells are washed away, there remains a cellulose structure which can be employed in a range of regeneration techniques. Cartilage tissue can be grown on the structure, bone tissue can be made to grow, and wound healing products can be better applied to human tissues. Other plants are also being researched to use their vein-like structures as platforms from which to engineer biocompatible material.

Artificial lungs are in development, joining the artificial hearts that are now in regular use, and which are carried around in something that looks a bit like a backpack. Hearts, being relatively simple pumps, are quite easy to replicate mechanically, but lungs are more complex. That having been said, early experiments in sheep show that artificial lungs can be made to work for at least six hours.

As an aside, an Italian neuroscientist, Dr Sergio Canavero, is preparing to conduct a human head transplant in 2017 or 2018, though the details are sketchy – and, rather oddly, it is to be financed by a reality TV show.

A major problem in organ transplantation is the successful transport of organs from place to place, given that most are only viable for a few hours after harvesting, and that existing cryopreservation techniques can lead to toxicity and/or unsuccessful "thawing".

Arigos Biomedical, a private California company, has a proprietary whole-organ preservation procedure which is designed to do two things: 1) to better preserve organs in transport: and 2) to allow freshly produced tissue slices to be successfully transported to

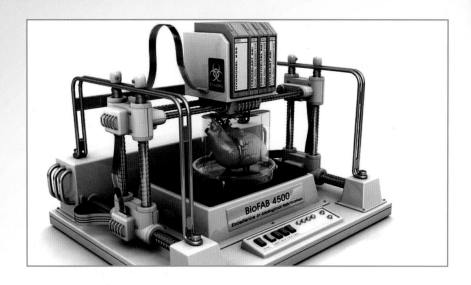

labs around the world. The process eliminates ice formation and stress fractures, and achieves a significant reduction in the use of cryoprotectant agents, which can be toxic. The process uses a technique called persufflation, in which blood is replaced with helium. This is a considerable improvement over current techniques of cooling organs, which require a much greater amount of anti-freeze material in order to avoid ice crystal formation.

In the field of printing tissues and organs, one investable company stands out. Organovo Holdings Inc. (NASDAQ: ONVO) bio-prints and already sells human tissues (liver and kidney tissue) for research purposes. In less than two or three years, it is possible that it will be able to make tissue which can be surgically transplanted, and ultimately that whole or partial organs will be printed using the 3D techniques that the company employs.

The first of these is likely to be sections of the liver. As liver tissue can regenerate faster than that of any other organ, the company's goal is to have such tissues ready within 3–5 years. Some 3D-printed hollow organs, such as bladders and urine tubes, are already being manufactured, along with windpipes, and in the latter case these have been transplanted successfully.

This type of 3D printing consists of a cell seeded scaffold, and the technique, being refined continuously, was first developed by Thomas Bolland of Clemson University in the early 2000s. The materials used in 3D bioprinting are usually polymers (alginate or fibrin), mixed with cellular adhesion molecules designed to allow the attachment of cells, and the material is termed "bioink".

One of the main obstacles to bioprinting is the incorporation of a blood supply in the bioprinted organ, known as the vasculature. This is still at a relatively early stage of development, but we are pretty confident that within five years, a simple bioprinted organ will be fully transplantable.

HOMEOSTATIC CAPACITY AND FUNCTIONAL LONGEVITY

Homeostatic capacity is the magnitude of the challenge against which an autoregulatory system can maintain functional homeostasis. Analogous concepts include resilience, robustness, antifragility, and strength, as well as allostatic, autoregulatory, compensatory and buffering capacity. We propose a model for healthy, functional longevity based on assessing and increasing homeostatic capacity.

Homeostatic capacity is sufficiently effective in our youth, such that we only tend to become more aware of it through its loss as we age, when allostasis (the process of achieving homeostasis) becomes less effective. Indeed, the myriad features of ageing may well be epiphenomena of eroding homeostatic capacity that reduce our

ability to contend with ubiquitous stressors and entropy. For example, the erosion of our autoregulatory control of blood pressure, blood glucose, tumour surveillance, and inflammation could partially explain hypertension, diabetes, cancer, and various inflammatory diseases, independently of more widely accepted factors.

If eroding homeostatic capacity explains the diverse features of ageing, could increasing homeostatic capacity help avert senescence and enable sustainable health? For acute ailments, the proximate and ultimate goals of intervention are symmetric – restoring homeostasis. For chronic conditions, including senescence, we propose shifting the proximate goal to increasing homeostatic capacity as a path to the ultimate restoration of functional homeostasis. This small conceptual change portends a radical transformation in the way we approach chronic conditions.

Current "Whack-a-Mole" remediations for chronic dysfunctions can promote a weakening of homeostatic capacity, leading to tachyphylaxis (a reduction in responses to drugs), increasing addiction to therapy, and exacerbating the need for additional therapy. Plenty of people, including those in medicine and in pharmaceuticals, benefit from the current approach, but the long-term benefit for patients is less clear.

Instead, let's ask a question: what if we used hormetic, (i.e. low stimulatory), oscillatory doses of eustress (beneficial stress) to paradoxically promote homeostatic capacity – and use it as a way to ameliorate various chronic dysfunctions? For instance, could hormetic doses of prohypertensive interventions be pulsed to increase allostatic capacity and reduce baseline blood pressure? Such counterintuitive approaches are already validated by examples such as exercise, muscle training, ischemic reconditioning, and vaccination.

Lifestyle interventions would be transformed as well. Current static recommendations related to certain diets, exercises, and stress reduction methods would shift to dynamic recommendations that emphasise variance over fixed habits as ways to increase the body's tolerance and dynamic range. For example, exercises and diets would vary in every dimension, and exposure to variance in light, temperature, and other eustress patterns would be encouraged.

While these approaches may temporarily ameliorate specific homeostatic insufficiencies, we are more interested in modulating central genes and fundamental pathways that regulate homeostatic capacity. Energetics, control systems, repair mechanisms, and biological clocks are examples of foundational processes that regulate, and dysregulate because of antagonistic pleiotropy, feedback loops and homeostatic capacity. Thereby fractally connecting molecular and cell senescence regulation to organismal senescence. Interventions that improve a large composite panel of relatively uncorrelated measures of homeostatic capacity, functional outcomes, are more likely to confer systemic benefit than interventions that improve just a single measure.

We also envision a fundamental shift in how we measure biology and health. Dynamic systems such as biological ones are better evaluated by using dynamic models than by static ones. We have heretofore been far too reliant on static variables as biomarkers. Annual checks of blood pressure, heart rate, and cholesterol levels to assess health risks are tantamount to a seismic engineer relying on the degree of angular declination, instead of resilience, to predict collapse risk.

Examples of dynamic tests that already exist include baroreceptor sensitivity, flow-mediated vasodilation, heart rate variability, gait balance, postprandial glucose and triglyceride tolerance tests, pupillary light reflex, and recovery time after cardiac stress. For every current state variable test, we envision the development of a dynamic version of the test with better capabilities for continuous or high-frequency sampling. Dynamic diagnostics, response diagnostics, and stress testing after contextual changes or allostatic loads to evaluate system dynamics will transform our understanding of homeostatic capacity and health.

Although a body's potential homeostatic performance under all possible conditions, including every magnitude, pattern, type, and duration of stress, cannot be reduced into a single measure, approximations of homeostatic capacity are possible through establishing standards, population-wide age-based normative values, and composites of relatively uncorrelated variables.

The normative or personal values at peak levels during youth can then be used as benchmarks for monitoring an individual's measures of homeostatic capacity as they experience chronologic ageing.

Homeostatic capacity is a fundamental trait of living systems, filtered by evolution at all scales of biology and all temporal epochs. Innovations that fundamentally increase homeostatic capacity will serve as a foundation for developing strategies that can help avert the natural ageing process and promote functional longevity. We envision a future in which homeostatic capacity levels beyond normative peak levels can be pursued and sustained for the purposes of enhancing our healthy, functional longevity through capacity building and intervention. The end of ageing would be the end of healthcare as we know it. The feed-forward relationship between healthcare innovation and increasing future consumption would finally be decoupled. If homeostatic capacity is restored, enhanced, and indefinitely sustained, humans would be able to persist at the low annual mortality rates currently enjoyed by young adults. Healthy lifespan could telescope to a much larger number of years beyond what might have been imagined. Human capacity to live longer lives, and to make effective contributions for a much, much longer time, would thus be unleashed.

The text for this section has been kindly provided by Joon Yun, M.D, President, Palo Alto Investors.

WILT AND WICT – WILD IDEAS?

Although derided by some members of the scientific community, the ideas behind WILT and WICT are interesting, if only to highlight what some people are suggesting as being possible in terms of human life extension, beyond the "bridge" being built by modern science.

WILT stands for "whole-body interdiction of lengthening of telomeres" and is the SENS (Strategies for Engineered Negligible Senescence) (see Key

Opinion Leaders. Page 158) proposal for the eradication of cancer (de Grey et al., 2004; de Grey, 2005).

The idea is to remove, or "knock out", the telomere-related genes that cause lengthening of the telomeres in cancer, which gives them their immortality. Cancers are unable to survive in the absence of telomerase or, in about 10% of cases, the absence of ALT – Alternative Lengthening of Telomeres (Kim et al.).

The problem is that we do require telomerase for at least some of our cells, particularly for stem cells – so that they can survive and replicate. So, while the answer to this roadblock is periodic injections of fresh stem cells (approximately every ten years), eventually our stem cells (in an environment of zero endogenous telomerase) would run out of telomeres and die.

It appears to SENS, though not to all others, that telomerase has no function other than to lengthen telomeres, so the removal of the genes that maintain it would have no effect, other than to create the need to replace stem cells on a periodic basis.

Certainly, this is a radical and highly interventional approach – but as with so much of Aubrey de Grey's work, it is challenging and provocative, rather than representing a currently viable scientific solution. However, the idea of "turning off" telomerase is not so outlandish: Salk Institute scientists led by Victoria Lundblad have managed to do just that in yeast, by exploiting what appears to be a natural "off switch", designed to inhibit the growth of aberrant cells.

In contrast, de Pinho et al have observed that mice which have had the telomerase RNA component (mTERC) knocked out, did develop different types of cancers, and lived short lives, despite the fact that they were unable to produce telomerase. Furthermore, mTERC deletion mice were unable to repair DNA and to maintain chromosomes as effectively as normal mice. So, the story is confusing. And until some serious money is deployed, we are guessing that WILT will remain wilted.

WICT stands "for whole-body induced cell turnover". The idea here is to periodically replace the cell population of our bodies in order to overcome several forms of accumulated age-related cellular damage (Cortese, Aguiar and Santostasi, 2017). "Homeostatic turnover" or "tissue renewal" denotes the regular turnover and replacement of renewing tissues (e.g. skin, blood, etc.) with cells derived from tissues' local adult stem cell populations. The aim of induced cell turnover (ICT) is to externally mediate the turnover and replacement of adult cell populations with human pluripotent stem cell (hPSC)-derived

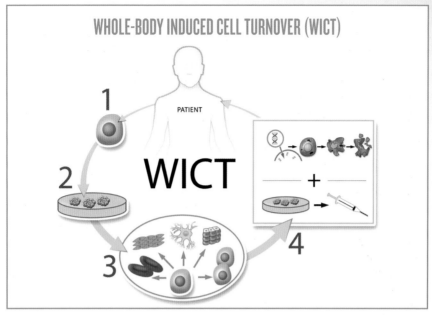

(1) Derivation of patient-specific human pluripotent stem cells (hPSCs). (2) Culturing of hPSCs to produce a sufficient quantity of exogenous cells. (3) hPSCs directionally differentiated into desired cell types. (4) Administration of directionally differentiated, partially-differentiated or undifferentiated hPSCs (bottom panel) in coordination with suicide gene-mediated targeted cell ablation (top panel) at tissue-specific rates in a gradual, multi-phasic manner so as to effect the extrinsically-mediated turnover of whole tissues and organs. Reprinted and adapted with permission from Rejuvenation Research 19/4, published by Mary Ann Liebert, Inc., New Rochelle, NY.

cells, cultured in vitro, which lack the forms of age-related damage present in the patient's adult cells.

The aim of WICT would be to apply this process to all of the cells in the human body, gradually over the adult lifespan of the patient, in order to remove several forms of age-related damage that have accumulated in the body's cells, including telomere depletion, genomic DNA and mitochondrial DNA damage and mutation, epigenetic mutations, and accumulated cellular

and intracellular junk – essentially all forms of non-extracellular age-related damage that can be removed by the ESC or iPSC-creation process and that can be prevented from re-accumulating during their expansion in the lab.

Many studies have shown that stem cells (including ESCs and iPSCs) lack many of the forms of age-related damage that accrue in adult somatic cells and adult stem cells. They are immortal, in the sense that they can divide and self-renew indefinitely without accumulating the typical forms of age-related cellular damage just listed. This provides the foundation for the idea of deriving patient-specific stem cell lines via somatic cell nuclear transfer (SCNT) or nuclear reprogramming, or of using existing stem cell lines immunologically matched to the patient, as a source of replacement cells to provide the fuel for this theoretical procedure.

This external turnover process would occur in a very gradual manner, in which a small portion of the cells making up a given tissue are "ablated" in a targeted manner and replaced with administered stem cell-derived cells of the same cell type as the ones they are replacing. The idea is to perform this procedure very gradually to avoid the temporary absence of too many cells at one time. All tissues lose a certain number of cells with age, which shows that they can sustain the loss of a certain number of cells without going haywire. The idea, then, is to ablate a small number of cells and replace them, and to do this iteratively until whole tissues and organs are replaced, without at any one time inducing tissue failure due to the ablation of too many cells at once.

Different tissues and organs vary in the number of cells they can have temporarily absent without experiencing tissue failure because different tissues vary in the total number of cells they are composed of. Thus, very small organs would be able to sustain a smaller number of lost cells than larger organs. For this reason, tissue- and organ-specific ICT rates would need to be applied in accordance with the size and specific function of each tissue and organ. This can be mediated by using cell type-specific ablation methods, such as the administration of suicide genes controlled by tissue-specific promoters, or the use of tissue-specific drug delivery systems to deliver apoptosis-inducing drugs. Since circulating stem cells typically only engraft at locations of existing cell loss, the patterns of ablation would guide the correct replacement cell types to the right locations so that they can engraft. The scientists behind the idea also think that this can be accomplished in an even easier manner for renewing tissues and organs by applying the process to tissues' adult stem cell niches exclusively, so that their regular renewal by their adult stem cell populations would serve to replace their differentiated cell types automatically.

The originators of this proposal consider ICT to be a novel third branch of regenerative medicine, with features that differentiate it from the field's two main pillars, cell therapy and tissue/organ engineering. Whereas cell therapy can only account for existing cell loss, and is limited to taking the place of cells that have already died, ICT aims to systematically create new vacancies for stem cells to "engraft"

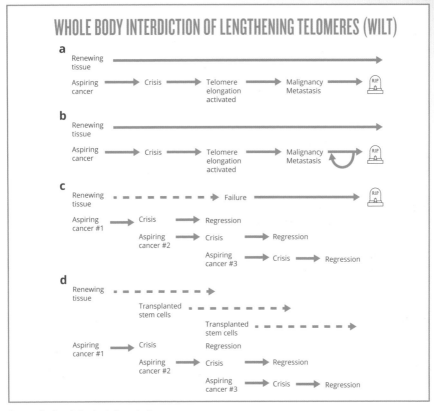

Source: Ending Aging by Aubrey de Grey

in order to increase the forms of age-related damage treatable by cell therapies beyond just existing cell loss. Similarly, tissue and organ engineering aims to create new tissues in the lab and transplant them into the body. By contrast, ICT aims to accomplish the same aim as tissue engineering – namely, the replacement of entire tissues and organs – but without the need for surgery, in a very gradual manner in situ (i.e. inside the body), so that the functioning of the tissue or organ is never interrupted throughout the course of the procedure. They also think that it has the potential to repair non-transplantable tissues like the vascular system, lymphatic system, skin and the brain.

In the words of the therapy's originators: "We view ICT as a novel branch of regenerative medicine and a novel method of in situ tissue regeneration. First and foremost, we feel that it could lift the main barrier limiting the clinical efficacy of stem cell therapies, namely the fact that administered cells can only engraft at locations of existing cell loss, severely limiting their ability to replace cells that are diseased or dysfunctional but refuse to die. While the notion of endogenous cell clearance has become routine for bone marrow transplants, it isn't really on the radar at all for solid tissues and organs. We'd like to change that. From the perspective of longevity, we feel that the eventual whole-body application of the therapy, while ambitious, might be a means of conferring the immortality of the germ line upon the soma, i.e. body. Every one of us are the offspring of a long line of cells that have continued functioning and dividing for billions of years, which we feel is the strongest evidence available that the lifespan of cellular systems can in principle be extended indefinitely.

Furthermore, the cloning of adult organisms with normal lifespans from adult somatic cells testifies to the fact that adult cells can be rejuvenated and used to produce a sufficient quantity of progeny to replace the sum of cells constituting adult organisms. Serial cloning experiments attests to this fact even more strongly. These are the facts that give us hope for the future potential of WICT. In principle, we feel that WICT would be capable of preventing or negating all forms of age-related cellular (i.e. non-extracellular) damage that can (a) be removed by the stem cell derivation process or the culture expansion process, and (b) be prevented from reoccurring during culture expansion or otherwise screened-out and removed during the culture expansion process. We feel that it is a much more tractable approach than trying to prolong the function of existing cells from the inside out. Why try and design a car that lasts a thousand years when you can simply replace the parts?"

Given its ambitious scope, there are plenty of potential pitfalls with the approach. For instance, how would a person's specific personality and memories be preserved throughout the turnover of the brain? How would very specific long-distance neural connections or nerves – ones that form in development and then grow in length over time with the organism – be preserved? And what if there are tissues where the temporary loss of even 1% of cells would lead to acute tissue failure?

Yes, WILD is the word for WILT/WICT – but without wild thinking, where would mankind be today?

Text kindly contributed by Franco Cortese, Deputy Director and Trustee, The Biogerontology Research Foundation.

GENETIC EDITIONS OF YOU

Gene therapy, genetic targeting, and gene editing are terms describing any intervention that changes genetic compositions – in mammals, organisms, or in plants. This might mean transferring genetic material from one organism to another, or it might mean changing one or several base pairs (A-T or C-G) in DNA sequences, or adding a copy of an existing gene to a host DNA, or "knocking out" part of an organism's DNA.

Any organism, including us humans, can be altered using such techniques. Hence the excitement around the startling emergence of brand new technologies.

The discovery of CRISPR, which took place only as recently as 2012, represents a quantum leap forward in genetic technology, and it would not be an exaggeration to say that the CRISPR system of gene editing is one of the greatest scientific advances of the past century. CRISPR and its ilk are kinds of a genetic cut-and-paste, one which uses highly accurate "scissors". These techniques have massive potential, both in health and in anti-ageing, as well as, of course, for investors.

CRISPR-Cas9 (to give it its full acronymic name) is found in nature, and has for millions of years been used by bacteria to defend against infections. CRISPR-Cas9, consists of two components, the CRISPR (clustered, regularly interspaced palindromic repeats) array and Cas (CRISPR associated) proteins. CRISPR sequences act as types of bookends at the termini of short stretches of DNA, and CRISPR targets DNA by using a small interchangeable RNA (which is the "guide" for what DNA to act upon) to attach to each new sequence of DNA that it is seeking to disrupt.

CRISPR-Cas9 is a natural product, just as are zinc finger nucleases (ZFNs) and transcription activator-like effector nucleases (TALENs), its somewhat cumbersome predecessors. Unlike them, CRISPR does not require a protein to be redesigned for each target DNA site, making it much more efficient.

At the outset, CRISPR suffered from what are known as unintended "off-target effects" i.e., it wasn't fully accurate. And in some cases, particularly those involving small-animal research in germline DNA, CRISPR still appears to go off-target. In May 2017, *Nature Methods* reported on a small study involving just three mice, one control, and two being treated for retinitis pigmentosa. The retinitis was successfully treated in the two disease-affected mice, but the CRISPR edits also altered their genomes at random sites. This is a very small study, and while cautionary it involves germline editing, where mutations can and do occur much more frequently than in somatic genetic editing.

With new iterations, however, CRISPR is now regarded as being pretty safe, and its applications are growing in number very rapidly. It is one of the areas of longevity science where there are already companies listed, some with great promise. We like Editas, CRISPR Technologies, Tool Gen and Intellia as examples (see Portfolios. Page 302).

There are two forms of medical genetic engineering now available to scientists using CRISPR and its derivatives.

One is Somatic Gene Therapy (SGT), where new genetic material is transferred to cells that are not germline (heritable) or to stem cells. This means that whatever trait is induced or knocked out is not inherited by the next generation. Currently, about 600 trials using SGT are being undertaken worldwide, most of them in the early stages.

The focus of these trials tends to be on diseases involving genetic defects (often monogenic defects), such as cystic fibrosis, haemophilia, immunodeficiency, Duchenne Muscular Dystrophy and thalassaemia.

The other type of therapy is germline gene therapy (GGT), where germ cells (eggs or sperm) have their genomes modified to alter the genetic makeup of the resulting offspring. All the cells of such offspring would thereby be permanently altered, and the implications of such radical therapy have caused 29 countries, including Australia, Germany, Israel and Canada, to ban the use of germline therapy outright. Additionally, many scientists, including Jennifer Doudna of CRISPR fame and David Baltimore, a Nobel Prize winner in medicine, have sought a moratorium on genetic alterations in medical practice, especially in human embryonic stem cells. They, like many others, are concerned about the ability of CRISPR and other technologies to genetically "engineer" humans. However, the first human embryo editing experiment using CRISPR, which successfully removed the malfunctioning gene MYBPC3 from the embryo's DNA, was performed by Oregon Health and Science University in July 2017.

Recently, work with 58 viable embryos has demonstrated that it is possible to edit out a specific genetic defect in most cases. This defect, known as a hypertrophic cardiomyopathy, is the leading cause of death in young athletes. It is caused by a mutation of the MYBPC3 and the work done by scientists in editing it out of embryos demonstrates two things: that CRISPR is becoming much less uncertain and more specific and that its use could circumvent the likelihood of inherited and often fatal disease.

As we age, the expression of our genes changes. This can influence the pace at which some individuals age relative to

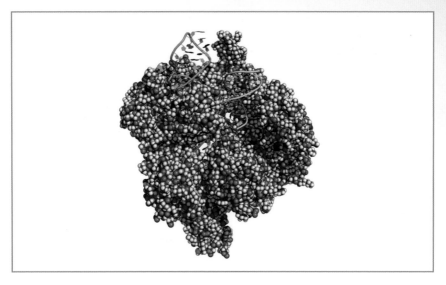

The CRISPR/Cas9 genome editing/engineering system. Cas9 can be used to cut target DNA at a site complementary to its loaded RNA. Space filling protein model, RNA in green, target DNA in yellow.

others, and therefore changing gene expression in later life is becoming a target for scientists – to both improve the quality of life, and to extend it.

As an example, George Church, a notable geneticist at Harvard, has examined the gene variants characteristic of long-lived people, particularly of supercentenarians (those who live to over 110). He has also looked at long-lived animals, apart from humans, as well as at models such as yeast, fruit flies and worms for clues.

His objective is to find genes that are related to longevity in other animals and organisms. This is an immensely difficult task; looking at animals that are long-lived relative to others in their species may not yield much relevant information for humans, as their DNA is not generally that close to ours. Species which have genomes that are much more similar to those of humans, such as monkeys, rats and mice, will probably yield more useful results.

But even in other models, where the DNA compatibility is not so great (for instance worms, fruit flies and yeast), the stunning increase in lifespan that can be achieved by genetic manipulation does indeed hold significant promise for some equivalence in humans, although perhaps not by the same relative quantum. As examples, a single gene alteration in mice has thus far yielded an increase of 150% in lifespan, and a 10-fold increase in the lifespan of C. elegans. To quote Anne Brunet, Professor of Genetics at Stanford University (2015), "The range of lifespans seen in nature is truly astonishing, and we really have very little insight into how this has evolved or how this works...By having the genome of this fish (the killifish) and comparing it to other species, we start seeing differences that could underlie lifespan differences both between species and also within a species."

The history of genetic interventions is long, dating as far back as the dawn of agriculture. The attempts of our distant ancestors to breed different types of animals or plants by cross-breeding or engraftment represented the first, albeit unscientific, examples of genetic manipulation. For millennia, efforts have been made to "artificially select" traits over generations of plants or of animals. These fumbling, haphazard efforts have yielded results such as the wide variation in dog breeds, hairless cats and the production of sweetcorn.

Subsequently, the work of Mendel, involving the dominant and recessive traits of peas, in the middle of the 19th Century, and of Darwin and others around the same time, proved seminal. Dominant and recessive describe the inheritance pattern of certain traits of a phenotype passed from parent to offspring. Researchers such as Mendel and Darwin introduced scientific rigour into the process of altering and describing genetic traits in plants, animals and human beings. Darwin's ideas merged with Mendel's in the early 20th Century, and a unified theory of evolution and inheritance has gradually arisen. However, using biotechnology to manipulate genes to change life forms is a science of the modern era, and only dates back to the early 1970s. Right from the beginning, ethical scrutiny has been applied to the modification of genes by technology, and this persists today in the era of CRISPR.

Broadly speaking, the genetic engineering of today is not much different in many of its aspirations than selective breeding was in distant history. This was to improve the characteristics of organisms, to make them resistant to diseases, faster growing or more profitable. The genetic engineering of today is vastly superior to that of just a decade ago. CRISPR and its derivatives have revolutionised the ability of scientists to easily, quickly and cheaply alter DNA.

The compression of history into a brief five years is one of the remarkable features of CRISPR, and a short summary of the story of its discovery, and the battle over the potential economic spoils associated with it, is instructive. Before CRISPR, genetic technology was already being used to improve crops, and to synthesise chemicals and food. It was also the basis of the biologic drug revolution, which began in the 1970s, starting with recombinant DNA.

Anti-TNF factors used in inflammatory disease, anti-VEGF treatments for heart and eye conditions, and synthetic insulin, now used by diabetics around the world, all resulted from the advances of the past forty years.

The original recombinant DNA technology used enzymes to "cleave" or cut DNA, but relative to the CRISPR process, it was prehistorically inefficient. Nonetheless, the trajectory of improvement in genetic engineering since the 1970s has been impressive. The first genetically-modified mouse was created in 1974, the first non-human (porcine) insulin in 1983, the first genetically-modified (GM) plant in 1983, and the first GM food in 1993, such foods sometimes being referred to, rather unfairly, as "Frankenfoods".

A genetically-modified organism is one where genetic material has been transferred from one organism to another, either to a plant or to an animal, in order to "improve" the resulting variant. GM crops, for instance, have been developed to be hardy and to grow in inhospitable terrain; additionally, some animals have been genetically engineered to produce improved characteristics. An example is farmed salmon, designed to grow larger than its wild-type equivalents. These so-called transgenic organisms, where genes are altered (unlike in cloning), are now a very big business indeed, encompassing the agricultural, chemical and pharmaceutical industries, amongst others.

In particular, the use of the recombination of DNA has resulted in the now huge biologic drug industry. Biologics are drugs made inside living microorganisms, including plant and animal cells. These types of drugs have now edged out synthetic small molecule drugs as the biggest money spinners for the pharmaceutical industry.

Drugs such as Humira, produced by Abbvie and with US $15 billion per year in sales, used for inflammatory diseases such as rheumatoid arthritis and Crohn's, or Avastin, produced by Roche, with US $6 billion a year in sales, used in colorectal and other cancers, are huge drivers of profits for pharma companies. Additionally, synthetic insulin made via a recombinant process has now entirely replaced porcine insulin for diabetics.

We described the history of the invention of biologic drugs in our 2012 book, *Cracking the Code*, and so we won't go over it again in detail here. However, even more exciting than the invention of biologic drugs is the prospect for genetic engineering using CRISPR techniques. And the patent war that has raged around CRISPR which still rumbles on, has a parallel in the early patent disputes around recombinant DNA.

The fact is that when the human genome was first sequenced in the early 2000s, the way was opened for much more sophisticated forms of genetic intervention. About a decade later, conveniently and concurrently, and in a variety of labs around the world, CRISPR emerged.

In a nutshell, CRISPR and its offshoots represent an efficient, increasingly accurate and inexpensive way of activating or deactivating genetic traits. Today, with CRISPR and its derivatives, it is not in any way hyperbole to say that a genetic intervention for ageing or ageing-related diseases is within sight – and probably within one or two decades.

A variety of genome-editing techniques existed for quite a while before CRISPR; these were centred around ZFN and TALENs, and we also covered these in *Cracking the Code*. It was a few months after publishing this book, however, that the invention of the CRISPR-Cas9 system really jump-started the possibilities for genetic engineering.

The Buck Institute for Research for Aging, in collaboration with the University of Washington, has recently identified 238 genes that, when silenced, increase the lifespan of yeast, one of the four most popular research models. Buck researchers believe that about half of those genes are found in mammals, including in humans. Scientists at King's College London, in

the UK, have found that using CRISPR to delete a gene called LOS1 in yeast increases lifespan by 60%. LOS1 is linked to caloric restriction, which is well known to have some lifespan effect, albeit modest, in humans.

This sort of early research into the genetic manipulation of organisms, in order to extend life, holds a clue as to just how huge the potential is for human gene therapies in disease and in lifespan extension. We really believe that despite the usual resistance to progress, the ethical issues surrounding the technology, and the recurring complexities of introducing any new technology, it won't be long before genetic engineering becomes a key part of longevity strategies.

A recent study by the US-based National Academy of Sciences agrees with this view, but with some reservations. Those doubts centre on the need to carefully monitor the germline, or "heritable" manipulation of our genes, as well as those of other organisms. The possibility of "enhancing" babies or of creating "designer babies" is one that concerns scientists as well as many others. This potential for re-engineering humans is a huge area of ethical debate, but as with every other controversial scientific advance, the positive benefits, once understood, will quickly overwhelm the forces of resistance.

The CRISPR breakthrough came when scientists working independently

METHODS FOR GENOME ENGINEERING

Points of Comparison	Mega Nucleases	Zinc Finger Nucleases (ZNFs)	TALENs	CRISPR/Cas
Ease of Creating Large-scale Libraries	Difficult, requires intensive protein engineering.	Difficult, but requires substantial protein engineering.	Feasible, but technically challenging, complex molecular cloning methods.	Easy to create using standard cloning procedures and oligo synthesis.
Delivery	Ex vivo: electroporation, viral transduction. In-vivo: small size allows use of multiple viral vectors.	Ex vivo: electroporation, viral transduction. In-vivo: small size allows use of multiple viral vectors.	Ex vivo: electroporation, viral transduction. In-vivo: large size limits the number of viral vectors accessible; repetitive DNA sequence leads to unwanted recombination in lentiviral vectors.	Ex-vivo: electroporation, viral transduction. In-vivo: the availability of different Cas9 orthologs of different sizes facilitate viral vector selection.
In Human Clinical Development		Sangamo	Cellectis	Editas, Caribou Biosciences, Intellia, CRISPR Therapeutics.
Components	Endonuclease.	FOK1 nuclease fused to multiple zinc finder peptides.	FOK1 nuclease fused to multiple zinc TALE DNA-binding units.	Guide RNA complexed with the Cas9 nuclease of Cas variant.

Points of Comparison	Mega Nucleases	Zinc Finger Nucleases (ZNFs)	TALENs	CRISPR/Cas
DNA Recognition Motif	Large recognition site 18-40 nucleotides.	Multiple 3 nucleotide sites, (9-18 bp per ZNF monomer).	One-to-one recognition; one TALE subunit recognises one nucleotide (14-20 bp per monomer).	22 nucleotides (20 for guide sequence + 2 for PAM); 44 for double nicking.
Types of DNA Breaks	Double-stranded (DBS) DNA breaks.	Double-stranded (DBS) DNA breaks.	Double-stranded (DBS) DNA breaks.	DBS if used with wild-type Cas9 or single-stranded DNA nicks if used with Cas9 nickase.
Specifically Off-target Effects	Highly specific; few mismatches tolerated.	Can have off-target effects; some mismatches tolerated.	Highly specific; few mismatches tolerated.	Some off-target effects than can be by selecting unique crRNA sequences; multiple mismatches tolerated.
Targeting	Difficult to target to new sequence and maintain efficiency.	Prefers G-rich sequences.	Methylation sensitive.	Sequence targeted must be followed by a PAM.
Multiplexing	Difficult.	Difficult.	Difficult.	Easy.

Source: Cowen and Company, LLC

in different parts of the world discovered that bacteria have an "adaptive," or learned, immunity. When attacked by a phage (virus) they can acquire a piece of its genetic code and absorb it into "memory", so that if subsequently attacked, they have "learned" how to deal with it, and shred the viral genome. And these bacteria use the "spacer," or guide, contained within CRISPR to do this.

The history of the science of CRISPR began in Japan in the 1980s, where scientists observed REPEAT sequences (the last "R" of CRISPR) in "E. coli" bacteria. Subsequently, Francisco Mojica, a Spaniard, found that about half of all microbes have these repeat sequences within their genomes, and it was he who invented the acronym CRISPR to describe the phenomenon. Later, it was found that the repeats of DNA sequences in microbes are typically bordered by Cas enzymes. All this work, its significance not then understood, went unpublished until 2005, when it was described in the *Journal of Molecular Evolution*.

It was at this point that an arms race really began in CRISPR, and the foundations for the patent wars were established. It's a mightily complicated situation, and we won't go into too much detail. Suffice it to say that because of continuous evolution in the CRISPR system, the patent dispute may amount to nothing or not very much, as the science is moving on so rapidly that the original patents may just become historical curiosities.

The first salvo in this patent war was fired by two researchers from Northwestern University in the US. Marrafini and Sontheimer had worked out that CRISPR is specifically DNA-related, rather than RNA-related (although, confusingly, CRISPR does employ RNA). It is the fact that CRISPR is DNA-based which gives it its exceptional quality of accuracy versus RNA-based systems.

This particular patent was denied in 2010, because Marrafini and Sontheimer hadn't figured out how CRISPR actually worked. But Jennifer Doudna of The University of California, Berkeley (UC Berkeley) began to zero in on the key to CRISPR by identifying something called Proto-Spacer Adjacent Motif (PAM), which adds accuracy to CRISPR/Cas9 DNA cleavage. The PAM sequence always creates breaks at exactly 20-letter intervals on DNA sequences, and this really was a key and novel discovery.

Doudna then met Emmanuelle Charpentier of France, and along with Martin Jinek, a Czech, in 2012 the trio published the most important paper on CRISPR yet to emerge. This paper identified a linkage between CRISPR and an RNA (messenger sequence), termed a tracrRNA, which when added to Cas9 made the system operate as a precise editor of DNA. They also discovered that the whole CRISPR system could be transposed into organisms that didn't have it naturally, including into types of bacteria where it was absent.

So, with university patent departments much more on the ball than they had been in the early era of recombinant DNA, UC Berkeley which is where Jennifer Doudna was based, and the University of Vienna, where Charpentier had worked, filed patents around the system of "CRISPR associated guide RNA to cut DNA", and thereby creating the potential to successfully edit genomes.

Not so fast, was the riposte from the other scientists who had been working on more or less the same thing in different institutions. The Broad Institute of San Francisco, where Feng Zhang had been working, and Prashant Mali and Luhang Yang from George Church's Harvard lab, had all been developing refined versions of the Doudna/Charpentier/Jinek system.

Meantime, the scientists involved were busy forming companies around their versions of the new technology. The Broad Institute licensed its technology to a now-public company, Editas (see Portfolios. Page 317), and Doudna by now had established three companies, including Caribou Biosciences, also public (see Portfolios. Page 314). Charpentier's efforts via the University of Vienna were licensed to CRISPR Therapeutics, another public company, based in Switzerland.

The irony of this gold rush was that most of the early money to fund the CRISPR research had come from the US government, but now it was the universities and scientists who were furiously cashing in. And, at the same time, battling each other in the courts.

In a nutshell: in the recent past, the US Patent Office has ruled that the Broad Institute, along with Harvard and MIT, have a better case than that of UC Berkeley, notwithstanding Doudna's significant role in advancing the science, which has led to her winning numerous scientific prizes. The net result is that Feng Zhang, unless the Patent Office decision is overturned, appears to be the victor in this somewhat sordid scientific battle, at least in the US.

And CRISPR in a wide sense is an exceptional technology, with applications in rare diseases, cancer, organ transplantation, and of course, life extension, so theoretically, this is a significant win for the Broad Institute and its partners. But the victory accorded to the Broad Institute may yet turn out to be pyrrhic, because the science is evolving so fast as to render early patents redundant.

Based on precedent, the US Patent Office ruling is unlikely to be overturned in the courts or on appeal, and therefore Editas, for now, looks to be the key winner among the public companies in the space, with speeds of implementation in hitting targets of about ten times those of earlier generation CRISPR/cas9, though nothing is clear cut.

Meantime, the European Patent Office has taken a completely different tack, sitting on opposite sides of the fence, i.e. that Editas and the Broad Institute should be the losers, and Doudna and Charpentier the winners. Complicating matters is the fact that newer versions of CRISPR have emerged, ones which promise even greater accuracy than the original CRISPR/Cas9 system. One of these new systems uses a different nuclease to Cas9, named Cpf1, to establish the target, and this nuclease is considerably shorter, making it much more accurate. Cas9 requires two RNA molecules to cut DNA while Cpf1 only needs one.

Additionally, because Cas proteins are large, it makes them a difficult cargo to transport into cells to edit specific genes. Thus, the recent discovery by Doudna and others of small-sized CasX and CasY enzymes is important, and may be her best bet to obviate the Broad patent in the US, and to restore value to the companies associated with her and UC Berkeley.

The new discoveries are likely to level the playing field, and allow for commercialisation of the CRISPR/Cas process across a wide range of applications.

As well, a genetic technology named NgAgo has been identified, albeit a discovery surrounded by controversy. This NgAgo technology is based on guides that are DNA-linked, rather than RNA-linked. If NgAgo works (and many have their doubts), it should provide a much more accurate targeting mechanism than even the newest version of CRISPR. NgAgo uses the nanobacterium Gregoryi Argonaute (Ago).

Whereas CRISPR sometimes cuts the wrong gene targets, although increasingly less so, the NgAgo system is theoretically highly accurate. The technology has emerged from a university in Hebei in China, and is the brainchild of biologist Han Chunyu. (It should be noted that the quality and quantity of bioscience coming out of China has been rising dramatically in recent years. It is still not up to San Francisco, Boston, Oxford and Cambridge levels, but it is getting close to being a real competitor.)

Although this is a challenging field, the level of knowledge now accumulated in genetic biology is quite astonishing – and is expanding at a phenomenal pace.

CRISPR and associated versions are already being used in real-life applications. Cellectis, a French company listed in the US, has disabled genes that cause an immune reaction in a type of cancer therapy we discussed earlier called CAR-T, where a viral vector (delivery system) is added to a specific gene and fused with T-cells to make them attack specific cancer cells. In London, Professor Waseem Qasim of UCL has recently treated two young girls suffering from leukaemia by using the Cellectis paradigm and both are doing well.

In addition, scientists are working on ways to use CRISPR to deliver precise doses of anti-inflammatory therapies. These doses would downregulate pro-inflammatory cytokines in age-related autoimmune diseases, in other words, those where the body literally "inflames" itself. These cytokines, including IL-1 (interleukin1) and TNF-alpha (TNF-a) are implicated in such diseases as rheumatoid arthritis, and are debilitating to older people. Too much downregulation, however, and tissue repair can be inhibited. So, precision treatment is needed – and genome editing using CRISPR/Cas9 has been shown to be effective in creating engineered stem cells that effectively mediate IL-1 and TNF-1 levels.

A huge amount of venture and public funding is now being diverted into genetic engineering, with a focus on CRISPR. At least US $2 billion has been allocated to the area since 2014, and a lot more is bound to go its way. The key listed companies in the gene therapy field are:

- Editas Medicine
- Juno Therapeutics
- Caribou Biosciences
- Intellia Therapeutics
- CRISPR Therapeutics
- Cellectis
- Sangamo

We rank these companies in order of our preference in Long Lived Portfolios section of this book.

Additionally, the concept of "gene drive" will be an important contributor to the gene therapy industry in the future. Gene drives now are made possible by CRISPR, although they have existed as a theoretical construct since the 1940s. These "drives" are ones that selfishly promote their own heritability over that of all other genes, ensuring that whatever characteristics that they contain get passed onto successor generations.

So, for instance, in December 2015, researchers at the University of California, San Diego reported that they had successfully created the first working version of a gene drive in a population of mosquitos. The traits of these mosquitos, if carried into the wild, might well eliminate malaria; and variants of engineered insects may be able to address Lyme disease, yellow fever, and dengue fever, as further examples.

There is some concern among elite scientists about gene drive as theoretically, they could be used as bio terror tools, or indeed could result in bio errors. The US government has allocated US $65 million to study this.

There has recently been a revival in the prospects of what might loosely be termed "bioelectricity" – and the potential of this science in ageing-related regeneration.

It is well known that some creatures have a remarkable ability to regrow organs and limbs; the salamander and the planarian worm are the two most celebrated examples of this phenomenon, but there are others, although not to the same remarkable degree.

But humans have only two organs which can regenerate fully – the skin and the liver – and those only in a compensatory sense. If the liver is completely lost, unlike in the case of a salamander limb for example, it cannot regenerate.

Scientists are now trying to figure out the "bioelectric code" which appears to play an important role in tissue formation – and which, in regeneration, allows some animals to regrow their limbs but prevents most others from doing the same.

In the 1930s, Harold Burr of Yale University noted that bioelectricity is the "organising principle" that kept mammalian tissues from falling into entropic disrepair. Each cell has some sort of voltage associated with it (think of the "sparks" between brain cells), and this electrical charge is influenced by the balance of charged ions on either side of cell membranes. It is the differences between these ion charges, represented by electrical potential, and governed by ion channels, that carry the "information" governing regeneration.

Planarian worms can even survive having their ends cut off, and indeed if they are chopped into many different bits, each piece will regrow into a brand-new worm. So, it is believed that by altering the bioelectrical signalling of an organism, the "plan" for its development might be changed.

There are some rare diseases in humans that are caused by malfunctions of the ion channels responsible for the electrical transmission of information in our bodies. As a result, the electrical channels and their effects in human ageing and in disease are being actively explored.

Lastly, a technique called optogenetics, where cells are genetically engineered to respond to a laser light, may have applications in the brain, in heart disease and in cancer. So far, optogenetics is being used to study forms of paralysis and some immune cells. Indeed, it is now being enhanced by "synogenetics", first developed at the Salk Institute, a technique which uses ultrasound to control neural behaviour.

PPP ACTIVATION

Studies in fruit flies and in mice have shown that overexpression of the gene G6PD (Glucose-6-phosphate dehydrogenase) extends lifespan and increases activity levels and motor coordination. Recently, the Sinclair/Wu labs at the University of New South Wales have identified three compounds that activate the gene G6PD, which is a part of the PPP or "pentose phosphate pathway."

Endogenous activation of G6PD in humans is thought to have effects similar to those in animal models, potentially inducing healthy lifespan increases. It is certainly the case that deficiency in G6PD causes disease in humans; this condition is known as favism, after the fava bean (which, when ingested, is a trigger for the disease). The G6PD deficiency causes the destruction of red blood cells in its (mostly male) victims. It is a very common enzyme deficiency, but most of its carriers don't manifest problems and typically avoid triggers such as the aforesaid beans. Favism does cause about 4,000 deaths a year in the US though, so it is serious.

The early investigations into how G6PD overexpression might have protective characteristics are therefore interesting in more than just an academic sense. In combination with the metabolites NADPH and glutathione, G6PD is highly protective of red blood cells from oxidative damage. An allele (gene variant) of G6PD is known to be protective against malaria, and is commonly carried by people of Mediterranean origin and by about 10% of those of African origin. Investigations are so far at a very early stage, but we are monitoring this additional avenue of longevity research with interest.

KLOTHO

Klotho is a protein that appears to have some control over rodent and human sensitivity to insulin, and as a result may have a role to play in ageing. It was discovered in 1997 by Kuro et al. and it is named after one of the ancient Greek Fates. Klotho is encoded by the KL gene and reduced production of the Klotho protein has been observed in cases of renal failure in humans. Mutations of the KL gene have also been observed in bone loss, excessive alcohol consumption and in ageing.

Transgenic mice which overexpress Klotho live about 30% longer than

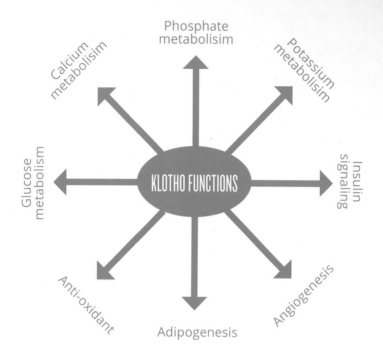

Calcium metabolisim

Phosphate metabolisim

Potassium metabolisim

Glucose metabolism

KLOTHO FUNCTIONS

Insulin signaling

Anti-oxidant

Adipogenesis

Angiogenesis

wild type mice. Indeed, low levels of Klotho appear to actually accelerate ageing. Mice with low Klotho develop atherosclerosis at an early age and it thus appears that Klotho may protect the cardiovascular system. The mode of action of Klotho is not yet understood, but its presence appears to improve cellular calcium homeostasis by increasing the expression and activity of the gene TRV5 and by downregulating that of TRPC6.

A paper by Kamri et al. in 2016 was inconclusive about the effect of Klotho in rodents. Total plasma triglyceride levels in rats overexpressing Klotho fell markedly, which is positive for heart health. However, blood pressure in these rats was not lowered, and there was no detectable benefit in averting atherosclerosis.

Klotho may have some effect on ageing and scientists are working to discover its specific effects. It is worth keeping an eye on this emerging field.

TAKING THE MYC

The Myc (**myelocytomatosis viral oncogene homolog**) family of transcription factor genes is important in cell division, metabolism and survival and they are present in the genomes of all animals. These transcription factor genes encode proteins involved in apoptosis. Jay Bradner, (see Key Opinion Leaders. Page 165) one of our interviewees, believes that targeting Myc with small-molecule drugs may be important in developing anti-cancer and anti-ageing therapies.

Myc, first discovered about 30 years ago, is a master regulator gene believed to control the expression of about 15% of all of our genes. Mutated versions of Myc, which then cause the overexpression of certain genes, are implicated in cancers, including aggressive forms of lymphoma, colon, breast, lung and stomach cancer. About 450,000 people are diagnosed each year in the US with a Myc-dependent cancer, making it an attractive target for drug intervention. It has been established that in mouse models, inactivation of Myc significantly improves survival rates in mice with Myc-related cancers.

Beyond this, however, Myc also appears to have an important role in developmental biology. As a result, targeting Myc in anything other than a carefully controlled way can cause unwanted toxicity. Because Myc lacks enzymatic activity, it is a difficult target for drug developers. Nonetheless, once thought to be "undruggable",

it is currently the subject of a great deal of research. Although inhibitors of Myc have so far proved elusive, there is considerable excitement over the drug stauprimide, which inhibits the Myc-family transcription factor NME2 and appears thereby to inhibit tumour growth in animal models, and this compound is being investigated in human glioblastoma, a type of brain cancer.

Researchers at Brown University have also found that mice with only one copy of the Myc gene lived 15% longer than mice with two copies. Humans have two copies also, so it could be that downregulation of Myc might have a positive effect on ageing and on longevity. It is true that animals can't live without Myc, but they seem to thrive with less of it. Because Myc is also implicated in inflammatory diseases, such as arthritis, downregulation of this gene may have an effect on improving overall tissue homeostasis.

There is no doubt that, because of the implication of Myc in so much human disease, research into this family of regulator genes is set to be very important indeed.

I'M NOT DEAD YET

It is vital to ageing research that single-gene mutations which appear to extend lifespan be fully investigated, particularly if the gene is conserved across multiple species. If such conservation exists, there is a possibility that drugs could target some common mechanisms that regulate ageing.

One such promising target is **INDY** (or I'm Not Dead Yet – seriously!).

The protein INDY, which is a sodium-coupled citrate transporter (also known as SLc.13a5), appears to be implicated in longevity, but in a negative way. In some studies when INDY was downregulated through mutations in models, notably fruit flies and mice, the lesser quantity seemed to extend the lives of the models. However, in the case of flies, this may have been the result of a uncontrolled genetic background (PLoS Genet. 2007 Jun;3 (6): e95), though this does not lessen the potential impact of INDY inhibitors in lifespan extension. INDY may be one of the most promising ways of mimicking and amplifying the effects of CR/DR.

It is estimated that a reduction of 25% to 75% of INDY's normal function results in an optimal level of life extension, and as a result development of INDY inhibitors is underway in several labs. For humans, it is thought that an INDY inhibitor could treat fatty liver disease, a condition which affects 20% of the US population, as well as extending lifespan.

Pfizer and Life Biosciences are very interested in INDY as a target.

NF-κB AS A POTENTIAL TARGET FOR ANTI-AGEING DRUGS AND GENE THERAPY

Inhibition of NF-κB has been proven to reverse some aspects of ageing, notably cardiac hypertrophy. This is where the heart muscle (myocardium) thickens, a condition generally due to high blood pressure, in itself a common aspect of ageing.

NF-κB is a transcription factor, meaning that it is involved in transcribing DNA into RNA, and thence into the production of proteins.

NF-κB is important to the immune system, but its effects are negative when it comes to lifespan. NF-κB seems to block the production of stem cells in aged individuals, and since the amount of NF-κB in humans increases significantly with age, particularly in the hypothalamus, it is regarded as pro-ageing.

Downregulation of NF-κB in middle-aged mice, using genetic manipulation, significantly extends lifespan; upregulation significantly decreases lifespan. Additionally, the downregulated mice performed better in memory tests, and were stronger, and had more supple skin.

So rather than just being a by-product of ageing, it appears that NF-κB is in itself causative of ageing. It also appears that gonadotropin-releasing hormone (GnRH), which is released in puberty and in adulthood, is inhibited by high levels of NF-κB. Increasing the levels of GnRH appears to increase memory in mice, though longevity has not yet been tested.

There are a number of cancer drugs in development in relation to NF-κB, but none specifically for ageing. We are watching with close interest to see when such drugs might emerge.

TRANSPOSONS

Increasingly transposons are thought to be implicated in ageing. Transposons are DNA sequences that change position within genomes, and can cause genetic alterations. Transposons can break free of their surrounding DNA sequences, rather like breaking free of chains.

This escape from the norm happens more and more often in ageing cells; these transposons will then go on to insert themselves elsewhere in the genome, occasionally causing chaos and leading to tissue death. In this respect, they have a similarly destructive effect as free radicals/ROS. They were

discovered in maize in the 1940s by Barbara McClintock, and for this she eventually earned a Nobel Prize.

The genomes of all living beings with eukaryotic cells, including humans, have large sections where transposable elements exist, and the genes encoding transposons take up as much as 40% of the space in the nuclear DNA of the cells.

Stephen Helfand of Brown University in the US has done extensive research into transposons, and believes them to be heavily implicated in ageing. It is possible that these wayward elements could one day be manipulated by CRISPR-like technology to stay in their original designated places.

CRYONICS – ON ICE

Cryonics comes from the Greek for cold. It is in modern parlance a word describing the freezing of bodies or tissues in the hope that at some future date, when medical technology has advanced sufficiently, resuscitation of the patient or some part of him or her (usually of the head) can take place.

There are several places, mostly in the US, where you can have yourself frozen at the point of death, in the hope that you can be revived and eventually cured of whatever felled you. At present, several hundred bodies are in a state of cryopreservation – and new state-of-the-art facilities are being built to accommodate even more.

Although we firmly believe that new technology will indeed extend our lifespans significantly, we are sceptical about cryopreservation – at least as it currently exists.

The world's biggest practitioner of cryonics, the Alcor Life Extension Foundation in Scottsdale, Arizona, admits that current methods of reviving cryopreserved people will most likely not be successful. They are depending on advances in technology, and in particular nanomolecular technology, to make this possible. Ray Kurzweil, he of "singularity" fame, is probably the most famous "member" of Alcor (www.alcor.org).

If even Alcor, with at least one hundred and fifty bodies stored in their facility, is sceptical, then so should we be.

There are several reasons for such scepticism. Most notably, these are whether human bodies can be successfully unfrozen, and thereby potentially cured, and also whether the operators of the cryonics facilities can be trusted to stay open for the decades necessary to allow medical technology to advance sufficiently to be able to resuscitate its customers.

Procedures to freeze or "vitrify" people are only legally allowed post death. Technically, they should really be performed within a few minutes of death, and at that point the blood of the recently expired is replaced with cryoprotectants (think anti-freeze), and after that the body is subjected to "vitrification" (turning the tissues into a glass-like structure) to prevent damaging ice crystals from forming.

James Bedford, a US-based doctor, was the first person to be cryopreserved, in 1967. Since then, about 300 people have been cryopreserved, most of them in the US, but also in Russia. About 1,500 are on the waiting list for cryopreservation, assuming that they are close enough to a facility at the time of their deaths.

Freezing takes place down to a temperature of below -130°C, typically using liquid nitrogen. Sometimes the whole body, and sometimes just the head, is frozen (cephalon is the name for this one). The idea of freezing just the head came about because some people think that long-term memory and therefore "self" is all that needs to be preserved indefinitely, though this is definitely an "out there" opinion. But of course, there are lots of those sorts of opinions amongst the anti-ageing community!

It is expensive to be cryopreserved, upwards of a couple of hundred thousand dollars, and this is generally financed by a life insurance policy. Bodies are stored communally in what are known as "dewars", a name for what are essentially large thermos flasks.

Without cryoprotectants, cells cannot be revived, as salt concentrations build up during freezing and wreak massive damage, making effective thawing impossible. Attempts to recover large animal models by thawing have consistently failed, but in the 1990s solutions were introduced that successfully achieved vitrification (which, unlike freezing without cryoprotectants, does not result in the salt problem). However, although these cryoprotectants do stop cellular damage, they are also somewhat toxic. Finally, large organs can develop fractures.

In 2016, McIntyre and Fahy at 21st Century Medicine (private), a cryopreservation company, demonstrated that a form of vitrification called aldehyde-stabilised cryopreservation could preserve a rabbit's brain in perfect condition when vitrification and freezing at -130°C were combined. Although the rabbit's brain was indeed in perfect condition, at least in terms of maintaining circuitry, the gunk involved in preserving it caused chemical crosslinks which entangled all the molecules, rendering

Quite probably the people who have been cryopreserved up till now will never be successfully revived but though they will, of course, never know the difference. But it is likely that sometime in the future, techniques will be improved and for some people it will become a viable option.

There are also those who believe that brains could be "uploaded" and implanted into a "new body" or just remain as disembodied holograms – something that has been described as "philosophical zombiedom". Mark O'Connell's book *To Be a Machine* is excellent and brilliantly describes the whole transcendence and singularity movement in a tongue-in-cheek and somewhat comedic way.

There are lots of legal issues around cryopreservation; it is, for example easier to have it done in Russia than in the US, and it is impossible in most European countries. A 14-year-old British girl who died in 2016 was cryopreserved, against her father's wishes, but the procedure did nonetheless take place in the US at Alcor.

The argument that encourages people to sign up to be cryopreserved is one akin to Pascal's Wager. And a relatively low cost of earthly insurance versus the priceless

8th Century France, that the small cost of believing in God (and thereby forgoing some earthly pleasures) was worth it in return for the chance of eternal life, versus the alternative .e. eternal damnation.

Stephen Valentine, an architect, is trying to build an elaborate and impregnable structure in Comfort Texas, (yes, t's a real place) designed to house hundreds of bodies in a cryopreserved state. It is called the Time Ship and will encompass the preservation of human beings, tissues, DNA and many other forms of life – a kind of latter-day Noah's Ark. It's an expensive project costing about US $200 million by the

latest estimates and it may neve funded. But there is certainly p of interest in his project, m from men (men outnumber wc three to one in today's body cou cryopreservation).

As Valentine puts it: "If y cremated, you have zippo chan coming back [as] who you are." T cryopreservation in a nutshell. S people who believe in the idea th don't need to die prematurely, p to be frozen and unfrozen – ever an uncertain chance of success.

LIFE EXPECTANCY AND LONGEVITY
WHAT TO EXPECT

About four billion years ago, two amino acids collided and formed the basis of life on earth.

The development of mortal creatures began about 1 billion years ago, but it is only now that some people are contemplating life without the absolute necessity of death. Even now, for the majority, that contemplation remains in the realm of science fiction. The reality is that the best we can hope for, at least for those of us alive now, is a significantly longer period of healthy life – way beyond what we currently think of as "normal". And why should such an extension be regarded as shocking? It shouldn't, is the short answer.

After all, in countries with reasonably accurate birth and death records, life expectancy grew by only 3% between 1500 and 1700, 8% between 1700 and 1800, 9% between 1800 and 1900 and then by an amazing 42% between 1900 and 2000. What would truly be shocking would be if we didn't experience a dramatic rise in life expectancy during this century, especially given the scientific advances now at our disposal.

By 2020, for the first time, there will be more people on earth over the age of 65 than under the age of five. Two-thirds of those who have ever reached the age of 65 in the history of the world, are currently alive. By 2050 more than a third of the population in the UK is expected to be over the age of 65. Already, that portion of the population represents 15% of the total, and numbers 11.6 million. It is now a fact that once people have reached 65 (and thereafter manage to avoid accidents and pathogen-related diseases) they are likely to live for quite some time yet. This also means that the influence of over 65s are having on society is increasing.

As an example, Age UK makes the point that one-third of the UK population today is over 50, and these people have 80% of the nation's net disposable wealth. Furthermore, most of the over 65s today do not consider themselves to be old, but rather, middle-aged. They may be right. What's more, it is quite probable that the first person to live to 150 years is amongst us today. As recently as 20 years ago, people making this type of pronouncement were regarded as crackpots, but the idea of a 150-year-old human is no longer immediately dismissed in polite society as pure fantasy.

The conventional wisdom today among scientists is indeed that life expectancy will rise fairly quickly. Unfortunately, they just can't agree on why or how that will happen, let alone when. For now, world life expectancy continues to rise, although in some developed countries it has somewhat stalled. This hiatus will prove to be temporary, as the average worldwide life expectancy is certainly going to rise sharply in the next twenty years or so.

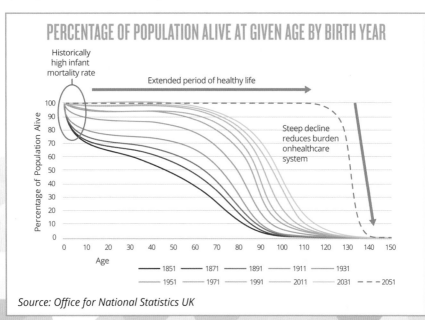

Source: Office for National Statistics UK

FUTURISTS

The roboticist Hans Moravec, in his 1988 book *Mind Children*, outlined a world in which humans would merge with machines and desert their physical bodies. This vision is now shared by a fair number of so-called transhumanists, the most famous of these is Ray Kurzweil, now of Google. Mr Kurzweil thinks that one day soon, our minds will be uploaded to some type of electronic system, allowing for much faster processing of information and thereby a world of almost unlimited possibilities. Unshackled from our failing biological bodies, we could then be whatever we would like to be. To get there, we would employ a variety of what Silicon Valley calls "substrates", ones that emulate (or "carbon copy") our brains, but with massively improved performance.

There is actually quite a lot of interest in this, frankly, quite disturbing idea. Bryan Johnson, a wealthy entrepreneur, has set up a pool of capital, the OS Fund, which invests in companies seeking to "rewrite the operating systems" of life. Many people in Silicon Valley see everything in terms of code, and some think that our biological brain systems are no more than long lines of code, waiting to be rewritten. In some ways this is true, but our research suggests that those who think that every problem can be "cracked" by computers may be indulging in wishful thinking.

We don't think that there are that many people who would forgo social interaction, the chance to play sports, to fall in love, to go to the pub, to listen to music in a live venue — and to generally live the human life – for a place in a disembodied hologram, no matter how smart it is. But the fact that so many in Silicon Valley are pouring their money into trying to find the elixir of eternal life

FUTURISTS

has got to be a good thing. The roster of rich entrepreneurs – almost all men, incidentally – who are prepared to fork out millions of dollars to "solve" the problem of death is impressive. Oracle's Larry Ellison, Google's Sergey Brin and Larry Page, The Milken Institute's Michael Milken, PayPal's founder Peter Thiel and Amazon's Jeff Bezos, are amongst them. No doubt some are splashing their cash out of self-interest, others may have philanthropic aims, while others are displaying the curiosity that is characteristic of the tech entrepreneur and in particular of those who inhabit the Valley.

Their search for immortality isn't new. In fact, it goes back a long, long way but the only difference today is that science may be able to deliver on at least part of the promise that these wealthy people are looking for - a very long life.

Historical examples of people searching for the key to eternal life stretch back millenia. Papyruses from Ancient Egypt, as well as the Sumerian Epic of Gilgamesh, mentioned longevity and the possibility of living highly extended lives. Somewhat later, scientists, such as Robert Boyle (1627-1691), a proponent of swapping old blood for new, (see Targets in Ageing. Page 178), and philosophers such as René Descartes (1596-1650), as well as Francis Bacon (1561-1626), all spoke enthusiastically, if mistakenly, about the extension of life beyond proscribed limits.

In more recent years, science has begun to catch up with aspiration (one of our favourite phrases!). Starting in the 1970s, a plethora of books predicting longevity increased have appeared. *No More Dying*, a book on human life extension by Joel Kurzman and Philip Gordon, both futurists, came out in 1976, and proved to be highly popular. Subsequent books with titles such as *Maximum Lifespan* and *The Life Extension Revolution* appeared in the 1980s, and innumerable tomes of a similar nature have appeared since.

In 2003, Doubleday published *The Immortal Cell: One Scientist's Quest to Solve the Mystery of Human Aging* by Michael D. West, one of our interviewees. West forecast at that time (and, rather, prophetically) that embryonic stem cells would play an important part in life extension. (see Targets in Ageing. Page 206)

Longevists such as Gennady Stolyarov have also been prominent in recent years. Stolyarov wrote that death is "the enemy of us all, to be fought with medicine, science, and technology "– and adding our own postscript, only now are the armaments for that fight available to scientists.

The American Academy of Anti-Aging Medicine, founded in 1992, has about 26,000 members, almost all of whom are doctors, and all with a specific interest in ageing and longevity, as opposed to straightforward gerontology.

In 2003, Aubrey de Grey (see Key Opinion Leaders. Page 158) and David Gobel formed the Methuselah Foundation, which gives financial grants to anti-ageing research projects. Aubrey de Grey then went on to found the SENS Research Foundation in California (see SENS. Page 158) and more recently Google (now Alphabet) funded Calico, a longevity company, with such biotech luminaries as Art Levinson and Cynthia Kenyon at the helm (see Key Opinion Leaders. Page 169). Additionally, Google/Alphabet has funded a medtech/venture capital business called Verily, which recently invested US $75 million in a European fund run by Medicxi, where Novartis is also a key investor.

Craig Venter (see Key Opinion Leaders. Page 163) another visionary biologist, and a leader in sequencing the first human genome, founded Human Longevity Inc in 2014. This company has the specific and punchy goal of ending ageing through genetic engineering and cell therapy. Eric Drexler wrote about

FUTURISTS

cell repair machines in his book *Engines of Creation*, published in 1986, and Ray Kurzweil believes such nanorobotic systems could be available by as early as 2030.

Even political parties have sprung up to promote longevity, in countries such as Russia, the US, Israel and the Netherlands, although they have received scant support as yet. Many commentators wonder whether slowing ageing and delaying death wouldn't just result in a growing but increasingly elderly population, thereby putting far too many pressures on the scarce resources of the planet.

For instance, Leon Kass, former chairman of the President's Council on Bioethics, has stated his opposition to life extension with the words: "simply to covet a prolonged life span for ourselves is both a sign and a cause of our failure to open ourselves to procreation and to any higher purpose. [The] desire to prolong youthfulness is not only a childish desire to eat one's life and keep it; it is also an expression of a childish and narcissistic wish incompatible with devotion to posterity." Dr Kass does sound like a grumpy killjoy!

Others, including Nick Bostrom of Oxford University, argue that life extension technologies must not just be the preserve of the rich. Aubrey de Grey believes that populations need not increase unmanageably fast if we all live longer. In those circumstances, menopause would be postponed or even eliminated, and therefore pregnancies could be spaced out over many more years.

We cover these issues further in a later section.

Life expectancy is best defined as the age at which people can expect to die, and is calculated as an average. Actuaries calculate this based on mortality tables, and make projections depending on what their present expectations of people's lifespans are. Given all the science happening around longevity, actuaries are using the wrong assumptions.

The so-called "Gompertz equation of human mortality", first identified by a British actuary in 1825, states that our probability of dying in any given year doubles every 7 to 8 years from the age of 30 onwards — and this formula, amazingly, works throughout the rest of life, at least up to the age of 80 or so. (It also works in animals: for dogs, the doubling period is three years, and for lab mice it is about four months.)

This Gompertz curve doesn't care in which country the calculation of life expectancy takes place, or whether average life expectancy is high or low, true it the seven to eight-year rule still applies. And this is still true for ages of 30 to 80 years (though, intriguingly, not beyond).

So, for instance, a British or American or German person, when aged 33, will have a 1 in 1,500 chance of dying in the next year, but by the time he or she reaches 41, that chance will have risen to 1 in 750, and at 49, to 1 in 375, and so forth.

For us to break free of this mortality doubling, we need new technologies and strategies – and of course, several are available to us right now.

Beyond that, scientists are investigating why some creatures live so long. For example, the Californian bristlecone pine is thought to live to over 5,000 years old. Usually, individual members are less long-lived than colony-based life but this pine seems to be the exception to the rule.

Other life forms that do not display signs of ageing include the hydra or anemone, jellyfish, planarian worms, and coral, possibly making them functionally immortal. It is certainly the case that all of those creatures have almost entirely different cells to those they started out with – and Hayflick thinks that that this means that they are not immortal.

But, countering Hayflick, let's remember that all adults are composed mostly of cells that they didn't start out with as babies. Are they therefore not still the same "people" in old age?

The real problem with using very long-lived pines, jellyfish and planarian worms as models to predict what might happen to humans is that those creatures are very different to us, and indeed are not even sexually reproducing. Undoubtedly, their long lives must hold some clues as to how

their regenerative capacity, which is seemingly endless, might have some bearing on our own capacity to regenerate, but there is no simple linkage.

The oldest organisms whose lives can be measured are generally trees. For instance, the Huon Pine colony (a "clonal" colony) in Tasmania is about 10,000 years old, and individual trees are as much as 3,000 years old.

Among animals that are sexually reproducing, Adwaita, a giant tortoise, died in India in 2006 at an estimated 255 years old. Jonathan, another tortoise who lives in the Seychelles, is thought to be about 184 years old.

The tuatara lizard can live to well over 100, and one of them, Henry from New Zealand, only recently mated for the first time at 111 years old. He and his 80-year-old "wife" now have 11 offspring. In addition, Ming, an ocean-going quahog (basically a clam), has been measured to be 507 years old.

If we could, as all of the above creatures appear to do, repair tissues, rejuvenate cells, and reverse epigenetic changes and extend our telomeres, we might similarly halt ageing, or at least slow it considerably.

Liberation from Gompertz will require this kind of leap of the imagination. We humans are already very long-lived compared to other comparably sized mammals (possibly because of our superior brains), and given the current configurations of our bodies, ultra-long life is not likely for most people, even with the potential elimination of some of the categories of diseases that are related to ageing.

Simply changing our metabolisms won't be enough. We will need fundamental cellular change and regeneration. That said, the pace of our decline into death has dramatically decreased in the past two centuries. And the next quantum leap in our average life expectancy is well within sight.

Average lifespan, which is the age of death of a given group of people, has already increased significantly. Huge falls in infant and maternal mortality, as well as a higher average age of death in older adults, have taken developed world life expectancy at birth to over 80, up 33 years from the 47 years people could be expected to live on average as recently as 1900.

Only 20% of the deaths in the UK are now sudden or unexpected, another one fifth occur pretty quickly over a number of weeks or months, but the majority, about 60%, happen after years of illness and intermittent recovery. This was certainly not the case in earlier eras, where sudden illness, mostly due to infections,

accidents and so forth, would carry people off very quickly indeed.

Montaigne, writing in the 16th century, said that death when old was "rare, singular and extraordinary."

But none of that stunning increase in average lifespan has occurred because people have biologically changed, nor is the increase because humans have somehow evolved to live longer.

Life expectancy has risen because our surroundings and our environment have improved. Sanitation, antibiotics, fewer wars, fewer famines, fewer accidents, as well as improved surgery and drugs, are all external factors. Our internal factors have remained the same.

If the people of the early 1900s had been given the conditions that we enjoy today, they would have lived as long as we do. Certainly, the verified record for the longest-lived human has increased. This is, however, because records can only go only one way – higher and higher. In the 1890s, T E Young, president of the English Society of Actuaries wrote that he had identified 4 people who lived (in the 1870s) to 108, 109, 110 and 113 years old.

In the early 1900s there were people who lived nearly as long as Madame Calment. The difference then was that

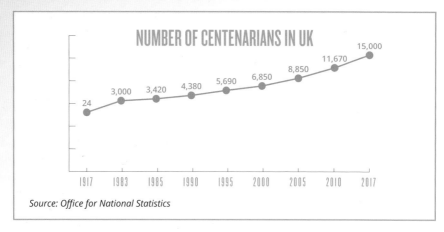

NUMBER OF CENTENARIANS IN UK

24 — 1917
3,000 — 1983
3,420 — 1985
4,380 — 1990
5,690 — 1995
6,850 — 2000
8,850 — 2005
11,670 — 2010
15,000 — 2017

Source: Office for National Statistics

there were a lot fewer of them, as the conditions necessary to become a so-called "superager" (over 100-105 years old), before disease or something else got you, were a lot less favourable than they are today.

As a result of the improved "environment" for human existence, the number of centenarians in the UK has quadrupled in just the past 30 years, and it will quadruple again by 2035. The figure now stands at about 15,000, but will reach at least 60,000 in less than 20 years. The Queen no longer sends telegrams to people on their 100th birthday and quite soon she might even stop sending letters. Her Majesty herself, of course, *deo volente,* will be joining the ranks of the centenarians in the relatively near future. Worldwide, the Pew Research Center estimates that the number of centenarians will rise from 95,000 as recently as 1900 to 3,676,000 in 2050.

It is no surprise that claimed centenarian rates are much higher in countries where there is poor record-keeping of births and deaths. It is a comedic paradox that as people get to be over 85 years old, some of them tend to lie about their age and in an upward direction. This is probably because they get a kick out of the fame associated with being older than everyone else around them.

Countries such as Indonesia, Pakistan and Georgia have or have had more centenarians per head than any of the developed countries, some of them with improbably high ages, as a consequence of this phenomenon.

When asked, many very long-lived people attribute their long lives to a variety of what are mostly stock factors: Spartan conditions, hard labour and a strong sense of community. Madame Calment attributed hers to smoking till she was

117 and to not being too interested in men, among other random things.

It is also important to note that the greatest advances in sanitation and healthcare, in the form of antibiotics and vaccinations, didn't occur until the 1940s and 1950s, so there is a long way to go to see how those changes will affect the number of centenarians, some 20 or 30 years out.

The answer is likely to be that there will be many more of them than is currently projected. So, in summary, life expectancy continues to rise but more slowly than ten or twenty years ago. The low hanging fruit has been mostly harvested.

In the context of today, for overall life expectancy to rise dramatically, it must be because older people live much longer, rather than because younger people die less frequently. In other words, not only must people who are currently elderly live even longer than they otherwise might do, but the life expectancy of the young and middle-aged people must rise also.

The "saving" of the young from early death has already more or less occurred, even in the developing world. This means that apart from the coming reduction in the impact of the Deadly Quintet of age-related diseases (and this is, in the case of cancer and CVD, well within sight), we need more fundamental treatments of "ageing".

The extra 30 years we need to live on top of current life expectancies, to make our forecast of ultra-long lives come true, can only happen if those anti-ageing treatments are made available in the relatively near future.

The good news is that most people do potentially have the physical capacity to live to 115-120 years now, and what prevents the majority of us becoming superagers is the late-life expression of "bad" gene variants, those such as ApoE4, which increases the chances of cardiovascular disease as well as of Alzheimer's.

ApoE4 carriers, who number about one fifth of the population, have higher LDL (or bad) cholesterol than the rest of the population, and if exposed to unhealthy diets, they develop atherosclerosis much more frequently than the general population.

There are many other genes associated with ageing (see Key Genes. Page 400) and of course lifestyle, accidents, suicides, cancer, neurodegeneration, heart disease, obesity, as well as other factors, ensure that in today's circumstances most people don't reach their "maximal" potential lifespans of 115 to 120.

The rapid development of treatments for most cancers, type 2 diabetes and cardiovascular disease, as well as a reduction in smoking in the developed world, is contributing to what are still rising life expectancies. Currently, among the leading 35 industrialised countries, South Korea has the longest life expectancy at birth — 91 for women and 84 for men. But that's still very low compared to what we think it could end up being just 20 years out.

One way of getting to a higher figure is to attack the key diseases of ageing. If cancer were totally curable (and this is a distinctly foreseeable possibility), it itself would add only 3.3 years to an average lifespan. Removing cardiovascular disease entirely as a risk factor for death might be expected to add a further four years. Neurogenerative disease being totally eliminated would add about another two, and even if we were lucky enough to dispense with all of the diseases of ageing, the average life span would extend only into the mid-nineties. The arithmetic to get to 110 is not there unless that there are other ways of enhancing lifespan. And we believe there are.

To live much longer, to the endpoint of our first bridge, with lifespans of about 115-120 being regarded as routine, scientists will have to address ageing itself.

It is important to note that positive trends in life expectancy are not just confined to the rich world. Life expectancy in almost every part of the world is increasing steadily, as the benefits of sanitation and medicine, now well established in the developed world, spread to developing countries as well. Bill and Melinda Gates have been instrumental in this process and absolutely deserve honorary sainthoods.

However, inequality in access to healthcare and the abuse of opioids (the "opidemic"), along with gun crime and suicide, means that the United States, despite its wealth, has one of the lowest life expectancies in the developed world. The US has 5% of the world's population and consumes 80% of the world's opioids. It is believed that Alzheimer's may have also contributed to the recent, though slight, decrease in life expectancy in the US.

It is also worth mentioning the Hispanic paradox, which is the fact that Latinos in the US live somewhat longer than their richer and typically better-educated white counterparts. This stands in contrast to everywhere else in the world, where longevity is at least in part determined by economic and general health status.

This paradox cannot simply be explained by reference to the "salmon bias", which is where immigrants quite often go back to where they come from in order to die, raising the life expectancy of the remaining immigrant population; nor can it be explained by a hypothesis that migrants are healthier than native populations, because of the fact that they are self-selected from the best or most competitive of their compatriots.

Whatever the cause, it probably hints at psychosocial aspects of ageing. Perhaps stronger family bonds among Hispanic people in the US compensate for lesser incomes and education.

This underlines an important factor in longevity and disease: less stress equals better health and longevity outcomes. Whatever the lessons for ageing research of the Hispanic paradox, the US remains a poor performer in the average life expectancy stakes in the developed world.

By 2030, Imperial College researchers believe, life expectancy at birth in the US will only be 80 for men and 81 for women (admittedly in the absence of the scientific advances that we expect to come), about the same as Mexico. This is despite the fact that the US spends almost one-fifth of its national income on health care. It clearly spends it very badly, especially if you happen to be poor.

Imperial College will be proven wrong, at least in the more distant future, because they are extrapolating current trends without considering presently available but little-used technologies, as well as future scientific advances. The combination of these will change everything to do with modern actuarial thinking.

The US isn't the only country with a healthcare problem, however. The UK is also in a pretty unhealthy state, as are Australia and Canada.

As with the US experience, average life expectancy at age 65 in Britain has also declined modestly in recent years, supposedly due to Alzheimer's.

However, overall British life expectancy at birth continues to

rise, unlike in the US. In the decade to 2013, life expectancy in the UK rose by three years for men and by 2.3 years for women. Andrew Scott, co-author of *The 100 Year Life,* has brilliantly pointed out that gaining this life expectancy each and every decade is like having a few extra hours added every day. It opens all sorts of choices for individuals and life, according to Andrew, will become multi-staged rather than the three stages it is now.

With very low fertility rates in most developed countries, and now in quite a few developing countries, including China, overall population sizes are falling. In some developed countries, such as Spain, Italy and most strikingly Japan, the potential decline in population is dramatic. Japan's population of 127 million today is expected to fall, according to the Japanese National Institute of Population and Social Security

Research, to just 88 million by 2065, and to 50 million by 2115. Against a fertility rate per woman of 2.1 births required to keep a population at a stable level absent net immigration, the Japanese fertility rate is just 1.44. Low fertility rates are also prevalent in most European countries, and the US also has a falling fertility rate.

Life expectancy has some familial characteristics. If one of your parents is, or was, long-lived, you too are more likely to be older than average when you die. There is a genetic component to this observation, but also an environmental one: longer-lived parents have probably conferred better nutrition, developmental care, and medicine on their offspring.

The offspring of most semi-supercentenarians (subjects who have reached an age of 105 to 109 years) have a lower epigenetic (i.e. biological) age than their peers (by about 5.1 years, measured by blood analysis). In addition, the epigenetic clock, described by Horvath, shows that the cerebellum part of the brain ages much more slowly in the grey matter of centenarians. It is also interesting to note that female breast tissue always seems to biologically age faster than its owner.

It is certainly the case, as Michael Denton says in *Evolution – Still a Theory in Crisis*, that: "genes cannot be the sole unidirectional determinants of organic form, as Weismann and most geneticists throughout the twentieth century believed". Genes play a major, but not exclusive, role in the extended longevity of superagers. But, there is no transparent blueprint for life. Thus, the mechanisms of human ageing are influenced by genetic factors as well as by lifestyle (Bishop and Guarante 2007) and for normal people the genetic part is thought to be 20 to 25%, and the lifestyle and luck parts 75 to 80%.

But interestingly, this genetic component becomes much more important the older we get. Clusters of long lives have been noticed in the families of people who live to be over 100 (Perls et al., 2000). There are also pockets of people in parts of the world who seem to have "protective" genes: An example are the 250 or so inhabitants of the Cretan village of Mylopotamos; they have very low levels of triglycerides and LDL ("bad") cholesterol.

Additionally, smaller people tend to have marginally longer lives than taller ones, most likely because of reduced growth hormone expression, although the science around this observation is also confusing and complex, and not necessarily robust.

Studies of why some people are very long-lived relative to others suggest that superagers exhibit geroprotection (anti-ageing) as a result of genetic traits (or alleles).

The obvious objective of such studies of superaged populations is to discover what specific traits make them long-lived and to try to induce or introduce those same traits into the general population. It is thought that people who live beyond their nineties have these aforementioned "protective alleles" in their genes, typically including ApoE and the FOXO (FOXO1 and FOXO3) family. These alleles seem to protect against oxidative stress or ROS (see Theories of Ageing. Page 68) (Broer et al., 2015).

In particular, an allele of FOXO3A, an insulin-regulating transcription factor, is common in superagers, and this has now been confirmed by eight different studies. FOXO, which has been conserved all the way through C. elegans worms to humans, has been shown in multiple research papers to be important in ageing, and is a very important component of insulin signalling through the IGF-1 pathway. FOXO is thought to be a member of the pro-longevity family of genes in most of its iterations (Webb and Brunet 2014) and its overexpression is thought to be important to proteostasis (see Proteostasis. Page 72).

FOXO is vital to autophagy and to the ubiquitin-proteasome system (see Autophagy. Page 132), both of which (in most people, but not so much in superagers) decline with age. A study of 1,762 German centenarians/nonagenarians, contrasted with younger "controls", identified FOXO3A polymorphisms or alleles, and the results show that possessing these alleles is correlated with reaching an exceptional age. This association was substantially stronger in centenarians than in nonagenarians (Flachsbart et al., 2009). Additionally, those people with two copies of an allele (450V) of the CETP (cholesterol ester transfer protein) gene enjoy lower LDL or bad cholesterol and higher levels of HDL or good cholesterol. This allele is found in many people over 90 and is also protective against Alzheimer's.

Additionally, what is clear is that superagers don't suffer much from the usual panoply of age-related diseases until the very last part of their lives (typically the last 5%, for people over 110). This contrasts with the general population, where people suffer from one or more serious diseases for the last 18% of their lives. However, interestingly, studies in Finland have revealed that at least half of those over 90 have what are known as cardiac transthyretin (TTR) amyloidosis, which are misfolded protein amyloid fibril. These gradually impair tissue structure and function, though they may not be a specific cause of death in the super-aged Nonetheless, familial TTR disease is quite prevalent in people, and this observation is being "reverse engineered" in studies to see if it throws up specific genetic "secrets" common to superagers.

Credible practitioners are now beginning to regard ageing as a disease, albeit one that is terminal, with the terminus moving further and further out in time. So the key questions for us are: what is it that makes ageing less rapid in some individuals and not in others, and can that longevity genetic benefit be extended to all?

The hunt is on to discover drugs that might replicate the allele polymorphisms that seem to confer super-long life on a small number of people. People like Aubrey de Grey believe that drugs and therapies can reverse us to more youthful states and thereby allow us to remain in our bodies, while extending lifespans and average longevity to undreamt-of numbers.

Others such as Ray Kurzweil, now on Google's payroll, believe that we will eventually merge with mechanical bodies and/or with the internet cloud. Here we enter the realm of science fiction, at least for several decades to come. Possible though it may be, it seems like a stretch too far for all but a handful of Silicon Valley fantasists.

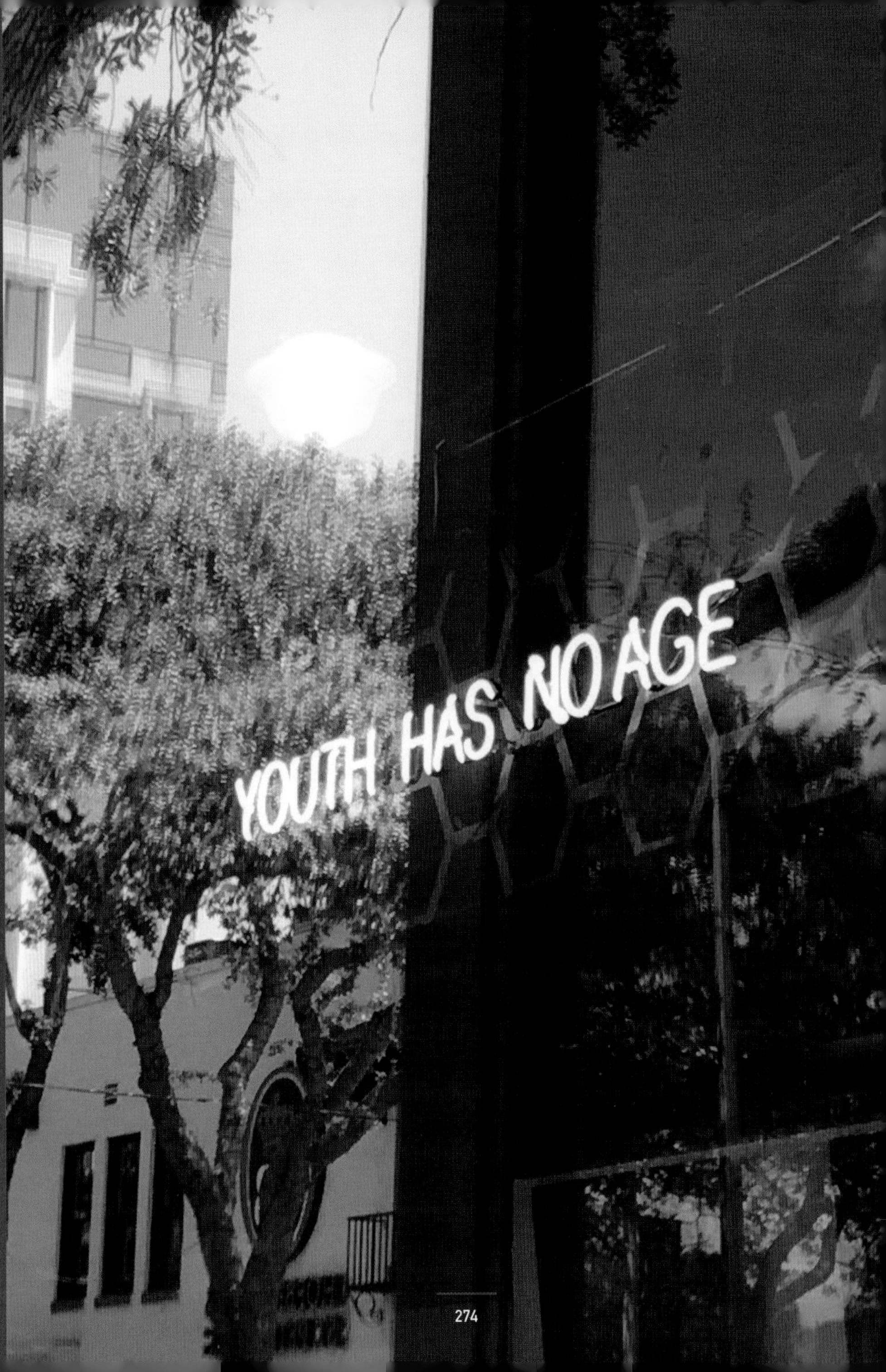
YOUTH HAS NO AGE

DEMOGRAPHICS, LONG LIFE, WORK, LEISURE AND THE TRAJECTORY OF LIFE

We are undeniably the most successful species to have ever occupied our planet.

Consequently, the human population is at an all-time high, and because of this our very presence and actions are having a greater influence over the fate of all the other life forms that also consider Earth to be their home. Collectively we influence what happens to the oceans, air, land and atmosphere (despite what climate change deniers may say).

Although the human population has reached 7.5 billion, before 1800 there were less than a billion people living on Earth. As the impact of the industrial revolution began to gather steam, the population grew by 65% over the next hundred years and that exponential growth rate continued to where we are today. The graph overleaf illustrates just how sudden and rapid the human population growth has been.

We first wrote about demographics (the study of human populations)

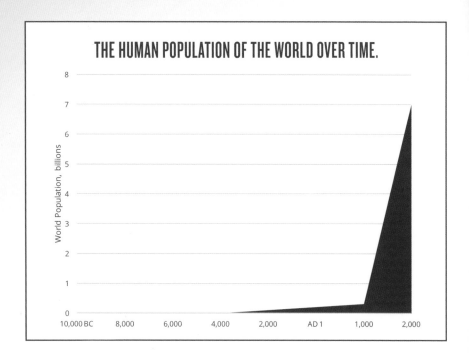

THE HUMAN POPULATION OF THE WORLD OVER TIME.

World Population, billions

8
7
6
5
4
3
2
1
0

10,000 BC   8,000   6,000   4,000   2,000   AD 1   1,000   2,000

over a decade ago in our first book, *Wake Up! Survive and Prosper in the Coming Economic Turmoil.* Back then, it was in the context of the economic burden that an ageing population will impose on the governments of most developed countries and how we should all strive to be financially self-reliant in our retirement years. The ageing of populations in developed economies is accelerating; in the decades ahead, governments may simply not be able to afford to hand out state pensions at such a young retirement age relative to life expectancy. Global ageing is a pervasive trend that is expected to

continue for the foreseeable future, and its impact on societies will be far-reaching.

The first state pension scheme was introduced in Germany back in 1889 by its then Chancellor Otto von Bismarck. In 1916, long after Bismarck's death, the retirement age was lowered to 65.

In the UK, the first modern state pension system was introduced in 1908 with the passing of the Old-Age Pensions Act by David Lloyd George. When it was launched, it was means-tested and it paid out somewhere between 10 and 25 pence per week from the age

Chancellor Otto von Bismarck of Germany (1862-1890), who introduced the first state pension system in 1889. (Source: https://commons.wikimedia.org, Kabinett-Photo, author AD.BRAUN & Cie Dornach)

of 70 in a time when life expectancy was around 45 and only about a third of men and 40% of women lived to see their 65th birthdays. After World War II, the government passed the National Insurance Act 1946, requiring all workers to make weekly contributions into the National Insurance Fund in order to be entitled to a state pension, as well as a range of other benefits, including unemployment and sickness. Implemented in 1948, the pension scheme paid out when a man turned 65 and when a woman turned 60.

This worked well for a few decades as there were plenty of young workers contributing towards National Insurance in the UK relative to the number of retirees drawing from it. In 1950, the ratio of workers to retirees was just over 7, but by 1970 it had fallen to 4.3 and by 2010 it was down to 3.6. By 2050 this ratio is expected to fall further to 2.4. So, while there used to be 7 workers contributing towards funding each pensioner, we now have half as many and this is set to fall further by mid-century. This is a direct consequence of (a) people living longer and (b) couples having fewer children. It means that the make-up of our population is changing and over 65s will account for a greater percentage of the population. As we mentioned earlier, globally, two-thirds of all people who have ever lived past the age of 65 are alive today. In the UK the imbalance in the pension pot is set to worsen with an ageing population and the annual deficit is set to rise to £15 billion by 2060. Offsetting this would require a 4% income tax hike for those still working, or the government could increase the retirement age.

The Office of National Statistics predicts that, by 2035, there will be around 58,000 people living in the UK over the age of 100 – a quadrupling from today's figure. So clearly we should expect people to continue working to beyond today's very "young" retirement age of 65. The UK government has taken some steps to increase the state pension age and is currently moving to equalise it for both men and women. It is currently 65 for men and 63 for women, but by 2018, it will be 65 for both. It is then set to gradually increase towards 70 by the middle of the century. If the government is going to expect people to keep working well beyond the age of 65, it needs to take steps to improve the elderly workforce's general health, otherwise they will not be in a fit state to keep working. Unfortunately, the healthspan of people has not been keeping up with the increasing life expectancy, especially in men.

Not surprisingly, life expectancy across the world continues to increase. The Population Division of the United Nations Department of Economic and Social Affairs (UN DESA) released its 2015 revision of World Population Prospects in which it published life expectancy at birth by country. Top of the rankings for life expectancy at birth for both sexes is Hong Kong, where it is 80.91 years for a male and 86.58 years for a female, putting Hong Kong just ahead of Japan, where it is 80.00 years and 86.49 respectively.

Interestingly, the UK didn't make the top 10, nor even the top 20,

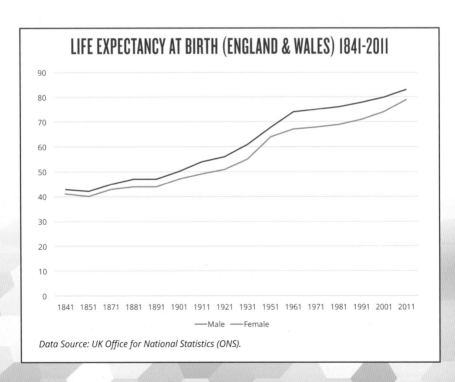

LIFE EXPECTANCY AT BIRTH (ENGLAND & WALES) 1841-2011

Data Source: UK Office for National Statistics (ONS).

Rank	Country	Overall	Male	Female
1	Hong Kong	83.74	80.91	86.58
2	Japan	83.31	80.00	86.49
3	Italy	82.84	80.27	85.23
4	Switzerland	82.66	80.43	84.74
5	Singapore	82.64	79.59	85.61
6	Iceland	82.30	80.73	83.84
7	Spain	82.28	79.42	85.05
8	Australia	82.10	79.93	84.28
9	Israel	82.07	80.18	83.82
10	Sweden	81.93	80.10	83.71
...				
28=	United Kingdom	80.45	78.45	82.39
...				
43	United States	78.88	76.47	81.25
...				
201	Swaziland	49.18	49.69	48.54

Life Expectancy at Birth for 2015 by Country.

Source: United Nations Department of Economic and Social Affairs.

but came in 28th (78.45 years for a male and 82.39 years for a female), while the United States was even further down the rankings at number 43 (76.47 years for a male and 81.25 years for a female.) Granted the overall life expectancy across the top 40 countries varies by less than 5 years, but it is still a valuable general indicator.

Of the 201 countries and territories included in the report, 124 of them had an overall life expectancy at birth of over 70 years.

By 2030, the number of people in the world aged 60 years or over is projected to grow by 56% to 1.4 billion, rising further to over 2 billion by 2050. The number of people aged 80 or over will also grow, reaching 434 million by 2050, versus around 125 million today.

HEALTH EXPENDITURE AS A SHARE OF GDP, 2013 (OR NEAREST YEAR)

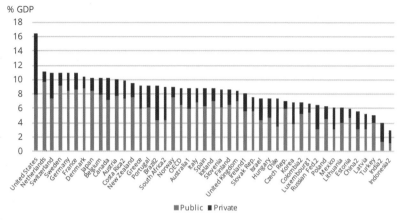

1 alongside a country's name refers to 2012. 2 alongside a country's name denotes that the data includes investment whilst all overs do not.

Surprisingly, East Asia is ageing faster than any other region in the world. According to US Census Bureau forecasts, by 2050 the top 5 countries with the highest percentage of their population over the age of 65 are all in Asia. Japan remains firmly in the number one spot with 40.1%, the next four countries being South Korea (34.7%), Thailand (27.4%) China (26.7%) and Singapore (23.9%). China represents a daunting number of people – with a projected population of 1.38 billion, it translates to 381 million people. No doubt China's one-child policy has distorted the natural demography; even though it has recently been relaxed to some extent, it will take many more decades to see the effects.

There is no denying that society is changing as a consequence of our ageing populations. Older people think differently, have different priorities, invest differently, buy differently and even vote differently. We can expect the overall social mood to change as the elderly continue to grow as a proportion of the population and we can also expect their collective voice to grow louder, highlighting issues that concern them more.

In terms of healthcare, older people require more care and support than younger members of society. The UK's National Health Service (NHS) regularly makes the front pages of the newspapers as stories emerge of just how much the system is struggling to cope with the sheer volume of patients. It is a healthcare system that was designed for a different era, when the population was smaller; when the country as a whole was much younger and life expectancy was lower. The NHS costs the British Government around £116 billion per year, or 9% of GDP to operate. According to the Congressional Budget Office, the United States Government spends around US $1 trillion, or 6% of GDP on healthcare (Medicare and Medicaid) but private healthcare spending accounts for another US $2.2 trillion annually, so overall the US spends around 18% of its GDP on healthcare even though its life expectancy is about one year lower than that of the UK, illustrating that more healthcare spending does not result in longer life expectancy.

Much of the NHS's workload today is geriatric care, which will continue to increase in the coming decades. We are not going to write about how the NHS could be redesigned to cope with the diseases of tomorrow (that's a separate book in itself); we are merely pointing out that demand for geriatric care is set to grow for the foreseeable future.

The changing demographics mean that geriatric diseases will become more prominent and will put further strain on the already stretched NHS system. In addition to cardiovascular disease, geriatric diseases include cancer, cognitive conditions, joints

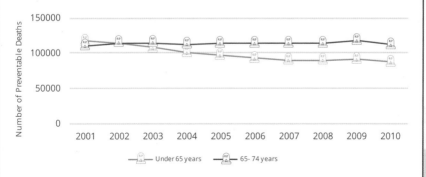

IMPORTANT PROGRESS HAS BEEN MADE, BUT MORE IS NEEDED TO CONTINUE TO SAVE LIVES, PARTICULARLY FOR PEOPLE UNDER 65 YEARS

Number of Preventable Deaths

150000

100000

50000

0

2001 2002 2003 2004 2005 2006 2007 2008 2009 2010

Under 65 years   65- 74 years

Source: https://www.cdc.gov/vitalsigns/heartdisease-stroke/infographic.html

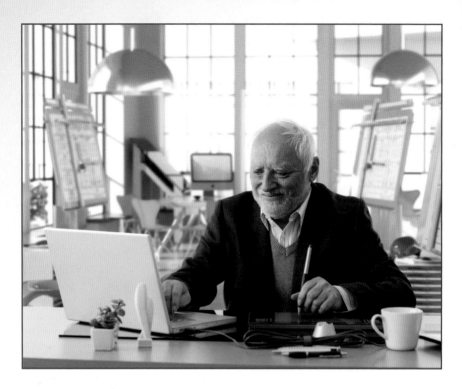

and bones, obesity, neurological diseases, loss of sight and hearing, and urinary incontinence.

On the other side of the equation, the healthcare system itself needs to be better prepared for the age wave. It's not just a matter of throwing more funding at the NHS; there is also a matter of better aligning its capabilities with the cases it sees. An increase in the number of diseases that mainly affect the elderly means we need more geriatricians, i.e. doctors that specialise in the health of the elderly. Robotics and automation will also start to pick up more meaningful roles in patient diagnosis and care, though probably not for another decade or so.

OUR GOLDEN YEARS WILL BE WORKING YEARS

With life expectancy continuing to rise and retirement ages creeping upwards, it would be fair to say that the vast majority of people working today will not have enough money to be able to retire at the traditional age of 65. The current state pension in the UK for people who have contributed towards National Insurance for 35 years is £155.65 per week. This works out to be an annual income of around £8,000, which for most people will not be enough to maintain their lifestyle, even though the government has nearly doubled the amount from a decade earlier.

According to Legal & General, a UK financial services company, the median value of a private pension fund is only £46,900, which in today's interest rate environment would pay an annual annuity of just £2,500.

A report by Aviva released in 2016 noted that "over-45s expect their pension fund to generate £12,590 a year on top of the state pension – but their current savings will deliver less than a third of this target income."

Owning your own home without a mortgage by retirement age is an added advantage and will reduce the amount of money required in later life, but it turns out that this is not as common as it used to be: fewer than 48% of people aged between 55 and 64 have no mortgage on their homes, and just under 25% are still renting. One in 10 of those aged 65 and over still have a mortgage.

The obvious solution to the pension shortfall is to keep working well into our 70s and possibly even our 80s, but we can expect the working hours to be fewer than when in full-time employment. To achieve this, we will need to re-skill ourselves in our golden years and find a useful role to fulfil in society. On the flip side, it means that employers will have to learn to accept older members of staff in the work place, something that is not the cultural norm in many parts of the developed world.

The prospect of working well into and beyond our 60s should not be a daunting one as it is actually better for our overall health and longevity. In the section of the book on lifestyle conditioning, we discussed how some of the most detrimental things to health in later life are being sedentary, not challenging our brains, and loneliness. Working, even part-time, will keep us socially engaged, active and mentally challenged. Plus, we get to earn some money at the same time for good measure. More people used to work in their 60s; early retirement is a relatively new phenomenon. In 1970, 81% of men aged between 60 and 64 worked in the UK, but by 1985 this number had dipped to 49.7%. Today, almost one-third of people in the UK aged between 50 and 64 are not working and yet, by 2020, one-third of the workforce will be over 50.

Working in later life does assume that the individual is in good physical and mental health. Nowadays, only a small fraction of the workforce is involved in physically demanding work such as mining, so most of us

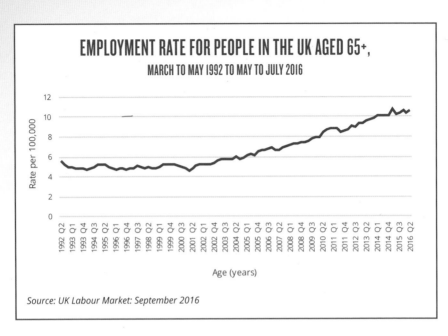

EMPLOYMENT RATE FOR PEOPLE IN THE UK AGED 65+,
MARCH TO MAY 1992 TO MAY TO JULY 2016

Rate per 100,000

Age (years)

Source: UK Labour Market: September 2016

should reach retirement without any serious work-related health issues. But for those whose health has been affected by their physical jobs, the prospect of working beyond the age of 65 may not be easy. Nevertheless, there are still jobs available that are not physically demanding. For those who cannot bear the idea of working beyond retirement age, relying on the state pension alone could prove to be challenging. If the state pension can be supplemented with a private pension, it may be possible to maintain a decent standard of living.

Alternatively, retirees who are not able or willing to work beyond the official retirement age can consider moving to a country where the cost of living is lower. Many British retirees favour Spain for their retirement, for example; pensioners often trade their UK homes for a comfortable residence in Spain. Their £8,000 annual state pension, plus any private pension scheme, goes a lot further there too. Of the official 300,000 Britons living in Spain, 108,000 are claiming the UK state pension. Other EU countries are also popular with British citizens: Ireland has a British population of 255,000 and France has 185,000 Brits living there. In total, there are 1.2 million British citizens living outside the UK in the EU.

For retirees with a more modest budget, there are more further afield locations to consider: in Europe, options include Cyprus, Turkey and Greece. In Asia, there are countries such as Sri Lanka, Philippines, Thailand and Malaysia. Many of these countries have expatriate retirement schemes. There are also a number of options in Central and South America.

However, as exotic and exciting as these countries may sound, unless you have some sort of connection with one of them, it is very difficult to just pack up and relocate to a new land in your golden years unless you are very outgoing and enjoy the thrill of such things.

For the rest of us who are still in our working lives, we would be wise to take advantage of our income-earning years by saving more earlier on, so that we will have more options when we reach our 60s. We need to be a little smarter with our investments and savings even though we are living in an incredibly challenging economic environment where interest rates are artificially low in most Western countries and debt remains at unhealthy high levels.

THE WORLD WILL BE CHANGED BY LONGER AND BETTER LIVES

In the developed world, it will soon become rarer and rarer for people to live for less than eighty, then ninety, then a hundred years.

And it is this fact that will transform societies around the world.

Learn, earn, burn out, retire and expire is about to be replaced with a new life paradigm. Older people will need to be rebooted and retooled on a regular basis, and instead of being sent out to pasture at 65, and often reluctantly, they will not only be hired or re-hired, they will be required.

We are pretty sure that our research has taken us to the correct conclusion – that life expectancy will indeed rise sharply in the next couple of decades. In those circumstances, it isn't hard to see that many of our known and accepted societal constructs will change. While we are only going to touch on this subject, important as it is, there is some terrific reading material out there. *The 100 Year Life* by Lynda

Grafton and Andrew Scott is very good in this respect, as is the work of the Milken Institute Center for the Future of Aging, headed up by Paul Irving. See the list of useful organisations in the Appendix, if readers are interested in exploring further.

At the moment, the conventional wisdom has it that our life paradigm is: birth, go to school, get a job, retire and then check out. It wasn't so long ago, of course, that the learning and retiring parts of life were a lot shorter than they are today. When Bismarck introduced the first universal pension, for people over 65, there wasn't a lot of demand for it, since very few people lived to over 65 in Germany or indeed, anywhere else. And, just 100 years ago most people didn't go to school after the age of 16.

Now, about half the population of the developed world can expect to be in higher education till about 20 or 21 years old, and most people enjoy close to two decades of retirement. The new life paradigm, however, will be very different to even this. It will go as follows: birth, start learning (you will be doing this bit for your whole life), earn (but in multiple careers), retire (at 80 or more), but even then, stay engaged with some form of "job" and eventually, at 110 or even more, expire.

The implications of this sea-change in life expectancy that is on the immediate horizon are pretty clear:

we will all need to work a lot longer, collectively we will have fewer children (this is already happening almost everywhere in both the developed and developing world), we will be continuously learning (or retooled), we won't work in the same job our whole lives, we will have much more leisure time, and we will live in a state of "wellderliness" for a lot longer.

If you want to be a lifelong employee anywhere in this new world of ultra-longevity, you will have to be a lifelong learner. We'd better get used to it, because this is going to be the new trajectory of our lives. And this is just the start of our escape from the Gompertz law. So much is going to happen in the next fifty years, that the world will look and operate completely differently to how it does today. Some pretty important implications arise out of this steepening and lengthening of the curve of lifespans.

Firstly, as we have stated before, fewer children will be born, all across the world. Prosperity and extended lives always have two effects; families no longer need to be large in order to provide either labour or "replacements", as in the days when people lived on farms and child mortality was common.

The other is, as women defer having children until later in life, in part due to extended or enhanced fertility (the result of longevity science), and partly because of career and family choices, fewer children will be born. The whole concept of "family life", indeed, will be recast. In most developed societies, the number of children women have is already below the "replacement" rate of 2.1. In fact, in countries like Japan, Russia and Italy, the fertility rate is regarded as something close to catastrophic and their populations are forecast to contract sharply in the next thirty years. Even in the developing world, and particularly in Asia and Latin America, fertility rates are declining sharply. Singapore has a fertility rate of just 0.82, Japan 1.41, the EU 1.61, the UK 1.89 and the US 1.87. China has fallen to 1.6, and Australia 1.77. All of these countries' fertility rates are below replacement levels. Countries such as Afghanistan (5.21) and Burundi (6.04), that still have high levels of fertility per woman. However, even these figures are declining, and will continue to do so (source: CIA).

In 1950 the world's population stood at 2.52 billion people. The UN estimates that the current world population of about 7.3 billion will reach 8.5 billion in 2030, 9.7 billion by 2050 and 11.2 billion by 2100. Our sense is that these numbers are probably too high, given that fertility rates are falling almost everywhere. Latter-day Malthusians, forecasting gloom and doom, due to overpopulation, soil erosion, climate change, a reduction in biodiversity, and energy depletion are likely

once again to be proved wrong. Technology and innovation have, are and will continue to provide ways for this planet to accommodate its by now slowly increasing but plateauing numbers of human inhabitants. World population growth has already slowed from about 2.2% in the 1960s to about 1% today, with most of that growth coming from Africa.

This slowdown, and future possible reversal of world population growth, is entirely due to prosperity. It is well known that billions of people have been lifted out of abject poverty by globalisation and by economic growth since the end of the second world war. There are, of course, concerns about how the developmental model so successful in countries such as China, involving low-tech manufacturing, will be able to persist in a world of automation and "on-shoring". This model, where cheap goods for exports are produced by rural migrants in factories, which act as the scaffolds of modernising economies, is now much less robust. This is because goods can be made more cheaply by machines, and can be made closer to the point of consumption.

Secondly, people are going to be older, everywhere. Centenarians are about to become commonplace: with just 24 of them in the UK a hundred years ago, when telegrams were first sent out, 3,000 in 1983, an estimated 15,000 today and at least 600,000 by

2080, according to the ONS. In the US, the last census indicated over 53,000 centenarians, but that was in 20101 and the figure will now be much higher; in Australia, there are presently over 4,500 centenarians, and that figure is expected to rise by nine times between now and 2055. The novelty of meeting a person who is hundred-plus years-old will soon be gone.

The world is ageing and that is despite the fact that, in countries such as the US or the UK, life expectancy has temporarily stalled. UK males, for instance, and expected to live 1.3% less at age 65 than ten years ago, and UK females 2% less. It is the same picture in the US, where mortality improvement peaked in 2004-2006.

But, the big picture is very positive. In the UK, life expectancy at birth has doubled in the past two centuries, and the oldest of the old – those over 100 – represent the fastest-growing cohort – and will continue to do so for a long time to come. And that trend, of the older segment of the UK population being the fastest-growing, is replicated worldwide. Currently, it is estimated by the UN that the over 60s accounts for 671 million people, or just under 10% of the global population. People over 80 only make up 1% of the total. But by 2050 the number of people over 60 will number 2 billion and those over 80 will number about 400 million, making up about 21% and 4% of the total world population respectively. In the developed world, the proportional figures will be much higher, with over a third of the populace being over 60 years old. Already, in Japan, Italy, Greece, Sweden, Canada and Hong Kong, people over 65 outnumber those in the 0-14-year-old age range – and, crazily, the retirement age in Japan is just 60! Every developed country will experience that phenomenon in the next twenty years or so.

The death rate internationally is generally continuing on the trend line which started during the industrial revolution i.e. downwards. Improved hygiene, the green revolution, nutrition, and antibiotics have been the key contributors. But, as we wrote earlier, that low-hanging fruit has largely been harvested, and further improvements are now coming through a decline in the mortality caused by the diseases of ageing in the future will come from the advances in medicine which we have detailed in this book.

The older end of the age spectrum is the fastest-growing in almost every country, including those of the developing world. Worldwide, the working population is expected to increase by 3% in the next decade, but the number of those aged 65 and older will increase by 39%. Additionally, the average age of the world's workforce is rising rapidly, and the age cohort that is most productive, 15-40, is only growing at about 0.5% per annum. The average age of the global workforce bottomed between 1980 and 1985 at around 33.9 years, and has been rising ever since. Numbers in the important 15–40 age cohort are growing much more slowly than in the 55-64 cohort.

Thirdly, education will be the key passport to prosperity for most people. Without embracing it as a lifelong continuum, people will find it difficult to get satisfying and well-paid jobs. Education will become a process that begins in early childhood and will continue to near death. So-called MOOCS (Massive Open Online Courses) (see *Fast Forward*), best personified by the likes of the Khan Academy and Coursera, are early indicators of how learning will spread to every generation. People will be required to relearn, retool and change to keep up with a fast-changing world. The education industry, both online and in person, will continue to expand rapidly. EdTechXGlobal, a consultancy, estimates that the worldwide education industry, at US $5 trillion, is already eight times the size of the global software industry and three times the size of the media and entertainment industry. However, education is only about 2% digitised and that will certiainly change. The edtech industry is expected to grow at 17% per annum and reach over US $250 billion of revenues by 2020.

This necessity of education on a continuous basis will be to avoid the sort of "work" in a world of dystopian automation envisaged by some forecasters. Will there be an elite, super class lording it over a biologically inferior caste of the "useless" feeders, in the nightmare scenario proposed by Yuval Harari in his book *Homo Deus*?

Certainly, we know that "work," as currently defined, will change, and it is pretty clear to us that human-to-human "connection" work, requiring sensitivity and empathy, will become more valued than it is today. Work involving proficiency in design, coding, the law, accounting, even medicine, will become less valued as artificial intelligence and other technology becomes more proficient than its human counterparts. This is actually happening today though most people in these types of jobs can't see what is happening to their own industries, instead are behaving rather like frogs being slowly boiled in water.

An example of a career that will become more valued, more skilled, and more specialised is the social care of humans. We already know that more and more people are becoming very old, and that frailty is still commonplace, despite medical advances. Those old people need –

and should get – the care that they deserve, rather than the mostly perfunctory and almost dehumanised experience they now receive. Already, disruptors are emerging in the home care market, particularly in the US, where the tech industry is applying its considerable brain power to improving the level of care in what is a highly fragmented market worth over US $30 billion a year. In this respect, Honor, a private but well-funded business, is worth following.

The crisis in social care across almost all of the developed world is primarily due to cost and to the smaller number of young people relative to the old (the so-called dependency ratio). Globally, the percentage of the population which is in the working age category has fallen from about 73% in 1965 to 53% today, with China, as an example, going from 77% in 1960 to just 37%. The amount of voluntary social care worldwide is huge; in the US, the estimated value of friends-and-family provision of care for the elderly exceeds that of Medicaid – US $522 billion a year, versus US $449 billion (Chari et al., 2015).

However, there are reasons for optimism about this social care crisis. Older people are going to be kept "wellderly" for much longer in

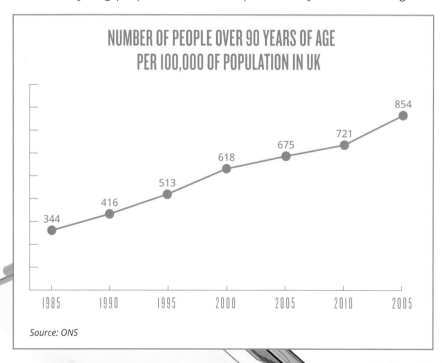

NUMBER OF PEOPLE OVER 90 YEARS OF AGE PER 100,000 OF POPULATION IN UK

854
721
675
618
513
416
344

1985   1990   1995   2000   2005   2010   2005

Source: ONS

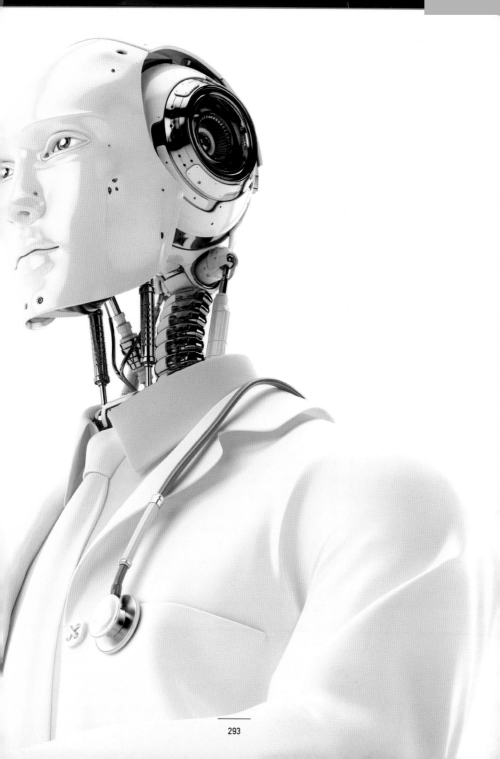

our brave new world, one in which the diseases of ageing are first rendered less onerous, and thereafter conquered. It is the diseases of ageing which cause the greatest need for social care, and which absorb huge portions of national health budgets. If these diseases could be lessened in terms of severity and, at least in one or two instances, eliminated, then those costs would go down sharply.

Furthermore, as these costs diminish, more money is liberated for other expenditures for instance, social care for those who have passed from wellderliness to illderliness. Almost everyone will have to go into some period of dependency but the good news is that it will be much shorter than it is today. The resources that are currently so stretched can be reinforced and applied to a smaller relative number of care-receivers. It is a fact that over 40% of the NHS budget in the UK is spent on people over 65 and any reduction in that figure will allow for larger amounts to be spent on better social care provision.

The Dutch have an interesting concept, now being rolled out across the whole country. It is called "Buurtzorg" which means "neighbourhood care". The Netherlands health authorities believe that the only people who should be administering social or domiciliary care should be health professionals, organised into teams of 12 people, each looking after 40-60 clients. There are now 900 such teams, and because at least 60% of the time worked by these health professionals is in direct contact with clients, apparently costs are significantly reduced. In fact, Buurtzorg is supposed to be saving the Dutch as much as 50% over conventional practice, with clients reporting much-improved service and outcomes. Teams of nurses act as "head coaches" for patients, offering lifestyle advice and encouragement. Smaller pilots of similar schemes are now being conducted in the UK.

In terms of a career, or one of multiple future careers, for those people just embarking on life at work, caregiving seems to us to be a worthwhile one to consider. The jobs in human-to-human connection will undoubtedly become more highly valued, and the market will continue growing. It's also a business area with insufficiently competent participants and thus provides the perfect recipe for career and business success.

Indeed, the US Bureau of Labor Statistics predicts that in the next decade, the fastest-growing occupations will be in social or medical care including carers, nurses, therapists, and healthcare employees. Robots just can't compete with human carers, and nor will they for a very long time to come. No compassion, no humour, no empathy whereas those characteristics not required in lawyers or accountants and so the algorithms that replace them are at no disadvantage in these respects. Since social care is currently miserably paid, with average salaries in the US of about US $23,000 and in the UK of about the same, an upgrading in the way that society values such carers is beyond due.

In contrast, will the doctors of the future just be front-office "receptionists", for computers such as IBM's Watson to provide diagnoses and recommend treatments? Will surgeons be replaced fully (as opposed to in part, as at present) by robots? A Boston-based start-up called FDNA is rolling out its Face2Gene platform. This consists of a photo database of people with more than 2,000 rare genetic diseases. Doctors take pictures of their patients and upload them to FDNA's mobile app, which then provides a list of diseases they might have by analysing facial features linked to those conditions.

Will lawyers and accountants be replaced by algorithms, will architects and builders be replaced by machines? Truck drivers and taxi drivers put out of work by autonomous vehicles? The answer is probably and, in some cases definitely.

Thus, education and careers will be fused together in lockstep: to remain relevant to the workforce, people will have to keep being trained, and retrained, and retrained again. Future careers may just be those among the least valued today such as education, caregiving, hospitality and tourism.

In a world where the average age is rising rapidly, discarding the wisdom, experience and empathetic abilities of older workers will not be just unwise, but pure folly. When so much of life is spent in retirement, a huge amount of talent and energy, and productive capacity, goes to waste.

Additionally, retirees consume money healthcare, savings, pensions, social care and they are not productive even if they wanted to be. Already, Warren Buffett has described the enormous burden of healthcare costs on the US economy as a "tapeworm", responsible for reducing the competitiveness of US companies against their global peers. The US already spends almost one in five dollars on healthcare versus one in twenty in China.

It will not only be an economic necessity for older people to remain in the workforce in some form or other: it will be a requirement. There will simply not be enough money in pension pots, be they government or otherwise, to fund graceful (and, perhaps, unwanted) indolence for all of the retirees who are joining the 65+ cohort in developed countries. It has been estimated that if things don't change radically, by 2050 the worldwide "pension gap", or shortfall, will be US $400 trillion – or about five times the size of the global economy.

Older workers will become increasingly valued for their empathetic skills and for their "wisdom", in the broad sense of that word. A recent study by Anglia Ruskin University in the UK showed that older job applicants were four times less likely to be offered an interview despite having more experience on their CV. Almost half of all unemployed people in the country aged 50 to 64 remain jobless for over a year. This has to change, and powerful lobbying groups, such as the AARP (formerly known as the American Association of Retired Persons) in the US, are pushing hard to reverse the discrimination against older job-seekers. Companies that don't make it a policy to hire older workers will soon find out that they are missing out on a key labour component.

Although it may be that people over 50 are less productive than younger peers in terms of raw output, a different picture emerges when other factors are taken into account, such as the transmission of intergenerational wisdom, the "soft "skills of older workers, and the fact that in some industries, despite automation, shortages of workers of all ages will soon emerge. For these reasons, older workers need to be embraced by forward-thinking companies.

In the UK, the large insurance company Aviva has begun to mobilise businesses to promote the idea of employing older workers. Andy

Joe Coughlin (MIT), Jim, Joan Ruff (current President of the AARP), Milken Institute Conference, 2017.

Briggs, the CEO of Aviva, has corralled other large companies, including Boots, the Co-op, and Barclays to increase the number of over-50-year-olds in their organisations by 12% by 2022. Adding a million more workers in the 50-69-year-old band would significantly raise the nation's output, reduce pension costs, and provide productive employment to a segment of the population that absolutely should no longer be regarded as "retirable".

In the US, companies such as American Express, Bank of America, IBM, Marriott, Steelcase, JP Morgan and Nestle are making serious efforts to embrace and accommodate the needs of older workers. In Germany, BMW is at the vanguard, in Brazil it's Bradesco and in France, Michelin.

A further reason to include older people in the workforce as a matter of course is the burden of pensions, which is ballooning in the developed world. In 2016, annual state pensions in the UK amounted to £108 billion, or about 5% of GDP; this figure is expected to rise sharply and will grow, on current trends, to at least 7% of GDP by 2066. Healthcare also is growing as a percentage of GDP, and is expected to rise to an eighth of total national output by 2066 unless something changes.

Globally, it is expected that there will be will be a US $400 trillion "pensions gap" i.e. a shortfall between what is supposed to be paid out versus what can be paid. This is about five times the size of today's global economy. There is a brewing crisis, and it is one that isn't too hard to solve, if only there was some concerted action by governments.

People living longer and in better health will require less expensive hospitalisation. Pensionable ages everywhere will have to rise, and a lot faster than the gradualist approach being taken by governments today. In the UK, a move to increase the retirement age by two years by 2028 is fantasy thinking. The retirement age should increase to 70 immediately, and gradually be worked up to 80. Otherwise, the burden of unfunded pension liabilities will just be too great. The World Economic Forum has recently produced a report showing that all around the world pension schemes, whether government or private, are simply inadequate to deal with the volume of retirees.

In summary, everyone will need to work and save for longer. The coming increase in life expectancy will change many societal constructs, including the age at which people have children, the number of children that they have, the nature of work itself, the concept of retirement, the current way in which education is organised and of course, the amount of our leisure time. Older people will be much more highly valued in the workforce, the jobs of the future will be in human-to-human connection (and there will be plenty of them) and the key industries of the future, which will require people as well as computers, will be in the caring, parts of healthcare, travel, hospitality and education.

In 1969, Zager and Evans had a one-hit wonder with "In the Year 2525"; it is a fine song, with great lyrics. However, their view of the future, then several hundred years out, was just plain wrong. What they forecast is actually happening right now. We really do live in a brave new world of extended life, rapid advances in medicine and limitless technological opportunities. We are about to live the 2525 life and about four hundred years ahead of the song.

THE LIFE INSURANCE BUSINESS — WINNERS AND LOSERS IN THE AGE OF LONGEVITY

It is hard to argue that rising longevity is anything other than a benefit for individuals and society as a whole. However, it also presents an increased financial risk to governments, to defined-benefit pension providers and to life insurers. Implicit in the pricing of life insurance policies is an expectation around life expectancy. If people live longer a life insurer may end up having to make more payments than was anticipated when the policy was priced. Life insurance policies can extend for decades and this exposes life insurers to any unexpected increase in longevity, particularly for their younger policyholders. Existing pricing assumptions include an expectation of rising life expectancy, yes but a step change in longevity would have massive financial implications.

Recent cutting-edge innovations from gene and stem cell therapies increase the likelihood that a life-extending breakthrough could be on the horizon. Furthermore, improvements in detection and health monitoring through, for example, wearable devices further leverage the continual improvement in medical technology. It might not be too long before your smartphone can be used to identify the biochemical residue of cancer cells in your breath. However, the lifestyle choices of many are contributing to increasing levels of obesity that threatens to somewhat offset the gains for society from technological progress.

The growing financial burden of an ageing population on public finances is well documented. Individual pensions are also significantly impacted. The International Monetary Fund estimates that adding an extra year to the average lifespan increases the world's pension bill by 4%, or around US $1 trillion.

Understandably, life insurers and corporate pension schemes continue to look for ways to offset this longevity risk. One way of doing this is by using the capital markets to transfer the risk to third parties through the issuance of instruments known as "longevity swaps". These pay out should policyholders live longer than expected.

Whilst an unanticipated rise in life expectancies would generally be bad news for the life insurers, it would be very much welcome news for their reinsurers. Life reinsurers help their insurance company clients navigate claims volatility; in the event of policyholders living longer, the point at which a reinsurer is required to pay a claim is extended. A leading global life reinsurer commented at its 2016 investor day that within its individual mortality book cancer accounted for 30-40% of death claims. There is growing optimism that diseases such as cancer will in time become much more of a chronic condition rather than a terminal illness. A handful of studies have suggested that a cure for cancer could add 3-4 years to life expectancies. For this company, the financial impact from just one year of unanticipated life expectancy improvement is equivalent to its annual premium.

THE LIFE INSURANCE BUSINESS

LONG LIVED PORTFOLIOS FOR LONG LIVED INVESTORS

When we write books, we aren't doing it for the royalties.

If we depended on book royalties, we'd be busking or scavenging. There isn't a lot of money in the printed word these days, but we are more than happy to be paid in reader satisfaction.

We write our books, including this one, to research and to develop strategies in respect of specific investment areas, ones that we think might appeal to us, as well as to our readers.

No subject has intrigued us as much as this one; the science of what is commonly known as longevity.

Not only do most people want to live longer, but they are going to need more economic fuel (a.k.a. savings) to keep them going as their life extends to a far-off horizon. With a market defined only by the size of the world's population, and with the science now catching up to the aspirations of life-extensionists, this is truly the biggest money fountain we have ever seen.

It will be bigger, and gush higher, than all the opportunities outlined in *Fast Forward* and in *Cracking the Code* combined. How lucky it is that we are all alive at this time in human history where the manipulation of our genetic make-up might well lead us beyond conventionally accepted maximal lifespans – ones that most people regard as hardwired into our biology.

We are also fortunate to be present at the birth of a new industry – the business of longevity. This industry will be bigger than technology, alternative energy, transportation, education, and the rest of the zeitgeist sectors du jour put together.

Yes, the medical and pharmaceutical industries are already huge, but their preoccupation with the diseases of ageing and not with ageing itself gives us and our readers the opportunity to find genuinely breakthrough technologies and identify promising companies before the investor herd gets to them. For once, the PayPal mafia, the big institutions, and the Wall Street penny loafer brigade will be behind the curve.

Because the science is so complex, and indeed contentious, this is not an area where darts can be thrown at the bull market. There will be multiple failures, several scandals (along the lines of Theranos), and many, many disappointments. Selection is key;

knowledge is vital – and hard work even more important.

This is an early and as yet quite primitive science.

In the same way that we tried to use the network effect, the superior knowledge acquired through curiosity, adaptability and application, in the construction of *Cracking the Code* and of *Fast Forward*, we try to do so here.

Of course, because this is a new industry, there are relatively few public company "pure plays" for investors to tuck away and indeed, not all of them are of sufficient quality, in our opinion, to be investible.

But the flow of public companies will come thick and fast. Already the area is attracting large amounts of money, and some big, enlightened companies (such as AstraZeneca and Novartis) are looking seriously at longevity as a business opportunity. Indeed, AstraZeneca plans to sequence the genomes of two million people in the next few years, partly to better understand the mechanisms surrounding the diseases of ageing.

There are companies that are transforming and disrupting the diseases of ageing. Immunotherapies for cancer are a good example, as are new therapies for diabetes and for heart disease.

But the really impressive gains will be made by investing in the companies that are now under the radar, or just emerging from the shadows, which, powered by science and entrepreneurship, will reshape the landscape of investment.

These companies, some of which we identify in this book, are not all investible, in the sense that they remain private. That is why the Juvenescence company has been established, to participate at a ground floor level in these types of businesses. This new venture will be named Juvenescence Limited and more will be announced in due course.

It is certainly the case that there is a shortage of directly investible Juvenescence-type investments that investors from outside of the biotech venture capital community can participate in. For the next few years we will expand, both through our own efforts and through being in the "know", the pool of available investments. This area should not be one cornered by the big boys.

We need to get started though, so in this section we identify a variety of companies, both public and private, that every investor should consider having some exposure to.

In the meantime, as with *Cracking the Code*, we provide three portfolios that we have created based on conservative, moderate and speculative approaches. The *Cracking the Code* portfolios have produced healthy returns since the book was published.

We are hopeful that these fresh portfolios will do even better. As more companies involved with longevity go public, we will update our website (www. juvenescence-book.com) to reflect the new opportunities and update readers with our opinions.

So, from immunotherapies, to repurposed "old" drugs, to senolytics, to gene therapies, to stem cells, to mitochondrial uncouplers, to mTOR pathway inhibitors (including the rapalogs), to NAD$^+$ precursors, to resveratrol and more, we lay our investment feast on the table for you, dear reader, to consider.

Company	Market Cap. (US $ m)
Novartis AG	217,752
Amgen Inc	126,658
Novozymes A/S	13,337
Kite Pharma Inc	5,862
Bluebird Bio Inc	4,699
Juno Therapeutics Inc	3,171
Spark Therapeutics Inc	1,860
Cellectis SA	914
Sangamo Therapeutics Inc	733
Editas Medicine Inc	694
Mesoblast Ltd	683
CRISPR Therapeutics AG	641
REGENXBIO Inc	609
Intellia Therapeutics Inc	576
PureTech Health Plc	384
Oxford BioMedica plc	299
Organovo Holdings Inc	275
Horizon Discovery Group PLC	261
ChromaDex Corp	176
MaxCyte Inc	156
Proteostasis Therapeutics Inc	117
Cohbar Inc	59
Living Cell Technologies Ltd	48
SalvaRx Group PLC	20
International Stem Cell Corp	5

CONSERVATIVE PORTFOLIO

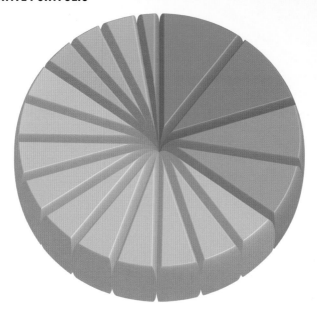

Company 🏛		Company 🏛	
Novartis AG	10.00%	REGENXBIO Inc	5.00%
Amgen Inc	10.00%	Intellia Therapeutics Inc	5.00%
Kite Pharma Inc	8.00%	PureTech Health Plc	5.00%
Editas Medicine Inc	7.50%	Bluebird Bio Inc	5.00%
Novozymes A/S	5.00%	Juno Therapeutics Inc	5.00%
Oxford BioMedica plc	5.00%	Cellectis SA	4.00%
Organovo Holdings Inc	5.00%	Sangamo Therapeutics Inc	4.00%
Mesoblast Ltd	5.00%	Spark Therapeutics Inc	4.00%
CRISPR Therapeutics AG	5.00%	SalvaRx Group PLC	2.50%
		Total	**100%**

MODERATE PORTFOLIO

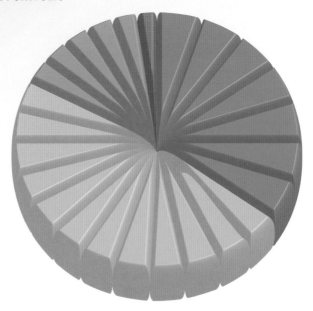

Company 🏛		Company 🏛	
Novartis AG	5.00%	PureTech Health Plc	4.0C
Amgen Inc	5.00%	Cellectis SA	4.0C
Kite Pharma Inc	5.00%	Sangamo Therapeutics Inc	4.0C
Editas Medicine Inc	5.00%	Spark Therapeutics Inc	4.0C
Novozymes A/S	5.00%	Horizon Discovery Group PLC	4.0C
Bluebird Bio Inc	5.00%	ChromaDex Corp	4.0C
Juno Therapeutics Inc	5.00%	SalvaRx Group PLC	3.0C
Oxford BioMedica plc	4.00%	MaxCyte Inc	3.0C
Organovo Holdings Inc	4.00%	Proteostasis Therapeutics Inc	3.0C
Mesoblast Ltd	4.00%	CohBar Inc	3.0C
CRISPR Therapeutics AG	4.00%	Living Cell Technologies Ltd	3.0C
REGENXBIO Inc	4.00%	International Stem Cell Corp	2.0C
Intellia Therapeutics Inc	4.00%	**Total**	**10C**

SPECULATIVE PORTFOLIO

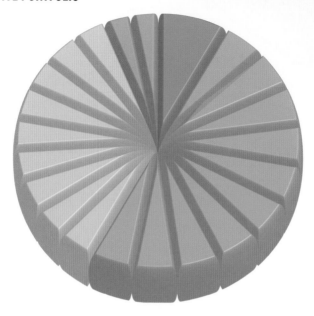

Company 🏛	
Editas Medicine Inc	8.00%
Novozymes A/S	5.00%
Oxford BioMedica plc	5.00%
Organovo Holdings Inc	5.00%
Cellectis SA	5.00%
Sangamo Therapeutics Inc	5.00%
Horizon Discovery Group PLC	5.00%
ChromaDex Corp	5.00%
Salvarx Group PLC	5.00%
MaxCyte Inc	5.00%
Proteostasis Therapeutics Inc	5.00%

Company 🏛	
Mesoblast Ltd	4.00%
CRISPR Therapeutics AG	4.00%
REGENXBIO Inc	4.00%
Intellia Therapeutics Inc	4.00%
PureTech Health Plc	4.00%
Spark Therapeutics Inc	4.00%
CohBar Inc	4.00%
Living Cell Technologies Ltd	4.00%
International Stem Cell Corp	4.00%
Bluebird Bio Inc	3.00%
Juno Therapeutics Inc	3.00%
Total	**100%**

AGEX THERAPEUTICS – PRIVATE – US

For further details, see Agex Therapeutics Inc, on page 216.

ALKAHEST – PRIVATE – US

Alkahest is a private Californian
company with a mission to "enrich
the health and vitality of humankind
through transformative therapies
that counterbalance the ageing
process." There is a danger of
bundling Alkahest in with all things
parabiosis – which isn't quite accurate
or fair.

What Alkahest is really working on
is identifying which specific factors
in the blood may be responsible for
the possible benefits promised by
parabiosis, particularly in Alzheimer's
disease. Tony Wyss-Coray, who sits
on the board of Alkahest, recently
co-authored a paper published
in *Nature* that showed that blood
plasma collected from the umbilical
cords of newborn infants possesses
some impressive rejuvenating effects.
Further work has linked the cognitive
benefits to a specific protein called
TIMP2.

AMBROSIA – PRIVATE – US

Ambrosia is a company that wants to
popularise parabiosis. The company
buys its blood from blood banks and
exclusively from paid donors under
the age of 25. It is charging people
US $8,000 to participate in a trial
in which they receive transfusions
and now have "about 100 paying
customers". Many people are critical
of this company for two key reasons:
that parabiosis is as yet unproven to
provide any benefit; and on ethical
concerns around having to pay to
participate in a trial.

AMGEN INC – AMGN: NASDAQ – US

Amgen is a NASDAQ-listed biotech
giant with a number of blockbuster
biotech products including Enbrel
(autoimmune disease), Neulasta (neu-
tropenia), Aranesp/Epogen (anaemia)
and Xgeva/Prolia (osteoporosis). Its
most recent product is Repatha (evolocumab, an anti-PCSK9 monoclonal
antibody), a drug for severe hypercholesterolemia and one that we are
particularly excited about, with mul-
ti-billion-dollar revenue potential.

At the time of writing, Amgen had a
market cap of US $118 billion and a
PE ratio of 14x. According to Cowen
and Company, Amgen will generate
US $11.2 billion in operating cash
flow in 2017 and will grow by more
than 5% p.a. into 2018 and beyond.
Trading cheaply, in our view, and one
of the few companies mentioned
in this book that pays a dividend,
this is a must-have holding for the
conservative portfolio.

ANTOXIS – PRIVATE – UK

Antoxis is a private pre-clinical drug discovery company based in Scotland. The company has a proprietary chemical scaffold that it uses to generate new chemical entities to address diseases in which either oxidative stress or mitochondrial dysfunction are implicated.

The company has two lead compounds: Proxison, for regenerative medicine applications which prevents reperfusion damage of transplanted stem cells, and Oncamex, a mitochondrial redox modulator for oncology applications which has been shown to sensitise animals to paclitaxel and TRAIL (a protein that activates apoptosis) resistant cancer cell lines.

ARIGOS BIOMEDICAL – PRIVATE – US

For further information, see Organs - Do it Like the Classics (Cars) page 220.

BENEVOLENTAI – PRIVATE – UK

A private company based in the UK, BenevolentAI is using its technology in a range of applications, with the first for drug discovery/lead identification (as opposed to drug development) targeting two novel targets of Alzheimer's disease in collaboration with an unnamed major US pharma company. This collaboration, dating from 2014, provides the company with the opportunity to earn up to US $400 million on achievement of early-stage milestones and up to US $400 million on achievement of later-stage milestones, plus royalties on sales of products should they be commercialised.

The company has raised US $88 million from significant institutional investors, including Woodford Investment Management of the UK. The most recent funding round valued the company at US $1.82 billion, a number that we find incredible. We are certain that AI has a role to play in drug discovery/development and in extending our lives, but Insilico Medicine, for example, is using deep learning techniques, and furthermore has a product on the market, Ageless Cell, in collaboration with Life Extension Inc. which makes Insilico a more attractive company in our view.

BIOQUARK – PRIVATE – US

Headquartered in Philadelphia, PA, Bioquark is a private company developing "combinatorial biologics" for the regeneration of organs and tissue. Combinatorial biologics mimic the regulatory biochemistry of the living human egg immediately following fertilisation which can perform all the necessary biological functions to create fully functioning humans.

In mice and fruit flies, Bioquark's lead product candidate BQ-A increased lifespan by 1.7 times and 2.2 times, respectively, versus control.

BQ-A will enter the clinic in 2017, although quite unusually will first be administered to patients in Latin America that are certified "brain dead". This has been dubbed first in human "Neuro-Regeneration & Neuro-Reanimation", but to be clear, they are not expecting some sort of resurrection. The company is simply hoping to observe some element of brain-death reversal using MRI imaging.

BIOTIE THERAPIES – PRIVATE – US

Biotie is a private subsidiary of publicly listed Acorda Therapeutics. It was acquired by Acorda early 2016 for US $363m, in cash, for its Phase 3 drug for Parkinson's disease called tozadenant, an oral adenosine A2a receptor antagonist. This clinical trial is due to read out in 2018. In addition, Biotie also had an oral, 5-HT6/5-HT2A dual receptor antagonist in Phase 2 development for Parkinson's-related dementia which is currently in Phase 2 clinical trials.

BIOVIVA – PRIVATE – US

BioViva is a US company founded by the controversial Liz Parrish, who we have met. Self-described as a "citizen

scientist" (with no formal scientific qualifications), it is clear that Liz is frustrated with the pace of drug development, the burden of regulation in developed markets and a "culture of risk aversion" in the drug industry.

In 2015, Liz travelled to Colombia in order to bypass regulators at the FDA and to become "patient zero" receiving two of BioViva's experimental gene therapies. BioViva is attempting to develop a myostatin inhibitor to address muscle loss and a therapy that supposedly lengthens telomeres. She claims that her telomeres have lengthened from 6.71 to 7.33 kilobases of DNA, but this is probably within the margin of error for measuring telomeres.

She has many critics, including Elizabeth Blackburn (see Shorter Telomeres. Page 200), but her terse response to these is *"what happens in human bodies is the ultimate test. I don't need researchers to agree with me."*

One of BioViva's key goals is to accelerate translation of therapies into humans. BioViva has accepted that this just isn't going to happen in the US or Europe, so it is opening clinics in jurisdictions such as Colombia and Kazakhstan.

In the short term, these therapies will be the preserve of the rich; Liz's telomere-lengthening therapy cost around US $1 million. However, the clinical data generated by these rich sentinel patients may well lead to broader access to gene therapies for all.

BIOZ – PRIVATE – US

Bioz has developed a search engine that aims to help researchers within the life-sciences industry make more informed decisions when conducting experiments. Combining computer science with in-house life-sciences expertise, its platform mines hundreds of millions of life-sciences papers and then cleans, tags and structures the data, ultimately speeding up drug discovery and increasing the rate of success in finding cures for diseases. Output data includes objective recommendations, ratings and insights for hundreds of millions of reagents, lab equipment assays, protocols and researchers.

BLUEBIRD BIO, INC.
BLUE: NASDAQ – US

Bluebird Bio is a biotech company listed in the US that is developing gene therapies for orphan genetic diseases as well as for cancer. Its two most advanced drug candidates are Lenti-D and LentiGlobin. Lenti-D is being evaluated as a therapy for cerebral adrenoleukodystrophy, a metabolic disorder that is characterised by the progressive deterioration of the nervous system. LentiGlobin,

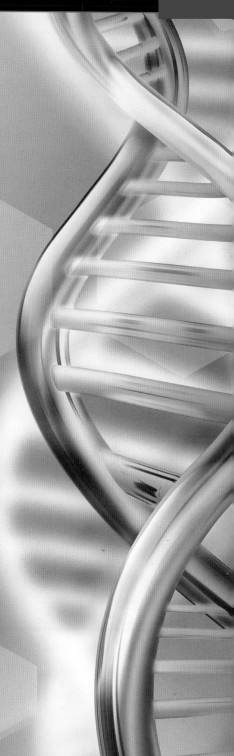

meanwhile, is being considered as a drug for transfusion-dependent β-thalassemia and severe sickle cell disease, both of which are catastrophic blood disorders. Bluebird Bio also has a gene-editing technology platform which is being tested for use in a variety of applications and disease areas, including haematology and oncology. Bluebird, along with the Chinese company Nanjing Legend, has recently revealed impressive results with CAR-T technology designed as an anti-B cell maturation antigen, expanding the range of blood cancers treated by CAR-T.

C4 THERAPEUTICS – PRIVATE – US

C4 Therapeutics was co-founded by Jay Bradner and is a private spin out of the Dana-Farber Cancer Institute based in Cambridge, Massachusetts. It was formed in 2015 and closed a US $73m Series A financing in early 2016 and is developing small molecule drugs that "trick" the machinery of the ubiquitin-proteasome system (UPS) to target disease-causing proteins implicated in cancer and other diseases.

The UPS system has two distinct functions: the labelling of defective/misfolded proteins and the disposal of the labelled proteins. C4's proprietary technology platform called Degronimid works by labelling the proteins and then allows the UPS to function normally by degrading and disposing of the waste through the blood stream and kidney.

CALICO LLC – PRIVATE – US

For further information about Calico and Cythia Kenyon see Key Opinion Leaders page 169.

CARIBOU BIOSCIENCES INC. PRIVATE – US

Caribou Biosciences is a leading private company in the application of CRISPR-Cas gene therapies. It was co-founded by Jennifer Doudna, who (along with other scientists from the University of California, Berkeley) played a vital role in the discovery of CRISPR. In May 2016, it announced it had closed its Series B funding round with US $30 million from investors including F-Prime Capital Partners, Novartis and Mission Bay Capital.

Outside human applications, it is using CRISPR technology for the precision breeding of crops exhibiting drought tolerance and disease resistance, as well as in industrial technology applications. These include getting microbes to "bio-produce" chemicals, as well as to produce enzymes that can't be synthesised by microbes' normal processes.

Caribou has multiple collaborations, the most notable of which are with the Novartis Institute for Biomedical Research, Intellia Therapeutics and DuPont. The company is based in California and, like many longevity-related companies, remains private and not yet investible to private investors.

CELLECTIS – ALCLS: EN PARIS – FRANCE

Cellectis is a publicly-listed French biotech company that is using TALEN and electroporation gene-editing technology to produce next generation CAR T-cell products for cancer. The company produces allogeneic products which are standardised off-the-shelf T-cells, although they still do require donated T-cells from healthy qualified donors.

The company's lead programmes are in various blood cancers. Its acute lymphoblastic leukaemia programme, partnered with Servier, generated very exciting data in two young patients. Its wholly owned programme in acute leukaemia started its Phase 1 clinical trials in the first half of 2017. At the time of writing, the company had a market capitalisation of US $875 million

and US $242 million in cash on the balance sheet.

CENTAGEN – PRIVATE – US

Centagen is a private company based in Boulder, Colorado, which is focussed on adult stem cells. The company's strategy is to enhance the stem cells' activity by improving the micro-environment around them using "multi path therapeutics". However, the company's website has scant information on its products.

COHBAR, INC. – CWBR: OTC – US

CohBar was co-founded by Nir Barzilai and Pinchas Cohen (both of whom Jim has met). CohBar is focused on the development of mitochondria-based therapeutics. Dysfunctional mitochondria have long been implicated in ageing, thus we are watching this emerging class of drugs with interest.

Specifically, the company is developing mitochondrial-derived peptides which address a broad range of age-related diseases, including obesity, fatty liver disease, type 2 diabetes, cancer, cardiovascular and neurodegenerative diseases. Currently progressing with IND-enabling studies, its lead candidate is in the indication of non-alcoholic steatohepatitis (NASH) and is expected to enter the clinic in early 2018.

CohBar currently has a market valuation of around US $65 million and we are speculative buyers.

CHROMADEX CORP
CDXC: NASDAQ – US

ChromaDex is an interesting US-listed company in the longevity space, and for two key reasons. Firstly, because in March 2017 it attracted the attention of Hong Kong billionaire Li Ka-Shing, who made a US $25 million investment. Secondly, and more importantly, because it is the sole manufacturer of commercially available nicotinamide riboside, a position that is protected by five issued patents, as well as by further patents pending.

To reiterate, our team at Juvenescence is very positive on the science surrounding NAD+ precursors and it seems that consumers are agreeing. In 2016, NIAGEN (ChromaDex's brand name for NR) revenues were US $11.9 million, representing 44% of the company's total. This represented growth in NIAGEN sales of 34% YoY from FY2015 to FY2016.

CHRONOS THERAPEUTICS
PRIVATE – UK

Chronos is a private Oxford, UK based company addressing degenerative and behavioural diseases of the brain and nervous system.

The company has a patent for the use of Fujimycin, a drug that suppresses the immune system already approved by the FDA in a number of indications. Fujimycin is believed to increase cellular lifespan through the disruption of OBD1, a sirtuin inhibitor.

CRISPR THERAPEUTICS AG
CRSP: NASDAQ – US

CRISPR Therapeutics is a Swiss-headquartered, but US-listed, leading gene-editing company. It has licensed its technology from the University of Vienna to develop transformative gene-based medicines for serious diseases.

CRISPR Therapeutics has a portfolio of wholly-owned and partnered programmes that will soon enter the clinic. The company's two most advanced programmes are partnered with Vertex Pharmaceuticals and are focused on beta-thalassemia and sickle cell disease.

EDITAS MEDICINE INC
EDIT: NASDAQ – US

Editas was the first company with CRISPR-Cas9 technology to list in the US, with a US $100 million raise on IPO in February 2016, having been founded only a couple of years earlier. Editas was widely expected to run the first FDA-approved clinical trial using CRISPR technology, but was pipped at the post by Sean Parker's (of Napster and Facebook fame) Parker Institute for Cancer Immunotherapy.

The company is currently focused on curing rare inherited diseases. Its lead programme targets Leber Congenital Amaurosis, a genetic form of retinal degeneration and blindness caused by mutations in the CEP290 gene. The company also has a collaboration with Juno Therapeutics in which they are creating chimeric antigen receptor and high-affinity T-cells (CAR-T) receptors to treat blood cancer.

So, a leader in gene editing with seemingly good IP – we like this one.

EGENESIS INC. – PRIVATE – US

eGenesis is a Cambridge, MA-based company co-founded by George Church and Luhan Yang of Harvard Medical School. The company is focusing on the xenotransplantation of tissues and whole organs grown in pigs, organs that are created using CRISPR technology in order to avoid issues of immunogenicity and porcine endogenous retrovirus infections.

The company is in its early phases with no identifiable commercial product as yet. In March 2017, it announced the close of a US $38 million Series A financing co-led by Biomatics Capital and ARCH Venture Partners.

ELYSIUM HEALTH INC – PRIVATE – US

Elysium Health Inc is a private company that already has a product on the market in the form of a nutraceutical. It boasts an impressive seven Nobel Laureates who are associated with the company.

Elysium's sole product is named Basis and is a once-daily supplement of nicotinamide riboside (NR), which is clinically proven to increase NAD+ (see Targets in Ageing. Page 189) levels that decline with age, as well as of resveratrol.

In general, we are positive on the science surrounding NAD+ and if you can get it fresh enough (because of its poor half-life) you should probably take it while keeping an eye out for better versions to come onto the market. There's a whiff of hype around Elysium, which is just a bit too slick for our liking.

EVERON BIOSCIENCES
PRIVATE – US

Everon Biosciences of Buffalo, NY is a private company led by Dr Alexander Polinsky, a scientist and biotech executive, and Dr Andrei Gudkov, the Senior VP Basic Science at Roswell Park Cancer Institute and Chair of the Department of Cell Stress Biology. Everon is studying the relationship between cellular senescence and organism-level frailty.

In partnership with Roswell Park, Everon has discovered a novel, undisclosed molecular mechanism that may underlie the ageing or senescence process. Everon believes that the products of this process, including senescent cells themselves, are the root cause of inflammaging. Everon's therapeutic development programmes focus on creating therapeutics that block the creation of these waste products or that restore the body's natural ability to clean them up.

To complement its therapeutic strategy, Everon is developing biomarkers of biological age. Everon's recently published Frailty Index is a composite score derived from simple blood biochemistry and physical examination. Everon has validated this score in mice; not only does the frailty index track chronological age in mice, it accelerates when the mice are placed on a high-fat diet and decelerates when they are given rapamycin.

EXSCIENTIA – PRIVATE – UK

Exscientia is a Scottish company that claims to be the first company to "automate drug design" using artificial intelligence.

The company's platform sifts through vast amounts of data, designs millions of novel compounds and pre-assesses each one for predicted potency, selectivity and other key criteria, before then selecting the best compounds for synthesis and assay. It claims to have generated candidates in roughly one quarter of the time of traditional approaches.

The company currently has collaborations and partnerships with Evotec, GSK, Sanofi, Sumitomo Dainippon and Sunovion.

FREENOME INC. – PRIVATE – US

Freenome's mission is to bring accurate, accessible and non-invasive disease screenings to doctors to pro-actively treat cancer and other diseases at early and, therefore, manageable stages.

Freenome is California-based and is backed by leading venture capitalist investors including Andreessen

Horowitz, Google Ventures and Founders Fund, from whom it has raised over US $70 million in private funding. Freenome has also secured several revenue-making deals with top-ten global pharma companies and is currently engaging in a number of retrospective and prospective clinical studies with leading academic and clinical centres to test its technology, on large scale, in different applications.

Freenome's technology uses a type of deep learning focused on circulating cell-free DNA derived from an individual's blood, in order to understand the dynamic changes in his or her genome through time. This is designed to detect age-related diseases if and when they occur. These circulating cell-free DNA samples arise from the death (necrosis and apoptosis) of the several hundred billion cells that turn over every day in every adult. Some 80% or more of the circulating DNA in the blood arises from the white blood cells of the immune system, which reflect the age of an individual, as well as of any diseases such as cancers.

Specifically, Freenome has developed proprietary software to detect and classify characteristic patterns in the circulating DNA – patterns that provide insights into gene expression changes, and to differentiate healthy samples from those with disease.

Freenome's primary focus is on detecting cancer earlier in asymptomatic people, so that as many tumours as possible may be removed in curative surgery; in addition, and where appropriate, to help recommend the most effective therapies, such as immuno-oncology drugs which will have the highest likelihood of response for a particular patient. Freenome aims to impact longevity in two main ways. Firstly,

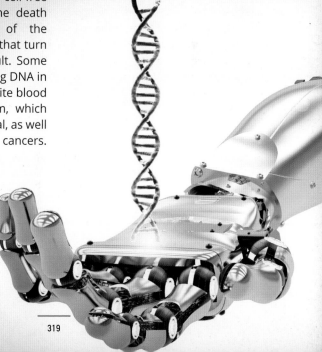

by increasing survival by reducing premature mortality from cancer through earlier detection. For instance, patients who have colorectal cancer tumours such as colorectal cancer, for instance, have a 91% five-year survival rate when caught early, versus only 11% when caught after having metastasised. Secondly, Freenome is working in the longevity field more directly – through undertaking research to understand the changes that occur in the genome in normal human ageing and analysing the success of interventions undertaken to slow or prevent the changes of ageing, with the goal of creating positive feedback loops. Such interventions include tailored lifestyle changes, such as diet modification, exercise regimes and stress-management (as well as other therapies as they become available) and when combined with Freenome's tests can be thought of as 'personalised wellness.'

GENESCIENT CORPORATION PRIVATE – US

Genescient is a private Fountain Valley, California-based company, founded in 2006, which sequences the genomes of the so-called Methuselah flies (Drosophila melanogaster). These flies have been artificially "selected" over 700 generations, thereby turning them into extremely long-lived animals. The company believes that this model of ageing is relevant to humans, because the Drosophila metabolic genetic pathways are highly conserved.

Genescient compared gene function in Drosophila with human orthologs and revealed over 100 genomic targets related to the primary diseases of ageing. The company is trying to "drug" these genes to address cardiovascular disease, neurodegenerative disease, diabetes and sepsis.

GERO – PRIVATE – RUSSIA

Gero is a private Russian company taking a big-data approach in identifying potential targets for ageing as well as for age-related diseases. Gero believes that traditional machine learning methods suffer from 'overfitting' (exaggerated emphasis on irrelevant details of training data), so it has developed new mathematical models to analyse 'omics' data.

These new models are derived from statistical physics and analyse the stability of so-called Gene Regulatory Networks (GRN) to predict their dynamics over time. Gero's work has shown that GRN dynamics strongly correlate with ageing.

The company is running a nematode study in collaboration with Robert Reis from Arkansas University, who holds the world record for extending life in animal models, by 10 times for nematodes.

GRAIL – PRIVATE – US

GRAIL is a high-profile spinout from the sequencing giant Illumina. In February 2017, the company announced that it had closed a massive US $900 million Series B funding round with support from investors drawn from the who's who of healthcare, including Johnson & Johnson, Merck, Bristol-Myers Squibb and Celgene, as well as the tech giants Amazon and Tencent.

GRAIL's mission is "to detect cancer early, when it can be cured", through the use of liquid biopsies, ones that detect even the faintest signals of cancer in the blood from circulating tumour DNA.

GRAIL is conducting one of the largest clinical study programmes ever undertaken. This programme will enrol tens of thousands of people to identify the patterns diagnostic of many types of cancer, and future clinical studies will enrol hundreds of thousands of people to confirm the clinical validity of the patterns. The company is currently

private and based in Menlo Park, California.

GUARDANT HEALTH – PRIVATE – US

Guardant Health is a private company based in Redwood City, California. Guardant uses digital sequencing to detect tumour DNA circulating in the blood stream via liquid biopsy. Digital sequencing is 1,000 to 10,000 times more accurate than standard DNA sequencing methods and offers 99.9999% specificity in its results, and in half the time of normal tissue biopsy sequencing.

The company's key product, Guardant 360, looks at 73 key alterations in the DNA of advanced solid tumours. This provides oncologists with a better chance of recommending a successful targeted therapy, that doesn't involve chemotherapy.

In March 2017, the company announced that it had raised US $360 million in a funding round led by SoftBank, with participation from other high-profile investors including Sequoia Capital and OrbiMed. This brings the total funding raised by the company to US $550 million - which sounds like a lot, but its competition includes Grail and Freenome, (see above) which have raised US $900 million (Series B) and US $65 million (Series A), respectively.

HORIZON DISCOVERY GROUP
HZD: LSE – UK

Publicly-listed on the London Stock Exchange, Horizon Discovery is a contract research organisation with expertise in gene editing and genetically modified cells. It is run by the highly competent Darrin Disley and its services span multiple gene editing technologies, including rAAV, CRISPR and ZFN.

Amongst its many activities, Horizon's reference standards were recently and successfully used as a positive control in support of a pre-market approval application with the FDA for a companion diagnostic in oncology. It has an international customer base of in excess of 1,400 organisations, including major pharmaceutical, biotechnology and diagnostic companies as well as key academic research centres.

HUMAN LONGEVITY INC
PRIVATE – US

Human Longevity is another high-profile private Californian-based company, one founded by Craig Venter and Peter Diamandis in 2013. Human Longevity has created the world's largest database of sequenced genomes and phenotypic data. The company received US $80 million in funding in its Series A offering in summer 2014 and announced a further US $220 million Series B financing in April 2016, which was fully subscribed.

As with all big data 'omics' companies, it uses machine learning to gain insights into data sets, insights that wouldn't be possible without machine learning.

The company currently offers four key products, namely: HLIQ Whole Genome, Health Nucleus, HLIQ Oncology and Open Search. The first three products are designed to provide personalised data for preventative health planning or personalised treatment, while Open Search is a browser-based portal for researchers to access data on 10,000 genomes.

INTELLIA THERAPEUTICS, INC
NTLA: NASDAQ – US

Intellia is yet another US-based publicly traded company working with CRISPR technology. Its lead programmes are focused on delivering the CRISPR/Cas9 system of gene editing to the liver with "single shot" efficacy. Its most advanced programme is partnered with biotech giant Regeneron Pharmaceuticals (REGN: NASDAQ) for the treatment of Transthyretin Amyloidosis (ATTR). The joint venture expects to be treating non-human primates in 2017 and hopes to complete IND (Investigational New Drug) enabling studies by the first half of 2018. Other targeted indications include Alpha-1 Antitrypsin Deficiency (AATD), hepatitis B and primary hyperoxaluria (PH-1).

At the time of writing, the company had substantial cash resources in excess of US \$250 million and a market cap in excess of US \$500 million.

INTERNATIONAL STEM CELL CORPORATION – ISCO: OTC – US

International Stem Cell Corporation is a Carlsbad, California-based company listed in the US. It is a clinical stage company using human parthenogenetic stem cells (hpSC) to treat severe diseases of the nervous system, the joints and the liver.

hpSCs are derived from unfertilised oocytes and have demonstrated efficacy in a number of animal models. The company's lead programme is a Phase 1/2a clinical study in Parkinson's disease.

This form of cell therapy is limited by the availability of safe immune-matched human cells which we believe will be superseded by other off-the-shelf cell therapy programmes like that of BioTime's new subsidiary, AgeX Therapeutics.

JUNO THERAPEUTICS
JUNO: NASDAQ – US

Juno Therapeutics is a US-listed immune-oncology company focused primarily on advanced blood cancers. The company has Chimeric Antigen Receptor (CAR-T) and T-Cell Receptor (TCR) programmes that have demonstrated impressive clinical data including unprecedented response rates and durability in patients with acute lymphoblastic leukaemia (ALL). So impressive are these results that Cowen and Company, among others, expects these CAR-T therapies to become the standard of care in spite of severe neurotoxicity issues (including two deaths!) in earlier trials.

The treatment for ALL is expected to have its commercial launch in the first half of 2018. Altogether, Juno's portfolio of products is expected to generate in excess of US \$1 billion in annual revenues by 2021.

JUVENON – PRIVATE – US

Juvenon is a west coast-based nutraceutical company with products created by Harvard Medical School Professor Dr Ben Treadwell and noted U.C., Berkeley researcher Dr Bruce Ames.

The company's key product is Juvenon tablets, which it claims helps repair mitochondria and reduce oxidative stress. The active ingredient in this product is acetyl-L-carnitine, which helps metabolise fat and has been shown in animal models to reduce oxidative stress and DNA damage and to improve memory.

JUVENTAS THERAPEUTICS PRIVATE – US

Based on research originating at the Cleveland Clinic in the US, Juventas Therapeutics is a privately-held biopharmaceutical company developing non-viral gene therapies for diseases including advanced chronic heart failure and late-stage peripheral artery disease.

JVS-100, its lead product candidate, uses a naturally occurring signalling protein (stromal cell-derived factor-1) to activate the body's own tissue repair pathways, inducing multiple changes that preserve or recover organ function. JVS-100 is currently enrolled in a Phase 2b study in patients with advanced peripheral artery disease.

KITE PHARMA, INC. – KITE: NASDAQ – US

A direct competitor of Juno Therapeutics, Kite Pharma is a well-funded pioneer in CAR-T therapies with an emphasis on blood cancers (lymphomas and leukaemias). As with Juno, KITE's therapies have demonstrated an ability to induce response rates in excess of 70% and multi-year responses in several types of cancer. CAR-T therapies are currently used for multiple myeloma, diffuse large B-cell lymphoma, ALL (acute lymphoblastic leukaemia), as well as for some less prevalent blood cancer.

Kite and Juno both offer engineered autologous CAR-T cell therapies, production of which consist of five broad steps, none of which are trivial or easy:

1. Isolating a patient's T-cells (regardless of their specificity),

2. Activating the isolated T-cells,

3. Transducing the T-cells with genes encoding tumour-recognising receptors,

4. Ex vivo proliferation of the transduced T-cells,

5. Infusion of the patient's transduced T-cells back into the patient.

The key trick for CAR-T companies is to move from autologous cell therapy, which is cumbersome and very expensive, to allogeneic or off-the-shelf approaches. If this can be successfully done, the market will be hugely expanded.

L-NUTRA – PRIVATE – US

L-Nutra is a private Los Angeles, California-based company founded by Valter Longo. The company develops Fasting Mimicking Diets (FMDs), which provide nutrients to the body while keeping it in fasting mode.

It has two main products: ProLon and Chemolieve. ProLon is a 5-day fasting programme that aims to improve longevity by managing body weight and improving health via supporting cellular protection, multi-system regeneration and rejuvenation. Chemolieve is a 4-day fasting programme for use with cancer patients, to protect the normal cells of the body and decrease side effects of chemotherapy. In addition, L-Nutra is developing a number of other FMD-based meal programmes that aim at preventing, delaying or treating chronic diseases. This seems to be essentially a company that markets non-patented nutraceuticals.

LIFE BIOSCIENCES – PRIVATE – US

Life Biosciences was launched in 2016 by Professor David Sinclair, CEO Tristan Edwards (Harvard Medical School) and by Professor Lindsay Wu of UNSW. Life Biosciences is private, but has a website, and investors should follow its progress there, particularly when it comes to the potential listing of daughter companies.

For more information about the company, see David Sinclair on page 149.

LIFE EXTENSION – PRIVATE – US

Headquartered in the Fort Lauderdale, Florida, Life Extension is a private company that specialises in nutritional supplements. It has partnered with Insilico Medicine to identify specific nutrient combinations that function as "geroprotectors" under the brand name GEROPROTECT. The first supplement in the GEROPROTECT line is Ageless Cell, which is designed to inhibit cellular senescence.

LIVING CELL TECHNOLOGIES LTD
LCT: ASX – AUS

Dual-listed on the Australian and US stock exchanges, Living Cell Technologies has a proprietary cell-based therapy that uses a unique heard of pathogen free pigs originally discovered in the remote sub-Antarctic Auckland Islands.

The company's technology platform called, NTCELL, uses neonatal choroid plexus cells harvested from these pigs. These cells are coated with another proprietary technology called IMMUPEL to prevent any immune response and are then implanted into a patient. Once implanted they produce cerebrospinal fluid and secret multiple nerve growth factors that promote new central nervous system growth and repair disease-induced nerve degeneration while potentially removing waste products.

The company had a market capitalisation of US $48 million at the time of writing.

MAXCYTE – MXCT: LSE – US

MaxCyte is US-headquartered, London listed company which has a cell-engineering platform designed to modify all cell types. The company's technology is based on generic transfection technology that it claims can deliver "virtually any molecule, to any cell, at any scale" and has the unique ability to transfect primary cells, stem cells and cell lines with efficiencies greater than 90%.

It provides its cell-engineering platform to biopharmaceutical partners engaged in drug discovery and development, biomanufacturing and cell therapy, including gene editing and immuno-oncology.

The company was capitalised at US $155 million at the time of writing.

MESOBLAST LTD
MSB: ASX – AUSTRALIA

Mesoblast is a publicly-listed Australian company involved in the administration of allogeneic or "off-the-shelf" MSCs. Its cells are being trialled in chronic heart failure, chronic lower back pain due to disc degeneration, graft versus host disease and rheumatoid arthritis.

The company does have a product on the market in Japan, TEMCELL HS Inj, for acute graft vs host disease. Subsequent to TEMCELL being approved, however, it has experienced challenges, notably when its commercial partner Teva returned the rights of its Phase 3 programme in chronic heart failure. This programme continues and in April 2017, the company announced the trial would continue following a pre-specified interim futility analysis.

MOUNT TAM BIOTECHNOLOGIES
MNTM: OTC – US

Mount Tam Biotechnologies is a publicly-listed company, collaborating with and based within the Buck Institute for Research on Aging's campus in California. It focuses specifically on the development of rapalogs that select for mTORC1 generated at the Buck.

The company is developing specific rapalogs to address autoimmune, neurodegenerative and rare genetic diseases where mTORC1 activity is elevated. All of its programmes are pre-clinical with its lead programme in lupus erythematosus currently being prepared for an IND.

The company had a market cap of US $6 million at the time of writing.

NAVITOR PHARMACEUTICALS
PRIVATE – US

Navitor Pharmaceuticals is based in Cambridge, Massachusetts, and is focused on restoring normal activity of mTORC1. Navitor distinguishes itself from others targeting mTOR with rapalogs and mTOR kinase inhibitors, because it is trying to selectively target mTORC1 without hitting mTORC2, which is a key challenge for scientists seeking to affect the key mTOR age related pathway.

Navitor is led by George Vlasuk, who ran the controversial Sirtris Pharmaceuticals after it was acquired by GlaxoSmithKline. The company's IP is based on the scientific work of Dr David Sabatini at the Whitehead Institute for Biomedical Research, also based in Cambridge.

In December 2015, the company raised US $33 million in a Series B financing, which included an investment from Sanofi-Genzyme BioVentures. However, this is the most recent announcement on the company's website and there is scant information elsewhere.

NOVARTIS AG
NOVN: SIX – SWITZERLAND

Novartis is a Swiss pharma behemoth with a market cap of over US $200 billion at the time of writing. It has a diversified business model with 67% of its revenues coming from branded products and 20% from generic products, sold through its subsidiary Sandoz. Out of the Big Pharma companies, and through its work within the Novartis Institute for Biomedical Research, it appears to be ahead of the curve in trying to understand ageing at a fundamental level, certainly as compared to most other Big Pharma companies.

In 2016, its key products included Gleevec/Glivec (for CML and ALL, both blood cancers – US $3.3 billion), Gilenya (MS – US $3.1 billion) and Lucentis (wet AMD – US $1.8 billion). While Gilenya continues to grow, Gleevec has come off patent and is now in steep decline as a result of generic competition, while the profitability of Lucentis is now subject to the off-label use of Avastin, a drug which costs considerably less per treatment (US $50 vs US $2,000) and is equally effective.

NOVOZYMES A/S
NZYMB: XCSE – DENMARK

Novozymes is a publicly-listed (in Copenhagen) Danish industrial biotech company. Novozymes develops and produces a wide range of enzymes and microorganisms for use in industry.

In 2017, it signed an agreement to explore uses for NgAgo, a protein

that could potentially be used for genome editing. Its enzymes and microorganisms have uses in a number of industries such as laundry and dishwashing detergents, biofuels as well as for improving the quality of bread, beer and wine.

In 2015, the company had a 48% share of the global market in industrial enzymes, with revenues of over US $2.1 billion. We will watch and see if NgAgo has real anti-ageing applicability.

OISIN BIOTECHNOLOGIES
PRIVATE – US

Oisin Biotechnologies was founded by Matthew Scholz and Gary Hudson (whom Jim has met and interviewed) and in part funded in its early days by SENS Research Foundation. It is developing a transient gene therapy approach to clear senescent cells which, according to the company, is a more powerful technology than that proposed by others, including Unity and SIWA.

Unlike other approaches to remove senescent cells, those particular cells aren't specifically targeted. All the cells of the body, whether healthy or senescent, are delivered a liposomal vector with a gene payload, but the relevant gene (a suicide gene in this case) is only transcribed to induce apoptosis if the relevant promoter, such as p16, is active in the cell.

Oisin has also shown that it can target senescent cells in mice treated with chemotherapy. However, it wants to spin its oncology applications out and to focus on age-related indications. We like the look of Oisin.

ORCHARD THERAPEUTICS
PRIVATE – UK

Orchard Therapeutics is a private London, UK-based gene therapy company, researching rare metabolic disorders and immune deficiencies.

The company uses ex-vivo autologous gene therapy, in other words making use of a patient's own stem cells, which are then altered using a lentiviral vector. Lentiviral vectors are derived from human immunodeficiency virus (HIV-I) and are used because of their ability to integrate into the genome of non-dividing cells, whereas other retroviruses can only infect dividing cells. Orchard's

lead programmes are for severe combined immunodeficiency, due to adenosine deaminase deficiency (ADA-SCID) and MPSIIIA (Sanfilippo A), a lysosomal storage disease. There is limited information on the MPSIIIA programme, but for ADA-SCID, the clinical data produced so far in 39 patients is encouraging, with a good safety profile and a high percentage of patients showing immune reconstitution. The ADA-SCID programme recently won an FDA rare pediatric disease designation.

The company is backed by F-Prime Capital, Fidelity's venture arm and one with very deep pockets.

ORGANOVO HOLDINGS, INC.
ONVO: NASDAQ – US

Organovo is a San Diego, California-based company, listed on NASDAQ, that creates functional 3D human tissue for research and therapeutic applications. The primary application in the near term is in bridging the gap between animal models and moving drugs into humans. It does not expect any significant revenues from commercial therapeutic applications in the very near term.

It has two key products: human liver and kidney tissue, sold under the brand ExVive. These tissues, organised in a 3D structure, are more representative of human tissue than cells in a 2D petri dish for the accurate testing of drugs.

Organova is moving towards the eventual goal of printing organs. Today this is only possible in the case of simple vessels and of part-organs such as skin replacements and windpipes. However, the bioprinting of entire complex organs with working vasculatures remains some way off and we don't attribute any value to that sort of activity for Organovo for some years yet. Still though, a step in the right direction.

OXFORD BIOMEDICA PLC
OXB: LSE – UK

Established in 1995 as a spin out of the University of Oxford, Oxford BioMedica is now publicly-listed in the UK.

Its LentiVector technology is a proprietary single dose gene therapy platform with which the company designs and develops medicines internally and for commercial partners.

Its pipeline includes treatments for cancer, Parkinson's disease and retinopathy. TroVax, its lead product candidate partnered with Novartis, is currently in Phase 3 clinical trials indicated in multiple types of cancer.

In addition to its partnership with Novartis, the company also has collaborations with GSK, Sanofi and Immune Design. At the time of writing, the company's market capitalisation was US $220 million.

PRANA BIOTECHNOLOGY LTD
PBT: ASX – AUSTRALIA

Prana is an Australian-based public company working on treatments for neurodegenerative diseases. Its lead drug candidate, PBT2, is being developed for Alzheimer's (in Phase 2b) and Huntington's disease (in Phase 2a).

Prana selected PBT2 from a proprietary library of over 1,000 Metal-Protein Attenuating Compounds (MPACs). The company is focussed on MPACs due to evidence that many age-related conditions are caused by interactions between metals and proteins.

The company's market cap at the time of writing was AU $27 million.

PROTEOSTASIS THERAPEUTICS
PTI: NASDAQ – US

Proteostasis Therapeutics is a Cambridge, Massachusetts-based, NASDAQ-listed company developing a new class of small-molecule drugs designed to maintain proteostasis.

The company's proprietary Disease-Relevant Translation (DRT) platform utilises genomic and proteomic data within a systems biology framework to identify disease, genetic mutations and environmental factors that cause imbalances within the proteostasis network. Its lead product is an amplifier and it is currently recruiting for its Phase 1 trial, for a compound which would be a breakthrough monotherapy for cystic fibrosis (CF). In vitro data indicates that amplifiers complement the activity of CFTR potentiators and correctors. Disruption of the CFTR gene is responsible for the clinical manifestations of CF.

With a market cap of less than US $100 million, following controversy surrounding the murder (yes!) of a healthy volunteer in the ongoing Phase 1 clinical trial, the company is somewhat down on its luck. However, the Phase 1 data readout, while delayed, is now due in late 2017 and it might turn the company's fortunes around. Worth a small punt.

PURETECH HEALTH
PRTC: LSE – UK

PureTech Health is one of the few publicly-listed UK-based longevity-

related companies, alongside SalvaRx Group and AstraZeneca. It has a market cap of around US $400 million and boasts a broad pipeline for indications including ADHD, schizophrenia, obesity and diabetes. However, the most interesting longevity-related programme was recently licensed from the Novartis Institute for Biomedical Research in March 2017, into a newly formed subsidiary resTORbio.

resTORbio will advance NIBR's work on everolimus and its role in the inhibition of mTORC1 to address immunosenescence. A Phase 2b trial will commence in late 2017, and has been preceded by two successful Phase 2a trials demonstrating that everolimus can boost the efficacy of vaccines in the elderly.

We believe that this is some of the most tangible and reproducible work in the anti-ageing field – and we are excited about it.

David Glass, in particular, believes that this is some of the most tangible and reproducible work in the anti-ageing field - and we share his optimism!

REGENXBIO INC. – RGNX: NASDAQ – US

REGENXBIO is a Rockville, Maryland-based gene therapy company that uses next-generation adeno-associated virus (AAV) vectors as delivery vehicles for the insertion of healthy copies of genes. The technology for its NAV Technology Platform is from discoveries and inventions of the Wilson laboratory at the University of Pennsylvania.

REGENXBIO has 5 internal and 24 external product candidates. The most advanced internal programme is in wet AMD and is due to begin enrolment in Phase 1 in mid-2017. For its 24 external programmes it has 9 partners, including the highly capitalised Shire and Biogen biopharma companies, which provides good validation of REGENXBIO's technology. Biogen, in particular, has board-level gene therapy experience (e.g. Dr. Sherwin and Dr. Mulligan) and has other collaborations with notable players in the genetics space.

REPLICEL LIFE SCIENCES
RP: TSX – CANADA

RepliCel is a publicly traded, Vancouver-based, regenerative medicine company developing autologous cell therapies. The company's lead programme is in chronic tendinosis, with additional programmes focussed on damaged or aged skin and baldness.

These programmes all stem from the company's fundamental understanding of the biological function of hair follicle cells. These particular fibroblasts can produce five times the amount of type 1 collagen than skin-derived fibroblasts, making them ideal 'factories' for pathologies where the underlying cause is a lack of collagen, such as tendinosis.

RETROTOPE INC. – PRIVATE – US

Retrotope is a private Californian company that claims to have created a new category of drug to preserve and restore mitochondrial health in degenerative diseases. Its platform is designed to prevent cellular damage and recover cellular function caused by lipid peroxidation due to oxidative stress. The company does not believe that this form of oxidative stress can be well controlled by antioxidants.

The company is currently preparing for a clinical proof of concept study in Friedreich's ataxia, a disease which is characterised by aggressive lipid peroxidation.

SALVARX GROUP PLC – SALV: LSE – UK

SalvaRx is a UK-listed immuno-oncology company that is addressing the resistance mechanisms to checkpoint inhibitors. It currently has an interest in four assets, all of which will be trialled in combination with Yervoy or Opdivo, in order to improve response rates in established tumour types, and to bring responses to new tumour types that have not yet been tried using current immunotherapies.

Its most advanced asset is Intensity Therapeutics' therapy INT230-6, which is a cisplatin and vinblastine combination coupled to a cell penetration enhancer. This combination has been designed to selectively diffuse and to disperse throughout tumours, while sparing normal healthy cells. When injected into a model tumour, the combo kills a large portion of the dividing cells, and recruits dendritic cells and T-cells to better process tumour neoantigens. This results in a vaccine-like effect, where the immune cells can clear additional non-injected tumours and prevent recurrences. In established tumour models, Intensity has seen up to 80% CR (complete remission) with long-term immunity to a specific tumour type for the entire life of the animal. This treatment has progressed into the clinic on humans in two countries and Intensity will be studying both superficial and deep tumours in these patients.

Its second asset is iOx Therapeutics, which has a series of small molecule immune-oncology compounds. The lead compound is IMM60, which is a liposomal formulation of an iNKT (invariant natural killer T-cell) agonist. iNKTs bridge the innate and adaptive immune systems. IMM60 has been shown to activate natural killer cells, dendritic cells, and B-cells leading to an increase in antigen-specific CD8 T-cells and a reduction of myeloid-derived suppressor cells.

SalvaRx also has two additional earliest-stage assets called Nekonal Oncology and RIFT Biotherapeutics.

SAMUMED – PRIVATE – US

Samumed is a private San Diego, California-based company focused on tissue-level regeneration through modulation of the Wnt (wingless integration site, which when disrupted in flies they don't grow wings) development pathway, using small molecule compounds. Wnt is the primary pathway regulating the self-renewal and differentiation of adult stem cells. When this pathway is disrupted, it almost always leads to disease in affected tissues.

Samumed is extremely well funded and a financing round in 2016 valued it at US $12 billion, based on its opportunity in arthritis and not its other products related to baldness in men and wrinkles in sun-damaged people. Its founder, Osman Kibar, is amongst other things a world-beating poker champion.

Samumed's lead programme is in osteoarthritis (OA) of the knee, which is the most common cause of disability in older adults. Wnt signalling plays a key role in determining whether stem cells in the knee become cartilage-forming cells (chondrocytes) or bone-forming cells (osteoblasts). In OA, elevated Wnt promotes the growth of bone and degrades cartilage which is the opposite of what is best for the patient.

The FDA recently granted orphan designation to its IPF programme SM-04646 which is administered locally via a nebuliser.

SANGAMO THERAPEUTICS
SGMO: NASDAQ – US

Sangamo Therapeutics is a NASDAQ-listed company based in Richmond, California. It utilises a combination of gene therapies, gene editing technologies and cell therapies to treat serious genetic diseases. Sangamo is the leader in ZFNs (zinc finger nucleases).

It currently has a Phase 1/2 clinical trial in haemophilia A & B, where the blood's ability to clot is compromised. In May 2017, Sangamo announced a significant collaboration with Pfizer on its haemophilia A programme. Sangamo received a US $70 million upfront payment, with potential milestones of up to US $475 million, while Pfizer becomes responsible

for the development, manufacturing and commercialisation activities.

Sangamo is also trying to address MPS (mucopolysaccharidosis) I & II, both of which are metabolic disorders and fall into the category of lysosomal storage diseases.

Sangamo has long been a favourite of ours and we retain an interest.

SIBELIUS NATURAL PRODUCTS
PRIVATE – UK

Sibelius is a private Oxfordshire, UK company developing natural products that modulate the activity of genes without altering the underlying DNA, in other words, recreating so-called epigenetic activity. Using its proprietary Chronoscreen platform, Sibelius has tested its product on C. elegans.

The company's main product, SIBE-LIUS SAGE, is a herbal extract, with benefits including supposedly significant improvements in memory performance of recognition and recall.

SIERRA SCIENCES – PRIVATE – US

Sierra Sciences is a private Reno, Nevada-based drug discovery

company, focused on the lengthening of telomeres. The company has screened over 250,000 small-molecule compounds that it believes could lead to an increase in the expression of telomerase. It has narrowed down its search and claim to have found a compound 3 times more potent than anything previously discovered at increasing the expression of telomerase in cells.

Telomeres and telomerase are definitely a part of the ageing story – but there is a sensationalist style to this company that makes us a little uneasy about the strength of its claims.

SIWA THERAPEUTICS
PRIVATE – US

SIWA Therapeutics is a private, Chicago, Illinois-based company, which is developing a monoclonal antibody to target senescent cells. Its CEO, Lewis Gruber, was the writer of the Neupogen patent for Amgen.

Its lead product, SIWA-318, has shown a statistically significantly reduction in senescent cells in mice, as measured by a reduction in p16INK4a expression. This was achieved with a 3-week study with a twice-daily injection routine. The reduction in senescent cells was coupled with a statistically significant increase in muscle mass,

restored back to levels comparable to young mice.

SPARK THERAPEUTICS, INC.
ONCE: NASDAQ – US

Spark Therapeutics is a Philadelphia-based gene therapy company using adeno-associated virus (AAV)-based delivery technology. This technology does not integrate a new gene into DNA which means that any changes are not passed down to succeeding generations.

Its lead programme candidate called LUXTURNA is for the treatment of inherited retina disease caused by mutations in biallelic RPE65. It received orphan drug designation from the FDA and has been assigned a PDUFA action date of 12th January 2018.

In addition to Spark's lead programme, it has programmes in Phase 1 with some impressive early data. One programme is in collaboration with Pfizer, providing significant validation for the platform.

TELOCYTE – PRIVATE – US

Telocyte is a private Grand Rapids, Michigan-based company developing telomerase therapies to treat Alzheimer's Disease. The company claims that telomerase resets the abnormal pattern of gene expression that results in Alzheimer's, where as other therapies such as those that clear amyloid and tau proteins only address the effects of the disease.

The company is currently speaking with the FDA regarding the pre-clinical toxicity work required before moving to IND. Once this is complete, it believes it will be in a position to dose its first patient in late 2018.

UNITY BIOTECHNOLOGY PRIVATE – US

Unity is a high-profile private senolytic company based in Brisbane, California, which raised US $151 million in its Series B financing in August 2017, backed by the likes of Baillie Gifford, Venrock and Fidelity Investments.

Its technology supposedly eliminates senescent cells and has applications in age-related diseases including osteoarthritis, atherosclerosis, eye diseases, and kidney diseases. It currently has two pre-clinical programmes, one in ophthalmology and the other in inflammatory joint diseases.

As noted previously, big money and high valuations bring with them high expectations. Very interesting – but the price could prove too high when public investors finally have the opportunity to invest.

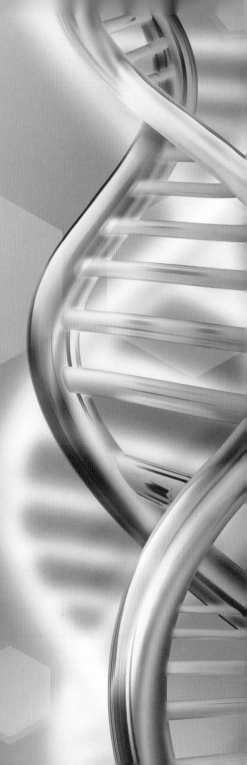

THE KEYS TO KEEPING HEALTHY
AND TO GETTING ACROSS THAT FIRST BRIDGE

Life expectancy in most of the world has been increasing steadily and for well over a century.

This is thanks to advances in medicine, improved hygiene and better nutrition. Yet, although people are living longer, the quality of life in the golden years is often marked by disease and what we call "illderliness".

One of the goals of this book is to prime our readers with information on how they might be able to take simple steps to increase their potential lifespans and, just as importantly, their "healthspans" too.

Healthspan is a term referring to the number of years which a person can stay healthy and free from disease. By increasing our healthspan, we defer the onset of geriatric diseases to much later on in life, and possibly even avoid them altogether. There are many exciting medical and technological breakthroughs in the pipeline and for that reason alone, we should want to hang on for as long as possible in order to take advantage of them.

Ageing is a fact of life (at least it is for now), but biologically some people seem to age more slowly than others. Why is it that there are some people who are still able to run marathons at 80, while others have limited mobility and are confined to a care home by age 70? The marathon runners may be older by a decade in a chronological sense, but biologically they are much younger.

There are a number of factors that influence the rate at which we age; certainly, the genes that we are born with play a part. Our genetic make-up is known as our *genotype*, which gives us our physical attributes. Ageing caused by our genotype is called the intrinsic rate of ageing. As we develop in the womb and throughout our life, our genotype interacts with the environment to produce the *phenotype*, also known as our *extrinsic rate of ageing*.

Lifestyle choices then play a major role in influencing our phenotype. For example, if we spend a lot of time out in the sun, we become exposed to higher doses of solar radiation, which puts us at greater risk in later life of skin damage and of skin cancer. Incidentally, there is a new drug emanating from the labs of the Massachusetts General Hospital that promotes melanin production (the body's own natural sunblock); early trials suggest that it allows the skin to tan without experiencing sun damage or sunburn. This drug might well serve to prevent melanoma and other skin cancers in the near future.

There is a second feature of our DNA, known as the epigenome, that also affects our longevity and how we age. Changes to the epigenome are alterations to certain genes that make them more or less active, but these changes are not to the DNA sequence itself. They can be caused by environmental factors such as smoking or pollution. As these changes accumulate, they take their toll on our bodies, damaging organs and muscles and leaving us more vulnerable to diseases.

Surprisingly, not all animals are destined to age. Senescence is the term for biological ageing, which can refer to ageing in a cell or in the organism as a whole. Unfortunately, unlike the cells of lobsters, which appear to be immortal, most of our cells have only a finite ability to replicate and renew themselves (see Hayflick Limit. Page 162). We need to take care of them so they can keep us in good health for the decades to come in anticipation of the break throughs that will transcend the hard ceiling of our current maximal lifespans.

So far, modern medicine has played a crucial role in keeping us alive for longer. The leading causes of death have dramatically changed over the past 100 years or so, bearing in mind that life expectancy at birth in the UK in 1900 was only 47 for a man and 50 for a woman. Back then, the leading causes of death were influenza and pneumonia, followed by tuberculosis (TB), diarrhoeal disease, heart disease and stroke. Through vaccinations, improved hygiene and antibiotics, the leading causes of death now look very different. Heart disease, stroke, respiratory disease, diabetes and neurodegenerative diseases, as well as cancers, are now the top killers globally.

LEADING CAUSES OF DEATH IN THE US 2014

CARDIOVASCULAR	747,381
CANCER	591,699
RESPIRATORY	147,101
ALZHEIMER'S	93,541
DIABETES	76,488
ACCIDENTS	136,053
INFLUENZA & PNEUMONIA	55,227
KIDNEY DISEASE	48,146
SUICIDE	42,773
OTHER	688,009

Source: Center for Disease Control and Prevention.

IN 2014 IN THE US:

The Deadly Quintet of diseases accounted for 63% of all deaths.

Cardiovascular disease and cancer alone accounted for more than 50% of all deaths.

In 1900, the top 3 causes of death were the infectious diseases - influenza and pneumonia, tuberculosis and diarrheal disease.

Age is now the most significant risk factor in the leading causes of death.

Even in richer countries, the top two causes of death (according to WHO) remain heart disease and stroke, and shockingly, Alzheimer's disease is in the number three spot. As life expectancy and the median age of the global population increases further, more people are likely to acquire Alzheimer's, though latterly the per capita incidence at any given age has been declining.

The best medicine of all is the preventative kind, so our best hope of avoiding these killer diseases is to maintain or adopt a healthy lifestyle.

This is apparently easier said than done, though: a study published by the Mayo Clinic in April 2016, led by Dr Paul Loprinzi, illustrated just how difficult it is. The study used data on around 5,000 adults from the US National Health and Nutrition Examination Survey to

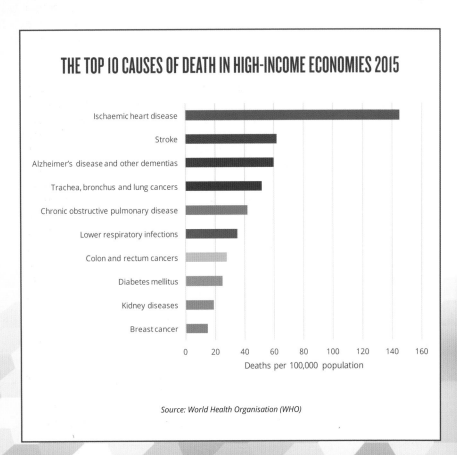

THE TOP 10 CAUSES OF DEATH IN HIGH-INCOME ECONOMIES 2015

Deaths per 100,000 population

Source: World Health Organisation (WHO)

measure four key health parameters: (1) being sufficiently active; (2) eating a healthy diet; (3) being a non-smoker; and (4) having a recommended body fat percentage. The study also analysed several cardiovascular biomarkers, such as blood pressure, cholesterol, fasting blood glucose levels and insulin resistance.

The results revealed that only 2.7% of the adults in the study had all 4 healthy lifestyle characteristics – a depressingly low percentage. It means that over 97% of adults in the US are living with an unnecessarily high risk of a premature death, especially from heart disease. Although this study was conducted on adults in the US, lifestyle and life expectancy in the UK is quite similar. It would not be an exaggeration to state that this is a tragedy on a supra-national scale. Taking action to change lifestyles today will immediately start to improve just about anyone's health prospects.

There is a dizzyingly large amount of published data in medical journals, as well as in the media, about what is and isn't good for human health and longevity. Sometimes, there are conflicting findings – often featured in the British tabloid press.

For example, there have been legitimate studies, properly conducted, that have concluded eating butter is good for our health, while others have linked its consumption to cardiovascular disease. There have also been findings for and against drinking coffee, but most recently (University of Sheffield 2017), it appears that three or more cups of coffee a day are likely to be beneficial for longevity.

A key thing to look out for with scientific studies is the sponsor behind them. If a dairy association funds a study on the health impact of regularly drinking milk, it should come as no surprise to anyone if the study concludes that drinking lots of milk is very healthy.

One of the most deceptive of such studies ever carried out took place in the 1960s and it was one which would shape the way people ate for 50 years. Funded by the US sugar industry, the study aimed to cast doubt on sugar's suspected role in causing heart disease. But, despite having found an inconvenient direct connection between the two, "false news" was propagated by the authors. They distracted the public by turning their guns onto fats, vilifying them as the major cause of heart disease instead of sugar.

The study caused mass hysteria about the impact of fats on health, even though it turns out that sugar was the real culprit all along. And so, more than half a century later, waistlines in America are larger and diabetes is rife because of this deceitful report.

Disinformation, thus, took a huge toll on public health.

The good news is that the health risk from eating refined carbs and sugars is becoming more widely known and many of us have become savvy enough to realise that when something is labelled as "low fat," it usually means it is high in sugar. A recent book by Robb Wolf, called *Wired to Eat*, suggests that we all react in different ways with carbs, which triggers different blood sugar responses. Wolf suggests that this variation in reactions is why many diets fail. *Wired to Eat* is definitely a book worth reading.

So, if we wish to adopt a healthy lifestyle, there are a few key things that we should and shouldn't do. We now discuss each one in more detail.

SMOKING

Let's start with the most obvious and easily addressable health threat – smoking. The fact that you are reading this book in the first place means that you care about your health and the health of your loved ones, so in all likelihood you are a non-smoker. But, if for some unfathomable reason you do smoke and have not found the right time to give up, do it now – and choose life! Without a doubt, smoking is the single most harmful thing you can do to your overall health; it causes a vast range of nasty diseases. The good news is that smoking is becoming less and less socially acceptable, and now only 15% of UK adults smoke. The tobacco industry, in the developed world at least, will soon be on its last gasp!

SUGAR - A SWEET DECEPTION

A diet high in sugar is probably the most detrimental thing to health – after smoking. Some people reading this may find that surprising and, indeed alarmist, but we believe that the public's perception of sugar will one day become similar to that of tobacco today: deadly, and to be avoided.

The chart below clearly shows how obesity and extreme obesity levels were relatively low until the introduction of high-fructose corn syrup in the United States, after which there was a sharp increase in both. Obesity levels have been rising steadily across all OECD member countries, with the US leading the way. *The New England Journal of Medicine* reported in 2017 that 10% of the world's population is obese, as defined by a BMI of 30+. Out of 195 countries surveyed, rates of obesity in 73 had doubled between 1980 and 2015.

Today in the UK, the US and Australia, two-thirds of the entire population are either overweight or obese. This

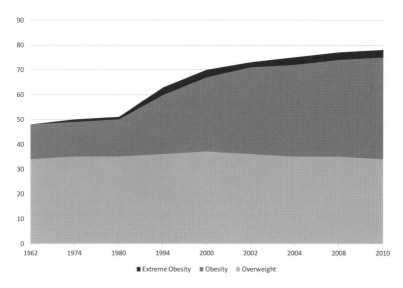

TRENDS IN OVERWEIGHT AND OBESITY AMONG ADULTS, UNITED STATES, 1962–2010

Chart from U.S. Department of Health and Human Services. NIH, National Institute of Diabetes and Digestive and Kidney Diseases.

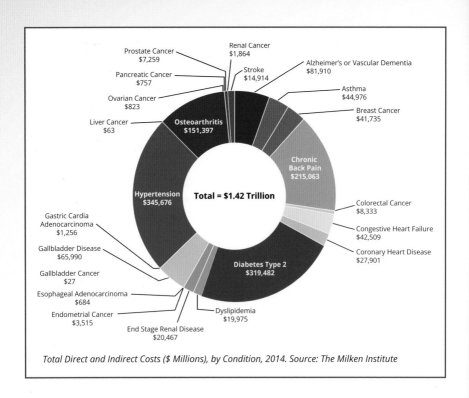

Total Direct and Indirect Costs ($ Millions), by Condition, 2014. Source: The Milken Institute

is a heavy (pun intended) price to pay for individuals and for society as a whole, as productivity suffers due to doctor/hospital visits and sick days taken. Being overweight or obese also renders people far more likely to die a premature death, as they have a higher risk of acquiring a serious disease. It is no wonder that healthcare systems such as the NHS in the UK, as well as the hospital system in the US, are struggling to cope with rising patient numbers.

Obesity raises blood pressure, as well as levels of LDL (known as "bad" cholesterol) and triglycerides (fats), and decreases levels of HDL ("good" cholesterol) in the blood. It also promotes chronic inflammation, which in turn accelerates cellular ageing. Obesity often triggers a negative feedback loop because one of its side-effects is a decrease in sensitivity to leptin, a hormone released by our body to make us feel full (satiated), which, when working, stops us eating too much. About 60% of the variation in human weight may be the result of a genetic predisposition to eating too much; the FTO appetite gene is highly implicated in this.

Type 2 diabetes is one of the most expensive of all health conditions. It is generally associated with being overweight or obese, and it accounts for just over a quarter of medical spending in the US. In 2014, US taxpayers, insurers and consumers spent $112 billion on treating 16.8 million acute cases of the disease, versus just $1 billion in 1962 (adjusted to 2014 dollars). This translates to just over 14% of total US healthcare spending, which in itself is monstrous.

Sugar is not specifically pro-ageing, but it does catalyse the diseases of ageing, notably diabetes, obesity, and quite probably dementia. It is also a factor in cardiovascular disease, and it represents a poisonous influence on public health, right up there with tobacco. Indeed, it is now thought that the concept of a "sweet tooth" is genetically encoded: a liver hormone coded by the gene FGF21 seems to regulate cravings for sweet things. (Gillum and Grarup, University of Copenhagen, 2017).

The prevalence of high-fructose corn syrup beginning in the 1970s, and the subsidies to farmers in the US to produce corn to make it, was the start of the process of institutionalising sugar as part of our diets. Fizzy and still drinks with sugar in them are a major cause of heart and metabolic disease.

A survey done by the American Heart Association and published in the journal *Circulation* in 2013 suggested that sugary drink consumption was associated with 184,000 extra adult deaths each year worldwide. About 100,000 people in Britain experience a stroke every year and only 60,000 of them survive, two-thirds of whom are left with a permanent disability. Sugar will for sure have played a part in many of those strokes.

Soft drinks, biscuits, cakes, snacks, pizza, bread and just about everything classified as fast food contains literally heaps of sugar. Sugar contains no essential micronutrients, and the calories it contains are rightly called "empty". Sugar is pure energy, and in excess, it does enormous damage to our bodies. Sugar is sometimes referred to as a simple carbohydrate. It comes in three main forms in our diet (if we ignore lactose, a sugar found in milk): these are glucose, sucrose and fructose. Glucose is the form of sugar that every cell in our body metabolises for energy. When you read about blood sugar levels, the reference is to blood glucose levels. The other two forms of sugar have to be metabolised into glucose before our bodies can use them for energy.

Sucrose is more commonly referred to as sugar, the type we are all familiar with. It is refined from sugar cane or sugar beet to form white, odourless crystals of sucrose. Sucrose (chemical formula $C_{12}H_{22}O_{11}$) is known as a

SUGAR TO GO - SUGAR CONTENT IN A RANGE OF DRINKS

The World Health Organisation "strongly recommends" limiting consumption of free sugars to 50 grams a day, while advising a further reduction to 25 grams. Just a few drinks can take you close to the limit.

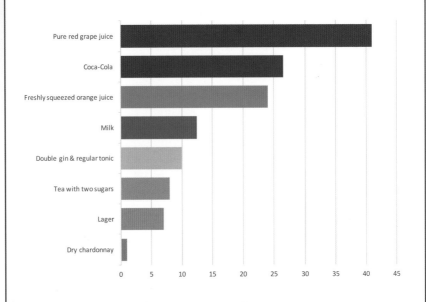

 One standard (330ml) can of Coca Cola gives you 140% of a daily 25g limit.

 Two pints (1136ml) of lager gives you 120% of a daily 25g limit.

disaccharide and is digested by the enzyme sucrase to form 50% glucose and 50% fructose. The glucose is released into the blood and is the source of energy for all of our body's cells. Excess glucose is temporarily stored in the skeletal muscles and the liver in the form of glycogen, sometimes referred to as animal starch, and this can be accessed as an energy source by the body very quickly. It is estimated that an adult can store up to 500 grams of glycogen, which equates to 2,000 calories.

Fructose is the sugar found in most fruits, but the good news is there are no apparent negative health effects found from consuming fruit in its natural form. It is only when fructose is added to foods, or when it is separated from the fruit and consumed as a juice, that it becomes a health threat. Drinking a glass of orange or apple juice is no healthier than drinking a can of a soft drink, as it contains just as much sugar. It is far better to eat the orange or the apple than to drink its juice. That's because fruit consumed in its natural form contains plenty of fibre, so the rate at which its sugar is absorbed into the bloodstream is greatly reduced. When we drink a fruit juice, we end up separating the fibre from the sugar, so our body absorbs the sugar very quickly, causing a spike in blood sugar levels shortly after drinking it. There is no link between developing type 2 diabetes and eating whole fruits, but the same cannot be said for drinking fruit juice.

Fructose cannot be metabolised by our cells directly; only the liver is able to break it down. The metabolic process of fructose in the liver is a complex one: up to half of it is converted to glucose, about a quarter is converted into lactate and about a fifth is converted into glycogen. The rest ends up being converted into triglycerides (a type of fat), uric acid and free radicals, none of which are conducive to good health.

Triglycerides can and do build up in the liver over time and impair its normal function. They can cause fatty liver disease and pancreatitis. High triglyceride levels are associated with atherosclerosis (a disease in which plaque builds up inside the arteries) laying the foundations for heart disease. Plaque comprises fat, cholesterol and calcium, as well as some other substances found in the blood. Over time this causes the arteries to harden and narrow, restricting their functionality.

Uric acid can build up and crystallise in the joints to form gout. It can also stop the body producing nitric oxide, a compound that is a powerful vasodilator, protecting our arterial walls from damage. Nitric oxide is often given as a medicine to treat patients suffering from angina.

There is really no such thing as "good sugar" (and that includes honey), as all sugars are broken down into two simple components – glucose and fructose. We produce glucose from all of our nutrients, in the form of ATP in the mitochondria, and excess production of glucose is damaging. But the worst of the lot is fructose, as we have no physiological need for it, and it can only be metabolised in the liver, and stored as glycogen. If there is an excess of glycogen in the liver, the surplus is converted to white adipose fat.

The new term "non-alcoholic fatty liver disease" (NAFLD), also known as NASH, or non-alcoholic steatosis, results from this phenomenon and is a condition that until a decade ago wasn't even a recognised disease. Today it burdens about 10% of Americans. When the liver is overburdened, some of the excess fat created in it becomes cholesterol, and this cholesterol is transported by the bloodstream around the body – potentially causing atherosclerosis, which is characterised by furring of the arteries.

In addition, excess glucose causes metabolic dysfunction, which can lead to diabetes, and this has now resulted in 8% of the world's adult population contracting the type 2 version of the disease. That total number, now estimated at 450 million, is growing by 3 to 5% per annum.

Excess glucose results in insulin resistance, and is the precursor to many of the diseases of ageing. Insulin resistance results from an overloading of the pancreas, which when overwhelmed can't make enough of the vital insulin hormone needed to counterbalance glucose surpluses.

Sugar can be, and often is, addictive, causing a dopamine "reward" reaction in the brain. The evidence is mounting that sugar, not fat, may be one of the leading drivers of heart disease, largely as a result of its harmful effect on metabolism.

The best thing to do to counterbalance the effects of sugar is to abstain from eating it, or to reduce its consumption dramatically. (Oh, and by the way, diet sodas are almost as bad as real sodas – but for different reasons as we discuss later).

There are also some new scientific developments which seek to reduce the effect of sugar in our diets. Scientists at the Salk Institute have been working with an experimental compound, which failed in earlier trials, called GW1516 (endurobol) and have been studying

its effects on mice to see if it could be revived in a new guise.

Sedentary animals dosed with the compound were able to run on a treadmill for 270 minutes before tiring. Untreated active mice could only manage 160 minutes by contrast. GW1516 works by activating the gene called PPARD (peroxisome proliferator-activated receptor delta), a gene used by mammals to switch between the burning of sugar and the burning of fat, which also activates nutrient sensors. As such, this gene receptor/activator might form the basis of a pill that could "select" which of fat or sugar should be burned, replicating the benefits of exercise.

This would be advantageous to those who are not able to exercise, such as the elderly, the bedridden, or the disabled. But first, GW1516 must be improved.

In earlier trials, it was shown to cause cancer and its development was abandoned in 2007. GW1516 is used as an illegal performance-enhancing drug, not approved for sale anywhere except in Russia.

Another PPAR-δ inhibitor, GW0742, appears to work somewhat better, and is also better absorbed than GW1516. For sure, a non-cancer producing PPAR-δ inhibitor will emerge in due course, and this will prove to be a useful weapon in the fight against sugar and ageing.

Until then, taking metformin (Glucophage, Glumetza, Riomet and Fortamet are some of its brand names) absolutely does reduce blood sugar and each pill costs less than 5 cents. Chromium is a mineral that appears to have a similar effect.

The final question to be asked here is: given that the consumption of sugar is so detrimental to public health, why isn't it universally taxed? Health systems around the world are creaking under the burden of age-associated lifestyle diseases, and sugar plays a big role in this burden. A tax on sugar, similar to that on tobacco, will see its level of consumption come down, plus it will generate additional revenues for the public purse.

But consuming excess sugar is not the only culprit when it comes to health: ingesting too much salt and saturated fat can be equally detrimental, as can consuming too little fibre.

A common misconception is that carbs and sugars are different. Not so. Carbs are simply long chemical chains of sugar, so eating starchy foods has more or less the same effect on blood glucose levels as drinking a glass of fruit juice or a can of cola.

This may come as a shock to some readers, especially those who are consuming specific carbohydrates in the belief that by doing so they are following a healthy diet. It turns out that eating carbs, such as a small baked potato or about 150g of long grain white rice or a 30g bowl of cornflakes, will all raise blood glucose levels as much as eating 9 teaspoons of sugar does. Conversely, eating foods rich in protein and fat does not affect blood glucose levels at all. Not only that, eating protein and fat leaves us feeling fuller for longer, hence there is a reduced likelihood of overeating. We will discuss diet and nutrition in more detail later on, but for now, let's move on to the next threat to health.

INACTIVITY

In terms of sustenance and abundance, we've never had it so good. We don't need to spend all day foraging for food, which preoccupied the short and brutish lives of our distant ancestors. Today, calories are cheaper than ever and accessible with minimal effort. Of course, in solving the problem of sustenance we have inadvertently created a health crisis. And an abundance of calories doesn't mean that we are properly nourished. Indeed, it could be said that billions of people remain malnourished in the sense that their diets are deficient in many vital nutrients.

Everyone who reads the news or watches TV is aware that being physically active is essential to keeping bodies and minds in a healthy state. The body craves movement and really needs to move often and vigorously. We evolved over millions of years to be constantly on the go. It is only since the industrial revolution, and more recently the invention of the television and the personal computer, that we have become significantly more sedentary creatures.

Physical activity is really the best wonder drug for our bodies. Activity has been shown to improve cognitive function, to lower blood pressure, to improve heart and lung function, to alleviate depression, to lower anxiety, to improve sleep, to improve digestion and bowel function, and to boost self-esteem. Our bodies and minds simply function better when we exercise them on a regular basis.

To further emphasise this point, a recent study from the University of Cambridge found that just a brisk 20-minute walk every day reduces a person's risk of a premature death by 25%. Another major study from the Mayo Clinic revealed that walking for just half an hour a day can dramatically diminish the risks of getting Alzheimer's disease, depression and type 2 diabetes.

Unfortunately, the UK is one of the least physically active countries in the world, with a quarter of the population doing less than 30 minutes of exercise per week. And activity levels don't seem to be improving. By 2035, Public Health England predicts that more than one in 10 people will be at risk of diabetes, and that is on top of the 8% of adults who already have the disease.

Choosing the right activity very much depends on the individual, but not all types of exercise have the same health and longevity benefits.

Regardless of the activity people prefer to take part in, we should all be spending more time walking in our everyday lives. The health effects are really too good to pass up.

Another study led by Oxford University, and published in the *British Journal of Sports Medicine*, analysed information on 80,000 people over the age of 30 in England and Scotland between 1994 and 2008 in an effort to find out the effects that different types of sports had on their longevity. The research concluded that people who played racquet sports on a regular basis reduced their risk of dying prematurely by 47% when compared to people who did no exercise at all. The next most beneficial exercise was swimming, which reduced the risk of dying by 28% followed by cycling with 15%. Unfortunately, the study found that running, football or rugby did not seem to have an impact on longevity. The scientists were stumped as to why this would be the case, but the key message from health experts is that we are far healthier when we exercise regularly as compared to leading a sedentary lifestyle. And on the subject of running, Duck

Chul Lee of the University of Iowa has recently published research in *Progress in Cardiovascular Disease* which contradicts British studies; he suggests that running adds more to lifespan than any other activity (one hour adding 7 hours to lifespan, on average) – so the bottom line is to get moving!

BEING OVERWEIGHT

As illustrated in the graph in the section on sugar, we are experiencing an obesity epidemic. This is no longer just a problem of the Western or developed world: many developing countries now have even greater incidences of obesity. According to WHO figures, 39% of adults worldwide are overweight and some 13% are obese. The countries with the highest proportion of overweight adults (defined as people with a BMI of 25 or higher) tend to be the Pacific island nations, such as the Cook Islands, Palau, Nauru and Tonga. Countries in the Middle East such as Kuwait, Bahrain and the United Arab Emirates are also in the top category. In these nations, 70 to 80% of adults are overweight. In 1980, there were only 857 million overweight and obese people in the world. Unfortunately, that figure had grown to 2.1 billion by 2013 and shows no sign of declining.

BMI stands for Body Mass Index and is a simple ratio that is derived by taking a person's weight in kilograms and dividing it by the square of that person's height in metres. It is not a perfect measure of health, but BMI is a good yardstick in determining whether a person is or isn't of a healthy weight.

BODY MASS INDEX

$$BMI = \frac{\text{WEIGHT IN KG}}{(\text{HEIGHT IN M})^2}$$

<18.5	18.5 TO 24.9	25 TO 29.9	30 TO 34.9	35 TO 39.9	40>
UNDERWEIGHT	HEALTHY WEIGHT	OVERWEIGHT	OBESE	SEVERELY OBESE	MORBIDLY OBESE

For example, a man with a height of 1.75 metres and weighing 90 kilograms would have a BMI of 29.4.

A study published in the *New England Journal of Medicine* (de Gonzalez et. Al, NEJM 2017) in 2010, and involving almost one and a half million adults who were non-smokers with no pre-existing medical conditions, is interesting: it concluded that overweight and obese people have a considerably shorter life expectancy compared to those with healthy weights. The negative effect of obesity on life expectancy was the same for both men and women. The study revealed that men and women with a BMI ranging from 20 to 24.9 had the lowest mortality rate. As one might expect, a higher BMI increased the risk of death, but what was surprising is that this risk increases exponentially as BMI increases; men with a BMI of 40 or more were 32 times more likely to die prematurely than those within the healthy BMI range.

A more surprising finding of the same study was that underweight people (those with a BMI below 20) also had an increased risk of death when compared to the group with a BMI in the 20 to 24.9 range. So, when it comes to weight, the message is clear: make sure your BMI is between 20 and 24.9.

Being overweight is also associated with an increased risk of developing and dying from many diseases, including cancer, type 2 diabetes and cardiovascular disease. A study published in the *BMJ* in February 2017 (BMJ 2017;356:j477) looked at the association between adiposity (the prevalence of white/yellow body fat) and the risk of developing or dying as a result of 36 major cancers and their subtypes. The findings showed that adiposity had a strong association with 11 of the 36 cancers, namely oesophageal adenocarcinoma, multiple myeloma, cancers of the gastric cardia, colon, rectum, biliary tract, pancreas, breast, endometrium, ovary and kidney.

The study also found that the greater the degree of overweight/obesity, the greater the risk of cancer: gaining just one stone (6.35 kg) can increase a person's risk of getting cancer by 50%. The backer of the study, the World Cancer Research Fund, warned that around 25,000 cancers in the UK could be prevented every year if people stayed in shape.

Despite near-universal awareness of the health risks associated with being obese, the trend is still moving in the wrong direction: in the UK, the NHS reported that between 2015 and 2016, there were 525,000 hospital admissions in England involving obesity as either the primary or secondary diagnosis. This represents a doubling of the figure from 5 years earlier and a 20% rise from just a year earlier.

CHRONIC STRESS

Our modern, hectic lifestyles are very conducive to stress, and essentially it comes down to three types: work stress, relationship stress and financial stress. How we deal with stress is vital to our health as it is too easy to let it overwhelm us – and this wreaks havoc on the body.

Usually, when there is a perceived threat, our body's fight-or-flight response kicks in, releasing the hormone adrenaline. This has the effect of increasing the heart rate, elevating blood pressure and boosting available energy supplies. The primary stress hormone is called cortisol, and it prepares the body for a conflict by increasing blood glucose and enhancing the brain's use of glucose. Cortisol also increases the availability of substances that repair tissues, just in case there is any physical injury, and suppresses certain non-essential functions as part of its reprioritisation efforts during a fight-or-flight situation, such as altering the immune response and suppressing the digestive system, the reproductive system and growth processes. It also affects the region of the brain that controls mood, motivation and fear.

Normally, the body will reverse these fight-or-flight responses once the perceived threat has passed. But if for some reason we constantly feel under threat, cortisol levels remain elevated for prolonged periods and this can cause serious damage to bodies. It is known as "chronic stress" and it is responsible for anxiety, depression, digestive problems, headaches, heart disease, sleep problems, weight gain and an inability to concentrate. Needless to say, chronic stress damages cells and can lead to premature ageing. Stress in life is inevitable, but we have to individually develop a coping mechanism that works for our particular set of circumstances. Some people are able to dissipate their stress very well by playing a sport or by working out, others prefer to de-stress through yoga or mindfulness/meditation, Tai Chi, Qi Gong, or breathing exercises.

Some choose to unwind through reading, playing games, or enjoying time with friends or family. In the journal *Frontiers in Immunology* (2017), British researchers followed 846 people and discovered that the expression of genes controlling inflammation was down regulated using de-stressing techniques.

CONDITIONING FOR A HEALTHY LIFE

We more or less understand what the greatest threats to our health are, so it's a fairly simple step to modify our lifestyles based on the latest scientific understanding, thereby improving our chances of living a long and healthy life, free from disease and injury.

We need to strike a balance between a decent quality of life and the compromises/sacrifices needed for the sake of good health and longevity. Each one of us will have a different equilibrium point. The quality of life should be the most important driver and an over-emphasis on longevity just for the sake of it is a somewhat questionable pursuit. After all, there is no point in living a long life if it has little meaning, or if it is plain boring or monastic.

LOSE EXCESS BODY FAT

To embark on our path to a healthy, long life, step one is clearly not to smoke as we've explained previously. Step two is to shed any excess body fat, so that the BMI is in the healthy range of 18.5 to 24.9.

To lose excess fat, we need to burn off more calories than we consume in a way that is not too painful or daunting. Fat yields 9 calories per gram, so one kilogram of fat contains 9,000 of them.

However, fat takes time to mobilise and to break down as an energy source; the body's priority is to burn readily available glycogen (also known as animal starch), which is mainly stored in the muscles and in the liver. Glycogen can be quickly converted to glucose, which is our primary source of energy when we move and exercise. When fully topped up, an adult body can store 1,500 to 2,000 calories of glycogen or about 500 grams of it in weight. It is worth pointing out that every gram of glycogen carries alongside it 3 grams of water and that this water is released into the bloodstream as the glycogen is used up. This is important in the context of weight loss because if all 500 grams of glycogen in the body are used up, then there will be an additional 1.5 kilograms of water lost with it, which is partly excreted as sweat (depending on exertion levels, temperature, humidity, etc.) and the rest in our urine.

This water loss associated with glycogen expenditure explains why, when starting a new weight-loss diet, many people manage to lose a good 2 kilograms or so initially, but then struggle to lose more weight.

Unfortunately, it is because that initial weight loss is primarily fluid loss and not fat loss. To burn stored fat, it is necessary to reduce insulin levels, which can only be done by reducing sugar intake, or by significantly upping the level of exercise.

There are two types of fat storage cells in our body, and they have competing objectives: white adipose cells store fat as an energy source for future use, while brown adipose cells burn energy for thermoregulation, i.e. to generate heat to keep us warm. Dr Benjamin Bikman, a professor of pathophysiology and a biomedical scientist at Brigham Young University, Utah, has conducted extensive research on how our body burns fat. His findings confirm that if we want to lose body fat, we must first bring down our insulin levels before our body initiates ketogenesis, the process by which we burn body fat for energy. Unfortunately, people with excess body fat, especially around the waist, are prone to insulin resistance, meaning the body has to produce more of the hormone to reduce blood sugar levels, and thus insulin levels do not reach a sufficiently low level to promote fat burning. This is why some overweight people find it more difficult to lose excess body fat. It's a really negative cycle, and it's a hard one to break.

The take-away message is clear: high insulin levels encourage white adipose cells to store fat; low insulin levels encourage the body's ketogenesis activity to rise, which encourage white adipose cells to convert to brown adipose cells (the cells that like to burn fat). This should always be kept in mind when starting any diet to lose body fat – cutting the carbs out is the main key to effectively losing body fat.

There are a few diets that readers might consider; all have merit, and maybe they could be "mixed and matched". There are plenty of other ones that we have looked at to get to this filtered list.

ATKINS DIET

A few decades ago, the *Atkins Diet*, named after its developer Dr Robert Atkins, emerged as an effective weight-loss programme. It is a diet essentially based on staying away from all carbs and with no limit on foods rich in protein and fat, such as eggs, meat, fish, nuts and non-starchy vegetables. Robert Atkins believed that eating starchy carbs was the main cause of weight gain, causing the body to overproduce insulin, depleting blood glucose and thereby making people feel hungry even after consuming more calories than their bodies needed. At the time, his diet was very controversial and, when he suffered a cardiac arrest in 2002 (which he survived), his critics took the opportunity to blame his high-fat diet for it. Unfortunately, Dr Atkins died a year later, not because of a heart condition but as a result of slipping on an icy New York pavement and hitting his head. He was 72. The luck of the draw.

Despite Dr Atkins being heavily criticised by his peers for prescribing his namesake diet to his many overweight patients, the scientific community has recently started to shift its stance and now supports at least some of his claims, notably that it is carbs that cause cholesterol levels to rise and that are the primary cause of weight gain, and not fats.

Additionally, eating foods high in cholesterol, such as eggs and steaks, does not raise blood cholesterol levels, but drinking cans of soft drinks or eating potatoes certainly does. This doesn't mean that we can eat as much fatty food as we would like without gaining weight; eating more calories than we burn off will always lead to weight gain. But the key distinction here is that consuming fat (and protein) does not cause our blood glucose levels to spike in the same way that eating carbs does. Opinion remains divided on whether fats are healthy, but everyone is in agreement that we should follow a balanced diet comprising protein, carbs and fats. Even within this advice, there is a broad range as to how this should be interpreted. The standard advice for a healthy, low-fat diet is that we consume 12% of our calories from protein, 8% from dairy, 40% from fruit and vegetables, 38% from carbs and 2% from fats.

PALEO DIET

The Paleo Diet is based on the premise that, before human beings settled down to domesticated farming around 10,000 years ago, we were hunter-gatherers, eating whatever we could get our hands on. It is assumed that this diet was helpful in ensuring survival but also reproduction. The proponents of the Paleo Diet suggest that 10,000 years is not a long time in an evolutionary sense, and that we really should still be eating as our hunter-gatherer ancestors did, before the dawn of farming.

The diet is based on eating unprocessed foods from all the major food groups such as fruits, vegetables, meats, seafood and nuts. These foods reduce the body's glycaemic load and contain a healthy range of fatty acids, proteins and carbohydrates, as well as all the vitamins and nutrients we need.

The health benefits of the Paleo Diet are unproven. We know that the average human life expectancy was much shorter during the Palaeolithic era (around 30 years) than today, but diet wasn't the reason. And while the Paleo Diet is certainly much healthier than the modern western diet, it is not clear whether it is actually conducive to living longer.

In general, the Paleo Diet allows you to eat until you feel full, which is one of its appeals. It is quite similar to the Atkins Diet in that respect, as it avoids most carbs, such as bread, rice and pasta. The general mix of caloric intake is about 35% from fats, 35% from carbs and 30% from protein. These are the core foods of the Paleo Diet:

- Meat
- Fowl
- Fish
- Eggs
- Vegetables
- Oils
- Fruits
- Nuts
- Tubers

THE ROSEDALE DIET: FOR LONGEVITY AND WEIGHT LOSS

A leading anti-ageing expert, Dr Ron Rosedale, is very much against having too much protein in our diet, stating that while the Paleo Diet may optimise us for reproductive success, it will not necessarily make us live longer because "nature doesn't care about longevity, its goal is to pass on our genes to the next generation." His recommendation is that we keep our protein intake to no more than 1 gram per day for every kilogram of lean body mass. Dr Rosedale doesn't like carbohydrates either; he calls sugar a "dirty" fuel, whereas fats burn more cleanly. His dislike of carbs as an energy source is expressed in a comment about our lifespan: "your health and likely your lifespan will be determined by the proportion of fat versus sugar you burn over a lifetime".

Dr Rosedale believes that, to live a long and healthy life, we should all be following a high-fat, ketogenic diet. This is when the body is deprived of carbs and resorts to burning fat as a source of energy.

Dr Rosedale believes that mTOR (see Targets in Ageing. Page 184) is the most important signalling pathway in the body; it is a pathway common to almost all living things, even bacteria. He also believes that virtually all cancers are associated with mTOR activation.

He initially discovered that his high-fat diet worked very well with patients suffering from diabetes and cardiovascular disease and now believes it should be a diet for everyone wishing to optimise health and longevity. In brief, keep carbs low, proteins moderate and fats high.

THE 5:2 FASTING DIET

This is one of the intermittent fasting diets that seem to us to be a good alternative to the misery that caloric restriction would impose on us, in order to eke out a little extra longevity.

A study published in *Cell* magazine, a leading scientific journal, found that both in mice and in early human clinical trials, with patients receiving chemotherapy, long periods of fasting (2 to 4 days over a 6-month period) significantly altered white blood cell counts. The fasting seemed to trigger

a regenerative switch which killed off older and damaged immune cells, while at the same time generating new ones. It is believed that this occurs because prolonged fasting reduces levels of PKA, an enzyme that needs to be shut down to allow stem cells to switch into regenerative mode. Furthermore, this diet reduced levels of IGF-1, a hormone strongly linked to ageing and cancer. (See Growth Hormone. Page 201).

It also appears that shorter periods of fasting, say for a couple of days, even just once or twice a year, have a hugely rejuvenating effect on the body, and while many may find it challenging to adhere to this kind of programme, the "suffering" only lasts a couple of days and it is a lot more pleasant and less punishing than following a calorie restricted, or calorie-restricted, diet on a regular basis. An option that is now wildly popular is what's often referred to as the "5:2 diet". Dr Michael Mosley, a BBC television presenter, is credited with developing this particular intermittent fasting diet, which he himself followed and thereby managed to reverse his type 2 diabetes. He also lost around 10 kg of fat in 3 months. Many people have achieved excellent results on this diet, largely because it is not too taxing on the body, as for 5 days of the week you eat normally (within reason). The dieting part only applies to 2 days of the week, ideally on non-consecutive days, where you only consume 600 calories per day for a man and 500 calories per day for a woman, so it is by no means a total fast.

EXERCISE REGULARLY

As we highlighted earlier, being sedentary is fundamentally damaging to both our bodies and our brains. We evolved to always be active, so we must all find time to incorporate some physical activity into our weekly routine. The NHS in the UK recommends that adults do at least 150 minutes of moderate aerobic activity every week, plus some strength training at least twice a week, to maintain muscle mass.

This becomes more important as we get older. A study by the Research Institute for Sport and Exercise in Canberra, Australia, found that exercise noticeably improved brain health in people over the age of 50. In particular, it was aerobic exercise that improved cognitive abilities (such as thinking, reasoning and reading), while strength training (such as weights) improved memory and the so-called executive functions, i.e. the ability to plan and to organise. The study found that there was a direct correlation between the amount of exercise done and cognitive function.

CARDIO

Aerobic exercise is a level of activity that gets the heart pumping faster to a sustainable level. It not only improves cardiovascular fitness but can also help to burn body fat, although, it takes 20 minutes before the body is able to start mobilising and burning fat for energy. Depending on age and level of fitness, the aerobic range for the heart can range from 100 to 160 beats per minute. The table below provides some guidelines based on age.

There is no lack of choice when it comes to selecting an aerobic activity or sport. If you already have a sport that you enjoy, stick to it. If you are looking for something new, consider something that you can reasonably sustain. Generally speaking, the more accessible an activity is, the more likely you are to stick at it. A walk, jog or run is probably the easiest, as these can be done anywhere, at any time and without an organised group, although for some people running as part of an organised group or event can sometimes be more fun. Cycling is also an accessible and increasingly popular activity, generally preferred to running by those with knee or hip problems as it is a low-impact activity.

Age	Target Heart Rate Zone 50-85%	Average Maximum Heart Rate, 100%
20 years	100-170 beats per minute	200 beats per minute
30 years	95-162 beats per minute	190 beats per minute
35 years	93-157 beats per minute	185 beats per minute
40 years	90-153 beats per minute	180 beats per minute
45 years	88-149 beats per minute	175 beats per minute
50 years	85-145 beats per minute	170 beats per minute
55 years	83-140 beats per minute	165 beats per minute
60 years	80-136 beats per minute	160 beats per minute
65 years	78-132 beats per minute	155 beats per minute
70 years	75-128 beats per minute	150 beats per minute

The table below provides some indicative figures of calories burned per hour during certain activities. The actual calories burned will obviously depend on age, weight and intensity level.

There is also a new type of cardio exercise that has really taken off since 2011; it is known as High-Intensity Interval Training or HIIT/HIT for short.

HIIT is an anaerobic form of exercise, meaning that it is performed in bursts of unsustainably high intensity levels for short periods of time, with short rests in between. There are a range of exercises that can be performed under HIIT for periods as short as 20 seconds. A simple example is to use a stationary bike to pedal as hard as physically possible for 30 seconds, then rest for 1 to 2 minutes and repeat for 3 sets.

HIIT has been shown to improve insulin sensitivity levels, making the body better at metabolising glucose, thus reducing the risk of diabetes.

STRENGTH TRAINING

Although sometimes overlooked as part of an exercise routine, strength training becomes increasingly important as we get older. After the age of 30, we start to lose 3% to 5% of our muscle mass per decade. Age-related loss of muscle mass is known as sarcopenia, and it tends

Exercise	Calories / hour for Men	Calories / hour for Women
Running	700	500
Cycling	600	450
Jogging	500	350
Tennis	500	350
Physical Housework	400	250
Walking	300	250

to accelerate in old age. We end up with smaller and weaker muscles, weaker bones, a diminished aerobic capacity and a decline in our metabolic function. Although this is a gradual process that takes place over several decades, by the time we reach old age, we are frailer and more susceptible to falls.

The good news is that sarcopenia can be arrested and even reversed with regular strength training, ideally twice a week. If you are not familiar with strength training, get a personal trainer to customise a workout for you that works all the muscle groups. Choose a weight or exercise that you are able to complete a set of 12 to 15

reps with; don't go too light as the muscles need to feel they are being stressed. If you don't have time to go to a gym, many equivalent exercises can easily be done at home.

A very simple and portable device that is ideal for strength training of the whole body is the TRX System (www.trxtraining.com), developed by a former US Navy SEAL. The TRX can be configured in a multitude of ways to work different muscle groups. It leverages the user's own body weight to effectively build strength, balance and flexibility. So even if you travel a great deal for your job, the TRX is easy to pack into a suitcase and set up in a hotel room.

Weight training has also been shown to significantly improve brain function, according to a study published in the *Journal of the American Geriatrics Society* in which 100 people aged 55 to 86 with mild cognitive impairment took part. The study lasted six months and focused on those who took part in twice-weekly weight training during which they worked to at least 80% of their strength. The study also showed that the stronger the person became, the greater the benefit to their brain. This supports the old adage that a healthy body is a healthy mind.

STRETCH AND BALANCE

Two often-overlooked aspects of exercise are stretching and balance.

As we age our muscles lose their elasticity, so we need to offset this by making sure that we incorporate a good stretch routine into our plan, ideally at the end of an exercise session. Stretching helps improve our posture, especially if we spend prolonged periods sitting at work, and it can also reduce the risk of injury when we do exercise.

Equally important is our sense of balance, which also unfortunately deteriorates with age. As we get older, having a fall can have serious consequences. More than 90 % of hip

fractures are due to falls and 80% of fall deaths occur in people over 65, according to Harvard Medical School.

One of the ways to bring both stretching and balance into our weekly routine is through practising yoga, an ancient discipline which not only helps flexibility and balance, but also offers a multitude of other benefits, such as improving muscle and bone strength, increasing circulation, draining the lymphatic system, increasing heart rate, reducing blood pressure, relieving muscular tension, and aiding focus and mindfulness.

Alternatively, there is the ancient Chinese art of Tai Chi, which offers similar benefits to yoga but at a lower physical exertion level.

EAT A BALANCED DIET

Next in our checklist for health and longevity is diet. Following a healthy, balanced diet is pretty challenging for almost all of us. We tend to lead hectic lives that don't afford us the luxury of planning what we eat far enough in advance. Consequently, we end up grabbing something quick for the sake of convenience and, more often than not, it tends to be fast food. Whether it is in the form of a burger, fish and chips or a ready-made frozen meal, fast food is a poor substitute for food cooked from fresh ingredients when it comes to nutritional content. It tends to contain processed meats (which have been linked to cancer), as well as being high in salt, fat and sugar and low in fibre and nutrients. Fast food should be thought of as an exception to our diet, not the norm.

The quality (and quantity) of the food we eat plays an important role in how we age and in keeping us healthy and disease-free. While many of us are concerned about what our diet will do to our weight, most of us neglect the broader health aspects of what we consume.

MACRONUTRIENTS

The primary nutrients humans need to consume in large quantities (macronutrients) are carbohydrates, proteins and fats, all of which we have mentioned briefly in the previous sections. Let's delve a little deeper into each of these macronutrients to give a better understanding of what they are, the foods in which they are found and the effects they have on our health.

First off, there are the much-talked-about carbohydrates, or carbs for short. These can be in the form of complex carbs, such as rice, bread, potatoes and pasta, or simple/ refined carbs, also known as sugars. Once ingested, complex carbs are broken down into sugars and provide our bodies with 4 kilocalories (often just referred to as calories or kcals) per gram. We are also starting to see more use of the kilojoule, the joule being the official measure of energy under the metric system. One calorie equals around 4.2 joules.

Next, there are proteins, which are broken down in our stomachs and small intestines into amino acids. Our bodies need a whole range of amino acids, some of which we must eat in their direct form (known as essential amino acids), while others our bodies can build by using some of the essential amino acids (known as non-essential amino acids). There are 9 essential amino acids and 11 non-essential amino acids, these being:

Essential Amino Acids	Non-Essential Amino Acids
Isoleucine	Alanine
Histidine	Arginine
Leucine	Asparagine
Methionine	Aspartic Acid
Lysine	Cysteine
Phenylalanine	Glutamic Acid
Tryptophan	Glutamine
Threonine	Glycine
Valine	Proline
	Serine
	Tyrosine

Amino acids are used in every cell of our bodies and can be considered to be building blocks, like Lego toy bricks, from which proteins are made, for example in building muscle tissue. When the body cannot access carbs or fat, it will break down amino acids for energy. Every gram of protein consumed yields 4 calories of energy, the same as carbs.

Lastly, there are fats. These contain the greatest amount of energy per gram, yielding 9 calories. Fats have been vilified for decades but are now coming back as an accepted healthy source of energy. There are three categories of dietary fat: saturated fat, trans fat and unsaturated fat.

Saturated fat is typically a solid at room temperature and is largely found in animal food sources, such as red meats (especially the likes of sausages, bacon and burgers) and dairy, although it is also found in some plant-based foods such as palm oil and coconut oil (which one study we read reported as being as bad as pork lard for our health). The American Heart Association recommends limiting saturated fat to no more than 7% of daily calorie consumption.

Trans-fat is largely a man-made fat, although it can be found in small quantities in beef and dairy products. It is made by heating vegetable oils with hydrogen gas, a process known as hydrogenation. The reason the food industry does this is because it increases the shelf life of the fat and makes it a solid at room temperature. Trans fat has very harmful health effects even in small quantities and must be avoided. Its harmful effects include: raising LDL and lowering HDL levels; creating inflammation; and contributing to insulin resistance. Trans fat is typically found in processed (especially fried) foods such as chips, crackers and cookies.

Unsaturated fat is the healthiest type of fat. It is a liquid at room temperature and is primarily found in plant-based foods. There are also two sub-categories of unsaturated fat: monounsaturated fat and polyunsaturated fat.

Cutting back on saturated fat and eating foods high in monounsaturated fat help lower LDL and raises HDL cholesterol levels. Foods high in monounsaturated fat include avocados, almonds and olive oil.

Polyunsaturated fat is found in high concentrations in walnuts, fish and flax seeds. A type of polyunsaturated fat is omega-3, which is an essential fat, meaning that the body is not able to make it so we must eat foods that contain it. It is used to make cell membranes in our body and is involved in regulating inflammation and the contraction/relaxation of artery walls. Omega-3 has received a lot of attention in recent years over its health benefits, especially in terms of helping to prevent heart disease and stroke, and may even play a protective role against cancer. Omega-3 also lowers blood pressure and heart rate, and improves blood vessel function.

Fatty fish, such as salmon, tuna and mackerel, are good animal sources of omega-3 fat. Good plant sources of omega-3 include vegetable oils, such as canola/rapeseed, flaxseed and soybean, as well as walnuts.

Rapeseed (or canola oil) is a good source of both *monounsaturated* and *polyunsaturated* fat.

The message about eating fats is clear: (1) they are high in calories (9 calories per gram) so don't consume more than you can burn off; (2) avoid trans fat as much as you are able; (3) minimise the amount of saturated fat in your diet; (4) unsaturated fat is the good fat and is the healthiest by far so try and consume most of your fat intake from unsaturated fat, especially monounsaturated fat (olive oil) and omega-3 (fatty fish, canola oil and walnuts).

GLYCAEMIC INDEX & GLYCAEMIC LOAD

The way we consume carbs, proteins and fats affects the way our bodies metabolise it, especially carbs, which quickly end up in our bloodstream as glucose. Different foods containing carbs are metabolised differently by the body, hence you may have heard the term "not all carbs are created equal." One way to explain what this means is through a measure referred to as the Glycaemic Index (GI).

First proposed by David Jenkins et al in *The American Journal of Clinical Nutrition* in 1981, the GI has become a recognised way of categorising carbs. It is a measure of how quickly carbs enter our bloodstream as sugar after being eaten. Good carbs have a lower GI than bad carbs, so the lower the number the better. The GI number is based on how quickly a food releases glucose into the bloodstream relative to glucose itself, which has a GI of 100. Some refined carbs can have a GI as high as 100.

Most fruits and vegetables, beans, unrefined grains, pastas and nuts have a GI of 55 or below, which is considered low; sugars from these foods enter the bloodstream slowly as they take longer to be broken down. Starchy vegetables such as potatoes, corn, white rice and couscous have a moderate GI (55 to 70.) Foods with a high GI (over 70) include white bread, rice cakes, bagels, cakes, doughnuts, instant oats, pretzels and croissants. These foods lead to a spike in blood sugar levels shortly after being consumed.

The problem with the GI is that it doesn't take into account the quantity of the food being eaten, which has a huge effect on how much sugar is released into the bloodstream. To factor serving size, another indicator, known as Glycaemic Load (GL), was created. The GL of a food provides a more accurate picture of a food's impact on blood sugar. GL is calculated by simply taking the GI value of a food, multiplying it by the serving size and dividing by 100. A GL of 10 or below is considered low

whereas a value greater than 20 is considered high.

The GI of a food can differ greatly from the GL for the same food. For example, ice cream has a GI of 62 but a GL of only 8, and watermelon has a GI of 72, but a GL of only 4.

Low-GI (and GL) foods tend to foster weight loss; the reverse is true for high-GI foods. This is because foods with a high GI result in an excess amount of insulin being released, which ends up removing more sugar from the blood than required, resulting in a return to hunger shortly thereafter. Low GI foods, on the other hand, such as chick peas, peanuts, avocados and soy beans, do not provoke the same insulin response and result in a slow, steady release of sugar into the blood, keeping us feeling fuller for longer. Food that is high in fibre is digested more slowly so the rate at which sugar is released into the blood is reduced.

Many natural foods are high in fibre; generally speaking, the more processed a food is, the more likely it is to have had its natural fibre removed, causing its sugar content to be more quickly absorbed into the blood when consumed, which in turn leads to a large release of insulin in an effort to bring down the blood sugar level.

For those of you out there reading this book while sipping a diet can of something, thinking that you are off the hook because diet drinks don't contain any sugar – not so fast. There is growing evidence to suggest that artificial sweeteners used in diet drinks, the most common being aspartame (sometimes marketed as NutraSweet), can upset the healthy balance of our gut bacteria, affecting the way our bodies digest food. Artificial sweeteners can also lead to an increase in sugar cravings, which is why diet drinks could actually be contributing towards making people gain weight. Israeli scientists recently discovered that such sweeteners change gut bacteria – and not in a good way. The best advice is to stay away from canned drinks altogether - but if you absolutely must have a carbonated drink, drink soda water and squeeze in a dash of fresh citrus fruit or zest, or try and find a drink that contains a more natural sweetener, such as stevia, which is extracted from plant leaves.

Also, beware of fads and unsubstantiated claims about certain foods. For example, adopting a gluten-free diet has been shown to yield no health benefits for the vast majority of people. A gluten-free diet can lead to deficiencies in fibre and micronutrients, such as vitamin B12, zinc, magnesium, selenium and calcium. It may also lead to a higher risk of developing type 2 diabetes.

MICRONUTRIENTS

Some natural foods are especially healthy for us and have been identified as being "superfoods" because they contain many of the ingredients our bodies need to help our cells repair themselves, fight infection and ward off disease.

That said, we don't fall for all the health claims made about some superfoods, which command higher prices, as often these claims are unwarranted or there is an equivalent superfood that is much cheaper. A study published in the *New Scientist* in 2016 (*Miracle meal or rotten swindle? The truth about superfoods* by Caroline Williams) dispelled a few myths. For example, all sorts of amazing health claims have been made about eating goji berries, but as far as the science goes, it's just another berry. There is no harm in eating goji berries, but equally, eating cheaper, local berries that are in season gives the same health benefits. Similarly, kale's cancer-fighting properties are not necessarily superior to those of other green, leafy vegetables such as the humble Brussels sprout.

Here's a quick summary of the findings from the *New Scientist* article, which we find useful in our own eating choices:

Goji berries: just another berry.

Kale: no better than other types of cabbage.

Quinoa: Eat it if you like it, but not for health benefits. There are none.

Blueberries: Super, though no better than many other berries.

Baobab: Nothing you can't get elsewhere.

Chocolate: Seems good for men in particular, in respect of heart health. No sugar though.

Chia seeds: Good, but oily fish packs more omega-3s.

Kimchi and Kefir: May be good for gut bacteria.

Coconut water: No better than water.

Wheatgrass: Whole shot of nonsense.

Beetroot juice: Good stuff, just don't overdo it as it contains sugar.

We have put together a table containing some of our favourite superfoods along with the health benefits they offer.

Food 🍴	Main Health Benefits ⊕
Nuts, especially almonds	Contain mono and polyunsaturated fats, omega-3, arginine, fibre and vitamin E. Possess strong anti-inflammatory properties.
	Improve heart health and help control blood sugar levels.
	Are made up of protein and fat and are low in carbs. Eating nuts promotes a healthy metabolism and digestive system and their high-fat content makes you feel fuller for longer and prevents over-snacking on carbs.
	Best to eat them raw, but roasted is definitely tastier.
Garlic	Anti-inflammatory properties
	Improves cholesterol
	Rich in antioxidants
	Boosts immune system
	Anti-bacterial and anti-viral properties
	Anti-cancer properties
Turmeric	Contains curcumin, the active ingredient
	Powerful anti-inflammatory properties
	Helps combat rheumatoid arthritis
	Rich in antioxidants
	Some indication that it boosts brain function and prevents dementia
	Cancer preventing properties, especially breast cancer, bowel cancer, stomach cancer and skin cancer
	Alleviates symptoms of depression

Food	Main Health Benefits
Olive Oil – the key ingredient of the Mediterranean Diet. *Make sure you get extra virgin olive oil as it contains more concentrated amounts of oleic acid.*	High in oleic acid, a monounsaturated fat that has anti-inflammatory properties Rich in antioxidants Reduces stroke and heart disease risk Protective qualities against diabetes Helps treat rheumatoid arthritis Anti-bacterial properties
Red/purple grapes and red wine *This is our favourite.*	Red wine and red grapes contain resveratrol, which has been linked to longevity. Resveratrol is a powerful antioxidant with benefits for muscle strength, anti-inflammation, metabolism, neurodegenerative diseases, diabetes, cardiovascular disease and even cancer. But, it's not all good news; there is some linkage between brain hippocampal atrophy and drinking wine, according to a recent study at the University of Oxford.
Soy beans/endamame	High in protein Lowers cholesterol Rich in vitamins and minerals

Food	Main Health Benefits
Kale, Brussel sprouts, spinach, broccoli and other green, leafy vegetables	Packed with vitamins and minerals, especially vitamins A, C and K Rich in antioxidants Lowers cholesterol Anti-cancer properties Protective qualities against diabetes (Tip: don't boil your vegetables as many of the nutrients will seep out and end up in the water. Best to steam or stir fry them to retain the nutrients and flavour.)
Blueberries and other berries	High in antioxidants Reduces DNA damage
Matcha green tea (Black tea has similar but less potent benefits)	Rich in antioxidants Contains epigallocatechin gallate, recognised for its cancer fighting properties. Matcha green tea contains over 100 times more epigallocatechin gallate than any other tea on the market. Contains amino acid L-Theanine (in the leaves) which promotes the production of alpha waves in the brain, inducing relaxation without drowsiness. Produces dopamine and serotonin, two chemicals that enhance mood, improve memory, and promote better concentration.

Food	Main Health Benefits
Fatty fish (such as salmon, mackerel and sardines)	Rich in omega-3 fatty acids, good for heart health Anti-inflammatory properties Reduction in the decline of brain function with age Rich in vitamin D, which we are often deficient in during the winter months (as our bodies produce it from the sun's rays on our skin) Vitamin D seems to have an additional benefit in relieving back pain.
Tomatoes (including tomato ketchup)	Rich in lycopene (give tomatoes their red colour), an antioxidant that is believed to have cancer preventing properties. Cooked tomatoes are five times more potent than raw ones; higher levels than in any other food.
Dark Chocolate	Contains resveratrol and other antioxidants. Contains important minerals such as iron, copper and manganese. Protects against heart disease. Lowers blood pressure.
Porridge/Oats/Oatmeal	Packed with slow-release energy (low glycaemic load) which means your blood sugar levels will hold steady and you will feel fuller for longer Lowers blood pressure Contains antioxidants and are high in fibre We should be starting our day with a hearty bowl of porridge at least once or twice a week. Note: try and avoid buying instant or quick oats as they are too refined and have a higher GL than Scottish oats (sometimes called steel-cut oats or rolled oats).

Food	Main Health Benefits
Vinegar – as part of a meal, such as a salad dressing. A couple of tablespoons per day are recommended. (Can be apple cider, balsamic, etc.)	Helps control blood sugar, improving insulin sensitivity Makes you feel fuller for longer Lowers triglycerides in blood Lowers blood pressure Lowers heart attack risk and may prevent heart disease

The super-foods we listed in the table above are rich in antioxidants which are micronutrients such as vitamins, minerals and phytochemicals that our body needs in very small amounts to function well. Many of the micronutrients found in colour-rich fruits and vegetables are called phytochemicals, "phyto" meaning plant.

ESSENTIAL VITAMINS

It is important to point out that of all the vitamins, only B and C are water-soluble, meaning that even if we overdose on these vitamins, our body can simply flush out the excess amounts through our urine with minimal side effects. The other major vitamins, namely A, D, E and K, are fat soluble; an excess of these vitamins can build up in our fatty tissues as there is no way for our body to dispose of the excess amount. This can have serious consequences, so we should always be careful with the vitamin doses we are taking, especially when they are in the form of supplements, where the vitamins can be concentrated many times more than the amounts found in natural foods. Also, it is important to take any fat-soluble vitamin supplements with a little fatty food to help their absorption in the body.

Let's run through the main vitamins to give you an idea of the foods they can be found in and the role they play in the body.

Vitamin A: This vitamin is found in different forms. In meat, fish, dairy, eggs and poultry, it usually takes the form of retinol. In plant-based form, it is found in carrots and other fruits and vegetables, usually as beta-carotene.

It is required by the body for general growth and development, especially of teeth, bones and skin. It also plays a role in maintaining the immune system and promotes good vision, especially in low light.

Overdosing on vitamin A can make us sick and could even result in birth defects, so make sure you don't exceed the recommended daily intake of your supplements.

Vitamin B Complex: There are 8 vitamins that fall under the vitamin B class; sometimes they are better known by their alternative names.

Vitamin B1 is also known as thiamine;

Vitamin B2 is also known as riboflavin;

Vitamin B3 is also known as niacin;

Vitamin B5 is also known as pantothenic acid;

Vitamin B6 is also known as pyridoxine;

Vitamin B7 is also known as biotin;

Vitamin B9 is also known as folic acid;

Vitamin B12 is also known as cobalamin.

The B complex vitamins play key roles in cell metabolism.

Unprocessed fruits and vegetables are rich in these vitamins as are some meats, such as turkey, tuna and liver.

Vitamin C: This vitamin is sometimes referred to as ascorbic acid. It is an antioxidant, meaning it neutralises free radicals, which harm our body. This vitamin is required for general growth and repair of tissues of the body and is one of the ingredients in making skin, tendons, ligaments, and blood vessels. It also plays a role in healing wounds and forming scar tissue. Vitamin C is also important in maintaining the health of stem cells and, in a recent study, has been shown to be a major factor in reducing mortality from sepsis, when combined with hydrocortisone and thiamine.

Vitamin D: This is an essential tool to allow our bodies to absorb calcium, a vital element in bones. A lack of it can lead to osteoporosis in adults. Not many foods naturally contain vitamin D, although fatty fish is one of the richest food sources. Also known as the sunshine vitamin, our bodies can produce it when our skin is exposed to sunlight. In fact, most people who like to spend time outdoors are probably getting all the vitamin D they need from the sun. 30 to 45 minutes a week of sunlight is all it takes to keep our vitamin D levels topped up. People with darker skin may need to spend more time in the sun as the melanin (pigment) in the skin is a natural sun screen.

In countries that receive very limited sunshine in the winter months, such as the UK, it is recommended that people take vitamin D supplements to make sure their bodies are still getting enough of the vitamin. It is estimated that one in five people in the UK are not getting enough vitamin D. Equally, take care not to overdose on vitamin D; according to findings by an NHS lab in Birmingham, UK, some patients are taking over 2,000 times the recommended dose. This can cause the body to absorb high quantities of calcium and can result in kidney and heart issues as well as in high blood pressure. Remember that vitamin D is a fat-soluble vitamin so any excess amount of it builds up in the body's fatty tissue.

In recent years, scientists are discovering additional health benefits of vitamin D that had previously been overlooked. According to Michael Holick, head of the Vitamin D, Skin, and Bone Research Laboratory at Boston University School of Medicine, "activated vitamin D is one of the most potent inhibitors of cancer cell growth. It also stimulates your pancreas to make insulin. It regulates your immune system."

Even more benefits of vitamin D are being uncovered, such as its ability to regulate mood and help ward off depression. Other studies indicate that it may also reduce the risk of developing multiple sclerosis and heart disease, as well as alleviating back pain.

Clearly this has been one of the most underappreciated vitamins until very recently, so make sure you venture outdoors once in a while, especially on sunny days, but be careful not to overdo it, as too much of the sun's UV rays will damage the skin and possibly cause skin cancer.

Vitamin E: This is another antioxidant vitamin. It promotes healthy skin and a strong immune system. It also plays a role in the formation of red blood cells.

For a while, vitamin E was touted as being a wonder vitamin that can ward off cancer, heart disease, diabetes, Alzheimer's disease, cataracts, and many other diseases. However, subsequent research has not been able to find any conclusive evidence to support these earlier claims. Further research is required to determine the specific benefits of this vitamin.

Some common food sources of vitamin E are vegetable oils, nuts (especially almonds) and seeds.

Vitamin K: This is the vitamin that most of us probably know the least about and is sometimes referred to as "the forgotten vitamin". Vitamin K exists in 2 basic forms:

Vitamin K1 (also called phylloquinone) is found in plants, especially green vegetables such as kale, spinach and broccoli, and when ingested goes directly to the liver and helps maintain healthy blood clotting.

Vitamin K2 (also called menaquinone) is made by the gut bacteria and goes straight to the blood vessel walls, bones, and tissues other than the liver.

Vitamin K is essential for building strong bones, preventing heart disease, and we are still learning more about its benefits. Interestingly, vitamins K1 and K2 have different health properties. For example, a study published in 2010 in the American Journal of *Clinical Nutrition* and undertaken by European Prospective Investigation into Cancer and Nutrition (EPIC) found that a high intake of vitamin K2 leads to a 30% lower risk of dying from cancer.

It also seems that vitamin K is most effective in conjunction with vitamin D and calcium: although consuming too much calcium might cause the arteries to calcify, vitamin K may play an important role in preventing this from happening.

SALT

Everyone has read about the health risks associated with having too much salt in the diet. Table salt, or sodium chloride (NaCl), is an essential nutrient and regulates many bodily functions and maintains the body's overall fluid balance. An adult body typically contains 250 grams of salt and a lack of it in our diets would kill us, but so would too much of it. How much should we be consuming?

The NHS guideline for healthy living recommends that adults consume no more than 6 grams of salt a day – that's just over one teaspoon. Given that the sodium makes up about 40% of sodium chloride by weight, this translates to 2.4 grams of sodium per day. This seems to be consistent with a number of US-based organisations' recommendations for sodium, namely:

- United States Department of Agriculture (USDA) recommends 2.3 grams of salt per day;

- American Heart Association (AHA) recommends 1.5 grams of salt per day;

- Academy of Nutrition and Dietetics (AND) recommends 1.5 to 2.3 grams of salt per day; and

- American Diabetes Association (ADA) recommends 1.5 to 2.3 grams of salt per day.

So, the general target should be around 2 grams of sodium or 5 grams of salt per day. It is important to emphasise that many natural foods already contain salt, and the recommended amount is inclusive of all salt intake.

Consuming an excessive amount of salt causes high blood pressure (hypertension), increasing the risk of strokes and coronary heart disease. Too much salt can also damage the kidneys and cause kidney disease; it is also a risk factor in osteoporosis as it can draw calcium out of the bones causing decreased bone density (even in the presence of a high calcium diet); and it is one of the leading causes of stomach cancer, or gastric cancer.

The NHS website lists the following foods as being high in salt, so they should be consumed with care and in moderation:

- anchovies
- bacon
- cheese
- gravy granules
- ham
- olives
- pickles
- prawns
- salami
- salted and dry-roasted nuts
- salt fish
- smoked meat and fish
- soy sauce
- stock cubes
- yeast extract

OTHER MICRONUTRIENTS

Iron: An essential element that plays a key role in transporting oxygen around the body as it is important to the formation of red blood cells. People who have an iron deficiency are called anaemic and have low red blood cell counts. Symptoms of anaemia include general fatigue, weakness and pale skin. Women are more susceptible to anaemia due to blood loss during menstruation. But anaemia could also be as a result of internal bleeding, so it is important to pinpoint the specific causes of the anaemia.

Anaemia can be treated with iron supplements or by eating foods such as red meats, nuts and green vegetables, all of which are rich sources of iron.

Magnesium: An often-overlooked but essential nutrient, magnesium is important for healthy bones. This metal is a co-factor in over 300 biological processes inside our cells, so every cell in our body contains magnesium.

Finding a good source of magnesium for our diet is easy - the magnesium molecule sits in the centre of a chlorophyll molecule (the molecule that gives leaves their green colour) so green vegetables are rich in magnesium. It can also be found in dark chocolate, in almonds, cashews and pumpkin seeds.

One of the most important roles magnesium plays relates to making ATP, a molecule responsible for transporting energy to where it is needed in the body. Magnesium is also involved in the DNA repair process.

Zinc: Zinc is also a metal. We only need a trace amount of it in our diet to keep us healthy. It is present in all our tissues and is required for healthy cell division. A couple of the important roles that zinc plays include boosting our immune system and supporting the clotting of blood. It is found in many foods, including meats, seafood, dairy products, nuts, legumes, and whole grains.

Chromium: Although our bodies only require a small amount of chromium, it plays an important role in metabolising fats and carbohydrates, as well as the hormone insulin. Chromium is another metal and is found in many of the foods we eat, such as meats, cheeses, cereals, fresh fruits and vegetables (especially potato skins). Sometimes, it is found naturally in hard tap water.

ALCOHOL CONSUMPTION

It has been general knowledge for some time that drinking a glass or two of wine every day is good for the health. One cardiologist, Dr William McCrea from the Great Western Hospital in Swindon, Wiltshire, recommends two 125ml glasses of red wine per day and has been prescribing this "medicine" to his patients for over a decade. Dr McCrea believes that the antioxidants in red wine reduce the risk of second heart attacks by 50% and the risk of stroke by 20%. But it is not just the antioxidants in the red wine that offer the health benefits, it is the alcohol content too.

An extensive study by researchers at the University of Cambridge and University College London, led by Steven Bell and published in the *British Medical Journal* on 22 March 2017, found that moderate drinking is associated with a lower risk of several cardiovascular diseases. The study followed almost 2 million adults in England aged 30 years or over between 1997 and 2010 (51% of whom were women) who initially showed no signs of cardiovascular disease. The study tracked 12 common symptomatic manifestations of cardiovascular disease, including myocardial infarction, coronary heart disease death and ischaemic stroke.

The findings revealed that not drinking alcohol was associated with an increased risk of the following cardiovascular diseases: unstable, myocardial infarction unheralded coronary death, heart failure, ischaemic stroke, peripheral arterial disease and abdominal aortic aneurysm, when compared with moderate drinking.

In the UK, moderate drinking for men is considered to be 21 units per week or 3 units per day; and for women it is 14 units per week or 2 units per day. Not surprisingly, heavy drinking, i.e. exceeding the recommended guidelines, resulted in an increased risk of cardiovascular disease.

DIET FOR HEALTH AND LONGEVITY

In this section, we refer to the word diet to mean a healthy, balanced diet for optimal nutrition – not one to lose weight. Once BMI has been lowered to a healthy range, it is a good idea to follow such a healthy, long-term diet on a daily basis.

In recent years, there has been a growing fascination with the so-called *Mediterranean diet,* spurred by a number of published studies suggesting that it may be the ideal diet for optimal nutrition and health. People living in Mediterranean countries have historically low rates of heart disease, which has been put down to a diet of moderate wine, fish and chicken, and plenty of nuts, olive oil and fresh vegetables.

Ancel Keys, an American physiologist, first recognised the benefit of the Mediterranean diet while researching and living in a small Italian village called Pioppi in the 1970s. Together with his wife Margaret, he wrote a book entitled *How to Eat Well and Stay Well the Mediterranean Way,* published in 1975.

His findings formed the basis of the now widely-recognisable Food Pyramid, originally published in 1977 by the US Department of Agriculture (USDA). This was the first time anyone had tried to categorise and quantify the types of food we should be eating for a healthy, balanced diet. The Food Pyramid has remained essentially unchanged for 40 years. Unfortunately, we now know that the proportions of the food groups in the pyramid do not promote a healthy weight and its emphasis on eating plenty of carbs, such as bread, rice and pasta, has been a major contributor to the obesity epidemic in the West. Equally misleading in the chart is the grouping of sugar and fat together and the recommendation that we keep our consumption of both to a minimum. Knowing what we know today about nutrition, it would be healthier to follow an upside-down version of this pyramid by grouping sugar with the carbohydrates instead of with fats and oils.

Keys recognised that the villagers of Pioppi seemed to make every meal a social occasion and that their diet was very low in sugar. Another interesting finding about the elderly people from the local region is that they tend to have unusually good blood circulation which helps keep their cells nourished and enables the efficient clearing of waste (see Autophagy. Page 132).

The key points we have gleaned from Pioppi and other regions in the world where people enjoy long and healthy lives can be summarised as follows:

1. Stay physically active. Keep moving and spend plenty of time outdoors.

2. Always give yourself a sense of purpose or a project to do. This could be in the form of a hobby, such as restoring a vintage car or learning a new language. Venture out of your comfort zone regularly and keep challenging yourself.

3. Learn to dissipate stress. Chronic stress shortens life expectancy. Don't let things get to you. Incorporate daily meditation/mindfulness into your daily routine if it helps manage stress levels.

4. Eat a sensible diet comprising plenty of fresh fruits and vegetables. Keep processed foods down to a minimum. Eat plenty of fish, and red meat only occasionally. Don't overeat. Put olive oil and garlic on everything!

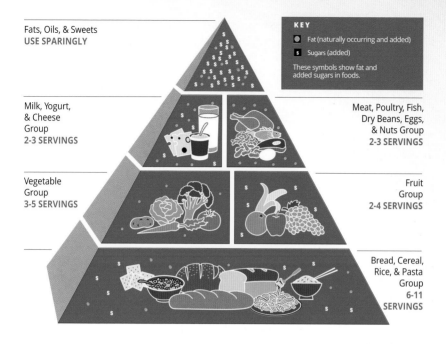

Fats, Oils, & Sweets
USE SPARINGLY

KEY

● Fat (naturally occurring and added)

s Sugars (added)

These symbols show fat and
added sugars in foods.

Milk, Yogurt,
& Cheese
Group
2-3 SERVINGS

Meat, Poultry, Fish,
Dry Beans, Eggs,
& Nuts Group
2-3 SERVINGS

Vegetable
Group
3-5 SERVINGS

Fruit
Group
2-4 SERVINGS

Bread, Cereal,
Rice, & Pasta
Group
**6-11
SERVINGS**

The Food Pyramid - Published by the US Department of Agriculture (USDA) in 1977. Now considered outdated!

LOOK AFTER YOUR GUTS

5. Drink in moderation, and stick to red wine. Drinkers tend to live longer than non-drinkers.

6. Family first. People with stronger family bonds tend to lead longer, more fulfilled lives.

7. Be friends with people who also support a healthy lifestyle, allowing you to share common values and activities.

We have been underestimating the role our intestines play in keeping us healthy. It turns out that we are hosting trillions of bacteria in our guts, so many in fact that we don't actually know how many. Reports range from 30 to 100 trillion and they are collectively referred to as the gut *microbiome* or gut *microbiota*. The actual number doesn't really matter; what is important is that the trillions of bacteria play an important role in our

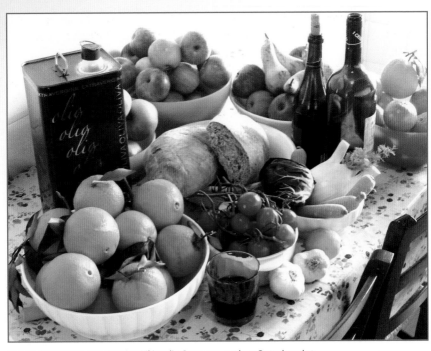

The Mediterranean Diet. Source: Wikimedia Commons, author: G.steph.rocket

overall health. The gut microbiome comprises thousands of different species and each one of us has a mix of around 150 types – a mixture that is as unique as our fingerprint, although 99% of the bacteria come from about 30 to 40 types. The most common type of gut bacteria found in healthy adults is *Faecalibacterium prausnitzii*, although you would be forgiven for being blissfully unaware of the name of your silent lodger.

Our gut bacteria contain more than 3 million microbial genes (that is 150 times more than the human genome) and this diverse and mysterious inner ecosystem is currently one of the hottest topics in human health as it has largely been overlooked and ignored until very recently. We are starting to understand just how important a role it plays in our overall metabolic health, from influencing how much we weigh to determining whether plaque is deposited on the inside of our arterial walls.

Gut microbiota also play an important role in how we age as they can influence our skin, immune system, cognitive function and our bone density, all of which determine our level of frailty in later life. The functionality of our neurons is influenced by our gut bacteria, because up to 70% of the neurons outside the brain are in the intestines. These neurons form a network of nerves that connect to the brain via the *vagus nerve*, a vital nerve that connects everything from the chest, lungs and abdomen to the neck and larynx.

A person's microbiota can, in total, weigh up to 2 kilograms. One-third of our gut microbiota is common to most people, while two thirds are specific to each one of us. Having a balanced diet should give us a diverse and healthy microbiota, although we tend to lose some of this diversity with age.

Some of the functions of our gut microbiota are:

- Helping the body to digest certain foods that the stomach and small intestine have not been able to digest.
- Helping the body produce certain vitamins (B and K).
- Fighting off attacks from other microorganisms.
- Maintaining health of the intestinal mucosa (the mucus membrane layer of the gut).
- Playing an important role in the immune system.

A healthy and balanced gut microbiome is key to ensuring proper digestive functioning.

Taking into account the major role the gut microbiome plays in the normal functioning of the body and the different functions it accomplishes, scientists and doctors are increasingly considering it as one of the organs of the body. However, it is an acquired organ, as babies are born without any gut bacteria and their intestine colonisation starts right after birth and evolves as they grow.

We are also discovering that the composition of our gut bacteria can be altered through changes in our diet and that an unhealthy gut results in malabsorption of essential nutrients and inflammation which lead to ageing of the body.

The gut is also host to the greatest quantity of immune cells in our bodies and these are protected from the gut bacteria by a mucus-like protein called *mucin* that is secreted onto the surfaces of the large intestine and serves as a protective barrier for the epithelium, a membrane. When this gut barrier fails, toxins can leak back into the body, forcing our liver and immune system to work harder to eliminate them.

PREBIOTICS
In the context of our gut microbiota, prebiotics are foods that promote the growth of certain types of gut bacteria. These foods are typically rich in insoluble (also known as non-digestible) fibre. When food containing prebiotics reaches our gut, it provides a substrate (surface) on which certain species of bacteria can live and grow.

Prebiotics are naturally present in vegetables and fruits, such as garlic, onions, leeks, asparagus, artichokes, tomatoes, bananas, plums and apples; in grains and cereals like bran; and in nuts like almonds. For this reason, vegetables, fruits and cereals should be part of a balanced and healthy diet.

As in many other fields, balance and variety are essential when eating prebiotic foods. Although a fibre-rich diet benefits gut bacteria, excess fibre may lead to discomfort or abdominal bloating in some people.

PROBIOTICS
Probiotics are live microorganisms which, when consumed in sufficient quantities, promote a healthy gut microbiome. These microorganisms partially resist the digestion process and provide a range of benefits for the body, such as a healthy digestive system and a strong immune system. They can also help rebalance the gut microbiota when it has been affected by poor diet or other factors, such as stress.

Probiotics were first suggested in the early twentieth century by Elie Metchnikoff, a Russian zoologist who was a Nobel Prize winner in Medicine for his work on immunity. He was also the deputy director at the Pasteur Institute.

Metchnikoff was one of the first scientists to study longevity and he believed that ageing was caused by toxic bacteria building up in the gut, and that to live a longer life, we should ingest lactic acid bacteria. He wrote *The Prolongation of Life: Optimistic Studies*. In this book Metchnikoff wrote about the problems, causes and mechanisms of dementia, and whether or not we should try to prolong human life. He strongly believed that optimists lived longer than pessimists.

He believed that "intestinal putrefaction" shortened life and that this was avoided by consuming lactic acid, an acid that is naturally present in many foods, formed by natural fermentation in cheese, yoghurt, soy sauce, sourdough, meats and pickled vegetables.

Metchnikoff's theory was based on his observation that Bulgarian peasants lived unusually long lives and that this was attributed to the milk they consumed that was fermented by lactic acid bacteria. Metchnikoff followed his own advice and drank sour milk every day, naming the bacterium Bulgarian Bacillus, now called Lactobacillus bulgaricus or L. bulgaricus, one of the main types of bacteria found in yoghurts today.

Lactobacillus is a broader name for a type of bacteria. In addition to L. bulgaricus, yoghurts are also made with L. acidophilus, L. animalis and L. casei.

There are two other groups of probiotics: Bifidobacterium and Streptococcus thermophilus.

Bifidobacterium strains include B. animalis and B. lactis. In total, there are at least 80 types of Streptococcus thermophilus found in yoghurts and cheeses.

So the next time you reach for a pot of yoghurt, take a moment to read the ingredients and find out how many types of bacteria it contains; the more the better, as diversity is good for gut health. Make sure that the yoghurt contains live bacteria (not surprisingly, given the games played by food manufacturers, not all yoghurts do).

Now that we understand how important our gut microbiome is to almost every aspect of our health, we can start to appreciate how devastating a course of antibiotics can be to our gut health. Whilst antibiotics have saved millions of lives over the past 80 years, scientists now realise that in many cases our gut microbiota was the collateral damage of ingesting antibiotics. One paper published

Elie Metchnikoff - the Father of Longevity? (Source: Library of Congress, Prints and Photographs Division, Washington, D.C. 20540 USA)

in *Genome Medicine* stresses the importance of reviewing the way we use antibiotics (Langdon et al., 2016). Their effects can leave lasting changes in children and adults and increase the likelihood of developing resistance to antibiotics due to their overuse. In 2015, an estimated 50,000 people died in Europe and the US as a result of antibiotic resistance and this death toll is projected to increase to 10 million worldwide by 2050 (Antimicrobial Resistance: Tackling a crisis for the health and wealth of nations).

LOOK AFTER YOUR BRAIN

As we get older, the health of our brain becomes an increasing concern. The concerns are justified given that the greatest known risk factor for dementia is advancing age. In the UK, some 500 people are diagnosed with dementia every day. Formerly more commonly referred to as senility, dementia is the general term for diseases that lead to the gradual deterioration in our ability to think and remember things due to physical changes in the brain. Although there are a number of different types of dementia, Alzheimer's Disease accounts for about two thirds of all cases. Unfortunately, almost all cases of dementia are detected after the patient starts to display physical symptoms of the disease, by which time it has already progressed and parts of the brain have been irreparably damaged. Early detection techniques remain elusive, as do effective treatments or even a cure.

Simply as a function of age, most normal brains will shrink at a rate of 5% per decade from the age of 40, accelerating after the age of 70. However, a study by scientists at Northwestern University in Chicago has revealed that superagers (a term used to describe people who are over 65 but have retained the mental acuity of their younger years) have brains that age at about 40% of this rate. Unfortunately, they have been unable to figure out why some people become superagers as their studies so far can see no common link between them.

A study by Professor Ian Deary of the University of Edinburgh concluded that brain ageing is only 25% due to our genes and 75% a result of our lifestyle choices.

The secret to age-proofing the emotional regions of the brain is to pursue both physical and mental activity: regular, vigorous physical exercise as well as frequent mental challenges. Contrary to what some readers may think, brain games such as Sudoku don't count as they are too "comfortable" for the brain. A mental challenge means taking your brain out of its comfort zone by tackling a new problem, something that would create some anxiety and positive stress. Break your routine, in other words. Try visiting www.brainhq.com or learn a new language.

A study from 2013 published in *Neurology* found that people who were bilingual developed dementia an average of 4.5 years later than monolinguists. They are also twice as likely to recover from a stroke and show slower cognitive ageing. For those of our readers who are monolinguists, it's never too late to take up a new language; the benefits apply to people learning a new language at any stage in life. It is believed that the ability to switch between different languages builds a higher cognitive reserve, keeping brain diseases at bay. We can highly recommend a couple of free language apps, one called *Duolingo* and the other called *Memrise*.

Another brain-challenging activity is playing a musical instrument. Playing an instrument has been shown to work both hemispheres of the brain, getting them to cross-communicate through the relay centre in the middle of the brain called the corpus callosum, which is thought to enhance the brain's neural network. It turns out that music is the only activity that stimulates the whole brain.

So, until a definitive cure for dementia comes along, which we think is still a decade away based on current research activities, it is best to try and keep the brain in an optimal state to reduce the likelihood of acquiring any of its forms.

Even though there is no guarantee that the brain will retain all of its memories and cognitive abilities, taking care of it and exercising it regularly will certainly improve your chances.

Another relatively new theory posits that Alzheimer's disease is a form of diabetes. This is because scientists have noticed that there is similar insulin-dependent molecular signalling in the pancreas and the brain. We have read some studies referring to it as type 3 diabetes; it provides yet another reason to avoid eating refined sugars.

Dr Preston Estep is the Director of Gerontology at the Harvard Personal Genome Project, Harvard Medical School. Dr Estep is convinced that the Western diet is the primary reason behind today's high rate of dementia. He points out those countries such as Japan and what he refers to as the "Mediterranean Rivieras" have a relatively long-life expectancy combined with low rates of dementia. In his book, *The Mindspan Diet,* Dr Estep accepts that even these countries are experiencing an increase in "Western" diseases, such as obesity, heart disease and dementia, but puts this down to the infiltration of the Western diet in these regions. But he highlights that people living in more rural parts of these countries have not had the same exposure to the Western diet and therefore still seem to be in good physical and mental health in old age.

Dr Estep boldly claims that he has found the reason for this, and that reason is iron, the essential micronutrient we mentioned earlier. His theory is that both the Japanese and the Mediterranean diets typically consume less red meat than the Western diet, and red meat is a rich source of iron.

Dr Estep states that *"iron is the most abundant and potent pro-oxidant in the body, and the more we have of it in our bodies, the more oxidative stress and damage."*

When something oxidises, it rusts, and Dr Estep believes that too much iron in our diet can lead to rusting in our bodies, and this rusting can result in the deposit of waste products in our brain cells, including plaques.

Although Dr Estep's view on the causes of dementia is not (yet) shared by the scientific community at large, his research is credible, and avoiding too much red meat is consistent with eating a healthy, balanced diet in any case, so we would suggest to keeping red meat down to just 2 to 3 meals a week.

GET ENOUGH SLEEP

For an activity that we are supposed to spend about a third of our lives doing, we know relatively little about sleep. We do understand, of course, that sleep is necessary for our brain and overall health, although we are on average getting two hours less of it per night than we used to in the 1960s, and that is not good news for our health. Long-term sleep deprivation increases the risk of cancer, heart disease, type 2 diabetes and obesity. A lack of sleep affects the brain more than any other organ in the body, even causing it to age prematurely.

Much of our sleep deprivation is linked to our modern, hectic lives, where we override our evolutionary instinct to sleep at sunset and wake up at sunrise. Artificial lighting allows us to sleep and get up whenever we want, and much of that lighting, including iPads, smartphones and LEDs, emits so-called blue light, a major disruptor of our body's *circadian rhythm*. This is our natural body's sleep-wake cycle and is responsible for controlling essential processes in our bodies, such as cell regeneration, hormone production, insulin regulation and brain activity. Artificial light is also to blame for shifting our sleep patterns – on average we are going to bed and waking up two hours later than we did a generation ago.

There are also genetic factors at work in insomnia; scientists in the Netherlands (Posthuma and van Someren, *Nature Genetics* 2017) have identified seven "risk" gene variants for sleep problems, most notably in the transcription factor MEIS9, which is also responsible for restless legs syndrome.

Sleep provides the opportunity to clear the brain of waste proteins that build up while awake. In sleep mode, the space between brain cells expands by 60%, allowing any harmful toxins that may have accumulated during the day to be more easily flushed out with cerebrospinal fluid.

How much sleep is enough for maintaining good health? Although no two people are identical, the overwhelming majority of us need somewhere between 7 and 8 hours of sleep every night. Some people claim they can get by on less sleep but the reality is only 3% of the population possesses the short-sleep gene. The other 97% trying to get by on less than 7 hours of sleep every night are sleep-depriving themselves to the detriment of their health.

Being sleep-deprived for just one night weakens your immune system and quadruples the chances of catching a cold. It also puts an additional 10% strain on the heart the next day. And if that's not enough of a deterrent, being sleep-deprived leaves you with poor concentration levels, slower reaction times and an increased appetite.

We should all dedicate adequate time for sleep every night, as a lack of it is making us all unnecessarily sick. The US Centres for Disease Control reported in 2008 that around a third of working adults in the US get less than six hours sleep a night, which is 10 times more people than it was 50 years ago. In a later study, it was also reported that nearly half of all the country's shift workers were getting less than six hours sleep.

A 20-minute nap during the day is worth an hour's sleep at night. The best advice on improving the quality of sleep is to have a device-free bedroom. Whatever that incoming message is, it can wait until the morning, when you will be refreshed and more alert to tackle the challenges of the day ahead.

Some of our prescriptions for a good night's sleep are:

1) Don't eat within three hours of going to bed. There are two reasons why going to bed with food still in the

stomach is bad for sleep: the first is that it can lead to indigestion and heartburn which causes restlessness; and the second reason is that the body is forced to expend energy to digest the food when it should instead be in energy-saving mode for maximum relaxation.

2) Exercise for at least 30 minutes. People who exercise during the day are around 50% more likely to get a great night's sleep.

3) Don't spend too long sitting down during the day. Get up and walk around every hour or so.

4) Avoid caffeine after 3pm.

5) Avoid drinking alcohol within 3 hours of sleeping. Although it may help with falling asleep faster, alcohol also causes our brains to spend less time in deep sleep and more time in REM sleep, which is less restful. This can cause us to feel more tired when we wake up.

LONELINESS

Being social and gregarious creatures, humans don't always deal well with loneliness and we are now aware that being lonely is, unsurprisingly, bad for our health. Being a form of stress, loneliness can damage us at a cellular level leading to disease. Most of us experience loneliness at some point during our life and short periods of it are not necessarily a bad thing. The elderly are the most likely to experience loneliness and as we are living in an ageing society, we can expect to see a surge of loneliness. The body's response to chronic loneliness is similar to that of chronic stress; it triggers an inflammation response, which, as we discussed earlier, results in our cells ageing prematurely. Some alone time is definitely a good thing but we need frequent human contact, so if you find that you are not interacting with other people on a regular basis, take steps to address this: take up a new activity or join a club. It could be tango lessons or a bridge club or anything that interests you, because the social aspects are just as important as the activity itself. A study carried out in the Netherlands found that loneliness increased the risk of developing dementia by as much as 65%. Social activities have a huge positive impact on the brain and being lonely is worse for health than smoking 15 cigarettes a day, being an alcoholic and being morbidly obese, according to Professor James Goodwin, chief scientist at Age UK.

REGULAR HEALTH CHECKS

After the age of 40, we should all be getting regular health checks. In the

UK, the NHS provides this service free of charge and clinicians look for any signs of heart disease, diabetes, kidney disease or stroke. For over 65s, the check will also look for any signs of dementia.

EARLY CANCER DETECTION

COLONOSCOPY

At the age of 50, it is also advisable to have a colonoscopy. This is an uncomfortable but potentially life-saving procedure that looks for any polyps (also referred to as adenomas) in the large intestine. Any polyps found can be removed during the colonoscopy. If left alone, they will eventually develop into bowel (also called colorectal) cancer, so in that respect, a colonoscopy is one of the most effective preventative ways to prevent bowel cancer.

BREAST CANCER SCREENING

One in 8 women will be diagnosed with breast cancer at some point in their lifetime. It is the most common cancer for women according to the CDC. Fortunately, breast cancer, if caught early, is one of the most survivable of cancers – the 5-year relative survival rate for a woman with stage 0 or stage I breast cancer is almost 100% If the cancer is detected late (stage IV), the relative survival rate drops to around 22%. So, like the

colonoscopy, a regular check-up can be a real-life saver by picking up any signs of cancer early.

PROSTATE CHECK

According to the CDC, prostate cancer is the most common type of cancer in men. It is also the second commonest cause of cancer death in men, so after the age of 40, it is advisable to have a prostate check. This is usually done with a prostate-specific antigen (PSA) blood test. It is always advisable to include this blood test as part of an annual medical check-up and it is also worth alerting your doctor if you find yourself getting up frequently to urinate during the night or if you are experiencing any problems or discomfort while urinating, as an enlarged prostate can block the urethra. Your doctor may elect to perform further checks.

SKIN CHECK

Overexposure to ultraviolet light is the cause of skin cancer. It is the most common type of cancer in the US. There are no skin cancer statistics for the UK, but it will not be as high, given that the UK does not get as much sunshine. However, that doesn't mean we should be complacent, as most of us like to visit sunny places on holiday and it is there where the sun's rays can do the most harm to our skin. The fairer you are, the more at risk you are from developing skin cancer, so be diligent with your sun block (at least factor 15) and, when in hot countries, try to avoid direct sunlight between 11am and 2pm.

The three most common types of skin cancer are basal cell carcinoma, squamous cell carcinoma and melanoma, the latter being the most dangerous and responsible for most skin cancer deaths.

As is the case with most cancers, skin cancer is highly survivable if caught early, so check yourself or get your partner to check you. If you are a high-risk case (fair skin with many moles and freckles), visit a dermatologist every year, as they will photograph suspicious areas of your body and pick up any malignant moles before they become life-threatening.

GET VACCINATED

A final and obvious tip to avoid getting sick unnecessarily is to make sure that you are up to date with all of your vaccinations. Effective vaccines exist to prevent us getting a broad range of diseases, so there is really no excuse for contracting measles, mumps, tuberculosis or tetanus, etc. There are vaccines for around 30 common diseases, so consult your doctor and find out which ones are relevant to you.

If you are over 65, make sure you also get your annual influenza vaccine. Remember that lower respiratory infections are the third leading cause of death globally, according to the WHO.

APPENDIX

KEY AGE RELATED GENES

Biological Description	Underlying Genes	Pathway	Protein / Enzyme	Comment
5' adenosine monophosphate-activated protein kinase	α – PRKAA1, PRKAA2	AMPK		AMPK is an enzyme that stimluates glucose uptake in skeletal muscle and is found in every cell in the body. It is considered a metabolic master switch because it influences a number of pathways of cellular metabolism.
	β – PRKAB1, PRKAB2			
	γ – PRKAG1, PRKAG2, PRKAG3			

Biological Description	Underlying Genes	Pathway	Protein / Enzyme	Comment
Adenosine triphosphate family	MT-ATP6		ATP synthase F_O subunit 6	ATP6 is a mitochondrial gene that provides information for making a protein that is essential for normal mitochondrial function.
	MT-ATP8		ATP synthase F_O subunit 8	ATP8 is a mitochondrial gene that acts to prevent futile rotation of the ATPase subunits relative to the rotor during coupled ATP synthesis/hydrolysis.
Adiponectin	ADIPOQ	AMPK / NF-κB	Adiponectin	Adiponectin is a protein in humans that modulates a number of metabolic processes including regulating glucose levels as well as fatty acid breakdown.
Apolipoprotein C-III	APOC3		APOC3	APOC3 is a component of very low-density lipoprotein and is believed to inhibit hepatic uptake. Increased expression of APOC3 levels induces the development of hypertriglyceridemia.
Apolipoprotein E	APOE		APOE	APOE is a class of apolipoprotein that has a role in the transport of cholesterol across different tissues and cells. The APOE gene is associated with the risk of Alzheimer or cardiovascular disease but its influence on exceptional longevity is uncertain.

Biological Description	Underlying Genes	Pathway	Protein / Enzyme	Comment
Cholesteryl ester transfer protein	CETP	HDL / IDL	CETP	CETP is a plasma protein involved in the transport of cholesteryl esters and triglycerides between the lipoproteins. Rare mutations leading to reduced function of CETP have been linked to accelerated atherosclerosis. In contrast, a polymorphism (I405V) of the CETP gene leading to lower serum levels has also been linked to exceptional longevity and to metabolic response to nutritional intervention.
Forkhead box family of transcription factors				These are members of the O subclass forkhead family of transcription factors:
	FOXO1	PI3K	FOXO1	FOXO1 is necessary for maintaining pluripotency in embryonic stem cells.
	FOXO3a		FOXO3a	FOXO3 has been implicated in ageing as it is found in most superagers regardless of ethnicity.
	FOXO4		FOXO4	FOXO4 is a transcription factor that senescent cells depend on for their survival.
Glucose-6-phosphate dehydrogenase	G6PD	pentose phosphate pathway	G6PD	G6PD plays a role in supplying reducing energy to cells by maintaining the level of the co-enzyme nicotinamide adenine dinucleotide phosphate (NADPH). The NADPH in turn maintains the level of glutathione that helps red blood cells work properly.

Biological Description	Underlying Genes	Pathway	Protein / Enzyme	Comment
Insulin like growth factor	IGF1	IIS (GHRHR, GH1, IGF1, INS, IRS1)	IGF-1	Signaling through the insulin/IGF-1-like receptor pathway regulates ageing in many organisms. Despite the impact of this pathway on C. elegans longevity, mammals lack dauer development stages so direct applications of this finding into humans are potentially questionable.
LOS1	LOS1	mTOR	LOS1	LOS1 is influenced by mTOR which is associated with caloric restriction and increased lifespan. LOS1 influences Gcn4, a gene that helps govern DNA damage control.
Mamalian homolog of "I'm not dead yet"	mINDY		INDY	mINDY is a human homolog of the gene found in model organisms of the fruit fly and mice. Lower mINDY levels protect mice from a high-fat diet and ageing induced obesity through a mechanism resembling caloric restriction.
Mechanistic Target of Rapamycin	MTOR	PI3K/AKT/mTOR	mTOR	mTOR is a kinase that in humans is encoded by the MTOR gene. Decreased TOR activity has been found to increase lifespan in a number of organisms, and the mTOR inhibitor rapamycin has been confirmed to increase lifespan in mice. The PI3K/AKT/mTOR pathway is an intracellular signaling pathway important in regulating the cell cycle.

Biological Description	Underlying Genes	Pathway	Protein / Enzyme	Comment
C-myelocytomatosis	Myc	MAPK/ERK	Myc	The Myc family of transcription factor genes are important in cell division, metabolism and survival.
Sirtuins or NAD-dependent deacetylase sirtuin				Sirtuin proteins are regulators of ageing that may be able to modify the deadly quintet of age related diseases. There are seven sirtuins in total, each with different function, three of which are of particular interest to this book.
	SIRT1		SIRT1	SIRT1 is linked to mimicking caloric restriction.
	SIRT2		SIRT2	SIRT2 plays a role in development and function of adipose tissue.
	SIRT6		SIRT6	SIRT6 functions in multiple molecular pathways related to ageing, including DNA repair, telomere maintenance, glycolysis and inflammation.
Nuclear factor kappa-light-chain-enhancer of activated B cells	NFKB1 / NFKB2		NF-κB1 / NF-κB2	NF-κB1 is a protein complex that if regulated incorrectly has been linked to cancer, inflammatory and autoimmune diseases, septic shock, viral infection, and improper immune development. NF-κB has been proven to reverse some aspects of ageing, notably cardiac hypertrophy.

Biological Description	Underlying Genes	Pathway	Protein / Enzyme	Comment
Tumour protein p53	TP53	p53	p53	p53 is a protein that is an important tumour suppressor. p53 seems to protect cells from death induced by stroke or by peroxides generated by ROS.
Wingless-related integration site	WNT	Wnt	WNT	Wnt is the primary pathway regulating the self-renewal and differentiation of adult stem cells.
Homeobox protein family	HOXA9	Wnt, TGFβ, JAK/STAT & senescence signalling	Hox-A9	Hox-A9 is part of the homeobox class of transcription factors. The expression of HOXA9 appears to be reactivated in murine muscle stem cells after injury which leads to a decline in regenerative capacity.

THERAPIES AND SUPPLEMENTS

Currently Available	Prescription / OTC	Dose / Regimen / Comment
Do ✔		
Therapies/Supplements		
Agmatine	OTC	1,000 mg per day
Alpha linolenic acid	OTC	300 - 500 mg per day
Artichoke leaf extract	OTC	1,000 mg per day
Astaxanthin	OTC	5 mg twice per day
Astragalus root	OTC	1,200 mg per day
Barley	OTC	500 mg three times per day
Beta sitosterol	OTC	160 mg twice per day
Calcium	OTC	700 mg - recommended daily intake
Chamomile	OTC	9,000 - 15,000 mg per day
Flavonoids	OTC	750 mg per day
Geroprotect - Ageless Cell	OTC	One capsule per day
Hormone replacement therapy	Prescription	For women Oestradiol appears to boost the immune system
I3C (Indole 3 Carbinole) in combination with DIM (diindolylmethane)	OTC	80 mg and 14 mg per day respectively
Icariin	OTC	2,700 mg per day
Iodine	OTC	1000 mg per day
Lithium	OTC	1 mg per day
Lychopene	OTC	6.5 - 30 mg per day
Metformin	Prescription	500 - 1,000 mg per day
Mini aspirin	OTC	75 - 81 mg per day
N-acetylcysteine	OTC	Stem cell health
Omega3 fatty acids in fish oil	OTC / Prescription	Vascepa
Spermidine		
Statin	Prescription	10 mg per day - Crestor preferred
Vaccinations	Prescription	Flu and shingles (herpes zoster)
Vitamin B12 / folate	OTC	125 - 2,000 mg per day

Currently Available	Prescription / OTC	Dose / Regimen / Comment
Vitamin B3 / niacin / NR / NMN	OTC	1,000 mg per day
Vitamin D	OTC	Countries with limited sunshine only
Zinc	OTC	15 mg per day

Lifestyle:		
Aerobic activity		150 minutes per week
Strength training		Twice per week
Sleep		7-8 hours per night
Manage stress		
Become bilingual		
Lose excess fat		Target BMI between 18.5 - 24.9
Yoga		

Diet:		
Limit saturated fats		7% of daily intake
Limit protein		Max 1 gram per day per kg of lean body mass
Sugar		Minimise
Apple cider vinegar		2 tablespoons per day
Limit salt		6 grams per day
Red wine		250mL per day
Calorie restriction		5:2 intermittent fasting diet
Prebiotics		Promote microbiome
Probiotics		

Don't ✖		
Smoke		
Eat within 3 hours of bed time		
Become lonely or disengaged		

Near Future	Comment
Rapamycin / rapalogs	Clinical trials commenced - see Targets in Ageing. Page 184.
Senolytics	Unity entering human trials in 2018
Sestrins	
Blood factors	Derivative of parabiosis - GF-11
Brown adipose tissue	Transplantation for non-shivering thermogenesis
Induced tissue regeneration	Cox7a1 inhibition
Mitochondrial uncouplers	Metabolic management
CRISPR editing	Various diseases
NgAgo	Various diseases
G6PD activation	Pentose phosphate pathway activation

Further in the Future
Cartilage restoration
Down regulation of INDY
Down regulation of Myc
Down regulation of NF-κB
GHRH up regulation cell therapy
Printed organ transplants
Telomeres lengthening
Transposon manipulation
Upregulation of Klotho
WICT / WILT
Xenotransplantation of organs

You all know it, but please be sure to seek professional advice before taking supplements or medicines.

GENETIC TESTING

www.23andme.com – 23andMe: DNA Genetic Testing & Analysis.

www.myheritage.com – My Heritage: Free Family Tree, Genealogy and Family History.

www.livingdna.com – Living DNA: Ancestry DNA Test.

www.dnacentre.co.uk – DDC DNA Diagnostics Centre: Best UK DNA Testing.

www.ancestry.co.uk – Ancestry UK: Genealogy, Family Trees & Family History Records.

www.pathway.com – Pathway Genomics: A Genetic DNA Testing Company.

www.genehealthuk.com – GeneHealth UK: Genetic Cancer Testing and Genetic Counselling.

www.viamedex.co.uk – VIAMEDEX: Genetic and Drug Testing Laboratory.

www.genebygene.com – Gene by Gene.

www.myriad.com – Myriad Genetics: Breakthrough Innovations in Molecular Diagnostics.

www.nsgc.org – National Society of Genetic Counselors.

www.geneplanet.com – GenePlanet: Genetic Testing for Diseases, Medications, Nutrition and Sports.

www.ibdna.com – International Biosciences: DNA Testing and Paternity from International Biosciences.

www.mayoclinic.org/tests-procedures/genetic-testing/home/ovc-20325301 – The Mayo Clinic.

www.easy-dna.com – EasyDNA: DNA Testing and Home DNA Test Services.

www.color.com – Color Genomics: Hereditary Cancer Risk Genetic Testing.

www.gtldna.co.uk – Genetic Testing Laboratories: Home & Legal DNA Testing Kits.

www.bsgm.org.uk – The British Society for Genetic Medicine.

www.ukgtn.nhs.uk – UK Genetic Testing Network.

USEFUL ORGANISATIONS IN THE LONGEVITY FIELD

AARP (formerly the American Association of Retired Persons) – This non-profit, non-partisan, US social welfare organisation supports a membership of 38 million over 50 year olds to deal with the many issues facing older people including financial security, healthcare and long term care. *www.aarp.org*

Ability is Ageless Award – Award ceremonies for outstanding mature workers that promote the employment of mature workers and teach the public to be aware of the value of mature workers to the work place and to the community. *www.tafep.sg/multimedia/ability-ageless*

Aegon Center for Longevity and Retirement – A Dutch outfit specialising in retirement preparedness and security as well as demographic ageing. *www.aegon.com/en/Home/Research/TheCenter*

Age Smart Employer NYC – Based in the Columbia University Mailman School of Public Health, this organisation awards and supports employers in the New York City area that are innovating in how to retain and benefit from older staff. *www.agesmartemployer.org*

Alliance for Aging, Inc. – A private, not-for-profit, nationwide network of more than 650 Area Agencies that distribute funds to, offers care and services to older people locally. The association was established in Miami, Florida, in 1988, and operates around the US. *http://www.allianceforaging.org/*

The American College of Financial Services – The American College of Financial Services is a non-profit, accredited, degree–granting institution that offers continuing education to people of all ages, primarily through distance education. *www.theamericancollege.edu*

American Society on Aging – The society's goal is to support the commitment and enhance the knowledge and skills of those who seek to improve the quality of life of older adults and their families. *http://www.asaging.org/*

Babylon Health – Babylon is a subscription health service that lets you book virtual GP consultations with professional physicians, monitor symptoms and receive prescriptions. Currently, the service is available in the UK, having a subsidiary in Ireland. *www.babylonhealth.com*

Buck Institute for Research on Aging – The Buck Institute is the USA's first independent research facility focused solely on understanding the connection between ageing and chronic disease in pursuit of the mission to increase the healthy years of life. *www.buckinstitute.org*

Calvert Foundation Age Strong Fund – A fixed impact fund that aims to deliver returns while providing new funding for organisations looking to meet the needs of vulnerable people over 50. Age Strong is an initiative of AARP Foundation, Capital Impact Partners, and Calvert Foundation. *www.agestronginvest.org*

Center for Retirement Research at Boston College – A primarily economic research institute focused on social security, pensions and the funding of long term care. *http://crr.bc.edu/*

Centre for Ageing Better – This independent charitable foundation aims to bring about change for people in later life today and for future generations. *www.ageing-better.org.uk*

Certified Age Friendly Employer Programme – Designed to identify the best employers for workers aged 50 and over, in the US. *www.retirementjobs.com/about-us/certified-age-friendly-employer-programme*

The Center on Aging and Work at Boston College – The centre promotes the rich and thoughtful exchange of innovative ideas about ageing and work among business leaders, academics, and policy makers. *www.bc.edu/research/agingandwork/*

The Eisner Foundation – The foundation, founded in 1996 and based in California, identifies advocates for, and invests in, high-quality and innovative programs that unite multiple generations for the betterment of communities. *www.eisnerfoundation.org*

Eldercare Workforce Alliance – The Eldercare Workforce Alliance is a group of 31 US-based organisations working to address issues related to staffing in the care industry. *www.eldercareworkforce.org*

Elder Justice Initiative – A programme to coordinate the US Justice department's effort at combatting crimes that frequently affect the elderly including neglect and financial scams. *www.justice.gov/elderjustice*

Encore.org – Encore aims to connect people in later life with socially beneficial work opportunities, in the US. *www.encore.org*

Generations United – Generations United promotes programs and public policies to promote intergenerational cooperation. *www.gu.org*

The Gerontological Society of America – The principal mission of the Society – and its 5,500+ members

is to advance the study of ageing and disseminate information among scientists, decision makers, and the general public. *www.geron.org*

Global Coalition on Aging – The Global Coalition on Ageing is a group of international firms with interests in the effect of ageing populations on the economy and policies to help ensure future growth. *http://www.globalcoalitiononaging.com/*

Global Institute for Experienced Entrepreneurs (GIEE) – The GIEE aims to help older people start their own businesses through research and dedicated incubator programmes. *www.experieneurship.com*

Grantmakers in Aging (GIA) – A networking group for grant makers in fields relating to ageing. *www.giaging.org*

International Longevity Centre Global Alliance – The ILC Global Alliance aims to help societies address ageing in positive and productive ways. *www.ilc-alliance.org/*

Leadership Council of Ageing Organizations – The LCAO is a US-based coalition of national nonprofit organizations concerned with the well-being of America's older population and committed to representing their interests in the policy-making arena. *www.lcao.org*

Institute for Ageing – Newcastle University – The Institute's vision is to examine and seek better understanding on all aspects of ageing, in order to create a society where we all "live better for longer". *www.ncl.ac.uk/ageing*

Leading Age – Founded in 1961, LeadingAge is a group of non–profit organisations serving the needs of the elderly, in the US. *www.leadingage.org*

Max Planck Institute for Law and Social Policy – An interdisciplinary institute that conducts comparative research into systems to safeguard against social risks including old age, long term care, and old age. *www.mpg.de/149954/sozialrecht / www.mckinsey.com/mgi/overview*

Methuselah Foundation – Founded to shed light on the processes of ageing and find ways to extend healthy life. Through regenerative medicine, it envisions cures for many of today's most debilitating conditions. *www. mfoundation.org*

Milken Institute Center for the Future of Aging – It aims to improve lives and strengthen societies by promoting healthy, productive and purposeful ageing. It focuses on promoting policies and practices to enable lifelong productivity and change the perception of older adults in policy,

business, media, and other domains. It encourages investment and innovation in the longevity economy. *http://aging. milkeninstitute.org/*

MIT AgeLab – The Massachusetts Institute of Technology AgeLab is a multidisciplinary research programme that works with business, government, and NGOs to improve the quality of life of older people and those who care for them. *http://agelab.mit.edu/*

Modern Ageing Initiative – The Modern Ageing Initiative is run by ACCESS Health International and aims to empower entrepreneurs to create business meeting the needs of the elderly. *www.accessh.org/modern–aging*

Multicultural Coalition on Ageing – The MCA builds and sustains a network of consumer, health, social service and governmental agencies serving culturally diverse elders. *www.mcaboston.org*

National Association of Area Agencies on Ageing (n4a) – The n4a aims to provide a voice in Washington for Title VI Native American ageing programmes. *www.n4a.org*

The National Aging in Place Council – A senior support network dedicated to helping meet the needs of an ageing population, and assist so that more elderly people can remain independent in the housing of their choice. It has several chapters around the US. *www.ageinplace.org*

National Council on Aging – The National Council on Ageing has advocated for elderly people in the US for over 65 years. *www.ncoa.org*

National Institute on Aging – NIA, one of the 27 Institutes and Centers of National Institutes of Health, leads a broad scientific effort to understand the nature of ageing and to extend the healthy, active years of life. *www.nia.nih.gov*

The Oxford Institute of Population Ageing – The UK's first population centre on the demography and economics of ageing populations whose aim is to undertake research into the implications of population change, particularly ageing. *www.ageing.ox.ac.uk*

Palo Alto Longevity Prize – The Palo Alto Prize is a newly established Silicon Valley–based initiative set-up to encourage collaboration, foster innovation, and build a community to address the underlying causes of ageing. *www.paloaltoprize.com*

ReFraming Aging Initiative – ReFraming Ageing Initiative aims to better public understanding of older adults' needs and contributions to society, in America. *http://agelab.mit.edu/*

The Robert Wood Johnson Foundation – Focused on improving the health and healthcare of all Americans. *www.rwjf.org*

The Robert N. Butler Columbia Aging Center – Seeks to develop the knowledge base necessary to inform ageing-related health and social policy locally, nationally, and globally, in addition to training a new generation of thought leaders to address issues facing societies of longer lives. *www.aging.columbia.edu*

Saga – Saga is a FTSE 250 firm that provides services specifically tailored to serving the needs of the over 50s in the UK. *www.saga.co.uk*

SENS Research Foundation – The SENS Research Foundation is a registered charity looking to transform the way the world looks at the ageing process and to develop technologies in the field of regenerative medicine. *www.sens.org*

Society for Human Resource Management – A US professional body for HR professionals: 285,000 members in more than 165 countries. *www.shrm.org*

Stanford Center on Longevity – The Stanford Center on Longevity aims to develop workable solutions for urgent issues confronting the world as the population ages. *http://longevity.stanford.edu/*

The SCAN Foundation – Supports the creation of a more coordinated and easily navigated system of high–quality services for older adults that preserve dignity and independence. *www.thescanfoundation.org*

Transamerica Center for Retirement Studies – A division of the Transamerica Institute, a non–profit, private foundation dedicated to educating the American public on trends, issues, and opportunities related to saving and planning for retirement and achieving financial security in retirement. *www.transamericacenter.org*

The USC Leonard Davis School of Gerontology – The mission of the USC Leonard Davis School of Gerontology is to promote healthy ageing for individuals, communities and societies through leadership and innovation in research, education and practice. It explores all aspects of human development and ageing. *http://gero.usc.edu/*

WorkingNation – Exists to expose hard truths about the looming unemployment crisis as a result of automation and other advances in technology that are eliminating (or showing potential to eliminate) jobs, hoping to keep America working. *www.workingnation.com*

WHO Global Network for Age-friendly Cities and Communities – Established to foster the exchange of experience and mutual learning between cities and communities worldwide of their efforts to promote healthy and active ageing and a good quality of life for their older residents. *www.who.int/ageing/projects/age_friendly_cities_network/en/*

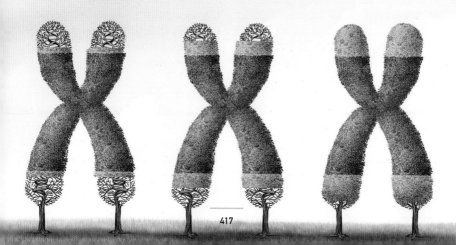

GLOSSARY

Acetyl group: a small molecule that can be attached to histones and other proteins and thereby change the protein's shape and function.

Adaptive immune system: learned or acquired immunity (see Inflammaging. Page 60).

Adenosine monophosphate-activated protein kinase (AMPK): an enzyme that plays a critical role in the regulation of our energy balance, particularly in maintaining mitochondrial function.

Adenosine triphosphate (ATP): a molecule used in cells as a coenzyme (they cannot by themselves catalyse a reaction but they can help enzymes to do). ATP is the molecule that carries energy to the place where the energy is needed.

Allele: a gene variant or alternative form of a gene.

Analog drug: a drug with either a similar function or chemical structure compared to another.

Antagonistic pleiotropy: where a single gene controls more than one trait and at least one of these traits is beneficial to the organism's fitness and at least one is harmful.

Apoptosis: the normal process of regulated cell death as an organism grows or develops (see Apoptosis. Page 198).

Autophagy: a normal and orderly process of degradation and recycling of damaged cellular components (see Autophagy. Page 132).

Aβ and tau: two proteins that sometimes accumulate in the brain which are strongly associated with the degeneration of neurological function and Alzheimer's disease. The development of compounds to clear these proteins is currently the focus of much research.

Biogerontology: the study of the ageing process and its effects.

Biomarker: a specific substance, physical trait, gene, etc. that can be measured to indicate the presence or progress of a pathology.

Brown adipose tissue (BAT): a highly specialised form of fat primarily located around the neck and large blood vessels of thorax that generates heat by non-shivering thermogenesis (see Targets in Ageing. Page 218).

Caloric restriction (CR): reducing macronutrient intake while maintaining the intake of essential micronutrients.

Cell: the components that make up human and other bodies. Cells come in many different forms, and they pack together to form organs and tissues. Cells consist of multiple structures, including the nucleus and the mitochondria.

Chaperone proteins: proteins which assist other proteins to fold correctly.

Chromatin: material consisting of DNA plus histones in combination, as well as proteins and RNAs that bind to it.

Codons: three consecutive bases in a messenger RNA strand. Each of the codons specifies a single amino acid in the protein that the messenger RNA encodes.

Conserved pathway: a molecular pathway that exists in a variety of different species.

CpG Island: these are clusters of C bases adjacent to G bases, linked by phosphate groups and close to gene transcription sites. Methylating the C base within a genecan change it's expression.

CRISPR (Clustered Regularly Interspaced Short Palindromic Repeats): segments of DNA containing short repetitive base sequences.

CRISPR/Cas9: a revolutionary genome-editing technology that enables permanent and precise modification of genes in a variety of organisms and tissues (see Genetic Editions of You. Page 235).

Cryonics/cryopreservation: The freezing of bodies immediately after legal death without causing much damage, in the hope that they can be revived in the future (see Cryonics – On Ice. Page 252).

Cytokines: small proteins secreted by cells which alter the behaviour of cells around them.

Cytomegalovirus (CMV): a common virus belonging to the herpes group which stays in the body for life. Generally, only causes real problems with pregnant women, newborn babies and/or people with weak or compromised immune systems, but indirectly also in ageing (see Inflammaging. Page 60).

Cytoplasm: content of a living cell with exception of the nucleus.

Deoxyribonucleic acid (DNA): the molecule that carries genetic information.

Dietary restriction (DR): is a robust nongenetic, nonpharmacological intervention that is known to increase active and healthy lifespan in a variety of species.

Endogenous: substances and processes that originate from within an organism, tissue, or cell.

Entropy: a measure of disorder or randomness.

Enzymes: proteins that act as catalysts for biological reactions.

Epigenetic clock: a type of DNA clock based on measuring natural DNA methylation levels to estimate the biological age of a tissue, cell type or organ e.g. Horvath's clock.

Epigenome: all of the modifications of the genome and the other components of chromatin which affect gene expression. The epigenome exhibits changes in different cell types.

Eukaryotic cell: a cell of an organism with a variety of internal membrane-bound structures and a distinct nucleus.

Exogenous: something originating from outside, externally.

FOX protein: a family of transcription factors that play important roles in regulating the expression of genes involved in cell growth, particularly in embryonic development.

Gene: a fragment of DNA that codes for a specific protein or RNA.

Genomic sequencing: the process of reading and recording the sequence of a DNA molecule.

Genotype: the genetic make-up of an individual.

Germ cell: a cell that can undergo meiosis to produce gametes (e.g. sperm and egg cells in humans).

Gerontogenes: genes which have a positive effect on longevity, and including mediator genes, genes involved in mitochondrial function, as well as genes involved in apoptosis and cellular senescence.

Growth Hormone-Releasing Hormone (GHRH): the naturally occurring hormone that stimulates secretion of growth hormone.

Haematopoiesis: the process by which blood cells are formed. In about half of those over the age of 75, clonal mutations in the cells that underpin haematopoiesis develop, leading to an increase in leukaemia and cardiovascular disease. (Rudolph, Leibniz Institute on Ageing, 2017).

Haematopoietic stem cell (HSC): a cell found in bone marrow, peripheral blood and the umbilical cord which can develop into all types of blood cells.

Hayflick Limit: Leonard Hayflick's finding that a cell's ability to divide is limited to approximately 50 divisions, due to the shortening of telomeres upon each cell division.

High-density lipoprotein (HDL): often referred to as "good cholesterol".

Histone: a type of protein which binds to DNA and assists in packing the DNA into nucleosomes that form chromatin.

Homeostasis: the state arising from the maintenance of a controlled environment within cells which is partly regulated by hormones produced by the endocrine glands. As far as humans are concerned this is the steady state when our bodies are in balance.

Homolog: a gene related to a second gene by ancestry.

Hormone Replacement Therapy (HRT): any form of therapy whereby the patient receives hormones to supplement or substitute naturally-occurring hormones.

Immunosenescence: deterioration of the immune system associated with ageing.

Idiopathic pulmonary fibrosis (IPF): a form of interstitial pneumonia which is generally fatal within 5 years and is characterised by scarring of the lung and progressive lack of pulmonary function. It is generally a disease of the elderly.

Immunosurveillance: process by which cells of the immune system look for and recognise foreign pathogens, such as viruses and bacteria, or pre-cancerous and cancerous cells in the body.

Immunotherapy: where the immune system is manipulated/restored to identify and destroy targets that it otherwise overlooks.

Induced pluripotent stem cell (iPSC): artificially created stem cells, genetically "reprogrammed" by the introduction of particular genes to assume a stem cell-like state.

INDY (I'm Not Dead Yet): a protein-encoding gene implicated in ageing in the model organism Drosophila melanogaster.

Inflammaging: the low-grade pro-inflammatory status of the immune system that appears to contribute to the ageing process.

Innate immune system: natural immunity which is the body's first line of defense against infection.

Insulin-like growth factor 1 (IGF-1): a hormone, similar in molecular structure to insulin, produced to promote cell growth and division.

Klotho: a protein that appears to have some control over rodent and human sensitivity to ageing and thereby to have a role in ageing.

Krebs cycle: the process of removal of electrons from nutrients, allowing the cellular respiration by which most living cells generate ATP to distribute energy.

Kleiber's Law: the law named after Max Kleiber which postulates that an animal's metabolic rate scales to the ¾ power of the animal's mass.

Low-density lipoprotein (LDL): often referred to as "bad cholesterol".

Mechanistic target of rapamycin (mTOR): a protein in humans encoded by the mTOR gene that has been implicated in ageing.

Medawar-Williams Theory: a theory of ageing which posits that accumulated mutations in our genome put an eventual limit on our existence.

Meiosis: a type of cell division in sexually reproducing organisms that creates egg and sperm cells.

Mesenchymal stem cell (MSC): a type of stem cell that self-renews and can mature into a large number of cell types including connective tissue, fat tissue, bones, and cartilage.

Messenger RNA (mRNA): a strand of RNA that encodes a protein.

Metabolism: the network of chemical reactions that occur within a living organism.

Metformin: an oral, diabetic drug that helps control blood sugar levels in people with type 2 diabetes.

Microbiome: all of the microorganisms, and their collective genetic material, present in or on the human body or in another environment.

Mitosis: the standard type of cell division, involving DNA replication alternating with cell splitting.

Molecular pathways: a series of interactions among molecules in a cell that leads to a certain endpoint or cell function.

Mutations: heritable, permanent changes in DNA sequences in chromosomes.

Myelocytomatosis viral oncogene homolog (Myc): a family of master-regulator transcription factor genes that are important in cell division, metabolism and survival (see Targets in Ageing. Page 249).

Nicotinamide adenine dinucleotide (NAD/NAD+ and NADH): a co-enzyme which is found in all living cells. It exists in two forms, oxidised (NAD+) and reduced (NADH) - see Targets in Ageing.

Nicotinamide Riboside (NR): a compound which acts as a precursor to NAD+ and has been linked to improvement in mitochondrial production and functionality.

Nuclear DNA: the blueprint for the production of proteins and processes that make "us" us.

Nuclear factor kappa B (NF-kB): a transcription factor, i.e. a protein involved in transcription of DNA to RNA, and thence into the production of proteins. NF-kB inhibition is proven to reverse some aspects of ageing - (see Targets in Ageing. Page 251).

Nucleus: this is in most cells, and is a compartment containing the cell's chromosomes.

Nucleotide: a building-block for DNA.

Oocyte senescence: decline in production and/or quality of eggs with age in mammals.

Organelle: a structure suspended in the cytoplasm of a cell, with a specialised function.

Parabiosis: a surgical technique in which two living organism's circulatory systems are joined together.

Pathology: the study of the essential nature of a disease, or the disease state itself.

Phenotype: the physical characteristics of an organism which are determined by its genes interacting with the environment.

Phylogenetic tree: a visual representation showing the evolutionary interrelations of a group of organisms derived from a common ancestral form.

Polypeptide: a chain of amino acids that form a protein molecule.

Prokaryotic cell: a single-celled organism with no true nucleus or other membrane-bound organelles.

Proprotein convertase subtilisin/ kexin type 9 (PCSK9): a protein that, when inhibited, leads to lowered levels of circulating LDL in the blood stream.

Protein: a large molecule consisting of a string of amino acids; proteins have multiple functions, including structural, metabolic and anti-infective.

Proteostasis: a set of cellular processes that maintains or restores the integrity and shapes of the proteins in a cell.

Rapamycin: a drug that can suppress the immune system, which is currently used to prevent the rejection of transplanted organs (see Targets in Ageing. Page 184).

Rapalog: an analog of rapamycin.

Rate of living theory: the theory that the slower the metabolism of an organism, the longer its lifespan.

Reactive oxygen species (ROS): unstable molecules that arise as unintended by-products of respiration and are potentially harmful to living cells.

Regenerative Medicine: a branch of translational research, including tissue engineering and stem cell biology, which deals with the process of replacing, engineering or regenerating human cells, tissues or organs to restore or establish normal function.

Resveratrol: a polyphenol antioxidant that has been shown to influence gene expression to turn on factors that promote longevity in cells (see Targets in Ageing. Page 189).

Ribonucleic acid (RNA): a single-stranded molecule that can hold genetic information but is also involved in the transfer of information carried by DNA to manufacture proteins within a cell.

Second Law of Thermodynamics: the law that as energy is transferred or transformed, more and more of it is wasted and that there is a natural tendency of any isolated system to degenerate into a more disordered state (see Theories of Ageing. Page 78).

Senescence: the process of deterioration with age.

Senescence-Associated Secretory Phenotype (SASP): the cocktail of factors and proteins released by senescent cells.

Sestrins: a class of proteins that play a key role in metabolism and ageing.

Sirtuins: a class of proteins that regulate many cellular functions, including metabolism, cellular death, inflammation and longevity. Activators of sirtuins include cocoa, kales, olives, green tea, tofu, turmeric, capers and parsley (see Targets in Ageing Page 189).

Somatic cells: any cells of a living organism other than the germ cells – (see Genetic Editions of You. Page 235).

Speciation: the formation of new and distinct species in the course of evolution.

Stem cell: an undifferentiated cell which can divide to produce one or more other types of cells while the other daughter cell is still a stem cell.

Stochastic: having a random probability distribution.

Telomerase: a reverse transcriptase enzyme which uses a template in elongating telomeres.

Telomere: the tip at the end of each chromosome, rather like a cap on a shoelace.

Tetrahydrocannabinol (THC): the psychoactive ingredient in cannabis that appears to restore memory in older people (see The Deadly Quintet. Page 109).

Transcription factors: the proteins involved in regulating the process of copying, or transcribing, DNA into RNA.

Transgenic: relating to an organism whose genome has been altered by the addition of a gene(s) from another organism (see Targets in Ageing. Page 248).

Transposons: a DNA sequence that can change position within a genome (see Targets in Ageing. Page 252).

White adipose tissue (WAT): loose connective tissue with the primary purpose of storing energy in the form of lipids. It also cushions and insulates the body (see Conditioning. Page 362).

WILT: Whole Body Interdiction of Lengthening of Telomeres, the SENS proposal for the eradication of cancer (see Targets in Ageing. Page 229).

Xenotransplantation: the transplanting of organs between organisms of different species (see Targets in Ageing. Page 220).

Yamanaka transcription factors: four transcription factors highly expressed in embryonic stem cells that can induce pluripotency in somatic cells (see Targets in Ageing Page 235).

Zygote: this is the single cell produced when egg and sperm fuse; zygotes then divide to produce two-celled embryos and eventually the mature organism.

BIBLIOGRAPHY

The 100-Year Life: Living and Working in an Age of Longevity, Lynda Gratton and Andrew Scott, Bloomsbury Business; reprint edition (2017)

50 Ideas You Really Need to Know: Biology, JV Chamary, Quercus (2015)

The 8-Week Blood Sugar Diet: Lose weight fast and reprogramme your body, Michael Mosley, Short Books Ltd (2015)

Abundance: The Future Is Better Than You Think, Peter Diamandis and Steven Kotler, Free Press; reprint edition (2015)

The Ageless Generation: How Advances in Biomedicine Will Transform the Global Economy, Alex Zhavoronkov, Palgrave Macmillan (2013)

Ageing by Design: How New Thinking on Ageing Will Change Your Life, Theodore Goldsmith, Azinet Press (2014)

Biocode: The New Age of Genomics, Dawn Field and Neil Davies, OUP Oxford (2015)

The Biology of Ageing: A Practical Handbook, Gurcharan Rai and Aza Abdulla, CRC Press (2012)

Biology of Ageing, Roger B. McDonald, Routledge (2013)

Boon and Bane of Not Being Subject to the Hayflick Limit: What effects does it have in cancer cells and what is it used for in life extension science? Miriam Herbert, GRIN Publishing (2015)

Cellular Ageing and Replicative Senescence (Healthy Ageing and Longevity), Leonard Hayflick and Suresh Rattan, Springer (2016)

The Crack in Creation: The Crack in Creation, Jennifer Doudna and Samuel H Sternberg, Houghton Mifflin (2017)

The Deeper Genome: Why there is more to the human genome than meets the eye, John Parrington, OUP Oxford; reprint edition (2016)

Disrupting Ageing in the Workplace, Lori A. Trawinski AARP (September 2016)

The effects of antibiotics on the microbiome throughout development and alternative approaches for therapeutic modulation, Amy Langdon, Nathan Crook and Gautam Dantas, Genome Medicine (2016)

Ending Ageing: The Rejuvenation Breakthroughs That Could Reverse Human Ageing in Our Lifetime, Aubrey de Grey and Michael Rae, St. Martin's Griffin (2008)

Evolution: Still a Theory in Crisis, Michael Denton, Discovery Institute (2016)

Fat Chance: The Hidden Truth About Sugar, Obesity and Disease, Robert Lustig, Fourth Estate (2014)

Freezing People Is (Not) Easy: My Adventures in Cryonics, Bob Nelson, Kenneth Bly and Sally Magana, Lyons Press (2014)

The Gene: An Intimate History, Siddhartha Mukherjee, Vintage (2017)

Gene Editing, Epigenetic, Cloning and Therapy, Amin Elserawi PhD, AuthorHouse (2016)

The Grain Brain Whole Life Plan: Boost Brain Performance, Lose Weight, and Achieve Optimal Health, David Perlmutter, Yellow Kite (2016)

Homo Deus: A Brief History of Tomorrow, Yuval Harari, Vintage (2017)

How and Why We Age, Leonard Hayflick PhD, Ballantine Books (1994)

How Emotions Are Made: The Secret Life of the Brain, Lisa Feldman Barrett, Macmillan (2017)

Human Genetic Engineering: A Guide for Activists, Skeptics, and the Very Perplexed, Pete Shanks, Nation Books (2005)

In Pursuit of Memory: The Fight Against Alzheimer's, Joseph Jebelli, John Murray (2017)

Introducing Epigenetics: A Graphic Guide, Cath Ennis and Oliver Pugh, Icon Books Ltd (2017)

Life's Ratchet: How Molecular Machines Extract Order from Chaos, Peter Hoffmann, Basic Books (2012)

Longer Lives, Stronger Families? The changing nature of intergenerational support, Nigel Keohane, Social Market Foundation (2016)

Longevity Now: A Comprehensive Approach to Healthy Hormones, Detoxification, Super Immunity, Reversing Calcification, and Total Rejuvenation, David Wolfe, North Atlantic Books, U.S. (2013)

Metformin, Clifford Bailey and Ian Campbell, Wiley-Blackwell (2007)

Metformin: therapeutic option in people at high cardiometabolic risk, Petya Kamenova, Scholars' Press (2016)

Millennials and Longevity: Matthew Baredes and Jay Rabinowitz, UBS (2014)

Modern Prometheus: Editing the Human Genome with Crispr-Cas9, Jim Kozubuk, Cambridge University Press (2016)

Molecular Biology of Ageing (Cold Spring Harbor Monograph), Leonard Guarente, Linda Partridge and Douglas Wallace, Cold Spring Harbor Press (2008)

Pathophysiology of Heart Disease: A Collaborative Project of Medical Students and Faculty, Leonard S. Lilly, Lippincott Williams and Wilkins; 6th edition (2015)

The Pioppi Diet: A 21-Day Lifestyle Plan, Aseem Malhotra and Donna O'Neill, Penguin (2017)

The Power of Time Perception: Control the Speed of Time to Make Every Second Count, Jean Paul Zogby, Time Lighthouse Publishing (2017)

The Prolongation of Life; Optimistic Studies, Elie Metchnikoff (1908)

Redesigning Life: How genome editing will transform the world, John Parrington, OUP Oxford (2016)

Regenesis: How Synthetic Biology Will Reinvent Nature and Ourselves, George Church and Ed Regis, Basic Books; reprint edition (2014)

Reverse the Signs of Ageing: The revolutionary inside-out plan to glowing, youthful skin, Nigma Talib, Ebury Digital (2015)

Sapiens: A Brief History of Humankind, Yuval Harari, Vintage (2015)

The Selfish Gene, Richard Dawkins, OUP Oxford; 40th anniversary edition (2016)

Stem Cells: A Short Course, Rob Burgess, Wiley-Blackwell (2016)

Super-Ageing: The Moral Dangers of Seeking Immortality, Mark Moorstein, iUniverse (2010)

The Telomere Effect: A Revolutionary Approach to Living Younger, Healthier, Longer, Elizabeth Backburn and Elissa Epel, Orion Spring (2017)

Telomere Time Bombs; Diffusing the Terror of Ageing, Ed Park, MD, self-published (2013)

Thrive: The Third Metric to Redefining Success and Creating a Happier Life, Arianna Huffington, WH Allen (2015)

To be a Machine: Adventures Among Cyborgs, Utopians, Hackers, and the Futurists Solving the Modest Problem of Death, Mark O'Connell, Granta Books (2017)

Transcend: Nine Steps to Living Well Forever, Ray Kurzweil and Terry Grossman, Rodale Pr (2010)

Type 1 Diabetes (Oxford Diabetes Library Series), David Levy, Oxford University Press; 2nd edition (2016)

Weighing Down America – The Health and Economic Impact of Obesity, The Milken Institute (November 2016)

We Live Too Short and Die Too Long: How to Achieve and Enjoy Your Natural 100-Year-Plus Life Span, Walter Bortz, Gazelle Drake Publishing; revised edition (2006)

What is Life?, Erwin Schrodinger, Cambridge University Press; reprint edition (2012)

Why We Age: What Science is Discovering About the Body's Journey Through Life, Steven N. Austad, John Wiley & Sons (1997)

Wired to Eat: How to Rewire Your Appetite and Lose Weight for Good, Robb Wolf (2017)

Workers are Working Longer – and Better, John Hanc, NYT (March 2017)

World Population Ageing Report 2015, United Nations, Department of Economic and Social Affairs, Population Division

MAGAZINES, NEWSPAPERS AND WEBSITES

Alzheimer's Association
www.alz.org

Alzheimer's News Today
www.alzheimersnewstoday.com

Alzheimer's Society
www.alzheimers.org.uk

Aubrey de Grey
www.sens.org

Babraham Centre for Healthy Ageing
www.babraham.ac.uk

BBC News
www.bbc.co.uk/news

British Heart Foundation
www.bhf.org.uk

British Medical Journal, The BMJ
www.bmj.com

The Broad Institute
www.broadinstitute.org

Cell
www.cell.com

The Daily Telegraph
www.telegraph.co.uk

David Sinclair
www.hms.harvard.edu/ageingresearch

The Economist
www.economist.com

Fight Ageing!
www.fightaging.org

The Financial Times
www.ft.com

George Church
arep.med.harvard.edu/gmc

The Guardian
www.theguardian.com

International Society for Stem Cell
Research
www.isscr.org

Jennifer Doudna
rna.berkeley.edu

The Journal of Insulin Resistance
www.insulinresistance.org

Kyoto University, Yamanaka Lab
www.cira.kyoto-u.ac.jp/e

The Lancet
www.thelancet.com

Logan's Run
**en.wikipedia.org/wiki/
Logan%27s_Run**

Matthew Freeman
**users.path.ox.ac.uk/~mfreeman/
Freeman_Lab/Welcome.html**

The National Institute of Diabetes
and Digestive and Kidney Diseases
www.niddk.nih.gov

The National Institutes of Health
www.nih.gov

Nature
www.nature.com

New England Journal of Medicine
www.nejm.org

New Scientist
www.newscientist.com

The New York Times
www.nytimes.com

Nir Barzilai
**www.einstein.yu.edu/centers/
ageing/longevity-genes-project**

NPR
www.npr.org

Salk Institute
www.salk.edu

Senescence info
www.senescence.info

Science
www.sciencemag.org

Scientific Advisory Committee on Nutrition (SACN) Carbohydrates and Health Report
www.gov.uk/government/ publications/sacn-carbohydrates- and-health-report

Scientific American
www.scientificamerican.com

UCSF Ageing and Memory Center
memory.ucsf.edu

University of Southern California, USC
www.usc.edu

US Department of Health and Human Services, The Weight-control Information Network (WIN), a national information service of the National Institute of Diabetes and Digestive and Kidney Diseases (NIDDK), part of the National Institutes of Health (NIH).

US Bureau of Labor Statistics
www.bls.gov

WebMD
www.webmd.com

The Weight-control Information Network
www.niddk.nih.gov/ health-information/health- communication-programs/win/ Pages/default.aspx

World life expectancy
www.worldlifeexpectancy.com

OTHER TITLES BY
JIM MELLON AND AL CHALABI

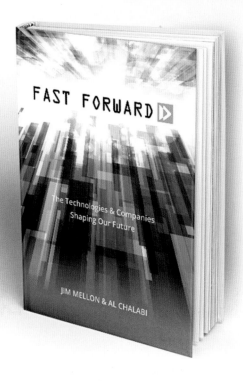

Fast Forward: The Technologies and Companies Shaping our Future.

As the pace of technological progress intensifies, agile businesses and entrepreneurs are discovering new applications that take advantage of faster and cheaper computer processing power. The status quo is being upended across all industries, and in some cases totally new industries are being created. *Fast Forward* is a book that filters this chaotic landscape and identifies the areas that will have the greatest impact to our lives, highlighting investment opportunities along the way. These disruptive technologies span the fields of robotics, transportation, the changing internet, life sciences, 3D printing and energy, all of which are experiencing tremendous growth.

AVAILABLE TO BUY FROM

amazon.co.uk

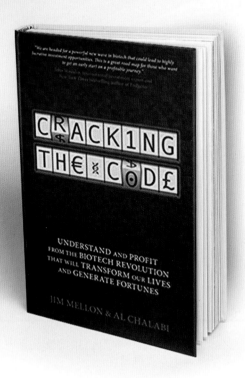

Cracking the Code: Understand and Profit from the Biotech Revolution that will Transform our Lives and Generate Fortunes.

Within most people's lifetimes, the developments in the biotechnology sector will allow us to live increasingly long and healthy lives, as well as provide us with technological innovations that will transform the way we live. But these innovations offer more than just hope for a better life, they offer hope for better returns too. Financial returns of incredible magnitude await savvy investors and businesspeople who can see the massive changes on the horizon. This book details these fast-moving trends and innovations and offers extensive advice on how to profit from them in business and investing.

AVAILABLE TO BUY FROM

amazon.co.uk

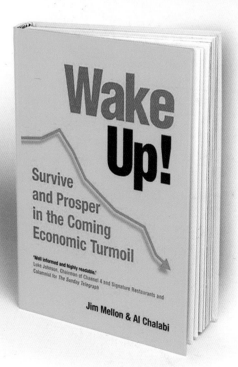

Wake Up! Survive and Prosper in the Coming Economic Turmoil.

"This book is a dramatic wake-up call to investors. It portrays an apocalyptic future of high risk and low rewards. It is well informed and highly readable. While some may dispute the author's bleak vision, this is nevertheless required reading for anyone who wants to understand the massive changes hitting the world's economies in the coming decades."

Luke Johnson, Former Chairman of Channel 4 and Signature Restaurants.